Barbara Dancygier, Wei-lun Lu, Arie Verhagen (Eds.)
Viewpoint and the Fabric of Meaning

Cognitive Linguistics Research

Volume 55

Viewpoint and the Fabric of Meaning

Form and Use of Viewpoint Tools across Languages and Modalities

Edited by
Barbara Dancygier
Wei-lun Lu
Arie Verhagen

DE GRUYTER
MOUTON

ISBN 978-3-11-057857-7
e-ISBN (PDF) 978-3-11-036546-7
e-ISBN (EPUB) 978-3-11-039307-1
ISSN 1861-4132

Library of Congress Cataloging-in-Publication Data
A CIP catalog record for this book has been applied for at the Library of Congress.

Bibliographic information published by the Deutsche Nationalbibliothek
The Deutsche Nationalbibliothek lists this publication in the Deutsche Nationalbibliografie; detailed bibliographic data are available on the Internet at http://dnb.dnb.de.

This volume is text- and page-identical with the hardback published in 2016.
Typesetting: PTP-Berlin, Protago-TEX-Production GmbH, Berlin
Printing and binding: CPI books GmbH, Leck

♾ Printed on acid-free paper
Printed in Germany

www.degruyter.com

Table of contents

Part III: **Across modalities**

List of contributors

Ad Foolen
Department of Linguistics
Radboud University
The Netherlands
a.foolen@let.ru.nl

Arie Verhagen
Leiden University Centre for Linguistics
Leiden University
The Netherlands
a.verhagen@hum.leidenuniv.nl

Barbara Dancygier
Department of English
University of British Columbia
Canada
barbara.dancygier@ubc.ca

Chie Fukada
Kyoto Institute of Technology
Japan
chieft@kit.ac.jp

Ditte Boeg Thomsen
Department of Nordic Studies and Linguistics
University of Copenhagen
Denmark
ditte.boeg@hum.ku.dk

Elisabeth Engberg-Pedersen
Department of Nordic Studies and Linguistics
University of Copenhagen
Denmark
eep@hum.ku.dk

Esther Pascual
School of International Studies
Zhejiang University
China
pascual@zju.edu.cn

Eve Sweetser
Department of Linguistics
University of California at Berkeley
USA
sweetser@berkeley.edu

Hans Hoeken
Utrecht Institute of Linguistics OTS
Utrecht University
The Netherlands
j.a.l.hoeken@uu.nl

Jeroen Vanderbiesen
Department of Linguistics
University of Antwerp
Belgium
jeroen.vanderbiesen@uantwerpen.be

José Sanders
Centre for Language Studies
Radboud University
The Netherlands
j.sanders@let.ru.nl

Kashimiri Stec
Centre for Language and Cognition
University of Groningen
The Netherlands
kashmiri.stec@gmail.com

Katsunobu Izutsu
Hokkaido University of Education
Japan
idutsu@gmail.com

Kobie van Krieken
Centre for Language Studies
Radboud University
The Netherlands
k.vankrieken@let.ru.nl

Lieven Vandelanotte
University of Namur and KU Leuven
Belgium
lieven.vandelanotte@unamur.be

Maria Josep Jarque
Department of Developmental and Educational Psychology
University of Barcelona
Spain
mj_jarque@ub.edu

Mitsuko Narita Izutsu
Fuji Women's University
Japan
mizutsu@fujijoshi.ac.jp

Toshiko Yamaguchi
Department of English Language
University of Malaya
Malaysia
tyamag@um.edu.my

Wei-lun Lu
Faculty of Arts
Masaryk University
Czech Republic
weilunlu@gmail.com

Arie Verhagen

Introduction: On tools for weaving meaning out of viewpoint threads

Human beings are unique in the animal kingdom for a variety of reasons. One of them is their extensive high levels of social cognition. The capacity to take the knowledge, feelings, and attitudes of other people, and the ways these relate to their own cognitive and emotional states, into account in coordinating their activities, definitely is a major "root" of human sociality (Enfield and Levinson 2006). Colloquially put: people are normally very good at assessing other people's "point of view" on matters that are of interest to them. The study of viewpoint has a long history in the scholarly study of narrative discourse: (linguistic) narratology, stylistics, and (cognitive) poetics. An essential feature of stories (whether fact or fiction) is that they represent the speech, thoughts, attitudes, and emotions of characters. In processing narrative discourse, listeners/readers construct conceptualizations of the ways these different viewpoints are connected into a meaningful fabric, and moreover connect it to their own point of view, thus adding a further dimension of meaning. The study of the complexities of viewpoint in narrative discourse thus provides an especially interesting window on core characteristics of human cognition, while theories of social cognition and its evolution may shed light on the delight that humans universally take in storytelling and the role of viewpoint in it (cf. Zunshine 2006, Boyd 2009, Van Duijn, Sluiter and Verhagen 2015).

In the humanities, the study of viewpoint goes back until at least the middle of the 19th century, and its history has shown a development, reflected in the present volume, from interest in a specific type of narrative viewpoint mixing, to a much larger and varied set of viewpointing tools and techniques, some of them beyond traditionally recognized linguistic categories. The specific type of "mixed viewpoints" that has been studied intensively from early on (and still is in present day research), is that of the so-called Free Indirect Discourse, as it appears to constitute a prototype of mixing. Direct Discourse ('quotation' as in *She thought: I may be president tomorrow*) minimizes the responsibility of the narrator and the distance between the reader and the character; Indirect Discourse (complementation as in *She thought that she might be president the next day*) maximizes them; but Free Indirect Discourse (*She was lost in thought; she might be president tomorrow!*) constitutes a 'mixed' variety. It was characterized by Jakobson ([1957] 1971) as a special type of one of the four crucial "duplex" structures in language (reported speech being a message representing a message), and has been in the centre of attention in various linguistic, narratological and stylistic studies. In these studies, tense, mood/modality and deixis have been identified as the major 'parameters' of Free Indirect Discourse as distinct from both Direct and Indirect Discourse; each type is in principle thought to be characterized by a specific, distinct combination of values of these parameters.

These distinctions refer to different ways of representing discourse (spoken or thought) of characters in a narrative (Speech and Thought Representation). However, early studies (including Jakobson [1957] 1971) already have pointed out that languages need not converge on the repertoire of linguistic resources they make available for construing the mixing of viewpoints. For instance, whereas Russian, as Jakobson points out, lacks a verbal grammatical category of evidentiality (marking of the relationship between the narrator and the source of evidence for the information involved), this is obligatory in many other languages; in the latter type of languages, this grammatical property implies a continuous computation of the relations between the source of the message and both the characters in the narrative and the narrator, which constitutes a kind of viewpoint mixing that is not only different from Free Indirect Discourse, but in fact not strictly a type of Speech and Thought Representation. So, with the inclusion of such obviously related phenomena into the overall study of viewpoint, first steps are taken to broadening the scope of this domain of investigation, mentioned above.

Furthermore, some languages, like Dutch and German, are known for their wide range of modal particles, which provide a variety of options for evoking a specific relationship between the viewpoint of the present Speaker and/or Addressee and some other one, of which the 'anchor' often is to be inferred from the context (see also Engberg-Pedersen and Boeg Thomsen on Danish particles in this volume). On the other hand, some (other) languages may lack a structural distinction between main and (supposedly) 'subordinate' clauses, and thus also a basis for distinguishing direct from indirect discourse; they definitely provide their speakers with tools for social cognition as well, but they simply are not of exactly the same type (cf. Evans 2010, ch. 4). Overall, partly as a result of its breadth, even the generally used category of Free Indirect Discourse has so far escaped a rigorous definition. Clearly, there is as much need for zooming out (broadening the range of languages and linguistic phenomena taken into account) as for zooming in (taking the details of specific forms of 'mixing' into account) in order to make further progress in understanding viewpoint mixing in general (cf. Dancygier 2012b for an overview of relevant conceptual and empirical dimensions).

Recent work in cognitive linguistics has identified important avenues in the investigation of the ways multiple viewpoints are managed and related to each other in discourse. The approach to intersubjectivity in grammar developed in Verhagen (2005) and its application to complementation constructions opened the traditional issue of Indirect Discourse to a new set of questions. Also, constructional-functional approaches (cf. Vandelanotte 2009) have offered new views on the specificity of the Free Indirect Discourse category, including the hypothesis that it may only be one of several more 'mixing' categories. At the same time, other studies identified a broader range of viewpoint markers in language use (Sanders 2010, Dancygier and Sweetser 2012), or developed a comprehensive theoretical framework for the analysis of complex viewpoint structures in narrative texts and of their effects (Dancygier 2012a). This recent work suggests the existence and relevance of more general strategies of viewpoint allocation, maintenance or shift. Bound together by the common capability of viewpoint construction, they offer an additional set of tools which can be used to elucidate mixed viewpoint phenomena.

The linguistic diversity, and possibly inconsistency, of the span of linguistic means that define forms of Speech and Thought Representation have not been an explicit focus of research. As a result, the potential of linguistic and cultural-cognitive diversity for understanding both universal and culture specific features of the construal of represented speech and thought, and for the interaction between grammar and cognition in this domain, has, at a minimum, remained under-exploited (Evans 2010). The same holds, and even to a greater extent, for the contribution that gestures can make to viewpoint construction in oral narration (cf. Sweetser 2012, and chapters in Dancygier and Sweetser 2012), and the possible cultural diversity of these. It is all the more important for linguistics and cognitive science to redress this situation in view of the tight connection between social cognition – the highly developed human capacity to have a deep understanding of the inner life of others – and narrative discourse.

While we do not and cannot aim to achieve this goal in this volume, it constitutes a collection of studies that each aims to provide a step towards realizing it. They find their origin in the theme session "Linguistic manifestations of mixed points of view in narratives – Cognitive and typological perspectives" at the 12th International Cognitive Linguistics Conference, held in Edmonton, Canada in 2013. Papers from that session have been reworked to a greater or lesser extent, and were selected (after revision) by the editors on the basis of reports from two independent reviewers.

Overview of the chapters

Part I: The ubiquity of mixed viewpoints

The chapters in part I of this volume confront existing approaches and concepts in linguistics and cognitive science with wider ranges of data, from several languages. Dancygier and Vandelanotte show that multiplicity of viewpoints is not an exceptional feature of a special kind of discourse – like the mixture of narrator's and character's voices in literary narratives known as Free Indirect Speech – but rather the norm in texts of any size and any genre. Moreover, multiplicity of viewpoints may be introduced and managed in flexible and context dependent ways by linguistic elements of various kinds, not just by 'dedicated' (combinations of) linguistic signals such as those traditionally associated with Free Indirect Speech. Using examples from such different genres as literary narrative and political speeches, they demonstrate that also 'minor' signals (the demonstrative determiner *this*, a negative particle, etc.) may cue the construction of multiple viewpoints. And while a specific phrase in a specific type of context (*Said no one ever* on an "e-card") does have the character of a more or less fixed formula indicating the absurdity of the expression to which it is added, it quickly and in a dynamic way gives rise to extensions in other communicative environments and situations. While all local viewpoints in a text participate in a global understanding at the level of the Discourse Space, they do not become undistinguishable – viewpoint 'mixing' in a stretch of text does not lead to a 'merger' of the viewpoints into a single one. What provides coherence to the way a text is understood is the entire network resulting from the integration of local viewpoint signals.

Vanderbiesen takes his starting point in a general definition of viewpoint in language: viewpoint is present when an expression represents a person's judgement or when that person is responsible for the expression. Mixing of viewpoints then occurs when a single (complex) expression evokes more than one conceptualiser to whom judgements and/or responsibility may be ascribed. Given this conception, two types of viewpoint mixing may be distinguished: the first is called 'quotative': besides the Speaker producing the text (the 'Narrator' in narratives), at least one other person is present in the discourse as a conceptualiser in her own right. The other is 'reportive', and relates to evidentiality (see above): the other person evoked functions as a source of information for the Speaker/Narrator; the focus remains with the latter's viewpoint, the person associated with the second viewpoint is not an independent conceptualiser. With the help of these distinctions, Vanderbiesen undertakes a detailed analysis of a large number of viewpoint mixing constructions in German, ranging from several subtypes of reported speech constructions to modal auxiliary constructions, from which he ultimately concludes that the two types just distinguished actually constitute the endpoints of a single quotative-reportive *cline*, not independently identifiable categories. In fact, many mixed viewpoint expressions turn out not to belong to either one type or the other, but they exhibit features of both of them in varying degrees, with different combinations of grammatical and lexical characteristics providing cues for the relevant interpretation of the mode of viewpoint mixing.

Izutsu and Izutsu also provide a study of viewpointing in two specific languages (in fact, in a specific genre), comparing the forms used in Ainu and Japanese with traditional categories of Speech and Thought Representation. They analyse viewpoint fusion in traditional folktales from Japan. As they are recited by performers in a first-person retelling, they involve a complex set of connected layers of viewpoints 'from the very beginning'. The authors argue that in these folktales, some specific devices actually serve to let some of these layers 'merge', specifically those of Speaker and Narrator on the one hand, and Addressee and Audience on the other. Archaic Japanese evidentials normally mark a shift from Speaker to Narrator, but when their use and non-use alternate, as they do in the folktales, in the telling of the same narrative content, the result is that the distinction between Speaker and Narrator is blurred, which in turn gives the whole narrative a higher sense of "realism". In Ainu, the distinction between inclusive and exclusive first person plural pronominal forms is exploited to distinguish the viewpoint of divine narrators (excluding the human audience and addressees) from that of human ones (inclusive). In both cases, the roles and viewpoints of addressee and audience are merged, again producing an enhanced sense of realism. The authors compare the viewpoint devices they analysed here with patterns of viewpoint mixing like Free Indirect Speech in terms of the Mental Spaces framework.

Given the omnipresence of mixed viewpoints in human communication, it is important to raise the question of the relationship between the ability to understand and process viewpoint mixing and social-cognitive problems. Engberg-Pedersen and Boeg Thomsen investigate the relationship between the development of social cognition ('Theory of Mind') and the use and acquisition of a set of three Danish particles by means of which participants in a conversation can signal their understanding of the interaction in relation to the propositional content of their talk. Based on previous semantic analyses, the authors hypothesize that these particles, labelled dialogue particles, indicate different specific configurations of shared knowledge or lack thereof, and they then develop an experimental way of testing these hypotheses. It turns out that adult speakers of Danish exhibit a high degree of consensus, corroborating the hypotheses and the feasibility of the test. Subsequently, the authors investigate the command of the use of these particles in both normally developing children and children with autism. The capacity to use each of these elements appropriately requires a relatively sophisticated level of socio-cognitive development of children acquiring Danish, corresponding to second-order false belief tasks. A test such as the one developed here might thus provide (a contribution to) a tool for measuring (problems in) socio-cognitive development. Normally developing children aged between 11 and 14 show more variation than adults, and the children with autism, as a group, also perform significantly worse than the control group (while being matched for other aspects of cognitive development). But there is also considerable variation within the group of autistic children tested, and the authors discuss a number of factors potentially involved in this variation.

Part II: Across languages

While the common denominator of the chapters in part I is to confront approaches and concepts with data, stemming from a variety of languages, the three chapters in this part explicitly aim to compare viewpoint mixing *across languages*. Van Krieken, Sanders and Hoeken look at a single genre – journalistic narratives of shocking events – in two languages, English and Dutch. In this genre, there is an important role for eye-witnesses in the narrated content, and a basic communicative goal of engaging the readership, turning them into *mediated* witnesses. The viewpoints of eye-witnesses are represented in similar ways in the two languages, especially by means of verbs of perception and cognition. Also, legitimization is achieved in the same way; by giving information in direct quotations, a narrative-*external* discourse space is accessed: the presentation as literal quotation evokes a witness-report *after* the event. However, dramatization is achieved differently in the narratives in the two languages; whereas the Dutch story uses present tense narration to this end, the American narrative employs free indirect discourse – maintaining the past tense of the story. The authors consider the possibility of different cross-linguistic conventions for blending viewpoints, and argue that their present study provides a good analytic framework to further explore this possibility in a larger corpus and, presumably, also across more languages.

In a somewhat similar vein to Vanderbiesen, Lu and Verhagen show that a specific combination of grammatical and typographical characteristics of English is employed systematically in Lewis Caroll's *Alice in Wonderland* to achieve the effect of a smooth gradual transition from a mixed, narrator-dominant viewpoint construal to a character-dominant one. Using four translations into Chinese as their material, they go on to argue that the lack of some of these characteristics in Mandarin – especially of the option to put a reporting clause in medial position –

apparently makes it difficult for translators to consistently achieve a similar effect. The same difficulty arises in the opposite direction where English lacks a straightforward conventional equivalent of the high frequency deictic movement verbs of Mandarin. Lu and Verhagen argue that translations, as parallel text corpora, provide an important addition to the methodological toolkit of cross-linguistic viewpoint research.

Also using translations as their data, Foolen and Yamaguchi undertake a comparative study of the way viewpoints are managed in different languages by looking at the translations of a Japanese novel (*Beauty and Sadness* by Yasunari Kawabata) into English, German, and Dutch. They start from the assumption that such differences need not be limited to differences in forms and structures, but that they may actually involve different conventional conceptualizations of viewpoint. Relating their discussion to the narratological tradition of perspective analysis, their linguistic approach demonstrates that several other viewpoint phenomena also have to be taken into account – for example granularity (high granularity suggesting closeness). Within this broader framework, they formulate some expectations about differences between the Japanese original and the translations into three West-Germanic languages. Eventually, they find some support for the expected preferences in Japanese, but the three European translations do not exhibit a consistent pattern that contrasts with Japanese. The authors attribute this (at least partly) to the challenging nature of representing the complexities of viewpointing, given the variety of different elements in each language that play a role in guiding the interpretation of viewpoint.

Part III: Across modalities

The last part of this volume extends the scope of viewpoint mixing research beyond the traditional boundaries of linguistic analysis, usually set by a limitation to spoken and/or written texts. The chapter by Fukada considers how viewpointing is effected by the combination of visual and verbal information, in the Japanese picture storybook *Usagi*, and how potential discrepancies between visually and verbally represented viewpoints are dealt with. The visual features investigated include colour, size of characters (cf. the granularity also discussed by Foolen and Yamaguchi), facial expression and gaze direction. The verbally represented viewpoint characteristics comprise direct speech, repetition, deictic expressions, and onomatopeia. The verbal representation turns out to provide a relatively stable view of the world of the two rabbit-characters in the story, but the viewpoints suggested by the pictures vary considerably throughout the book, and include subjective ones that invite a high degree of involvement from the reader with one or both characters. Fukada reports results of an experiment testing how readers deal with apparently conflicting cues, showing that the text actually plays an important role in the construction of readers' perspective on the events being represented.

The chapter by Sweetser and Stec is concerned with the role of one specific feature of co-speech gesturing in viewpoint management in oral narration, viz. gaze. First of all, they show that gaze does not (just) support the spoken channel, but plays an independent role in the on-line construction of meaning: It may mark one viewpoint while the spoken channel represents another. Second, the precise role that gaze plays is in turn heavily dependent on the configuration of Mental Spaces available at a particular moment in the narrative, for example, what portion of the Real Space has been assigned to a particular character in a previous stretch of discourse. Or, again dependent on both properties of the discourse situation and the content of the story being told, gaze is sometimes used to check mutual understanding between the actual Speaker and Addressee, or to enact an aspect of a conversation between characters in the story. Sweetser and Stec's analysis thus underscores both the crucial role of Mental Spaces in discourse understanding and the flexibility of gaze to be used as a meaningful, in fact indispensable, type of co-speech gesture.

Whereas language-specific characteristics investigated in previous chapters involve differences between conventions, the chapter by Jarque and Pascual addresses a type of difference that may be immediately related to the actual physical and perceptual properties of modality in which the language is realized, viz. signed, spoken, and/or written. They examine the construction and function of markers of viewpoint shifting – standardly associated with direct speech – in narratives conducted in sign language, using Catalan Sign Language (LSC) as their material. Researchers of spoken language agree that direct discourse in a conversation serves as an enactment or 'demonstration', rather than as an attempt or claim to reproduce someone else's words as they supposedly have been produced before (cf. the use of exactly the same devices of viewpoint shifting for 'fictive interaction', or in the internet memes discussed by Dancygier and Vandelanotte). Building on this view of spoken interaction, the authors first establish how factual discourse, i.e. quotation, is marked in signed interaction in LSC (among other things: interrupting eye contact with the actual interlocutor and shift of gaze to the position in sign space representing the addressee of the reported utterance); they then go on to show that exactly the same set of devices is employed to convey hypothetical and conditional statements, intentional and attitudinal states of characters, as well as evidentiality (marking that sources differ in their account of the same event). They relate the general, grammaticalized use of the same viewpoint shifting tools for representing both factual discourse and imagined thoughts and attitudes in LSC to a general tendency found in languages without a strong tradition of literacy.

In conclusion

As a whole, this volume testifies to the present state and direction of viewpoint research. On the one hand, the awareness of the variety of viewpointing tools and strategies within and across cultural communities is growing, and so is the insight into their specific character. But by the same token, it is also increasingly clear that there are general cognitive mechanisms and processes underlying the management of multiple viewpoints. Areas that appear to be relatively well charted – like that of Speech and Thought Representation – still see important innovations, both because of increasing cross-linguistic coverage and through integration with insights produced by the study of newly discovered (or recognized) viewpointing phenomena. New areas – like that of gesture – simultaneously benefit from the theoretical and analytical insights and tools developed in the long tradition of Speech and Thought Representation research, and create new directions of investigation and opportunities for deeper, generalized insights. The editors hope that the collection of studies in the present volume will inspire investigators to move this exciting cross-disciplinary field, that is so central to our understanding of what it is to be human, further forward.

References

Boyd, Brian. 2009. *On the Origin of Stories. Evolution, Cognition and Fiction*. Cambridge MA/ London: The Belknap Press of Harvard University Press.

Dancygier, Barbara. 2012a. *The Language of Stories. A Cognitive Approach*. Cambridge: Cambridge University Press.

Dancygier, Barbara. 2012b. Conclusion: multiple viewpoints, multiple spaces. In Barbara Dancygier & Eve Sweetser (eds.), *Viewpoint in Language. A Multimodal Perspective*, 219–231. Cambridge: Cambridge University Press.

Dancygier, Barbara, & Eve Sweetser (eds.). 2012. *Viewpoint in Language. A Multimodal Perspective*. Cambridge: Cambridge University Press.

Duijn, Max J. van, Ineke Sluiter & Arie Verhagen. 2015. When narrative takes over: The representation of embedded mindstates in Shakespeare's *Othello*. *Language and Literature* 24: 148–166.

Enfield, Nick J. & Stephen C. Levinson (eds.). 2006. *Roots of Human Sociality. Culture, Cognition and Interaction*. Oxford/New York: Berg.

Evans, Nicholas. 2010. *Dying Words. Endangered Languages and What They Have to Tell Us.* New York: Wiley-Blackwell.

Jakobson, Roman. 1957. Shifters, verbal categories and the Russian verb. Russian language project, Dept. of Slavic Languages and Literature, Harvard. [Reprinted in Roman Jakobson (1971), *Selected Writings, ii. Word and Language*, 130–147. The Hague: Mouton.]

Sanders, José. 2010. Intertwined voices: Journalists' modes of representing source information in journalistic subgenres. *English Text Construction* 3: 226–249.

Sweetser, Eve. 2012. Introduction: viewpoint and perspective in language and gesture, from the Ground down. In Barbara Dancygier & Eve Sweetser (eds.), *Viewpoint in Language. A Multimodal Perspective*, 1–22. Cambridge: Cambridge University Press.

Vandelanotte, Lieven. 2009. *Speech and Thought Representation in English: A Cognitive-Functional Approach.* Berlin/New York: Mouton de Gruyter.

Verhagen, Arie. 2005. *Constructions of Intersubjectivity. Discourse, Syntax, and Cognition.* Oxford: Oxford University Press.

Zunshine, Lisa. 2006.*Why We Read Fiction. Theory of Mind and the Novel.* Columbus: The Ohio State University Press.

Part I: **The ubiquity of viewpoint**

Barbara Dancygier and Lieven Vandelanotte

Discourse viewpoint as network

Abstract: This paper argues that multiplicity of viewpoint is the norm in discourse, and is best studied in terms of networks of local viewpoints contributing to and supervised by a higher-level Discourse Viewpoint: rather than a hierarchical 'list', then, viewpoint in discourse involves networked configurations. Depending on the viewpoint network required for interpretation, one and the same linguistic form (even a lowly grammatical form such as a pronoun or a determiner) may carry a different meaning, and viewpoint functions emerge in a wide range of contexts, which necessitates study of a broad range of data, not just narratives. The examples discussed in this paper thus include, alongside narrative excerpts, quotes from film discourse, examples of a popular internet meme, and a contemporary piece of video art, all of which evince multiple viewpoint configurations every bit as complex as in traditional narrative, requiring among other things compressions and zoom-outs to be established between discourse, belief and narrative spaces; defocusing and refocusing; and decompression of a discourse and its embodiment. In all cases, we propose that the different viewpoints are reconciled and understood at the level of the Discourse Viewpoint space, regulating and supervising the network.

1 Introduction

Multiplicity of viewpoints is a topic that has often been discussed in the context of narrative discourse (e.g. Mey 1999), where linguistic choices frequently signal the particular perspective of various subjectivities involved – fictional ones in the case of narrators and characters, or non-fictional ones in the context of journalistic prose and other genres (e.g. Sanders 2010). One prominent avenue of research has centered on the representation of speech or thought in various forms, such as direct and (free) indirect speech/thought, as recognizable clusterings of grammatical forms and lexical choices.

While we pay brief attention to this area below, the main aim of this paper is to broaden the scope of enquiry with the help of a range of examples collectively supporting the idea that multiplicity of viewpoint is the norm, not the exception. Part of this re-focusing requires looking not just at broad-ranging constructional clusters such as free indirect speech/thought but also at seemingly 'innocent' or 'viewpoint-neutral' lower-level constructions, down to the level of examples such as determiners or negation, which we will show can also function as viewpoint markers. Correspondingly, the range of text types considered needs to be enlarged: much as full-scale narratives remain important sites for the management of multiple viewpoints, some of our examples show similar complexities at work in far more condensed form, for instance that of an internet meme. At both lower and higher levels of discourse complexity, we suggest that viewpoints are organized hierarchically and in terms of a network, with local viewpoint choices achieving overall coherence in what one might call a top-level or 'Discourse Viewpoint' space, from which lower-level viewpoint choices are overseen.

Starting from an understanding of viewpoint as a discourse participant's alignment with an aspect of a frame or situation, we want to look at examples from different types of discourse forms – not just narrative – to study how viewpoint multiplicity and its particular configuration is dependent in equal measure on local and global viewpoint phenomena (for example, specific to a scene or organizing the text as a whole); these configurations change as the discourse unfolds. In addition, because the traditional focus on multiple viewpoints in individual sentences (for instance in sentences of direct or (free) indirect speech or thought) does not allow for a textured view of how viewpoints are expressed, shifted, manipulated, etc., we propose to move away from a sentence-based approach. In this respect, our guiding assumptions are as follows:

1. *Viewpoints are hierarchically ordered*; even if at any one point a given viewpoint is selected for 'local' purposes, it still participates in viewpoint construction at a higher level, as earlier work by Dancygier (2005, 2012a) on viewpoint compression has demonstrated for narrative fiction. Thus, for instance, in (1) below, a travel writer sees TV coverage of his own departure, and temporarily the narrative viewpoint is compressed with the viewpoint of the writer/traveller (*he*)-as-TV-viewer (*me*), rather than simply the writer/traveller-as-traveller (which would have yielded 'my face had a cheesy pallor' and 'I looked like a clowning greenhorn'):

(1) *The TV news went local. An Englishman had left Minneapolis that day in a small motor boat [...]. In the picture on the screen his face had a cheesy pallor. [...] He looked to me like a clowning greenhorn.* (Jonathan Raban, *Old Glory*; example quoted in Dancygier 2005: 109)

While what (1) presents is at one level a TV viewer's perception of a TV news report, at the same time it contributes to the higher level Discourse Viewpoint, in this case that of the narrator of *Old Glory*; otherwise, the reader would not be able to see that the writer is in fact talking about his own image on TV.

2. *Specific viewpoint configurations available at any given point in the text are structured through language choices*; these choices often coincide with "global" categories established in existing literature (e.g. categories applied to constructions or even discourse fragments, such as direct vs. indirect vs. free indirect speech/thought), but are more effectively considered as constellations of "local" (word, phrase or sentence level) individual viewpoint parameters: tense, pronouns, proper names, adverbs, syntactic embedding, clause sequence, modality and polarity, conjunction, expressive lexemes, etc. In addition, temporal viewpoint may be separate from and independent of emotional viewpoint or epistemic viewpoint, as in those celebrated cases where a narrator's past tense is used in speech or thought representation contexts where a character's heightened emotion state is represented. In (2), for instance, the pastness of *was* is understood with respect to the narrator, whereas the despondent feelings and questioning attitudes expressed are clearly those of the character Ursula. Combining the narrator's past perspective (*was*) and the character's present perspective (*tomorrow*) has come to be known as free indirect discourse, loosely speaking a construction, but the nature of that construction centrally depends on the two independent viewpoints represented:

(2) *Tomorrow was Monday. Monday, the beginning of another school-week! Another shameful, barren school-week, mere routine and mechanical activity. Was not the adventure of death infinitely preferable? Was not death infinitely more lovely and noble than such a life?* (D.H. Lawrence, *Women in Love*, Ch. XV)

Different linguistic choices regarding the representation of participants involved in the discourse thus yield different multiple viewpoint configurations.

3. *Viewpoints expressed in a text form a network, rather than just a hierarchical list*. While there needs to be a top-level, unifying viewpoint space, it can build on various configurations of lower-level spaces. Possible configurations may include embedded spaces, parallel spaces, alternative spaces, or even two independent networks of spaces, depending on the nature of the text; in fragmented narratives, for example, the text may develop rather elaborate networks before the unifying space becomes salient. To explain the final cohesion of such a network, we will rely on the concept of viewpoint compression (as described in Dancygier 2012a), as a phenomenon which allows viewpoint to be conceptualized coherently; importantly, in the reader's mind, all lower-level or sub-network viewpoints are naturally considered with respect to their role and salience in the relevant part of the network, rather than as sentence-level interpretations. This assumption

allows one to understand viewpoint emergence in more complex texts, where a sentence-level viewpoint configuration (e.g., a stretch of direct speech) may participate in higher-level textual viewpoint (e.g., construction of a character).

4. *Multiplicity of viewpoint is not restricted to the commonly recognized categories; new constructions emerge in various contexts and genres.* The variety and flexibility of such examples require that we develop theoretical tools to deal with multiple viewpoints in a range of expressions, narrative and non-narrative alike. We hope to propose an approach which adequately deals with both well-described and new discourse forms.

2 Viewpoint and constructional forms

Free Indirect Discourse provides a textbook example of a construction widely considered to involve mixing of viewpoints – often couched in terms of "dual voice" (e.g. Pascal 1977; see Vandelanotte 2009: 244–255 for discussion and references) – of the current speaker (or 'narrator') and the represented speaker (or character). In example (2), quoted above, the thoughts of the represented speaker (the character Ursula) are rendered without the syntactic incorporation into the current speaker's discourse typical of Indirect Discourse, but, as we pointed out above, temporal expressions are not consistent – the word *tomorrow* signals the viewpoint of the represented speaker Ursula, while the choice of past tense takes into account the temporal distance between the 'now' of the current speaker and the temporal frame of the past story being told. This is, then, a true example of linguistic choices which signal multiple viewpoints. The construction as a whole is thus a good example of what has been called a 'mixed-viewpoint construction'.

However, describing various kinds of multiple viewpoint forms as 'mixing' the viewpoints involved is, in our view, not a fully descriptive term. The term 'mixed' may be understood to imply that the viewpoints, once combined, 'merge' so as to become indistinguishable, or yield a constructional level at which they are fused, while in fact, each individual viewpoint expression in (2) is easily assigned to a specific participant. It seems possible to talk about fusion or mixing when multiple viewpoints of participants are built into one form (as is the case, for example, in expressions which Evans (2005) and others have referred to as 'triangular' kin terms, which reflect the relation of both speaker and addressee to the referent). But even in those cases, the intended multiplicity is recognizable at the meaning level. In more elaborate constructional forms, such as the "*Past + now*" construction (often signalling Free Indirect Discourse) described in Nikiforidou (2012), or in some of the examples discussed below, viewpoints may be allocated to various independent expressions within a higher frame of the construction. In such cases, it is not quite accurate to talk about mixing. What can be argued, though, is that the independently expressed viewpoints become participants in a configuration which compresses them to a higher level viewpoint of the whole construction.

Constructions such as Direct, Indirect and Free Indirect Discourse are far from being the only constructions relying on viewpoint allocation. As Sweetser (2012) argues, viewpoint phenomena are pervasive, and individuals cannot escape viewpointed conceptualizations (even if only because of their temporal and spatial location), but, at the same time, a single mind can access multiple viewpoints on the same scene – if we see an object on our left, we are also aware that the same object is perceived as being on the right by the person facing us. These examples should not suggest that viewpoint is primarily spatial or temporal. In another context, we are fully capable of understanding that while we are ourselves satisfied with a tiny car, a person who has a large family may need to buy a van. While such dimensions of viewpoint may not yield themselves to straightforward grammatical analysis, there are in fact constructions which specialize in the expression of experiential viewpoint and profile it through grammatical means. An example of this is a range of constructions in English which use the genitive form as an experiential viewpoint marker (Dancygier 2009):

(3) *One person**'s** trash is another person**'s** treasure.*
*Benghazi may turn out to be Hillary**'s** Waterloo.*
***My** Vancouver includes the East Side.*

Each of the genitive forms in (3) profiles a person's viewpoint – objects may be valuable or not in the view of a given person, an event may put a politician in a situation analogous to Napoleon's defeat at Waterloo, and a resident's evaluation of the nature of the city may make them more or less understanding of differences in wealth and standard of living. Similarly, negation may be used to reject a viewpointed understanding of a situation, rather than negating the truth of a fact (Dancygier 2012b):

(4) *Q: What do you hope to gain by behaving in this way? A: I **don't** hope to gain **some**thing. I'm just doing what I think is right.*

In (3) and (4), low-level grammatical forms such as genitive or negative markers provide a viewpointed construal of the situations described, rather than possession or negation. At the same time, this does not preclude the emergence of full constructions which rely on such minimal viewpoint markers in important ways. For example, *One person's X is another person's Y* is a common construction which goes beyond marking one viewpoint. It contrasts two possible viewpoints on an object or a situation, and relies on rich frames associated with the X and Y expressions. The trash/treasure contrast is naturally imbued with viewpoint, but not all uses of the construction require that. For instance, in the example *One person's city street is another person's home*, used to comment on the issue of homelessness and lack of compassion on the part of some city inhabitants, *street* and *home* are not inherently viewpointed in the way that *trash* ('negative') and *treasure* ('positive') clearly are. It is the viewpoint-contrasting strength of the construction that yields the comparison, and the attendant evaluation, but while the contrast is a more broadly constructional matter, the viewpointed meaning relies on the genitive.

These examples suggest, then, that while constructions as wholes are meaningful structures, possibly engaged in viewpoint expression, their components may provide the lower-level viewpoints that the construction then organizes in more elaborate structures. We argue that this is true also of the standard speech and thought representation constructions. We cannot engage here in a full analysis of all potential viewpoint markers involved, but we will discuss examples where compositional analysis of viewpoint yields a more accurate analysis of the data at hand.

The next two sections start out from observations on pronouns, featuring first person pronouns relying heavily on the broader viewpoint network for their interpretation in section 3, and relating findings on pronoun choice and verbs of seeing to broader questions in section 4. In section 5 we show particular viewpointed deictic functions of determiners, to next consider broader discourse patterns in sections 6 (on the *said no one ever* meme) and 7 (on a piece of video art characterized by a disconnect between discourse and embodiment). A concluding section rounds off the paper.

3 Pronouns, viewpoint networks and viewpoint compression

In this section we consider examples where the use of the same grammatical form (in this case, the pronoun *I*) yields different meanings because of the different structure of the overall viewpoint set-up. First person pronoun *I* is typically considered in the context of one discourse space, with a single deictic centre (space, time, speaker, hearer). In this standard set-up, the pronoun *I* refers consistently to the speaker of the discourse presented in the discourse space. However, in narrative examples such as (5), this is not the case:

(5) *He started off on Aragon – had I read* Le Paysan de Paris*? Did I remember the Passage Jouffroy in Paris? What did I think of St. Jean Perse? Or* Nadja *of Breton? Had I been to Knossus yet? I ought to stay a few weeks at least – he would take me over the island from one end to another. He was a very hale and hearty fellow and when he understood that I liked to eat and drink he beamed most approvingly.* (Henry Miller, *The Colossus of Maroussi*; example quoted in Dancygier 2012a: 187)

The fragment represents a conversation between the first-person narrator and a Cretan man. They talk about literature, and about the attractions of Crete. The Cretan asks a number of questions, while the narrator is the addressee. The first question asked, then, was actually 'Have you read *Le Paysan de Paris*?'. The tense is shifted into the past to represent the fact that the story is told from the present viewpoint of the writer, while describing the past visit to Crete. The form of the question is preserved, and the pronoun 'you' is shifted into the first person 'I', thus connecting the Cretan's discourse to the flow of the first person narration. This (rather specific) form of discourse representation has been described by Vandelanotte (2004, 2012a) as DIST – Distancing Indirect Speech or Thought. It is characterized by a single, constant deictic centre (as contrasted with the two operative in example (2) above), such that all discourse of the narrative is subjected to one shared viewpoint of the first person narrative. The pronoun *I* is thus not cross-linked to the actual speaker (the Cretan man, Mr Tsoutsou), but to the addressee and narrator, which occasionally confuses readers, who expect *I* to consistently refer to the current speaker, not the represented addressee. In this case, the embedding of the conversation in the narrative discourse provides a higher level Discourse Viewpoint which subordinates all lower level deixis to the highest level deixis of the first person narrative. This is what we mean by saying that the viewpoint of a grammatical form results from the structure of the network, not an isolated sentence participating in that network.

For comparison, the ostensibly Direct Discourse fragment in (6) represents a different pattern:

(6) *I am a politician, which means that I'm a cheat and a liar, and when I'm not kissing babies I'm stealing their lollipops, but it also means that I have options.* (*The Hunt for Red October*)

Although the politician speaking refers to himself as 'I' (predictably), he is not really describing himself from his own perspective. On the contrary, when he calls himself a cheat and a liar, he is sarcastically echoing descriptions which might have been offered by people who do not think highly of politicians. This makes (6) a good example of what Clark has discussed under the rubric of "staged communicative acts" (1996: 368–378), in which interlocutors knowingly engage in joint pretence within a single communicative act, in order to "mutually appreciate the salient contrasts between the demonstrated and actual situations" (Clark 1996: 368). Staged communicative acts include not just irony and sarcasm, but also, for instance, teasing, rhetorical questions, under- and overstatement, and hyper- and misunderstanding (on the latter two notions, see e.g. Brône 2008; Brône and Oben 2013).

One reading of Clark's argument seems to suggest, however, that there is a hierarchy of viewpoints, where the "serious" attitude is in a sense in the scope of the "nonserious" one. While the final interpretation indeed suggests shared pretence, the details of how such meanings are construed require clarification. We argue that the configuration and the process are in fact more complex, with the "serious" and "nonserious" takes co-existing, and the clash between them being resolved at a higher level, which we label "Discourse Viewpoint space". This brings our interpretation in line with the recent interpretation of irony, offered in Tobin and Israel (2012), wherein the clash of viewpoints can only be resolved from a higher, zoom-out perspective.

In (6), the belief that politicians are cheats and liars and the discourse representing that belief are incorporated into the discourse of the speaker. As a result, the viewpoint has to be incorporated into the viewpoint structure in which *I* does in fact refer to the actual speaker (the politician). What needs to be resolved in the previous example (5) is, one might say, "who's who" within a single speech event (such that it becomes understood the Cretan Mr. Tsoutsou did not actually say "Had I read *Le Paysan de Paris*" but rather "Have you read *Le Paysan de Paris*"). The present example (6), on the other hand, can only be resolved once it is understood to relate to a second speech event or discourse space, in which people voice their strong mistrust of politicians.

Figures 1 and 2 attempt to capture this difference from the point of view of the reader's or viewer's interpretive processing (cf. Rohrer 2005). In these diagrams, we distinguish 'discourse/belief spaces', containing some discourse participant's discourse or belief, from 'narrative spaces', which may contain spatial and temporal settings, events, characters and narrators, and which participate in the story which emerges when readers read narrative texts (cf. Dancygier 2012a: 36). Dotted lines show correspondences between discourse participants. The overarching, "global" viewpoint that is construed by the network of lower-level viewpoints is ultimately located in what we call the Discourse Viewpoint Space.

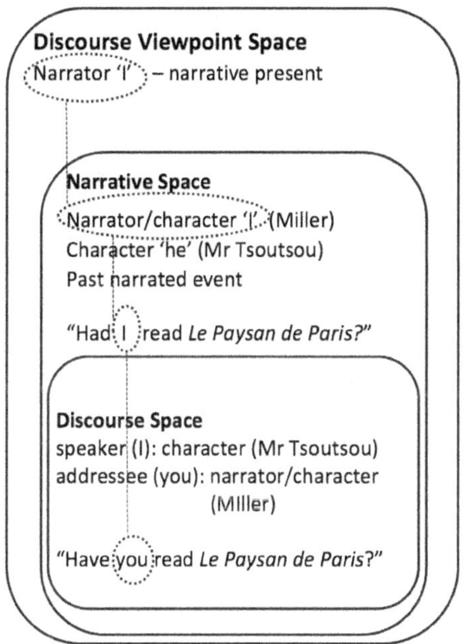

Figure 1: Resolving the Miller example (5): one discourse space embedded in a narrative space

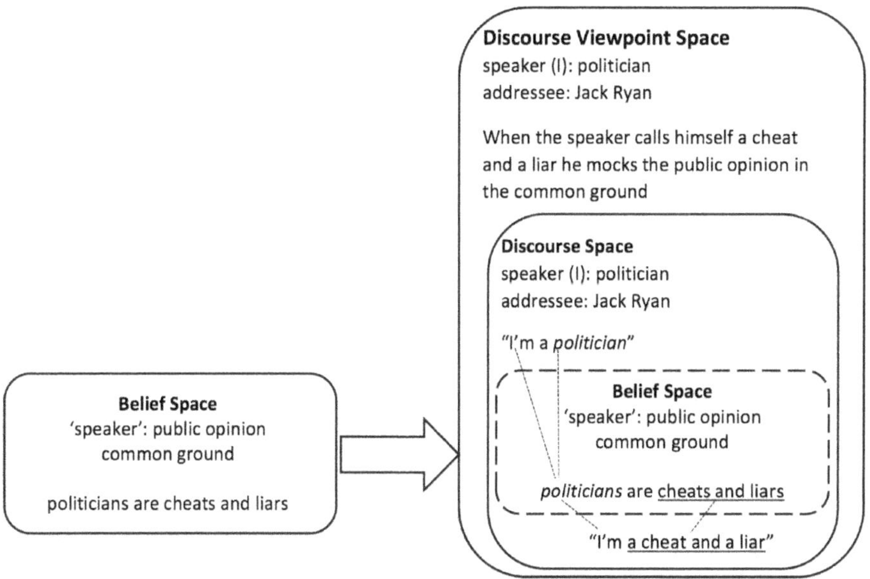

Figure 2: Resolving the *Red October* example (6): a discourse space and a belief space

In Figure 1, the Discourse Viewpoint Space of the narration is deictically linked to the narrator's present time and first person identity. The story includes many narrative spaces, including one represented in (5); this narrative space, in turn, contains a discourse space – a conversation. Each of these spaces has its own topology (time, place, participants, etc.). However, in this case, even though in the bottom level of the Discourse Space the narrator is an addressee (*you*), viewpoint compression aligns the network with the Discourse Viewpoint Space, where he is represented as *I*. The network structure determines the form and its meaning.

The network in (6) is different from the one in (5). While the listener initially has access only to the Discourse Space, where the politician and Jack Ryan are participants, what is said evokes a Belief Space, which represents public opinion in the common ground. The two spaces are parts of independent networks, but interpreting (6) requires that they are incorporated into one network (the outlined arrow indicates the projection of one space into another). As a result, the viewpoint of the Belief Space is projected into the Discourse Space, where it expands the discourse understanding of who a politician is and yields the ensuing self-mocking description. The discourse fragment is now governed by the discourse viewpoint which is informed by the Belief Space and gives meaning to the Discourse Space. The *I* in the expressions *I'm a politician* and *I have options* is directly aligned with the deictic set-up of the Discourse Space, but, because there is no speaking participant or temporal alignment in the Belief Space, the *I* is further projected to the mock-echoic expression *I'm a cheat and a liar*. The choice of the pronoun is dictated by the network again, even though this network is very different from the one in (5).

4 Pronouns and verbs of seeing

The analyses above suggest that viewpoint configurations have an important role in our understanding of pronouns. It is interesting to consider these observations in the context of experimental studies of simulation prompted by pronouns. One such study (Brunyé et al. 2009; cf. Bergen 2012: 113–114) tested the response to pronouns using (matching or non-matching) pictures of activities such as slicing a tomato or ironing pants. The activities were shown either from an internal perspective (where a viewer would feel engaged in the activity) or an external one (where the viewer would be an observer of somebody else's action), and subjects were expected to press a "yes" or "no" button ("yes" for pictures matching the event description, "no" for a mismatch, i.e. when the relevant objects were depicted but were not being used in the action described). The study showed how grammar influences the viewpoint from which to simulate a scene: it found that the subjects were responding faster to participant perspective pictures ('internal') following *you* sentences and to observer perspective pictures ('external') following *he* sentences. However, the results for the use of first person pronouns were less straightforward. There the responses were faster if the pronoun *I* was used with participant perspective pictures ('internal') accompanying short sentences (*I am slicing a tomato*), but when a more elaborate context was added (*I am a 30-year-old deli employee. I'm making a vegetable wrap. Right now, I'm slicing a tomato.*) subjects responded faster to observer perspective pictures ('external', i.e. simulating *someone else* slicing a tomato). Brunyé et al. and Bergen suggest that the effect may be due to the fact that a more elaborate context makes it clear who the referent is.

In their discussion of this experiment, Sanford and Emmott (2013: 162–169) agree that the experiment shows the importance of linguistically driven cues to viewpoint, but they do rightly point out that, even in the condition in which some context was added, the materials used in the experiment remain much simpler than real narratives. Other factors, including lexical choices, style, and text types should be taken into account; in particular, they (2013: 166–167) argue, presence vs. absence of internal perspective cues in the text, including verbs of seeing (e.g. *I noticed*), certain deictic expressions (e.g. *right in front of me*) or markers of vagueness or lack of knowledge (e.g. *something*), constitutes a more decisive factor than length of context provided.

We agree with Sanford and Emmott that the nature of textual viewpoint clues matters significantly for viewpointed interpretation, but we also argue that it is very difficult to establish the effectiveness of such means without also considering the network involved. We consider two textual examples of narrative reliance on vision, (7) and (8) below, which, in Sanford and Emmott's interpretation, should prompt for internal perspective. The examples illustrate different ways in which presence vs. absence of seeing verbs need not correlate directly with presence vs. absence of internal perspective. In the first, the explicit marking of 'seeing' arguably makes the perspective less rather than more internal:

(7) *I see us turn and walk away toward the gap in the dunes that led to Station Road. A corner of Chloe's towel trails in the sand. I go along with my towel draped over one shoulder and my wet hair slicked down, a Roman senator in miniature. Myles runs ahead. But who is it that lingers there on the strand in the half-light, by the darkening sea that seems to arch its back like a beast as the night fast advances from the fogged horizon? What phantom version of me is it that watches us – them – those three children – as they grow indistinct in that cinereal air and then are gone through the gap that will bring them out at the foot of Station Road?* (John Banville, *The Sea*; example quoted in Vandelanotte 2010: 220)

If we compare *I see us turn and walk* to *We turn and walk* we find that the expression *I see us* is in fact a case of 'distanced' narration yielding a 'floating eye' style 'view of a viewpoint'. In this case, a conceptualizing subject takes himself (along with two others) as the object of conceptualization (*I* see *us*). Furthermore, there is a zooming out effect (cf. Tobin and Israel 2012) prompted by going from the use of *us* (inclusive 'we', including the I-narrator) over *them* (personal pronoun marking high accessibility in the sense of Ariel 1990) to *those three children* (distal demonstrative pronoun). In this case, the narrative network dampens the embodied effect of *see*.

Our next example suggests that while 'see' may be important as a means of evoking the 'internal perspective', it may in fact be implied rather than explicitly used. In example (8), a photographer is describing her first experience with a traditional camera:

(8) *It was a summer afternoon in 1917. My father hung upside down in the little lozenge of glass; my mother's chair was stuck in a canopy of flowers where my beautiful brother Orlando's toes were planted...* (Paul Theroux, *The Picture Palace*; example quoted in Dancygier 2012a: 94)

It used to be the case that looking through a camera lens yielded an upside down image (which then appeared the right side up in the photograph). This is the experience the fragment describes, without ever referring to it as seeing. The description of a striking image makes sense not as an act of visual perception, but as an element in the complex network of narrative spaces and frames, where what the photographer sees is the image on the lens, not the actual situation. This is, quite naturally, an internal perspective, but it has to be first appreciated as such, to be then understood as an act of seeing. To conclude, seeing, whether mentioned or implied, may involve an internal perspective, but not automatically. In the context of a narrative, the nature of the network and its specific profiling of subjectivity capable of taking an internal perspective plays an equally important role. We assume that the same may appear to be the case if other 'internalizing' means mentioned by Sanford and Emmott are involved.

5 Deictics as viewpoint markers

In this section we turn to examples of deictic *this* functioning as viewpoint marker, where it serves to navigate the multiple viewpoints present in a network rather than to yield a properly 'mixed' perspective. Here again, then, as discussed in section 2, there is multiplicity but not mixing. The first example comes from a novel:

(9) *I will come home and the door will be open, wide. The babysitter will be gone and there will be silence. (...) At the steps up to Toph's room there will be blood. Blood on the walls, handprints soaked in blood. (...) I will be to blame. (...) There will be a hearing, a trial, a short trial –*

How did you come to meet this man, this baby-sitter?
We found a posting, on a bulletin board.
And how long did your interview of him take?
Ten, twenty minutes. (...) (Dave Eggers, *A Heartbreaking Work of Staggering Genius;* example quoted in Dancygier 2012a: 38)

Dancygier (2012a: 38–40) discusses this example at length to point out various viewpoint phenomena. The story presents the main character, who left a child (his brother Toph) with a babysitter, worrying about the situation and spinning very unlikely scenarios to flesh out the worries. The man, Dave, imagines the babysitter as a murderer and goes on to imagine himself being put on trial for trusting the wrong person. There are many important viewpoint phenomena here. The imagined future situation (finding the child murdered) and the imagined future trial in which Dave is asked questions are all contained in a higher space of the narrative, that of the time spent driving when Dave lets his imagination flow. The represented thoughts of Dave take the form of direct discourse in the trial, so that in effect direct speech has the function of free indirect thought. Temporal viewpoint is also tricky, as in the context of the trial the past event of the murder is in fact an imagined future event in the main story.

However, for the purposes of our discussion here, we want to focus on the use of the proximal demonstrative *this*. When the imagined prosecutor asks *How did you come to meet this man, this baby-sitter?* he is referring to a person who is absent: strangely, the fantasy does not even assume Stephen, the baby-sitter, to also be on trial for the murder, and the nameless reference to him as a *man* and *baby-sitter* further suggests that he is considered perhaps with contempt, but in any case as an unimportant nonentity not relevant to the case in hand; in Dave's fantasy, he alone is to blame, hence the choice of expressions. Given Stephen's absence from the scene, spatial proximity is not the issue in using the proximal *this*. Also temporal proximity seems unlikely, given that the prosecutor is using a distal past tense to talk about the event of Stephen and Dave meeting for the first time. Our explanation is that the prosecutor's repeated use of *this* here resets the viewpoint of the exchange from the events of the murder, to the point of Dave having made the wrong decision in hiring Stephen as baby-sitter; the specific point may seem irrelevant to the murder, but is uniquely relevant to the fantasy concocted so that Dave can indulge in blaming himself for all the potentially bad decisions he makes as a guardian of his brother. The proximal demonstrative here maintains its indexical function, but it organizes viewpointed narrative spaces, rather than objects or people: from the reader's perspective, it creates a connection between the imagined space of the trial, with its embedded discourse between prosecutor and defendant, and the past (hence real, but actually 'distal') space of Dave interviewing and hiring Stephen. *This* is thus in effect a viewpoint marker, pointing to the narrative space currently in focus in the exchange – the trial, in which *this man* is currently being discussed and so 'proximal' in terms of discourse activation – and contributing to the overall Discourse Viewpoint, which portrays Dave as getting lost in exaggerated fears and self-doubt.

Our second example comes from Barack Obama's victory speech in 2008 – a different genre altogether. In the fragment, Obama talks about Ann Nixon Cooper, first introduced in his speech as "a woman who cast her ballot in Atlanta", more specifically a (then) 106-year-old African American woman who voted in the election, using a computer screen. The point is to highlight all the ways in which the 2008 election changed all the expected standards – it allowed an older person to use the benefits of the internet, and it allowed an African American woman to vote for an African American candidate for President:

(10) *A man touched down on the moon, a wall came down in Berlin, a world was connected by our own science and imagination. And this year, in this election, she touched her finger to a screen, and cast her vote, because after 106 years in America, through the best of times and the darkest of hours, she knows how America can change. Yes we can.*

In the fragment, Obama lists some crucial events and developments which resulted in freedom and access to technology[1] – the prerequisites of Cooper's ability to vote for him. Importantly, these events are described with indefinite articles, in spite of their uniqueness and clear referential status (Neil Armstrong, the Berlin Wall)[2]: they are such central referents within the common ground (cf. Clark 1996: Ch. 4) that the seemingly general description given is in fact sufficiently informative for listeners to identify the specific instances for Obama and the audience to jointly focus attention on. (For comparison, the unique identity of *a woman who cast her ballot in Atlanta* is not part of the common ground, so Obama in his speech quickly follows this NP up with the woman's proper name and further particulars.).

When, having discussed the frames of freedom and technology, whose advances come together in the life-story of Cooper, Obama returns to the issue of the election, he uses *this* (*this year, in this election*). As was the case with his choice for *a* (in *a man, a wall, a world*), with this determiner choice too he is manipulating the viewpoints in his speech. The events and people mentioned (such as the landing on the moon or, in an earlier part, various important moments in the Civil Rights movement) are not specific events he focuses his viewpoint on – they are just 'illustrative' material from the past he uses to highlight freedom and technology (Figure 3). But when he returns to the space which is in focus – the current election and its results – he uses the demonstrative proximal *this*, in ways similar to how it was used in example (9).

We argue, then, that in the context of complex discourse, basic grammatical forms (pronouns, determiners, tense, etc.) may be used not in their basic deictic function, but to manipulate the deixis of the event spaces involved. The indefinite article may then defocus a salient space, while *this* can designate a space as the one currently in focus. Both forms work as viewpoint markers, just like the pronouns discussed in Sections 3 and 4. It is interesting to note that the recent innovation in the quotative system in inner-city London, discussed as "*this is + speaker*" by Fox (2012), combines precisely the viewpoint focusing element of demonstrative *this*, referring cataphorically to the ensuing quote (cf. Vandelanotte 2012b: 187), with personal pronouns:

(11) [Airport security staff checks a potentially suspicious spray]
they sprayed the spray yeh (...)
like just to check that it weren't anything.

1 The discourse fragment relying on indefinite articles is in fact much longer, detailing major events in the struggle for civil rights in America.

2 We want to thank Adrian Lou for drawing our attention to this usage.

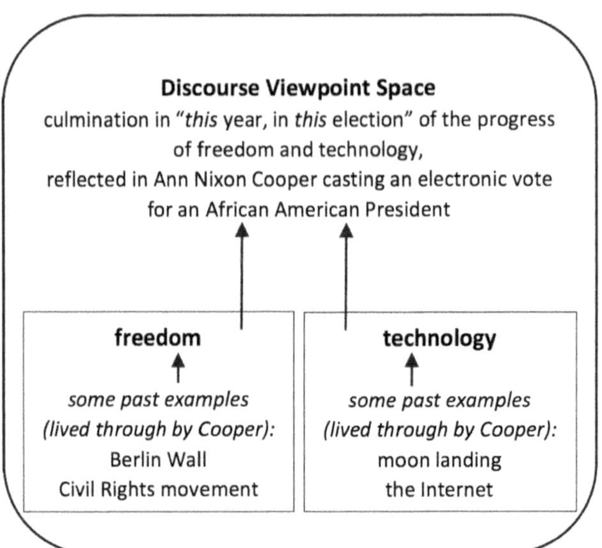

Figure 3: Defocused events contributing to the Discourse Viewpoint in focus

> bruv when I say they were smelling weed
> this is him. **this is them** "what's that smell that's coming out?"
> **this is him** "oh i dunno like it must be d.d. thing"
> (Fox 2012: 251; emphasis original)

The use of *this is + pronoun* seems a very explicit means of opening up and focusing on different speakers' discourse spaces. In the next section we turn to a much more subtle device opening up a discourse space which effectively turns out to have no appropriate accompanying speakers, but which nevertheless contributes significantly to the Discourse Viewpoint intended.

6 Unattributable discourse in an internet meme

Among the more interesting complex viewpoint constructions to have emerged in recent years is the use of *said no one ever*, particularly in internet memes[3] typically going round in the form of "e-cards". In their most formulaic form, e-cards

3 While "said no one ever" may have become a set expression, it is primarily interesting to us as appearing ubiquitously in so-called "internet memes". A pervasive form of on-line communication, memes also rely crucially on easily recognizable linguistic forms and varying visual images.

such as those featuring *said no one ever* combine text in a plain style with a stylized drawing of a man or woman, often in the style of 1950s or 1960s advertising, against a bright monochrome background, but other forms featuring full-colour photos of people and block lettering can also be widely found. We do not propose to consider the visual aspects in detail, but want to focus on the family of *said no one ever* and related forms in terms of the kind of viewpoint they present. Consider two typical examples below (Figures 4 and 5), taken (like all examples in this section) from the Internet, the first in the typical stylized format, the second in the freer picture-cum-lettering format:

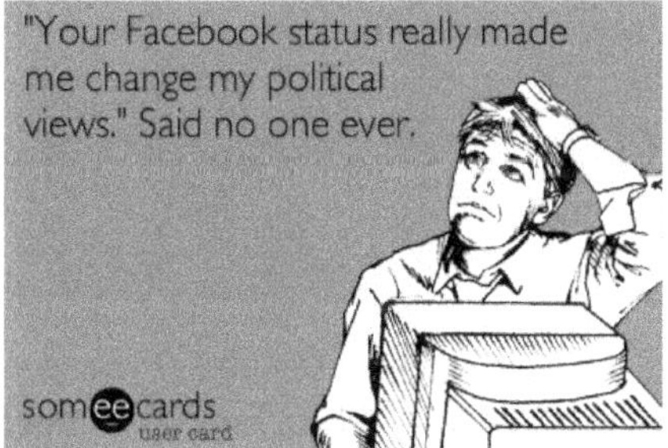

Figure 4: From someecards.com

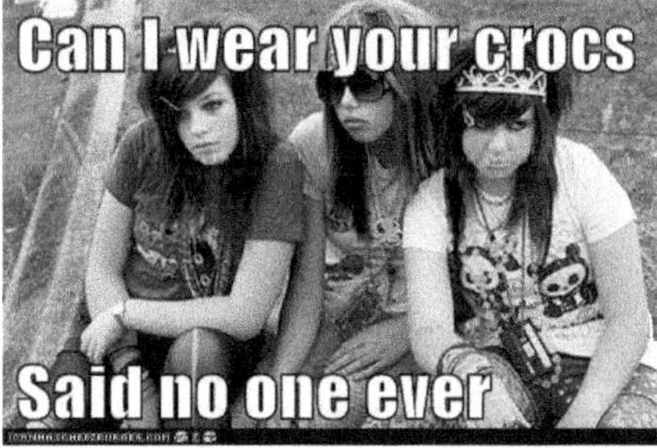

Figure 5: From cheezburger.com

The use of quotation marks as in Figure 4 is typically taken as a signal that Direct Discourse is involved, and thus as an instruction to locate the speaker in the discourse context, who is naturally assumed at first glance to be embodied by the person depicted in the card, presumably addressing the card's reader. In examples without quotation marks, such as Figure 5, the default assumption in online processing initially must be that *I* and *you* simply refer to a speaker depicted in the picture (one of the bored looking hipster girls in the case of Figure 5) and the card's recipient respectively. In both types of cases, when one gets to *said no one ever* it turns out that the expectation is not met, since apparently the preceding speech act (typically a statement as in Figure 4 but a request in Figure 5) cannot be attributed to anyone.

The "said no one ever" meme is different from occasional conversational uses of "non-quoting" Direct Discourse, as in (12) below, which fit into a family of conditional, counterfactual or negated uses, illustrating the point that direct speech

We argue that they provide very relevant data in the study of viewpoint (which distinguishes our approach from that represented by Shifman 2013a, b).

does not always "report" a pre-given "original" (see e.g. von Roncador 1988, Vandelanotte 2009: Ch. 4). In (12), the negated quote is used to underscore a point within a discourse context in which a lot of details are coloured in, relating to a parent whose talents do not lie in baking; note also that the negated *say* clause precedes the unattributable quote. In "said no one ever" memes as in (13), on the other hand, the negation indicating the quote's non-attributability necessarily follows the quote, and the construction is used unprompted, to make a clever sarcastic or amusing comment on people's typical behaviour.

(12) *No one has ever said: Nance, these are the best brownies I've tasted. And for my son's 11th birthday he begged me to buy, not bake, his cake. The child was right; I shouldn't bake.* (Cobuild corpus, National Public Radio)

(13) *"I love listening to all the crap you're going through, and you never asking about my crap. It's awesome."*
Said no one ever.[4]

In terms of viewpoint, we believe this construction is best understood in terms of the kind of "zoom out" proposed by Tobin and Israel (2012) in their account of irony: because of some perceived incongruity which prompts for a re-evaluation, attention shifts from a 'lower' mental space where viewpoint initially is located to a 'higher' one, the Discourse Viewpoint space. Thus, in Figure 4, the initial viewpoint *Your Facebook status really made me change my political views* has to be re-evaluated as a result of the *said no one ever* part, as not being said by the card's speaker to its reader, but rather being said by no-one to no-one. These two incompatible viewpoints are resolved in the final Discourse Viewpoint, according to which what people say on Facebook has no influence on people's political views (Figure 6): the idea that anyone would ever say their views were influenced by Facebook posts is effectively presented as being too ridiculous to contemplate. The initial viewpoint thus ends up being re-construed as its opposite very effectively and economically, in ways similar to the conversational use of *not* as a sarcastic, zooming-out follow-up (as in *That dress looks so cute on you. NOT*).

This type of example cleverly exploits an important aspect of Clark's notion of common ground, namely his observation that when we act on the basis of our common ground, "we are in fact acting on our individual beliefs or assumptions about what is in our common ground" (1996: 96), since we cannot take it as given

4 Examples (13) and following in this section are quoted from the Internet with punctuation, capitalization and (deliberate) line breaks between the initial part and *said no one ever* given as found in the e-card.

that we truly have corresponding mutual beliefs about something. The zoom-out operation described above serves to explicitly construe part of the common ground: the viewer's likely suspicion that *Your Facebook status really made me change my political views* cannot be a serious claim is confirmed by *said no one ever*, and allows the 'card writer' and 'card viewer' to jointly add the belief that Facebook posts never influence people's political views to the intersubjectively construed common ground.

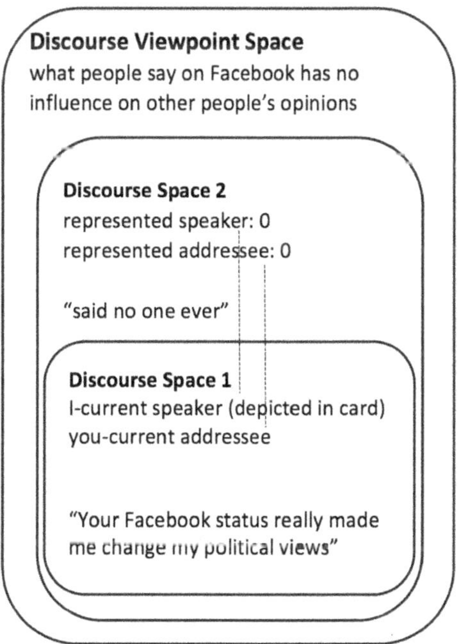

Figure 6: *Said no one ever*: Zoom-out to Discourse Viewpoint space.

In some respects, the network in Figure 6 is similar to Figure 2, which is not too surprising given that both require a reinterpretation of an ostensibly straightforward statement by the speaker. In both cases common ground changes the viewpoint of what is being said. There are important differences, though. In Figure 2 we saw a common ground belief incorporated into the discourse, yielding an actual utterance where the speaker presents himself and his political role in the worst possible way. Here we see the emergence of a proposed common ground, on the basis of embedding the ostensible (not actual) utterance, which is not in itself conspicuously odd, in a clause rejecting its utterance status and communicative validity. We are not suggesting that these differences distinguish some well-defined types of viewpoint configurations; rather, we are pointing out that the nature of these configurations is directly relevant to the emergent meaning. The need for incorporation of multiple viewpoints into coherent discourse structure is what is shared across all these examples; the specific patterns of incorporation vary.

A number of extensions from the constructional template illustrated in Figures 4–5 and (13) are worth noting. One is exemplified in (14–15), and concerns condensed forms in which the full clause *said no one ever* is shortened to *no one ever* or even just *nobody*, adopting the quotation style in which rather than quoting clauses and/or quotation marks, a long dash is used to introduce the source of the quote:

(14) *I love final exams.*
  – No One Ever

(15) *I love your crocs*
  – Nobody

As one reviewer pointed out, these condensed phrases (*– No One Ever*, or *– Nobody*) seem to function almost like emoticons or hash tags in computer-mediated communication: in the absence of prosodic and paralinguistic markers which can help signal the need for a sarcastic interpretation in face-to-face interaction, modern online communication has developed its own set phrases and graphic conventions to help activate layered meanings. Such examples also illustrate what Dancygier and Sweetser (2005) have termed “constructional compositionality”, by which the presence of even only a small subset of lower-level constructional forms can be sufficient to metonymically prompt the whole construction, such that here, for instance, *no one ever* without the *said*, or even just the subject *nobody*, propped up by the long dash which we know from other contexts of use can introduce sources, suffice to evoke *said no one ever*.

Another extension involves examples which restrict the class of improbable or impossible speakers, to whom the initiating utterance cannot believably be attributed, to a specific subset of people relevant to the utterance’s content, for instance Latino people where tacos are concerned or gamers where endless online gaming is concerned. Because they play on stereotypes that target certain groups of people specifically, *no one* is replaced in these examples by *no + noun*, with the noun typically being a common noun (e.g. girlfriend, man, gamer, student in 17–20 below), but possibly a proper name as in (16), in which Juan as a very typical Latino name is sufficient to frame-metonymically evoke Latinos in general:

(16) *I hate tacos! ... said no Juan ever.*

(17) *I'm mad at you and I'm gonna be very specific in telling you why said no girlfriend ever.*

(18) *"Date? Nah, you're like a sister to me." said no man ever.*

(19) *"I wanna play online, but no one's gonna be on the server early in the morning" said no gamer ever*

(20) *"I can't wait for class to start" said no student ever*

The initial viewpoint which ends up being re-evaluated in these cases is not one judged to be unattributable to anyone at all: there may well be people who hate tacos, don't want to date girls they are friends with, or think no one will be online to game early in the morning – only these are not viewpoints found among the most typical people likely to be involved with tacos, dating girls or online gaming (viz. Latinos, men and gamers respectively). Those people are the butt of the joke, whose overall effect is to reinforce stereotypes.

A final extension worth noting concerns examples turning the joke on the use of the "said no one ever" construction itself, as in (21), which cleverly draws attention to the meme's success in writing but apparent non-existence in ordinary conversation, or (22), in which the initial part which is subsequently re-evaluated consists only of the phrase *said no one ever*, whose well-formedness (or otherwise) is commented on from a normative English usage viewpoint:

(21) *"Remember when I said 'said no one ever' out loud in conversation?" said no one ever.*

(22) *"Said no one ever," said no one ever with a basic understanding of the English language.*

Further examples with different twists include (23), a one-off joke printed over a picture of a big number "1" which is unexpectedly pushed into the role of the (absent) represented speaker in ways similar to examples (16–20) above, and (24), which moves from one extreme (no speaker ever says X) to another (every single speaker says X constantly) to make a point about how annoying the *said no one ever* construction has become. (24), then, does not involve the kind of zooming out from an assumption of a current speaker addressing an addressee to there being no available speaker, but conversely zooms out from some individual speaker to a huge collective comprising all possible speakers universally finding the over-use of *said no one ever* incredibly annoying.

(23) *"I'm greater than two!" said no one ever.*

(24) *Your overuse of the phrase, "said no one ever", is "incredibly annoying", says everyone, all of the time.*

While *this is + pronoun* very explicitly draws a discourse space into focus, and *said no one ever* typically constructs discourse spaces not attributable to suitable speakers, our final example involves yet another type of discourse space – one embodied not by its speaker but by its topic.

7 Discourse vs. embodiment: *2 into 1*

In the striking short film *2 into 1*,[5] British artist Gillian Wearing quite literally "re-presents" interview material from two sides of a parent-child relationship. The opening view is of a middle-aged woman sat on a bench; when the sound comes on, however, we hear a young boy's voice to which the woman lip-synchs:

(25) *Um... I'm... intelligent... and sophisticated... I mean sophisticated means you know you know about, you know about the world so when you get... I mean obviously everyone does, but you know I'm only eleven (...)*

It is clear the speaker (or 'lip syncher') we *see* is not an eleven year old boy; when the image cuts to two teenage boys in school uniforms sat in chairs and we start to hear a woman's voice describing her sons, the initial confusion is resolved, as we understand the discourse and its embodiment have been switched:

5 At the time of writing, the full piece is viewable on YouTube at https://www.youtube.com/watch?v=36WUgFMDY-M.

(26) *My sons are unusual and they are absolutely adorable and they're very bright and very alive and full of life and they, um, they've got very very strong personalities and... and sometimes they, God obviously they drive me mad, but they... um... Well they love me I suppose. And they can be quite cruel, too. They do actually say to me "Now get in and make our dinner". I have had that a few times.*

The incongruity between the discourse and its embodiment is more than an amusing gimmick, as becomes clearer as the piece progresses and themes of cruelty and control in relationships emerge. The boys voiced by the mother criticize her among other things for being a slow driver, for her dress sense (or lack thereof), and for being forgetful and overly dramatic ("like a Laurence Olivier play"); the mother voiced by the boys professes her love for her boys while at the same time admitting they sometimes drive her mad and can be abusive to her. Of one for instance she says,

(27) *I think he's brilliant but he's er... got a terrible temper and he can be a real bugger at times. Oh, he said my teeth are yellow, I'm old and ugly, and I never finish anything. I say I'm going to do it and I don't. He has a way of putting his finger on the truth. Oh yes he says I'm a failure. He said I'm a failure, which has hurt because I think of myself as a failure.*

Apart from the pragmatic mismatch which as a viewer you pick up on relatively quickly, there is also a sense in which the 'incomplete' embodiment provides a clue to what is going on, in that the speakers/lip synchers in the video piece do not use any co-speech gesture, which in spontaneous speech would be highly unusual. Collectively the cues provided by the discourse mismatch, lip-synching and lack of gesture prompt the viewer (who is not guided in this by any narrating voice or screen titles) to construct their own understanding of 'who is who', and their own interpretation of the relationships between the different discourse participants involved.

The effect of this is not only the viewer's construction of a shared Discourse Viewpoint which allows them to attribute claims appropriately and also appreciate the complexity of the family dynamic represented. The re-construed embodiment also creates a disturbing effect. The way viewers naturally respond is to see the speakers as not simply mouthing other people's words, but in fact talking about themselves from a perspective that they are possibly aware of (the mother's words suggest that), but would express differently. There is an almost abrasive straightforwardness in the discourse with which people typically do not see themselves, suggesting that we generally view our own faults more generously than others view them. This idea of using discourse to put a crooked mirror in front of a person is here exploited purely through embodiment – presumably without the speaker's awareness of what is being done. But as viewers, we naturally assume that a speaker's words are a signal of their conceptualization, hence our complex emotional response to the video.

All along, the contents of what is being communicated are entirely serious, unlike in most cases of irony or in the case of *said no one ever* discussed above. The mother embodies the sons' discourse about herself without sarcastic comment, not even non-verbal, and likewise the sons and the mother's discourse about them. It is in fact interesting to compare example (6), which is a self-mocking rendering of the viewpoint clearly espoused by other people, critical of politicians, and the Wearing video, where critical views of others are also incorporated into the discourse of the person being described. The absence of sarcasm in the video seems to be due to the use of pronouns and discourse representation constructions. While the speaker in (6) is not allowing his critics to have a true voice, the mother quotes her son's words through Indirect Speech (*Oh, he said my teeth are yellow, I'm old and ugly, and I never finish anything*). But in the video, it is the son actually saying these words, so his hurtful criticism is put back in his mouth, but through the mother's actual voice. Still, he is referred to as *he* not *I*, and that precludes the viewer from reading it as the self-mocking sarcasm of (6), as the third person pronoun increases the distance between his own thoughts and the mother's response to them. Similarly, the good things the mother says

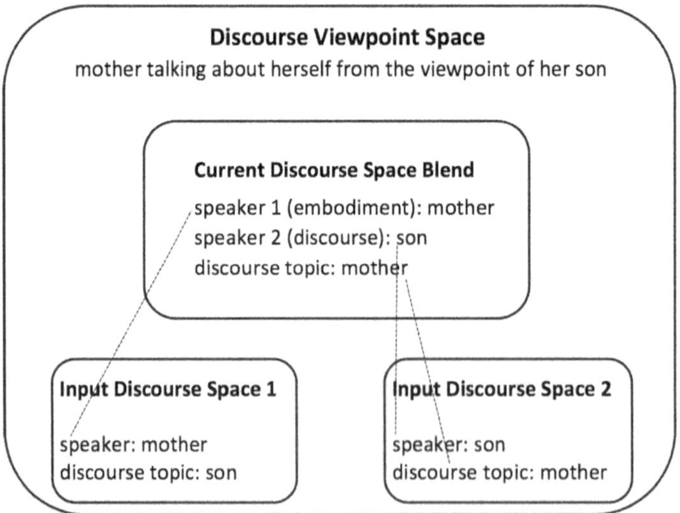

Figure 7: Discourse-embodiment blend in Gillian Wearing's *2 into 1*

about the sons are now said by them, again quite seriously. There is no appropriation of discourse, just the uncomfortable clash resulting from the fact that what people think and say privately becomes the discourse of the person talked about. Thus we need to understand what we are presented with as a blend of discourse spaces in which the discourse of one input is combined with the embodiment of the other (thereby indeed putting "2 into 1", as the piece's title has it). One side of this interpretive process is represented in Figure 7.

This example represents another viewpoint pattern, wherein two discourses are blended into one – rather than one being incorporated into another. This is perhaps the only case where the viewpoints are close to being mixed, and this happens not only because of the blend prompted, but also because of how we end up interpreting the discourse, which results from its embodied aspects, not just from a combination of discourses.

8 Conclusions

Just as studies increasingly show that multimodality in viewpoint is the norm rather than the exception (e.g. Parrill 2012, Green 2014), so do our examples suggest multiplicity of viewpoint in discourse is natural and ubiquitous, and not restricted to special constructions such as Free Indirect Discourse. At the same time, we have suggested this multiplicity is best studied in terms of complex networks of local viewpoints which contribute to and are 'supervised' from a higher level viewpoint, the Discourse Viewpoint, which guides comprehension in communication. These local viewpoints may be marked even by such small grammatical forms as genitives, negative particles or determiners, and one and the same form may carry a different meaning depending on the viewpoint network, as we illustrated with first person pronoun examples.

We have shown that various networks are required for actual expressions to be understood. In Figure 1, the lowest space is the discourse of the scene, while the actual text representing it is in a higher narrative space, in the centre of the network. In Figure 2, a belief in the common ground is incorporated into the discourse. In Figure 6, the actual discourse of the meme is at the lowest level, to be then embedded in the negative *said no one ever* and properly re-construed in the Discourse Viewpoint Space. Finally, Figure 7 shows the actual discourse of the video as a blend of discourse spaces that need to be recovered. In each case, the network is different, and the actual discourse of the text may be located at a different level. But in each case, the Discourse Viewpoint Space is the level which is necessary for comprehension to take place.

The analysis presented here also poses interesting questions regarding the approach to meaning, and especially constructional meaning. We have shown that grammatical forms may develop viewpoint functions on the basis of their widely recognized syntactic or discourse functions, working as the lowest-level elements in the construction of higher-level viewpoint. But the specific role an item plays in an expression or the discourse is determined by the emergent viewpoint network. Lower-level items provide the building blocks, but the meaning is as much a function of the network as it is a function of the lower-level meanings. We are not arguing for crude compositionality, but for a recognition that grammar operates at various levels of generalization, and that the interaction across levels is as much a component of the emergent meanings. The building blocks do their jobs, and complex syntactic expressions (like FIST) have recognizable functions. But there is a host of linguistic phenomena organizing the emergent structures, and they are in many cases driven by viewpoint.

The resulting picture is one of local multiplicity and complexity within global coherence. A visual analog for this discourse phenomenon is formed by the kinds of picture collages David Hockney is renowned for, where each individual picture has its own perspective, giving the viewer much more to look at and be involved in, while at the same time the complete work is perfectly coherent thanks to the viewer's effortless linking together of the different bits.[6] Further research into viewpoint phenomena in language and image can only be mutually enriching and point the way towards a fuller understanding of how viewpoint networks work.

References

Ariel, Mira. 1990. *Accessing noun phrase antecedents*. London: Routledge.

Bergen, Benjamin. 2012. *Louder than words: The new science of how the mind makes meaning*. New York: Basic Books.

Brône, Geert. 2008. Hyper- and misunderstanding in interactional humour. *Journal of Pragmatics* 40(12). 2027–2061.

Brône, Geert & Bert Oben. 2013. Resonating humour : A corpus-based approach to creative parallelism in discourse. In Kurt Feyaerts, Tony Veale and Charles Forceville (eds.). *Creativity and the agile mind: A multi-disciplinary study of a multi-faceted phenomenon*. Berlin/Boston: De Gruyter Mouton. 181–204.

6 One example is "Pearblossom Highway, 11th-18th April 1986", which is viewable online at http://www.hockneypictures.com/works_photos.php.

Brunyé, Tad T., Tali Ditman, Caroline R. Mahoney, Jason S. Augustyn & Holly A. Taylor. 2009. When you and I share perspectives: Pronouns modulate perspective taking during narrative comprehension. *Psychological Science* 20(1). 27–32.

Clark, Herbert H. 1996. *Using language*. Cambridge: Cambridge University Press.

Dancygier, Barbara. 2005. Blending and narrative viewpoint: Jonathan Raban's travels through mental spaces. *Language and Literature* 14(2). 99–127.

Dancygier, Barbara. 2009. Genitives and proper names in constructional blends. In *New directions in cognitive linguistics*, edited by Vyvyan Evans and Stephanie Pourcel. Amsterdam/Philadelphia: John Benjamins. 161–184.

Dancygier, Barbara. 2012a. *The language of stories: A cognitive approach*. Cambridge: Cambridge University Press.

Dancygier, Barbara. 2012b. Negation, stance verbs, and subjectivity. In Barbara Dancygier & Eve Sweetser (eds.). 69–93.

Dancygier, Barbara & Eve Sweetser. 2005. *Mental spaces in grammar: Conditional constructions* (Cambridge Studies in Linguistics 108). Cambridge: Cambridge University Press.

Dancygier, Barbara & Eve Sweetser (eds.). 2012. *Viewpoint in language: A multimodal perspective*. Cambridge: Cambridge University Press.

Evans, Nicholas. 2005. View with a view: Towards a typology of multiple perspective constructions. *Proceedings of the Annual Meeting of the Berkeley Linguisitics Society* 31. 93–120.

Fox, Sue. 2012. Performed narrative: The pragmatic function of *this is + speaker* and other quotatives in London adolescent speech. In Isabelle Buchstaller and Ingrid Van Alphen (eds.) *Quotatives: Cross-linguistic and cross-disciplinary perspectives*. Amsterdam/ Philadelphia: John Benjamins. 231–257.

Green, Jennifer. 2014. *Drawn from the ground: Sound, sign and inscription in central australian sand stories*. Cambridge: Cambridge University Press.

Mey, Jacob L. 1999. *When voices clash: A study in literary pragmatics* (Trends in Linguistics 115). Berlin/New York: Mouton de Gruyter.

Nikiforidou, Kiki. 2012. The constructional underpinnings of viewpoint blends: The *Past + now* in language and literature. In Barbara Dancygier & Eve Sweetser (eds.). 177–197.

Parrill, Fey. 2012. Interactions between discourse status and viewpoint in co-speech gesture. In Barbara Dancygier & Eve Sweetser (eds.). 97–112.

Pascal, Roy. 1977. *The dual voice: Free Indirect Speech and its functioning in the nineteenth century European novel*. Manchester: Manchester University Press.

Rohrer, Tim. 2005. Mimesis, artistic inspiration and the blends we live by. *Journal of Pragmatics* 37. 1686–1716.

Sanders, José. 2010. Intertwined voices: Journalists' modes of representing source information in journalistic subgenres. *English Text Construction* 3(2). 226–249.

Sanford, Anthony J. and Catherine Emmott. *Mind, brain and narrative*. Cambridge: Cambridge University Press.

Shifman, Limor. 2013a. Memes in a digital world: Reconciling with a conceptual troublemaker. *Journal of Computer-Mediated Communication* 18. 362–377.

Shifman, Limor. 2013b. *Memes in digital culture*. Cambridge, MA: MIT Press.

Sweetser, Eve. 2012. Introduction: viewpoint and perspective in language and gesture, from the ground up. In Barbara Dancygier & Eve Sweetser (eds.). 1–22.

Tobin, Vera & Michael Israel. 2012. Irony as a viewpoint phenomenon. In Barbara Dancygier & Eve Sweetser (eds.). 25–46.
Vandelanotte, Lieven. 2004. Deixis and grounding in speech and thought representation. *Journal of Pragmatics* 36(3). 489–520.
Vandelanotte, Lieven. 2009. *Speech and Thought Representation in English: A cognitive-functional approach* (Topics in English Linguistics 65). Berlin/New York: Mouton de Gruyter.
Vandelanotte, Lieven. 2010. 'Where am I, lurking in what place of vantage?': The discourse of distance in John Banville's fiction. *English Text Construction* 3(2). 203–225.
Vandelanotte, Lieven. 2012a. 'Wait till *you* got started': How to submerge another's discourse in your own. In Barbara Dancygier & Eve Sweetser (eds.). 198–218.
Vandelanotte, Lieven. 2012b. Quotative *go* and *be like*: Grammar and grammaticalization. In Isabelle Buchstaller and Ingrid van Alphen (eds.) *Quotatives: Cross-linguistic and cross-disciplinary perspectives*. Amsterdam/Philadelphia: John Benjamins. 173–202.
von Roncador, Manfred. 1988. *Zwischen direkter und indirekter Rede: Nichtwörtliche direkte Rede, erlebte Rede, logophorische Konstruktionen und Verwandtes* (Linguistische Arbeiten 192). Tübingen: Niemeyer.

Jeroen Vanderbiesen

Mixed viewpoints and the quotative-reportive cline in German: Reported speech and reportive evidentiality

Abstract: This paper discusses viewpoint mixing in German reported speech (direct and indirect constructions), in reportive evidentiality (by way of constructions with *sollen* 'shall') and in related constructions with *wollen* 'will'. First, it redefines the relation between reported speech and reportive evidentiality in terms of a functionally-oriented opposition between 'quotatives' (which attribute information to a source) and reportives (which justify information by referring to a source). Second, it shows how in both domains as well as in the *wollen*-constructions variations along a number of parameters reflect subtle viewpoint mixes, and that in fact a construction from one category may display traits that are more typical of another category. Third, these observations are taken as evidence in support of a cline (encompassing various sub-clines) that runs from quotatives (direct and indirect speech) over *wollen*-constructions to reportives (with *sollen*), where viewpoint variation is directly correlative to variation in other parameters and to the functions of attribution and justification. This cline, in turn, is discussed as evidence for a functional core shared between quotatives, reportives and *wollen*-constructions.

1 Introduction

Recently, it has become increasingly clear that there are many ways in which viewpoints can be represented in reported speech and thought. The present paper aims to tackle this subject in two ways. First, it will peruse some of the ways in which mixing of viewpoints occurs on different levels in German reported speech and reportive evidentiality, based on an analysis of both domains in terms of the notions 'quotative' and 'reportive'. Second, it will extrapolate from these observations towards a cline between reported speech and reportive evidentiality that captures gradual transitions between both domains in terms of viewpoint and a variety of other parameters.

Viewpoint is understood in the sense of Reinhart (1975: 170): "To say of an expression E that it is from a certain person P's point of view is to say that E represents P's judgements (wishes, etc.) or that P is responsible for E". By this definition, mixing of viewpoints occurs when in one construction there is more than one conceptualizer to whom judgements or responsibility may be ascribed, or alternatively, that the judgements expressed can be traced back to different conceptualizers, or that different conceptualizers are responsible for the information. Sections 2 and 3 will deal in some detail with (the viewpoint behaviour of) reported speech and reportive evidentiality, but a few basic assumptions should be outlined here. In the default case reported speech constructions bring more than one conceptualizer onto the scene, and mixing of viewpoints is thus inherent in them, though to varying degrees. In example (1) the viewpoints of the current (referring) speaker and the referred speaker (Riexinger) are syntactically, deictically and orthographically delineated: the referring speaker is responsible for the main clause that introduces the referred speaker, e.g. the tense morpheme *–te* in *sagte* 'said' refers to anteriority, to the time of referring. Riexinger is responsible for the sub-clause, e.g. the pronoun *wir* 'we' refers to a group that includes Riexinger, but not the referring speaker, and the quotation marks signal that the sentence is a foreign "insertion" into the referring speaker's discourse.

(1) *Riexinger sagte: "Wir verkörpern schon einen*
Riexinger say-IND.PST.3SG we embody-IND.PRS.1.PL EMPH a-ACC
Aufbruch."
revolution
'Riexinger said: "We do embody a revolution"' (FAZ/12-09/3)

In example (2), the referring viewpoint is clearly evident in the main clause, but the referred viewpoint (of the *Gerichtssprecherin* 'spokesperson for the Court') is less clearly present. Syntactically, the clause containing the referred information has been subordinated and looks less like an "insertion" into the referring discourse, and more like an integral part of it. Deictically, moreover, there is nothing referring overtly to the referring speaker (e.g. no first person pronouns, as in [1]); even the past indicative *wurde* (the passive auxiliary) could relate to either the referring or the referred viewpoint. Nonetheless, the referring information is construed as stemming from the spokesperson and thus as being her responsibility.

(2) *Eine Gerichtssprecherin betonte, dass über Gauweilers*
a court.spokesperson stress-IND.PST.3SG that about Gauweiler's
Antrag noch nicht entschieden wurde.
motion yet not decide-PST.PTCP become-IND.PST.3SG
'A spokesperson for the Court stressed that Gauweiler's motion had not been decided yet' (BMP/12-09/1)

By contrast, reportive evidentials typically focus heavily on the viewpoint of the referring speaker. Whereas they do make reference to another entity that functions as the source of the information, this entity is not a conceptualizer in its own right, as in the examples above. Rather, this other entity functions as a justification for the referring speaker for stating the proposition ("P, because I heard about P"), which may be called a judgement in the general sense of Reinhart's (1975) definition above. This is compounded by the fact that with reportive evidentials the source is typically not mentioned overtly, as in (3) from Basque (Boye 2012: 81, in reference to Jendraschek 2003: 49). Though the speaker does disavow responsibility for the proposition, there is no direct implication that some other (specific) person *is* responsible.[1]

(3) *Lapa-bonba-k* *pendulu* *mekanismo-a* *omen* *zuen*
sticky.bomb-ERG pendulum mechanism-DET REP have-PST.3SG
'The sticky bomb is said to have had a pendulum mechanism'

German already has a rich research tradition when it comes to viewpoint phenomena in reported speech. Works like Plank (1986), Fabricius-Hansen (1997, 2002), Günthner (2000) and Vliegen (2010) discuss how viewpoint interacts with syntactic embedding: as the prevalent viewpoint shifts from the referred to the referring speaker, the syntactic bond between the clause containing the referred information and the clause that contains the source strengthens; e.g. compare examples (1) and (2). For this reason, types of reported speech have traditionally been identified on a syntactic basis. The difference between direct and indirect reported speech is governed by the reference of deictic elements, and types of direct speech and indirect speech are differentiated based on the placement and syntactic relation of the referring clause (containing the reference to the source) to the referred clause (containing the information being related to the source). Functionally, this method has given rise to the representation of reported speech as a cline whose poles are direct speech and indirect speech, between which a variety of intermediary mixed forms is attested (cf. e.g. von Roncador 1988). The present paper will expand on this idea of reported speech as a cline by includ-

1 The source invoked by reportives is not in essence a conceptualizer who could be attributed a point of view (a referred viewpoint is not represented in example [3]), but is a form of justification for stating what is in the proposition. This places reportives on a par with other evidentials with sources of evidence (seeing, hearing, inference, etc.) are likewise not conceptualizers. In reported speech constructions, however, there is usually some indication of both a referring and a referred viewpoint: the former is at least needed to overtly identify the referred speaker and other elements of his speech situation, the latter is evident from the information being quoted.

ing more parameters than just syntax and deixis, thus showing that viewpoint mixing is much more varied and subtle than previously expected. Moreover, it will expand the cline to encompass non-reported speech forms (like reportive evidentials), which show the same type of variation (cf. also Mortelmans and Vanderbiesen 2011).

The data analyzed for this study come from a sample of German newspaper texts (cf. ten Cate 1996: 189–190; Jäntti 2002: 144–146 on the pros and cons of newspaper corpora).[2] It consists of both data extracted via COSMAS (Corpus Search, Management, and Analysis System) from the DeReKo (*Deutsches Referenzkorpus*) and data gathered manually by reading through editions of actual newspapers. Examples are either marked with a part of the code accorded to them in the DeReKo, or with a reference to the newspaper, its edition and the page number, in the case of the manually gathered data.[3] In total, 638 tokens of reported speech were gathered, in addition to 200 tokens each of constructions with *sollen* and *wollen* that in German have a similar but different function to reported speech. A token is one instance of a relevant construction. Usually there is one token per sentence, but in the case of reported speech there may be more.

The paper is structured as follows: Section 2 sets up a theoretical framework and defines the crucial terms 'reportive', 'quotative' and 'reported speech'. Section 3 offers up some case studies of German reported speech-, *sollen*- and *wollen*-constructions in terms of viewpoint mixing. Section 4 constructs a cline that includes all the forms discussed in the case studies, and Section 5 provides a conclusion.

2 Theoretical framework

Both reported speech and reportive evidentiality have received quite divergent definitions in literature, and both have been described in terms of the notion of 'quotatives' (see Vanderbiesen [to appear] for more). Of interest are thus concise definitions, but also the relation of the terms to each other. Therefore, Sec-

2 Traditional research tends to employ literary texts (e.g. Jäger 1971; von Roncador 1988; Breslauer 1996) and often invokes so-called *Erlebte Rede*, the representation of a character's thoughts, as a prime example of viewpoint mixing. In this paper's sample, such constructions do not occur, but nevertheless there is still plenty of mixing in the constructions that *are* attested.

3 The publications used for manual data gathering are *Bild* (B), *Berliner Morgenpost* (BMP), *Frankfurter Neue Presse* (FNP), *Münchner Merkur* (MM), *Frankfurter Allgemeine Zeitung* (FAZ) and *Der Spiegel* (DS).

tions 2.1. and 2.2. contrastively define reportive evidentials (or simply 'reportives') and quotatives, while Section 2.3. discusses reported speech.

2.1 Reportives

Boye (2012: 15–18) relates evidentiality to the traditional philosophical notion of knowledge, defined as "justified true belief". Evidentiality deals with the *justification* for knowledge, i.e. the various sources of information and kinds of evidence underlying the knowledge a speaker has.[4] It is not confined to a special type of (grammatical) marking – rather it is a functional-conceptual domain that can be linguistically encoded in various ways (cf. Boye and Harder 2009).

The traditional way of subdividing the domain of evidentiality is Willett's (1988) classification by type of evidence. Direct evidence depends on a speaker's direct experience of an event (e.g. seeing or hearing it). Reportives are part of the indirect branch of evidentiality, which includes elements that mark that a speaker has some justification for a proposition, but that this justification does not come from his or her own direct experience of the event described in the proposition. That being the case, reportives are here defined as elements that *i.* justify the use of a proposition P by a speaker S, by *ii.* evoking the notion of a source completely unrelated to S from which P originated, thus signalling that *iii.* S has only indirect access to P. The first and third parts of the definition identify reportives as indirect evidentials, the second part specifies its specific value. Reportives are a unique kind of evidential in that their source of information lies entirely outside of the current speaker. Whereas with an inferential a speaker bases on his own reasoning, with reportives the source is a different consciousness that *reports* on the situation, and which in turn may have had only indirect access to P. In other words, the speaker marks his own non-involvement in the proposition ([-SELF] in Squartini 2001: 938) and it is his relation to P that is the central concern of reportives. For this reason, reportives may be called deictic elements. The importance of the source is "secondary", being evoked only as a means to an end, i.e. to justify the proposition.[5] A German example is given in (4) (the reportive construction is underlined).

4 This is to be distinguished from epistemic modality, which encompasses the ways in which a speaker may *support* his belief in a proposition, which relates to the typical modal notions of (degree of) certainty and commitment (cf. de Haan 1999, 2001, Squartini 2004, Cornillie 2009, Boye 2010a).

5 The term 'evocation' is meant to capture that although the existence of an information source is necessarily *implied*, it does not automatically follow that the source is *identified overtly* in the

(4)

In	*der*	*Kreisklinik*	*Ebersberg*	*sollen*	*die*
in	the-DAT	community.clinic	Eberberg	shall-IND.PRS.3PL	the-NOM

Ärzte	*einen*	*Mann*	*falsch*	*behandelt*	*haben.*
doctors	a-ACC	man	wrong	treat-PST.PTCP	have-INF

'In the Ebersberg clinic doctors are said to have given a man the wrong treatment' (MM/12-09/14)

All evidentials, and thus also reportives, have propositional scope, meaning they relate to information that can be said to have a truth value. In a sentence like *I saw that he was writing a letter*, the speaker acquires some knowledge – that someone was writing a letter may or may not be true (cf. Boye 2012b). The same applies to examples (3) and (4): that the sticky bomb had a pendular mechanism or that a man was given the wrong treatment are pieces of knowledge acquired by the speaker that have a truth value and are justified by the reference to a speaker-external source. These are all opposed to a sentence like *I saw him write a letter*, where "him write a letter" is a state of affairs, i.e. something that occurs, an event, but not anything with a truth value. It is an act of perception, not an acquisition of knowledge. To the extent that evidentiality relates to knowledge and scopes over propositions, Boye (2012) calls it an 'epistemic' domain.

2.2 Quotatives

The term 'quotative' does not usually get a consistent definition in the literature, being used both as a synonym for and as a separate domain from reportives, cf. Vanderbiesen (2014: 169–170). For present purposes, quotatives will be defined as being separate from reportives, as elements that *i.* attribute some information expressed in their context, *ii.* to some person or "personal entity" thus identified as the source of this information, *iii.* thereby evoking the idea of a speech act relationship between the source and the information. The first two parts of the definition taken together encompass what is at stake in quotatives, namely the attribution of some information to a source. The identification of the source is primary: whenever a quotative is used, its function is both to point to the source of the information and to mark the information as "belonging to" that source. This means that quotatives are not evidentials, as they do not primarily serve the justification of some information. With them, a speaker underlines the involvement of another source, rather than his own non-involvement (cf. Squartini 2001:

sentence, or even knowable.

938: "[+OTHER]").[6] The typical way in which information can be attributed to a source is by signalling that the source "said" or otherwise produced the referred information, hence it can be said of quotatives that they scope over speech acts rather than propositions. A speech act is a way of interacting communicatively with language and as such is dependent on illocutionary forces or 'meanings', of which assertions, questions and commands are the three basic types (cf. Boye 2012: 187–195). Quotatives may thus have one of these types within their scope, as in example (5) from Kannada, cf. Sridhar (1990: 1). The particle *anta* attributes a whole speech act (the assertion that work is to be done, and the command to come immediately, enclosed in square brackets) to *amma* 'mother' – this is quite different from (3) and (4), where a proposition is justified by stemming from an unknown third-party source. The inclusion of an imperative (the typical clausal expression of a command) under the scope of *anta* shows that the referred clause has illocutionary potential in itself.

(5) *Amma* *barediddа:Le,* *[jaru:r* *kelasa* *ide,*
mother write-NPST.PRF.3SG.F urgent work be-NPST.3SG.N
ku:Dale *horaTu* *ba:]* *anta.*
immediately start-PTCP come QUOT
'Mother has written, "There is urgent work. Come immediately."'

This example does not signal the acquisition of knowledge by the speaker, nor is it the truth value of the mother having written something that is at stake. What *anta* signals is that the 'mother' is responsible for the assertion and the command expressed in the referred clause. It is thus not the current speaker's relation to P that is at stake here, but that of the source. Quotatives are therefore not purely deictic, like reportives, but encode what can be called 'deictic displacement', which means that the centre of perspectivization is not the actual I-Here-Now

6 The opposition between involvement (of another) and non-involvement (of oneself) as it is used here is meant to identify a difference in focus between reportives and quotatives. While it is true that the current speaker is typically not involved in the event described with both reportives and quotatives, the former tend to stress the fact that the current speaker is not involved, rather than another source being involved, whereas the latter do the opposite. This is also what Squartini (2001) captures: [+OTHER] and [-SELF] are different ways of viewing essentially the same thing. The behaviour of first person subjects is indicative of this contrast. They are rare in combination with reportive function (signalling non-involvement in something one was involved in), but not with quotative function (signalling one was involved oneself but at an earlier time is not far different from signalling the involvement of another). In German, reportive SOLL-constructions (cf. 3.4.) do not occur with first person subjects without altering their function, whereas quotative reported speech (cf. 2.3.) does (see ample evidence in Jäger [1971]).

of the current speaker, but rather that of the source speaker (cf. Diewald 1991: 113; Vanderbiesen 2015). As quotatives do not scope over propositions and do not relate to the notion of knowledge as defined above, they cannot be considered 'epistemic'.

Summarizing, reportives are evidential (and hence epistemic) forms that encode a speaker's justification for P by indicating that he or she gathered information about P from another consciousness. They are purely deictic forms (encoding the current speaker's relation to P) that have propositional scope. Quotatives are non-epistemic and non-evidential forms that encode a speaker's attribution of P to another consciousness. They are deictically displacing forms (encoding another speaker's relation to P) that have speech act scope.

2.3 Reported speech

Given the notions of 'reportive' and 'quotative', the question arises whether either of these labels applies straightforwardly to reported speech, as it has been analysed both ways in literature (cf. Vanderbiesen 2014: 169–170). Terminologically, *reported* speech seems biased towards one side of the distinction, but ultimately, its classification depends on its function in terms of justification or attribution.

The definition of 'reported discourse' by Güldemann (2012: 1) runs as follows: "Reported discourse is the representation of a spoken or mental text from which the reporter distances him-/herself by indicating that it is produced by a source of consciousness in a pragmatic and deictic setting that is different from that of the immediate discourse". By "text" Güldemann (2008: 6) means "a linguistic form which has the potential of instantiating an illocutionary act [...]. Text in this sense can range from a long discourse through complex or simple sentential forms to a one-word utterance. Thus, the relevant string of linguistic signs must largely retain the morphosyntactic form of an independent utterance". The two basic ways in which a construction can refer to another pragmatic and deictic setting are referred to as direct speech and indirect speech. Direct speech is the form where the viewpoint of the referred speaker is dominant, meaning he or she is the centre of perspectivization from which all deictic, expressive elements in the referred information are interpreted. In line with the findings of von Roncador (1988: 108), direct speech is a referentially shifted form, meaning its focus on the referred viewpoint is not somehow reflective of an 'original' viewpoint, but rather a deviation from the default viewpoint of the referring speaker. An example is (1) above. Indirect speech is the referentially unshifted form that anchors referential elements in the referring speaker and structurally integrates the referred information in the surrounding context, as in example (2) above.

There are typically two readings of the referred information: 'de dicto' and 'de re' (cf. Coulmas 1986; Hopper and Traugott 2003: 185). In a de dicto reading, the only option in direct speech, the linguistic elements in the referred information refer to parts of the discourse as linguistic elements. For instance, in *John said: "I am home"*, the referring speaker is not referring to himself by using "I", but rather points to the linguistic form "I" as it was uttered by John to refer to himself. In de re readings the referring speaker refers to the actual semantic content of linguistic forms, rather than the forms themselves. In *John said that he was home*, "he" refers to John, not to the linguistic form uttered by John (as he did not use *he* to refer to himself). Indirect speech may have both de re and de dicto readings, as such *John said that X is false* may go back to either John saying "X is false" (de dicto) or "X is not true" (de re), cf. Li (1986). The de dicto – de re contrast is a viewpoint phenomenon, as it keeps track of the influence of the referring speaker on the referred information. In indirect speech he or she may choose to adjust, for example, the reference of pronouns, or the structure of the sentence, or the choice of words, etc., to reflect his or her own viewpoint rather than that of the referred speaker.

Following the definition of Güldemann and the inherent viewpoint hybridity signalled by the de dicto – de re contrast, reported speech is best described as a quotative phenomenon. The representation of a text produced by another consciousness in another setting amounts to nothing more than attributing that text (which has illocutionary potential) to a person.[7] Note that this makes 'reported speech' a misnomer in two regards: it is not restricted to speech only, but it is also not 'report'. For ease of reference, however, the paper will continue to use the established term. Sections 3.2. and 3.3. will illustrate some of the ways viewpoint mixing actually occurs in (direct and indirect) reported speech, and in doing so will provide an empirical underpinning for the claim that reported speech is quotative. Section 3.4. will show the same viewpoint phenomena at work in reportive constructions (with *sollen*) and other non-quotative constructions (with *wollen*).

7 Chojnicka (2012: 173), whose view of reported speech is in some points at odds with the presently proposed one, also speaks of reported speech as bringing together "tools and devices used for *attributing knowledge to another speaker*" [emphasis mine].

3 Case Studies

3.1 Caveat: Syntax and viewpoint

Traditional research into viewpoint phenomena in German reported speech takes a “type-based” approach. Various reported speech constructions are classified into a relatively small number of types, usually on the basis of two criteria: the syntactic relation between the referring clause (containing the source) and the referred clause (containing the information being attributed), and the direct – indirect dichotomy as described above. Both criteria are said to correlate: as the referring viewpoint becomes stronger (in indirect speech), the referred clause becomes more embedded under the referring clause (e.g. from hypotaxis to subordination, cf. 3.2.). However, the syntax criterion makes this approach necessarily reductive. First, there are reported speech constructions where there is no syntactic relation between a referring and a referred clause, either because there is no referring clause, or because both clauses are simply “juxtaposed” (Hopper and Traugott 2003: 179–180), meaning they are two separate sentences, rather than one complex syntactic unit, as in (6) and (7) (the referred clause has been underlined, the referring clause is in bold).

(6) *Sieben Menschen seien verletzt worden,*
seven people be-SBJV.PRS.3PL injure-PST.PTCP become-PST.PTCP
berichteten türkische Fernsehsender. *Der Angreifer*
report-IND.PST.3PL Turkish television.channels the-NOM attacker
habe erst eine Handgranate geworfen und
have-SBJV.PRS.3SG first a-ACC hand.grenade throw-PST.PTCP and
sich dann in die Luft gesprengt.
REFL then in the-ACC air explode-PST.PTCP
‘Seven people were injured, reported Turkish television channels. The attacker first threw a hand grenade and then blew himself up.’ (FNP/12-09/3)

(7) *Das würde erklären, warum die Akte*
that will-SBJV.PST.3SG explain-INF why the-NOM acts
nirgendwo aufgetaucht sei,
nowhere turn.up-PST.PTCP be-SBJV.PRS.3SG
sagte er. <u>*„Eine solche Frechheit*</u>
say-IND.PST.3SG he a-ACC such insult
<u>*habe ich noch nicht erlebt.“*</u>
have-IND.PRS.1SG I yet not experience-PST.PTCP
'That would explain why the acts did not turn up anywhere, he said. "Such an insult I have not yet experienced."' (BMP/12-09/2)

Both examples attribute information to a contextually named source and are distinguishable on the basis of the direct – indirect contrast, but lack a syntactic relation between their referring and referred clauses. Though they are clearly reported speech, they are often not included on the cline of reported speech types.

Second, there are constructions where the syntactic relation is reversed, i.e. where the referred clause embeds the referring clause, rather than vice versa. (8) and (9) are again sensitive to the direct – indirect contrast, but especially in the indirect construction in (9) the referring clause is syntactically less, and not more, prominent than in the direct speech construction in example (1) above.

(8) *Seit 2008 wird dort, mitten in einer Hochburg*
since 2008 become-IND.PRS.3SG there middle in a-DAT stronghold
der Grünen, „Das Fest der Linken“ gefeiert
the-GEN Greens the-NOM feast the-GEN Left celebrate-PST.PTCP.
um „die Tür aufzumachen“, wie es der
to the-NOM door open.to.make-INF as it the-NOM
damalige Geschäftsführer Dietmar Bartsch formulierte.
former leader Dietmar Bartsch formulate-IND.PST.3SG
'Since 2008 the "Feast of the Left" is celebrated there, in a stronghold of the Green Party, to "open the door", as then leader Dietmar Bartsch put it.' (FAZ/12-09/3)

(9) *Wie aus Justizkreisen verlautete, sei ihnen*
as from judiciary.circles anounce-IND.PST.3SG be-SBJV.PRS.3SG them
aufgefallen, dass [...] Misshandlungsspuren an dem
remark-PST.PTCP that abuse.signs on the-DAT
Säugling sichtbar wurden.
infant visibly become-IND.PST.3PL
'As was announced from judiciary circles, it became apparent to them that signs of abuse became visible on the infant' (BMP/12-09/1)

In other words, while there are general tendencies, there is no perfect one-to-one correlation between viewpoint and syntax, and the latter should therefore not be a general classificatory principle. However, the direct – indirect contrast is valid. There are constructions where the distinction cannot be made, as in (10), where the indicative conjugation of *wurde* (the passive auxiliary) does not point to either direct or indirect speech in the absence of any other distinguishing marking (such as quotation marks). However, these examples are rare (12 cases of ambiguity in 638 tokens), and the distinction between referred- and referring-oriented reported speech constructions is cross-linguistically attested, though the (formal) means by which this distinction is marked may be widely different (see e.g. several contributions in Güldemann and von Roncador 2002).

(10) *Der Behördenchef wurde*
the-NOM administration.chief become-IND.PST.3SG
unter-Ausschluss-der-Öffentlichkeit befragt, wie der
in.camera question-PST.PTCP as the-NOM
Ausschussvorsitzende Edathy (SPD) mitteilte.
committee.chairman Edathy (SPD) communicate-IND.PST.3SG
'The administration chief was questioned in camera, as committee chairman Edathy (SPD) communicated' (FNP/12-09/1)

The following discussion will therefore be structured along the functional distinction between direct and indirect constructions, and a further subdivision on syntactic grounds will be abandoned. It will be shown that within direct and indirect speech constructions in German, variation is rampant along a whole range of parameters, of which syntax is only one. Even constructions that are similar in some respects (and might be put under the same 'type'), can still vary in other ways, and thus the cline of reported speech constructions is more fine-grained than traditionally assumed.

3.2 Direct speech

The sample employed for the present paper contains 193 direct speech constructions. Each of these has a number of structural and functional characteristics one can look at. For direct speech, they are exemplified in (11) and (12) below.

(11) *Der „Bunte“ sagt sie: „Ich habe zu*
the-DAT Bunte say-IND.PRS.3SG she I have-IND.PRS.1SG too
lange nach den Terminplänen meines Mannes
long according.to the-DAT schedule my-GEN husband
gelebt. Jetzt geht es um mich und
live-PST.PTCP now go-IND.PRS.3SG it about me-ACC and
meine Söhne.“
my-ACC sons
‘To “Bunte” she says: “For too long I have lived by my husband’s schedule. Right now it’s about me and my sons.”’ (B/12-09/5)

(12) *Der parlamentarische Geschäftsführer der*
the-NOM parliamentary leader the-GEN
SPD-Bundestagsfraktion, Thomas Oppermann, sagte
SPD-fraction Thomas Oppermann say-IND.PRS.1SG
zu Gauweilers jüngstem Eilantrag in Karlsruhe:
to Gauweiler‘s youngest-DAT rush.order in Karlsruhe
„Herr Gauweiler trifft schon einen wunden Punkt.“
Mr Gauweiler hit-IND.PRS.3SG indeed a-ACC sore point
‘The parliamentary leader of the SPD-fraction Thomas Oppermann said about Gauwiler’s most recent rush order: “Mr. Gauweiler indeed hits on a sore point”.’ (FNP/12-09/3)

First, both examples make explicit mention of their source in a main clause and establish a relation to the referred clause by means of the communicative verb *sagen* ‘to say’ (i.e. they have a referring clause). Reported speech sources may be subdivided according to whether they are actual persons (‘concrete’) or whether they are some kind of itself non-personal entity (‘abstract’) that may be composed of persons (e.g. a committee, a team), or may not be (e.g. information, a report). In turn, both source types may be singular or plural (John vs. the protestors, a report vs. indications), definite or indefinite (the killer vs. a witness, the letter vs. a statement), and abstract sources may additionally be animate or inanimate (the government vs. [the man’s] opinion). In both (11) and (12) the source is concrete, singular and definite, i.e. a uniquely identifiable individual. Information is most easily attributed to such a source (it is capable of being at the origin of a speech act, i.e. it can be quoted in the narrow sense of the word), and it is itself an entity that can have a certain viewpoint, i.e. that can make judgments and be responsible for things.

Second, the referred information looks much the same in both examples. It is a (string of) finite main clause(s) that is separated from the referring clause by means of quotation marks and a colon. In (11), additionally, there is a discrepancy in pronominal reference, as both third person *sie* 'she' in the referring clause and first person *ich* 'I', *mich* 'me' and *meine* 'my' in the referred clauses refer to the same person, i.e. the source. Hence it becomes clear that in the referred clause the referred speaker is referring to herself and that it is thus from her point of view. In (12) there is no deictic indication that the referred clause is indeed from the referred perspective, as the mood on the main verb is compatible with either viewpoint – here the attribution to the referred speaker is signalled unequivocally only by the quotation marks, and additionally by the speech act relation between the referred clause and the source speaker established by *sagen* 'to say'. In both examples, moreover, the referred information is composed of assertions, meaning that what is being attributed to the source in each case is a whole speech act rather than just a proposition.

Third, the syntactic relation between the referring and referred clauses is the same in (11) and (12). Hopper and Traugott (2003: 177–184) set up a cline of complex sentence relations with three cluster points that they call parataxis, hypotaxis and subordination.[8] Parataxis refers to two or more finite clauses that are relatively independent of each other – they do need each other to "make sense" pragmatically but have no further relationship. Hopper and Traugott give this relationship the labels −dependent and −embedded. Hypotaxis is a stronger degree of dependency: it consists of a finite clause with one or more clauses which cannot stand by themselves, but which are not constituents of the superordinate finite clause. This relationship is described as +dependent and −embedded. Subordination, finally, is complete dependency, and the dependent clauses are now in fact constituents of the superordinate clause. Examples (11) and (12) have a hypotactic relationship. The referred clause may not be the actual complement of the verb in the referring clause (as is typical in reported speech, cf. Munzo 1982: 304; Plank 1986: 306–307; Vliegen 2010: 213), but the referring clause would

8 The fact that they call it a cline implies that there may be degrees of each value, e.g. Vliegen (2010) talks about the difference in "strength" of the hypotaxis involved in various types of reported speech.

nonetheless be "incomplete" without it, as *sagen* 'to say' requires something that is said.[9]

Fourth, both constructions are set up to reflect and to put the focus on the referred viewpoint. On the one hand, it is syntactically, orthographically and (in 11) deictically separated from the referring viewpoint. On the other, it is represented in one or more fully specified main clauses that express one or more assertions that each represent a certain judgment in the sense of the definition in Section 1, e.g. in (12) that Gauweiler did hit on a sore point. By contrast, the referring viewpoint is not represented in a fully specified main clause, as it needs the referred clause to be semantically/conceptually complete. Moreover, the referring clause does not serve to reflect a judgment of the referring speaker as much as it serves to flesh out and elaborate on the referred viewpoint, by specifying details of the speech act (e.g. the addressee in [11] or the title and topic of the source in [12]). Notice, though, that *i.* the referring speaker is in each case the one "responsible" for (or perspectivizing) the contents of the referring clause (even if they do not express his or her 'judgments' per se), cf. Plank (1986: 296), and *ii.* there is clearly variation between (11) and (12) in how elaborate the referring speaker can be, and the more elaborate he or she is, the more his or her viewpoint comes to the fore. Each of the parameters discussed so far has an impact on the viewpoint: the overt mention of the source and its detailed specification, as well as its function as the centre of perspectivization in the referred clause reveal it to be the more important participant (while we know virtually nothing of the referring speaker's judgments or thoughts). The syntax and orthography of both constructions keep the referred viewpoint clearly separate, while the referred clause is a full main clause with its own illocution, which is dedicated to the referred viewpoint only.

Von Roncador (1988: 4–5) states that traits that recur often may be considered prototypical: therefore the constructions in (11) and (12) are prototypical examples of direct speech. Table 1 outlines the prototypical values in the sample of several parameters, all of which are evident in (11) and/or (12).[10]

9 In Cognitive Grammar terms the referred clause may still be said to elaborate the landmark of the relationship profiled by the verb.

10 The table contains a wide variety of different types of values (syntactic, deictic, conceptual), and more detail (or even more parameters) could certainly be included. Moreover, it is clear some parameters are more important than others (e.g. viewpoint vs. syntax), and that the parameters are to an extent intertwined, but the table is merely intended to give an overview of the characteristics a typical direct speech construction may have. It is not meant to be exhaustive in its detail.

Table 1: Prototypical values of direct speech

Parameter	Prototypical value	Number	Total
Source	overt (vs. absent)	182	(n = 193)
	concrete (vs. abstract)	144	(n = 182)
	explicit (vs. implicit vs. context)	127	(n = 183)
	clausal (vs. non-clausal)	106	(n = 130)
	main clause (vs. sub-clause)	99	(n = 106)
Referred information	non-deictic (vs. deictic vs. mixed)	119	(n = 193)
	clausal (vs. non-clausal)	174	(n = 193)
	finite (vs. non-finite)	171	(n = 174)
	main clause (vs. sub-clause)	173	(n = 192)
Syntax	hypotaxis (vs. other)	114	(n = 172)
Scope	speech act (vs. other)	193	(n = 193)
Viewpoint	referred (vs. referring vs. hybrid)	193	(n = 193)

Most of the values recorded in the table have been dealt with above. The value 'explicit (vs. implicit vs. context)' under the source parameter is based on Pütz (1989). 'Implicit' refers to source markings that are in the same simple sentence as the referred information, whereas 'explicit' relates to source markings that still fall within the same complex sentence , as in (11) and (12) above. 'Context', finally, applies when the source marking is in a different sentence altogether. The values referring to deixis under 'Referred Information' relate to how the reported speech is marked: if it is marked by means of shifts in deictic reference, then the marking happens deictically. If it happens only with quotation marks or through the communicative main verb, as in (12), then the value 'non-deictic' applies. 'Mixed' applies when the marking happens through a combination of both, as in (11). This parameter is one way in which the referred viewpoint is stronger in (11), as the referred speaker here overtly anchors some of the deictic markers in the clause. Finally, the value 'hybrid' under the viewpoint parameter applies when two viewpoints are expressed in the same construction, but cannot be easily distinguished from each other (this typically happens only in indirect speech; see section 3.3.). A given construction may vary along any of these parameters, and there is almost no limit to how "deviations" from the prototypical values of the parameters can be combined. This means that there is a wide variety of ways in which viewpoints can be mixed, only some of which will be addressed in the following paragraphs.

Both examples (13) and (14) qualify as direct speech constructions, as both have a referring clause that specifies a source and a referred clause that is bracketed off by means of quotation marks.

(13) *Das geht aus einem vertraulichen Papier vom Juli*
that go- IND.PRS.3SG out a-DAT confidential document of July
2012 hervor: „Es ist mit fremdenfeindlichen
2012 forth it be-IND.PRS.3SG with immigrant.hostile
Gewaltdelikten von Einzeltätern oder Tätergruppen
violent.crimes of sole.perpetrators or perpetrator.groups
in Form von Körperverletzungen zu rechnen.“
in form of body.injuries to count-INF
'This emerges from a confidential document from July 2012: "To be expected are violent crimes against immigrants by sole perpetrators or groups of perpetrators in the form of bodily harm."' (DS/37.12/17)

(14) *In zehn Jahren, hoffte er seinerzeit, werde*
In ten years hope-IND.PST.3SG he of.his.time will-SBJV.PRS.3SG
das ehrwürdige Pressefest so etwas sein wie
the-NOM honourable press.ball like something be-INF like
die einst legendären Pressefeste der
the.NOM once legendary press.balls the-GEN
„L'Humanité“ in Paris[...]: „Da muss man sein.“
L'Humanité in Paris there must one be-INF
'In ten years, he hoped back then, the venerable press ball would be something like the once legendary press balls of "L'Humanité" in Paris: "One simply has to be there."' (FAZ/12-09/3)

Still, these examples are quite different from (11) and (12). Example (13) has as its source *ein vertrauliches Papier* 'a confidential document', which is an abstract and fully non-personal source that cannot technically have a viewpoint of its own, or be involved in a speech act. While it cannot really be said that the document is a "source of consciousness" that "produced" a text (as per Güldemann's [2012] definition), it is still true that the referring speaker is attributing the information between quotation marks to the document (as per the definition of quotatives). The referring clause that contains the source is likewise different: rather than being a main clause that requires the referred clause to be complete, it is a syntactically fully specified main clause that could stand on its own. The relation between the referred and referring clauses is thus more paratactic than hypotactic, because while both clauses need each other to "make sense" pragmatically, they are as good as independent of each other syntactically. The referred clause itself is similar to that of example (12): while there is no overt deictic shifting to the referred viewpoint, the clause itself is a main clause containing an assertion and is marked by means of quotation marks. Plank (1986: 307) suggests parataxis is better for direct speech, as the weaker the syntactic link is, the more clearly the referring and referred viewpoints can be separated. The referred viewpoint thus gains in focus. But it also loses in focus because the source is construed as an abstract entity in a prepositional phrase, with no verb to indicate a speech act relationship. The referring clause still primarily serves the function of specifying the referred clause, rather than expressing the referring viewpoint, but gains in prominence through being in a fully specified main clause.

Example (14) has the typical concrete, singular, definite source (*er* 'he') and it is represented in a main clause that requires a sub-clause to be complete. However, this sub-clause in first instance is the indirect speech clause marked by the subjunctive on *werden* 'will'. Orthographically, this indirect speech construction is in turn connected to the direct speech clause (marked by quotation marks) by means of a colon, and thus *er* 'he' is revealed to be the source for the direct speech clause as well. In other words, the indirect speech construction (with its referring clause) syntactically functions as a referring clause for the direct speech construction, to which it has a paratactic relationship. Moreover, the verb *hoffen* 'to hope' is not a communication verb and thus does not serve to establish a speech act relationship on the referred level, but is rather an additional description of the source from the referring level. Considering that the influence of the referring viewpoint is stronger in indirect speech than in direct speech, example (14) juxtaposes a more referring- and a more referred-oriented perspective in one complex sentence.

In example (14), the clause containing the source (*hoffte er seinerzeit* 'he hoped at that time') is parenthetical to the indirect speech construction that it appears in. This happens in a variety of ways in direct speech too; consider (15) and (16).

(15) *„Mit einem Zufriedenheitswert von 7,11 liegt das*
with a-DAT contentment.value of 7.11 lie-IND.PRS.3SG the-NOM
südliche Bayern klar im vorderen Drittel", heißt es
southern Bavaria clearly in.the-DAT upper third it.is.said
im Glücksatlas.
in.the-DAT happiness.atlas
'"With a contentment value of 7.11 southern Bavaria is clearly in the upper third", it says in the Happiness Atlas' (MM/12-09/3)

(16) *Seit 2008 wird dort, mitten in einer Hochburg*
since 2008 become-IND.PRS.3SG there middle in a-DAT stronghold
der Grünen, „Das Fest der Linken“
the-GEN Greens the-NOM feast the-GEN Left
gefeiert um „die Tür aufzumachen“,
celebrate-PST.PTCP. to the-NOM door open.to.make
wie es der damalige Geschäftsführer Dietmar Bartsch
as it the-NOM former leader Dietmar Bartsch
formulierte.
formulate-IND.PST.3SG
'Since 2008 the "Feast of the Left" is celebrated there, right in the middle of in a stronghold of the Green Party, to "open the door", as then leader Dietmar Bartsch put it.' (FAZ/12-09/3)

Vliegen (2010: 218), in reference to Mikame (1986: 326), calls parentheticals weakly referring-speaker-oriented, and states that a parenthetical main clause typically allows for more types of verbs than the main clauses in constructions like (11) and (12). These verbs tend to be non-communication verbs and to not establish a speech act relationship, but rather to be interpretations or descriptions of the speech act by the referring speaker. This is true of *hoffen* 'to hope' in (14), but also of *schwärmen* 'to enthuse' in (17).

(17) *Sie ist und bleibt meine kleine Rosie,"*
she be-IND.PRS.1SG and stay-IND.PRS.3SG my-NOM little Rosie
schwärmt er.
enthuse-IND.PRS.3SG he
'She is and will always be my little Rosie," he enthuses' (B/12-09/4)

A parenthetical use thus reinforces the referring viewpoint, but at the same time it is a syntactic "demotion", as the referring clause behaves less like a superordinate main clause; cf. its word order and placement relative to the referred clause in (14)–(17). This demotion is even more evident in constructions like (16), where the referring clause is now actually the subordinate, dependent clause. On the one hand, a parenthetical use allows the referring speaker more freedom to express his or her own viewpoint and to place the marking of the source less centrally, but on the other hand, it promotes the referred clause to main clause status (cf. Hopper and Traugott 2003: 208–209).

A parenthetical use thus inherently provides more of a mix than a typical use as exemplified in (11) and (12), but here again one parenthetical use is not necessarily like the other. In terms of source, (15) is quite untypical. The source is *Glücksatlas* 'Contentment Atlas', an abstract, non-personal entity, and it is marked in a prepositional phrase. There is no real verb in the referring clause either, but rather *es heißt* 'it says, it is said', which places the focus on the referring speaker as the recipient of some information, rather than a referred speaker as the source of that information. In other words, both the type of source and the way it is marked favour the referring viewpoint. By contrast, in (16), the source is concrete and accompanied by a communication verb (*formulieren* 'formulate'), but the referred information (marked by quotation marks) is not a finite clause and acts more like an "aside" to what the referring speaker is saying, rather than the purpose of the construction.

Because the referring clause is the only part of a direct speech construction in which the referring speaker can reflect his or her viewpoint (though see von Roncador [1988] on "nichtwörtliche direkte Rede" 'non-literal direct speech' in German or Aikhenvald [2008] on semi-direct speech in Manambu), there tends to be a lot of variation in the way it is construed. One other guise is its appearance in reported speech constructions where it is not in the same sentence as the referred clause, cf. (18) (the relevant referred clause has been underlined).

(18)	*„Ich*	*bin*	*entsetzt“,*	*sagte*	*Edathy.*	*„Das*
	I	be-IND.PRS.3SG	dismayed	say-IND.PST.3SG	Edathy	that

	wird	*Folgen*	*haben*	*müssen.*
	will-IND.PRS.3SG	consequences	have-INF	must-INF

'"I am dismayed", said Edathy. "This will have to have consequences".' (BMP/12-09/2)

This example is itself not any different from examples (11), (12) or (17); indeed the only difference seems to be the syntactic relation between referring and referred clauses, and the even more clear separation between both viewpoints that follows from it. Besides their three "cluster points" of parataxis, hypotaxis and subordination, Hopper and Traugott (2003: 179–180) also discuss "juxtaposition", where "two or more nuclei [i.e. finite clauses, JV] occur next to one another and the semantic relationship between them is by inference only", e.g. *Fort Sumter has been fired on. My regiment leaves at dawn.* In (18), the quotation marks do prompt the reader to look for a source (which is readily available and marked in the typical way in the preceding sentence), but the referring and the referred clause do not form one complex whole and thus do not constitute clause combining. They might be described as being somewhere in between juxtaposition and parataxis proper.

In some constructions, this juxtaposition is taken further and a clear source marking is omitted. Because reported speech constructions are quotative, a source to whom the information can be attributed is necessary, which prompts readers to look for a source in the context if one is not readily available. A rather simple example of this is (19), where the source is in the preceding sentence, though 12 tokens out of 30 of this kind in the sample have at least one sentence between the sentence containing the source and the referred clause.

(19) *Michael Rösch startet für einen anderen*
Michael Rösch start-IND.PRS.3SG for a-ACC other
Nationalverband. „Ich gehe nicht im Groll.
national.association I go-IND.PRS.1SG not in.the-DAT grudge
Ich will wieder im Weltcup und bei
I want-IND.PRS.1SG again in.the-DAT world.cup and with
der WM starten."
the-DAT WM start-INF
'Michael Rösch is starting for another national team. "I don't hold a grudge. I want play the World Cup and the World Championship again".' (B/12-09/11)

There is nothing marking Rösch as the source, but the quotation marks (and pronominal shifts) indicate the following sentences have to be attributed to someone, and Rösch is the first viable instance in the context, being capable of having a viewpoint and being the topic of the preceding sentence.

In some rare cases a source may be omitted altogether (9/193 tokens). As Pütz (1989: 200) points out, the source marking may then be nothing more than "signals in the preceding context" or "pragmatic signals" or even "such signals that are recognizable by the speaker on the basis of his or her general knowledge of the situation" [translations JV]. An example of the latter is (20), where the source (supposedly the panel behind the Klassik-"Echo" prize) is identifiable only because prizes tend to have panels awarding them.[11]

11 This is the entire stub article – there is no mention of a source anywhere in the context.

(20) *Dirigent Daniel Barenboim 69 wird mit dem*
conductor Daniel Barenboim (69) become-IND.PRS.3SG with the
Klassik-„Echo“ […] ausgezeichnet. Begründung: „Barenboim
Klassik-“Echo” honour-PST.PTCP Reason: Barenboim
zählt zu den bedeutendsten Klassikkünstlern
count-IND.PRS.3SG to the-DAT most.important classical.artists
unserer Zeit.
our-GEN time
‘Conductor D.B. will be honored with the Klassik-Echo. Reason: “B. is one of the most influential classical artists of our time”.’ (B/12-09/4)

The omission of a referring clause has interesting consequences for viewpoint. On the one hand, the focus is drawn away from the source (as it is not even identified), but on the other hand, the referring speaker likewise has no “place” to express his own viewpoint relative to the referred clause – he or she is only recognizable orthographically through the addition of quotation marks, which mark an insertion into the referring discourse. Compared to the preceding direct speech examples, the referred viewpoint is construed with less “interference”, but in terms of the quotative function of reported speech (attribution to a source), examples such as (20) are less felicitous, and thus on the whole rare.

In conclusion, whereas there does seem to be a prototypical direct speech construction (based on the number of times certain values of the parameters in Table 1 co-occur), there is nonetheless extensive variation between individual constructions. However, this variation is mostly limited to the referring clause, i.e. the typical domain of the referring speaker in direct speech constructions. The referred clause varies less, showing significant variation only in the presence or absence of deictic shifts to mark the attribution (examples such as [16], where the referred clause is non-finite, are rare). Moreover, it is not always easy to determine the “direction” of the variation, i.e. which viewpoint is being strengthened. For instance, a parenthetical referring clause affords the referring viewpoint more freedom, but accords it less syntactic prominence, making it more of a crutch to “prop up” the referred viewpoint. The omission of a referred clause leaves the referring speaker no room to express his viewpoint in direct relation to the referred clause, but also leaves the source of the referred viewpoint out of the picture.

3.3 Indirect speech

The sample contains 457 tokens of indirect speech. It presents an even more varied picture than the direct speech sample, because the influence of the referring speaker now extends past the referring clause into the referred clause. This is reflected in the increased distribution across values for the 'Referred Information' parameter in Table 2, which also shows that while certain values still apply to most tokens in the sample, they are not as numerically dominant as they were in direct speech.

Table 2: Prototypical values of indirect speech

Parameter	Prototypical value	Number	Total
Source	overt (vs. absent)	434	(n = 457)
	concrete (vs. abstract)	309	(n = 434)
	explicit (vs. implicit vs. context)	224	(n = 434)
	clausal (vs. non-clausal)	248	(n = 318)
	main clause (vs. sub-clause)	229	(n = 248)
Referred information	deictic (vs. non-deictic vs. mixed)	240	(n = 457)
	clausal (vs. non-clausal)	405	(n = 457)
	finite (vs. non-finite)	381	(n = 405)
	main clause (vs. sub-clause)	372	(n = 405)
Syntax	hypotaxis (vs. other)	160	(n = 364)
Scope	speech act (vs. other)	338	(n = 457)
Viewpoint	hybrid (vs. referring vs. referred)	338	(n = 457)

While indirect speech may appear in more "configurations" than direct speech, there are nonetheless constructions that display all the prototypical values of Table 2, cf. (21) and (22) below.

(21) *Schäuble sagte, Gründlichkeit gehe vor*
Schäuble say-IND.PST.3SG thoroughness go-SBJV.PRS.3SG before
Schnelligkeit.
speediness
'Schäuble said thoroughness goes before speediness.' (FAZ/12-09/2)

(22) [Kritiker wundern sich angesichts der medialen Präsenz von Voßkuhle zwar über solche Aussagen, zumal der hochgewachsene Ostwestfale mit seinen Interviews hin und wieder für Wirbel sorgt.]

So	*betonte*	*er*	*einmal*	*unverblümt,*	*Deutschland*
for.instance	stress-IND.PST.3SG	he	once	frankly	Germany

dürfe	*nicht*	*noch*	*mehr*	*Kernkompetenzen*
may-SBJV.PRS.3SG	not	even	more	core.competences

an	*Brüssel*	*abgeben.*
to	Brussels	relinquish-INF

'[In the face of Voßkuhle's media presence, critics do wonder about such utterances, especially since the East-Westfalian is kicking up a storm everywhere with his interviews.] For instance, he once said outright that Germany should not relinquish more of its core competences to Brussels' (BMP/12-09/2)

In both examples there is a referring main clause with a concrete, singular and definite source that is put into a speech act relationship with the following hypotactically dependent referred clause. The referred clause itself looks like a typical main clause but differs from direct speech constructions by the mood of its main verb: a present subjunctive rather than an indicative. Much has been written on the subject of the present subjunctive in German (cf. e.g. Helbig 2007 and Askedal 2007 for an overview of some of the issues). For present purposes the focus will be on its core function as a marker of reported speech, cf. Jäger (1971: 26–27, 128), Fabricius-Hansen (1997: 19, 23) and Schecker (2002: 2). It is a sufficient marking of all finite types of indirect speech, and while it is not always strictly necessary (see infra), it is never considered to be redundant here.[12] In fact, its importance lies in the realm of viewpoint. The present subjunctive explicitly refers to the existence of another consciousness that is responsible for the referred information and marks the shift away from the referring speaker as the centre of perspectivization. In other words, it is a marker of deictic displacement, akin to the pronominal shifts in direct speech, but with one major difference. In direct speech the shift is evident because certain deictic elements (such as pronouns) are anchored in the referred viewpoint, (almost) to the exclusion of the referring viewpoint – the shift is evident from the referred viewpoint. With the present subjunctive, however, the shift is evident from the referring viewpoint, as it marks an explicit shift *away* from it. Therefore, the present subjunctive, though it points to the referred view-

12 It is also considered to have no epistemic-modal meaning (encoding a speaker's degree of certainty); neither does its alternation with the past subjunctive or the indicative (cf. ten Cate 1996: 198; Diewald 1999: 183–184; Fabricius-Hansen 2004: 122–125).

point, occurs naturally in more referring-oriented indirect speech. Moreover, notice that deictic elements such as pronouns are anchored in the referring viewpoint, as with *er* 'he' in (23), rather than the referred viewpoint, as with *ich* 'I' in (19). In other words, the 'reference shift' to the referred viewpoint is only partial in indirect speech – the existence of the referred viewpoint is implied, but no deictic elements are explicitly anchored in it.

(23)

Bundesfinanzminister	*Wolfgang*	*Schäuble*	*hat*	*seinen*
finance.minister	Wolfgang	Schäuble	have-IND.PRS.3SG	his-DAT

Gesprächspartnern	*in*	*der*	*Euro-Gruppe*	*bedeutet*
interlocutors	in	the-DAT	euro.group	intimate-PST.PTCP

er	*halte*	*das*	*Risiko*	*eines*
he	consider-SBJV.PRS.3SG	the-ACC	risk	a-GEN

Griechenland-Austritts	*für*	*vertretbar.*
Greece.exit	for	justifiable

'Finance minister Wolfgang Schäuble has intimated to his interlocutors in the euro group that he considers the risk of an exit by Greece justifiable' (DS/37.12/25)

The present subjunctive is a linguistic marker of deictic displacement, and by the definition offered in 2.2. therefore a quotative.

Even though (21), (22) and (23) all have the typical values listed in Table 2, they nonetheless vary with respect to each other. Whereas (21) is a simple representation of Schäuble's statement from the referring speaker's point of view, the referring viewpoint is more strongly present in (22), e.g. through the use of *so* 'for instance' and the adverb *unverblümt* 'frankly'. The former makes the referred information part of the argumentative structure of the referring speaker (an example to illustrate the preceding claims given in square brackets), while the latter is a direct comment on how the referring speaker perceived Voßkuhle's remark. By contrast, in (23) the referring clause is set up in much the same way as in direct speech, as an explicitation of the speech act that the referred information is part of (e.g. identification of addressees).[13]

13 Vliegen (2010: 220), in reference to Steube (1986: 360) and Zifonun et al. (1997: 1765), remarks that these types of constructions (where the referred clause is asyndetically dependent on the referring clause) always have a de dicto reading, i.e. that the words in the referred clause (apart from deictic elements) refer to the linguistic forms as expressed by the referred speaker. The very fact that an indirect speech construction, which inherently brings the referring viewpoint more to the fore, has a de dicto reading that relates to the referred viewpoint, makes the constructions in (21)–(23) truly perspectivally hybrid.

Individual indirect speech constructions may diverge from the prototypical values in many ways, only some of which can be addressed here. The same basic permutations of the referring clause in direct speech are also evident here, but the sample also contains constructions such as (24) that do not have a direct speech counterpart.

(24) *Der* *Freiburger* *Staatsrechtslehrer* *hat*
the-NOM from.Freiburg constitutional.law.professor have-IND.PRS.3SG
schon *öffentlich* *gesagt* *dass* *die* *Grenzen* *der*
already in.public say-PST.PTCP that the-NOM limits the-GEN
europäischen *Integration* *unter* *dem*
European integration under the-DAT
Grundgesetz *weitgehend* *ausgeschöpft* *seien.*
constitution largely exhaust-PST.PTCP be-SBJV.PRS.3PL
'The constitutional law professor from Freiburg has already said in public that the limits of European integration had already largely been reached under the constitution' (FAZ/12-09/2)

In Hopper and Traugott's (2003) terms, (24) is an example of subordination. The referred clause is embedded under the referring clause by means of the subordinator *dass* 'that, which' and has the verb in final position, as is typical of German subordinate clauses. This syntactic relation is indicative of a de re construal of the referred clause, whereby the referring speaker represents "the gist" of what was said, rather than adhering to a strict wording. In other words, compared to (21)–(23), (24) is a more extreme example of the referring viewpoint becoming central, even if the construction is ultimately still quotative, i.e. geared towards attributing the referred clause to the source, which is an overtly identified and clearly indicated individual.

However, the "salience" of either viewpoint may once again vary; cf. (25) and (26).

(25) *Die* *Prüfer* *kritisieren,* *dass* *das* *„bis* *dahin*
The-NOM inspectors criticize-IND.PRS.3PL that the-NOM until then
durch *ein* *eingeschränkt* *wirksames* *Gewehr* *G36*
by a-NOM restrictively functional rifle G36
ersetzt" *worden* *sei.*
replace-PST.PTCP become-PST.PTCP be-SBJV.PRS.3SG
'The inspectors criticize that the "up to then functional G3 rifle" was "replaced by the less functional G36 rifle".' (DS/37.12/19)

(26) *Es gibt nicht viele Menschen, die gefragt*
it give-IND.PRS.3SG not many people who ask-PST.PTCP
wurden, ob sie Bundespräsident werden
become-IND.PST.3SG if they president become-INF
wollen, und abgelehnt haben.
want-IND.PRS.3PL and decline-PST.PTCP have-IND.PRS.3PL
'There are not many people who were asked if they would like to become president and have declined' (DS/37.12/26)

Whereas (25) has an overt source, (26) relies on pragmatic inference to identify a source (it is only implied through the passive construction *die gefragt wurden* 'who were asked'). While in both examples the referred clauses are subordinated (once with *dass* 'that, which', once with *ob* 'if, whether'), they are noticeably different. In (25) the bulk of the referred clause is between quotation marks, which are clear indicators of the referred viewpoint, yet the main verb is in present subjunctive. In terms of viewpoint it is closer to direct speech constructions such as (11) or (12) than it is to (26). In (26) the referred clause (underlined) is only a part of a restrictive relative clause that belongs to the referring speaker's text, and a present subjunctive is either lacking or not formally distinguished.[14] Instead, the attribution to the referred speaker is signalled through the indication of a speech act relation by means of the verb *fragen* 'to ask' in the referring clause.

The present subjunctive is thus not a necessary marker of indirect speech, but it is a sufficient one. This is most evident in the type of construction underlined in (27), where the referred clause is a syntactically independent formal main clause.

14 The present subjunctive cannot be fully morphologically distinguished from the indicative in all verbs (cf. Fabricius-Hansen 1997), and the third person plural of both the present indicative and the present subjunctive is *wollen*. However, it is journalistic practice in German to resort to the past subjunctive form in order to distinguish from the present indicative. While both forms would again be equivalent for *wollen* (i.e. *wollten*), the peculiarity of either a past indicative or a past subjunctive in this context would suffice to mark reported speech.

(27) [AußenministerWesterwelle sagte bei einem Besuch des Europaparlaments in Straßburg, er erwarte ein „proeuropäisches Urteil“ der Richter.]
Das *Grundgesetz* *sei* *eine* *proeuropäische*
the-NOM constitution be-SBJV.PRS.3SG a-NOM pro.European
Verfassung, *es* *wolle* *die* *europäische*
constitution it want-SBJV.PRS.3SG the-NOM European
Integration.
integration
'Foreign Minister Westerwelle said during a visit to the European parliament in Strasbourg that he expects a "pro-European verdict" by the judges. The constitution is a pro-European constitution, it wants European integration' (FAZ/12-09/1)

Example (27) strongly resembles the prototypical constructions in (21)–(23) and is different from them only in the weaker (or absent) syntactic relation between the referring clause (in square brackets, marked by *sagte* 'said') and the referred clause. Ten Cate (1996: 196–197) remarks that his German newspaper sample has a remarkable predominance of constructions with asyndetically dependent referred clauses (i.e. subclauses that lack a subordinator and have main clause word order) and constructions such as (27), and goes on to state that in these forms the use of the present subjunctive specifically is almost obligatory.[15] In the sample used for this paper as well, asyndetic hypotaxis and juxtaposition are the most frequent syntactic relationships in indirect speech, and they almost always coincide with a present subjunctive marking (54/63 constructions with asyndetic hypotaxis, and 107/123 constructions with 'juxtaposition'). It is not surprising that constructions where the quotative marker (the present subjunctive) is almost obligatory would be most frequent in the sample if reported speech is indeed a quotative phenomenon. Coupled with the observation that syntactically "free" reported speech constructions such as (27) are rare in other languages (cf. e.g. Pütz 1989; Breslauer 1996; Fabricius-Hansen 2004; Mortelmans 2009), the present subjunctive thus gives German a functional diversity few other (Germanic) languages have.

As with direct speech, there are varying possible degrees of 'juxtaposition' between referring and referred clauses. Breslauer (1996: 125–131) sets up a hierar-

15 Interestingly, Askedal (1996: 299), who uses a literature corpus, comes to largely the same results, both in terms of the type of dependency (asyndetic and lacking altogether) and the use of the present subjunctive. This means the data in ten Cate's (1999) sample and the sample employed here are probably reflective of a more general non-genre-specific trend in the use of indirect speech.

chy of constructions of increasing autonomy (cf. also Pütz 1989): examples such as (27) only tend to autonomy, but in (28) no actual overt source is marked and it is therefore more autonomous.[16]

(28) *Xi habe sich beim Schwimmen am*
Xi have-SBJV.PRS.3SG REFL with.the-DAT swimming on.the-DAT
Rücken verletzt.
back injure-PST.PTCP
[*So wollte es das erste Gerücht wissen, das vergangenen Donnerstag entstand.*]
'Xi has injured his back while swimming. This according to the first rumour that started last Thursday' (BMP/12-09/4)

The referred clause is the opening sentence of a paragraph under a new section title in the original article, and does not refer to any preceding source. While the present subjunctive may occasionally refer to a source coming later in the context, in the case of (28), the addition of *Gerücht* 'rumour' explicitly refers to the absence of a known source. In these cases, the present subjunctive is the only reference to a referred viewpoint (and thus the only marker of any kind of attribution), and had an indicative been used, (28) would not have been recognizable as reported speech. Here the present subjunctive gravitates more towards becoming a marker of the referring speaker's relation to P rather than that of a referred speaker's viewpoint; Askedal (1996, also 1999, 2000) even speaks of a re-grammaticalization of the present subjunctive. Though rare, (28) presents a case where the referring viewpoint becomes dominant in a domain that is primarily centred around the inclusion and attribution of information to a referred viewpoint.

Some constructions focus even more strongly on the referring viewpoint; they are exemplified in (29) and (30).

(29) *Seehofer kündigte danach an, den vierfachen*
Seehofer announce-IND.PST.3SG thereafter PART the-ACC fourfold
Familienvater trotz der Niederlage in besonderer Weise
family.father in.spite.of the-DAT defeat in special way
in die Parteiarbeit einzubinden.
in the-ACC party.workings involve-INF
'After that, Seehofer announced that he wanted to involve the father of four in a special way in the workings of the party, in spite of the defeat.' (FNP/12-09/3)

16 See Marschall (2002: 100–101) for more types of "autonomy" in reported speech.

(30) *Israels Energie und Wasserminister Uzi Landau warnte*
Israels energy and water.minister Uzi Landau warn-IND.PST.3SG
eindringlich vor einer nuklearen Bedrohung durch den Iran.
emphatically for a-DAT nuclear threat by the-ACC Iran
'Israel's Minister for Energy and Water Uzi Landau warned emphatically for a nuclear threat from Iran.' (B/12-09/2)

Example (29) is an infinitival construction and (30) is a nominal one. In both cases there is hardly a referred clause: in (29) it is non-finite, and in (30) the referred information is not clausal, being instead represented by a nominal (*eine nukleare Bedrohung* 'a nuclear threat'). In Hopper and Traugott's (2003) view, (29) is a limiting case of subordination, whereas in (30) there is no longer a clausal relationship. Both infinitival and nominal constructions leave no room for any salient expression of a referred viewpoint. As such, these constructions are strongly de re, as the idea of a preceding utterance becomes exceedingly vague (cf. Coulmas 1986 on form vs. content). However, there is still a referring clause, on par with other indirect speech constructions, and it is the only marking of reported speech in (29) and (30). Whereas the 'free' construction in example (28) relies on mood marking in the referred clause to draw conclusions about the referring clause (in terms of identifying a source), (29) and (30) rely instead on the source marking in the referring clause to identify what follows as referred information. The referring clause may take on the function of marking the whole construction as reported speech in other indirect speech constructions as well (e.g. because of the indicative marking in [26]), but it is the only option in non-finite and non-clausal constructions. Therefore, these constructions very often exhibit the typical source marking (main clause with communication verb: 26/28 infinitival constructions, 47/48 nominal constructions) and source type (concrete, singular, definite: 12/27 infinitival constructions, 34/52 nominal constructions), as exemplified in (29) and (30). Moreover, it is typical of infinitival reported speech constructions in German that they are only possible with more subjective verbs of communication (e.g. *vorwerfen* 'reproach', *warnen* 'warn', *behaupten* 'claim', *betonen* 'stress'), *sagen* 'say' being notably excluded. This fits with the more referring-oriented character of infinitival constructions overall. Though not obligatory, many of the nominal constructions in the sample likewise combine with more subjective verbs of communication.

Contrary to the reported speech constructions treated so far, infinitival and nominal constructions cannot be said to have speech act scope. As the referred information is not represented in a finite clause, it has no illocutionary potential, i.e. it cannot express assertions, commands or questions. Coupled to the almost total absence of a referred viewpoint, these constructions are often considered atypical and/or as not being reported speech (e.g. Marschall 2002: 100; Bucalić 2007: 51; Güldemann 2008: 6). Because of the lack of illocutionary potential, Güldemann (2012, 2008: 6) excludes nominal constructions such as "they asked him about the whereabouts of George" from reported speech (cf. section 2.3.). However, like other indirect speech constructions, they can still be seen as attributing information to a source, and through the presence of a communication verb, they at least implicitly evoke the idea of a speech act relationship between the source and the information, even if the referred information itself is not a speech act. Therefore (29) and (30) are still quotative constructions, and if reported speech is defined as a quotative domain, they are also still reported speech (e.g. Leech and Short 1981; Coulmas 1986; Emberson 1986; Wiesemann 1990; Thompson 1994; McCarthy 1998 all include them as well).

There is less possibility of different degrees of viewpoint mixing in these constructions as compared to other indirect speech constructions, yet variation still occurs. Example (31) retains a politeness formula that is reflective of the referred viewpoint (*doch bitte* 'please'), while at the same time offering up a description of the referred speaker's clothes by the referring speaker as a type of scene setter. Example (32), by contrast, omits a clear source indication, relying instead on the broader context. This is an even more referring-oriented construal that is at the margins of what might be called reported speech, and a referred viewpoint is as good as absent.

(31)

Der	*Präsident*	*trägt*	*blaues*	*Hemd*	*und*	*Krawatte*
the-NOM	president	wear-IND.PRS.3SG	blue	shirt	and	necktie

und	*fordert*	*den*	*Besucher*	*sogleich*	*auf,*
and	invite-IND.PRS.3SG	the-ACC	visitor	straight.away	PART

doch	*bitte*	*auch*	*das*	*Sakko*	*abzulegen.*
EMPH	please	also	the	coat	to.take.off-INF

'The president is wearing a blue shirt and tie and tells his visitors immediately to please also take off their coats.' (DS/37.12/27)

(32)

Zunächst	*wurde*	*ihm*	*vorgeworfen,*	*eine*
at.first	become-IND.PST.3SG	him-DAT	accuse-PST.PTCP	a

Todesschwadron	*angeführt*	*zu*	*haben.*
death.squad	lead-PST.PTCP	to	have-INF

'At first he was accused of having commanded a death squad.' (FAZ/12-09/2)

For nominal constructions there may likewise be constructions that reinforce the referred viewpoint, e.g. (33), which introduces quotation marks, and (34), which does the same and introduces a present subjunctive in the relative clause of *Schönwetterhaushalt* 'a budget to smooth things over'. At the same time, the direct speech fragments are clearly non-clausal and fit the referring speaker's argumentative structure.

(33) *Entwicklungshilfeminister Dirk Niebel (FDP) lobte die*
foreign.aid.minister Dirk Niebel (FDP) praise-IND.PST.3SG the
Kehrtwende als einen „richtigen ersten Schritt".
turn.around as a true first step
'Foreign Aid Minister Dirk Niebel praised the turn-around as a "true first step".' (BMP/12-09/1)

(34) *Das sieht die Opposition zwangsläufig anders: Sie*
that see-IND.PRS.3SG the opposition necessarily differently she
redet von einem „Wahlkampf" und
speak-IND.PRS.3SG of a-DAT campaign and
„Schönwetterhaushalt" der mit „Taschenspielertricks" und
smooth.over.budget that with sleight.of.hand and
„Selbstbedienung" bei den Sozialkassen „unsolide" und
self.serving with the-DAT social.classes unsound and
„auf Kante genäht" sei.
accounted.for be-SBJV.PRS.3SG
'The opposition sees that necessarily differently: It talks about a "campaign" and a "budget to smooth things over" that with "sleight of hand" and "self serving" is "unsound" and "accounted for down to the last cent" for the social classes.' (FNP/12-09/2)

In conclusion, with indirect speech there is variation not only in the referring clause, but also in the referred clause. Whereas there are prototypical values for the parameters looked at in the sample, and there are constructions that have all these values, there are nonetheless quite extensive differences between individual constructions. Whereas they all share an increased focus on the referring viewpoint as opposed to direct speech, they differ in the strength of that viewpoint, as well as in the ways different viewpoints are evoked. Some constructions, such as those with asyndetic hypotaxis, may still revolve largely around the referred viewpoint, but other constructions, notably those with non-finite or non-clausal referred information, may lack any overt marking of that viewpoint. Indirect speech therefore has all the makings of a transitional domain: whereas direct speech focuses in a large part on the referred viewpoint, indirect speech displays much more of a hybrid viewpoint. In the next section it will be shown that not only is there a domain where the referring viewpoint is central by default, but also that this domain displays the same variation along more or less the same parameters as direct and indirect speech do.

3.4 *Sollen* and *wollen*

Both direct and indirect speech have been described as quotative phenomena that have as their basic function the attribution of information to an overtly identified source that typically is in a speech act relationship with the information. Though both types of reported speech vary with respect to how they mix the referring and referred viewpoints and how strongly each viewpoint is present in a given construction, the values in Tables 1 and 2 run more or less parallel. This is a reflection of their functional commonality as quotative constructions. However, German has other means at its disposal to mark non-firsthand information and its relation to its sources. At issue here are certain constructions with "grammaticalized", "deictic", "broad scope", "epistemic" or "subjective" uses of the modal verbs *sollen* 'shall' and *wollen* 'will, want' – (35) is a typical example of *sollen*.

(35) *Sein Vater soll im Yakuza-Milieu – so nennt sich die japanische Mafia – tätig gewesen sein.*

Sein	*Vater*	*soll*	*im*	*Yakuza-Milieu –*	*so*
his	father	shall-IND.PRS.3SG	in.the-DAT	Yakuza-environment	thus

nennt	*sich*	*die*	*japanische*	*Mafia –*	*tätig*	*gewesen*	*sein.*
call-IND.PRS.3SG	REFL	the	Japanese	mafia	active	be-PST.PTCP.	be-INF

'His father is said to have been active in Yakuza circles – that is what the Japanese mafia calls itself' (FAZ/12-09/10)

In (35), the referring speaker is indicating he heard, from some unspecified source, that the father of the person in question was a member of the Yakuza. The function of this construction is not the indication that some other source is responsible for the information (that it is from another than the referring viewpoint). Rather, the source serves as a kind of justification for the referring speaker's statement that the father was in the Yakuza. This means that according to the definition in Section 2.1, (35) is a reportive construction (Vanderbiesen forthcoming, gives more detail). This reportive *sollen*-construction will henceforth be called 'SOLL'.

Being reportive, it is different from reported speech, and this is reflected in the values in Table 3.

There are a few obvious differences with Tables 1 and 2. First, a new parameter 'Verb' has been added whose values relate to the verb *sollen* as it appears in the construction. In terms of its conjugation it quite often appears as a third person singular present indicative and it does so in the majority of cases in a main clause, rather than a dependent clause. There is also a new value under 'Referred Information', namely 'simple (vs. complex)'. It captures whether the complement of the infinitival main verb that *sollen* is the auxiliary of (in [35]: [*tätig*] *gewesen sein* 'to have been [active]') is clausal or non-clausal (i.e. [pro]-nominal). Most SOLL-constructions are clearly simple, as is (35). Moreover, the parameter of 'Syntax' has become redundant, as there is no longer a separate referring and referred clause between which a syntactic relationship could exist. The value 'main clause (vs. sub-clause)' under 'Referred Information', which keeps track of whether the referred information has the form of a main clause or not, is likewise redundant, as the referred information in SOLL-constructions is always non-finite.

Table 3: Prototypical values of SOLL

Parameter	Prototypical value	Number	Total
Source	absent (vs. overt)	144	(n = 200)
	abstract (vs. concrete)	44	(n = 56)
	implicit (vs. explicit vs. context)	30	(n = 56)
	non-clausal (vs. clausal)	34	(n = 40)
	main clause (vs. sub-clause)	4	(n = 6)
Referred information	deictic (vs. non-deictic vs. mixed)	200	(n = 200)
	clausal (vs. non-clausal)	200	(n = 200)
	non-finite (vs. finite)	200	(n = 200)
	main clause (vs. sub-clause)	N/A	N/A
	simple (vs. complex)	180	(n = 200)
Verb	3sg present indicative (vs. other)	149	(n = 200)
	in main clause (vs. in sub-clause)	165	(n = 200)
Syntax	N/A	N/A	N/A
Scope	proposition (vs. other)	200	(n = 200)
Viewpoint	referring (vs. referred vs. hybrid)	200	(n = 200)

Second, the values that are prototypical for the SOLL-construction are almost the complete reverse of what was found for the quotative constructions in 3.2. and 3.3. The "Source" parameter shows that SOLL-constructions often lack overt source marking, and that if they do not, the source is usually abstract rather than concrete, and given implicitly (in the same simple sentence as the referred information). An example is (36), where the abstract source is given in a prepositional phrase (*laut Medienberichten* 'according to media reports').

(36) *Als Folge* *sollen* *laut* *Medienberichten*
as consequence shall-IND.PRS.3PL according.to media.reports
weltweit *rund* *6700* *Stellen* *statt* *der* *zuvor*
worldwide around 6700 places instead.of the-GEN earlier
geplanten *4500* *Arbeitsplätze* *gestrichen* *werden [...].*
planned 4500 jobs strike-PST.PTCP. become-INF
'In consequence, worldwide around 6700 positions instead of the earlier planned 4500 jobs are said to be cut, according to media reports' (FNP/12-09/4)

Under 'Referred Information' SOLL seems to share the 'deictic' and 'clausal' value with indirect speech constructions. Though both (may) use deictic means to signal the relationship between the information and its source (*sollen* for SOLL and the present subjunctive for indirect speech), the type of deixis involved is fundamentally different, as *sollen* is not a marker of deictic displacement but rather of pure deixis (cf. Section 4 and Vanderbiesen [2015]). For SOLL the referred information is everything other than the verb *sollen* itself (and any additional source marking), and as (35) and (36) show, this "rest" is always and necessarily clausal (as it contains the main verb), but non-finite (as it is an infinitival form of the main verb). By contrast, in indirect speech the referred information tends to be a finite main clause. When it comes to the parameters of 'Scope' and 'Viewpoint', SOLL expectedly diverges from reported speech constructions. In (35), for instance, whether the father was indeed active in the Yakuza may or may not be true, which is typical of propositions. Moreover, in (35) it is clearly the referring speaker who is making a statement about the father (namely that he is rumoured to have been in the mafia) – there is no reason to attribute anything to a referred viewpoint.

Third, it is remarkable that certain values apply to all 200 SOLL-constructions, which would suggest there is perhaps not so much variation in SOLL. Note, though, that whereas Tables 1 and 2 encompass a whole range of sometimes quite distinct constructions, Table 3 looks at only one construction. Reported speech is much more prevalent in German than is the use of reportive markers such as SOLL, and hence there is more of a quotative "system". Nonetheless, variation within SOLL-constructions still occurs. Example (35) above is already a typical SOLL-construction, but it has an added clarification by the referring speaker between dashes, reinforcing the idea that the whole sentence is a statement by the referring speaker. Though absent sources occur in quotative constructions as well (cf. e.g. [32]), albeit rarely, they often allow for contextual or pragmatic identification of that source. In (35), however, there is no suggestion of who specifically is responsible for the content, hence SOLL-constructions often have the character of rumours or hearsay. Even when the source is overtly identified, as in (36), the attribution to that source is signalled by the preposition (*laut* 'according to'), not by *sollen* itself, and more often than not the source will not be an individual capable of holding and expressing a viewpoint, but rather an abstract entity that functions more as an information source from which the referring speaker "got" the information (cf. Carlsen 1994 and Diewald & Smirnova 2013 for more on combinations of *sollen* with 'according to'-style adverbials). Though mentioning the source does potentially bring another viewpoint onto the scene, it is done in a way that is not syntactically obligatory and such that it can be easily distinguished from the SOLL-construction proper.

The 'simple (vs. complex)' value in Table 3 also captures some variation within the SOLL-construction. The infinitival main verb of the SOLL-construction may itself have a clausal complement that allows for the expression of the referred viewpoint. In these "complex" constructions, *sollen* often appears alongside a reported speech construction, and 10 out of 20 verbs used in these constructions are communication verbs. This mixing of viewpoints may be rather subtle, as with the inclusion of a present subjunctive in (37), or rather blatant, as with the direct speech complement in (38). Note, though, that in both cases the SOLL-construction does not change its function: it does not serve any function within the accompanying reported speech construction, which is only a "complement" of the main verb and thus part of the proposition that *soll* scopes over.

(37) *In einer Sitzung mit Neugebauer soll Lamprecht*
in a-DAT meeting with Neugebauer shall-IND.PRS.3SG Lamprecht
darauf gepocht haben, dass sich das schnell ändern
Insist-PST.PTCP thereon have-INF that REFL that quickly change-INF
müsse, wenn man internationalen Standards
must-SBJV.PRS.3SG when one international standards
genügen wolle.
satisfy-INF want-SBJV.PRS.3SG
'In a meeting with Neugebauer Lamprecht is said to have been insisted that that had to change quickly if they wanted to live up to international standards' (DS/37.12/74)

(38)

„Das	*Tafelsilber*	*wird*	*verscherbelt“,*	*soll*
the	tableware	become-IND.PRS.3SG	sell.off-PST.PTCP	shall-IND.PRS.3SG

Dehm	*unter*	*anderem*	*gesagt*	*haben –*	*was*	*er*
Dehm	under	other.things	say-PST.PTCP	have-INF	which	he

bestreitet.
deny-IND.PRS.3SG

'"The tableware will be sold off", Dehm is reported to have said, among other things – which he denies'

The new 'Verb' parameter captures cases where the SOLL-construction appears in a dependent clause and is thus itself within the scope of a superordinate structure. Typically, these constructions serve to reinforce the referring viewpoint, as they make the SOLL-construction part of the argumentative structure that the superordinate construction sets up (31/35 dependent uses of SOLL are of this kind). An example is (39), where SOLL elaborates on the reason why both suspects may be given a separate treatment.

(39)

Beide	*müssen*	*sich*	*möglicherweise*	*aber*	*einem*
both	must-IND.PRS.3SG	REFL	possibly	however	a -DAT

separaten	*Verfahren*	*stellen,*	*weil*	*sie*	*ein*	*Videoband*
separate	procedure	expose-INF	because	they	a	videotape

von	*einem*	*Teil*	*des*	*Unglücksflugs*	*zerstört*
of	a-DAT	part	the-GEN	doomed.flight	destroy-PST.PTCP

haben	*sollen.*
have-INF	shall-IND.PRS.3PL

'Both possibly have to subject themselves to a separate procedure, because they are said to have destroyed part of the videotape of the doomed flight' (L99/MAR.09508 Berliner Morgenpost, 05.03.1999)

Occasionally, however, SOLL may be in the scope of a reported speech construction. Some researchers have argued that in these cases SOLL may actually serve a quotative function rather than its standard reportive one (e.g. Letnes 1997, 2008; Schenner 2009, 2010), whereas others have nuanced this (notably Diewald and Smirnova 2012, 2013: 14–15). Whatever the case, (40) is a prime example of viewpoint mixing in a SOLL-construction and shows some of the "layering" that may occur: the referring speaker indicates that the judicial director uttered that it is said that the 20-year-old was involved in a physical injury. SOLL is clearly within the scope of the reported speech construction, being marked with a present subjunctive, and as a part of the referred clause it is clearly reflective of the referred viewpoint, but nevertheless it seems to hold its reportive function (just on a different level).

(40) *Der 20jährige solle außerdem in eine Körperverletzung*
the 20.year.old shall-SBJV.PRS.3SG moreover in a-ACC bodily.injury
im April 1998 verwickelt gewesen sein,
in.the-DAT April 1998 involve-PST.PTCP be-PST.PTCP be-INF
äußerte *der Gerichtsdirektor.*
utter-IND.PST.3SG the-NOM judicial.director
'Moreover, the 20-year-old is said to have been involved in a bodily injury in April of 1998, uttered the judicial director' (L99/MAR.11074 Berliner Morgenpost, 12.03.1999)

Though the values that are typical for quotatives do appear in reportives and vice versa, there nonetheless seems to be a "gap" between the typical values of both domains, as they are almost entirely opposite. However, constructions with *wollen* as exemplified in (41) seem to bridge this gap.

(41) *Er will unabsichtlich in ein Rettungsboot*
he want-IND.PRS.3SG unintentionally in a-ACC lifeboat
gefallen sein.
fall-PST.PTCP be-INF
'He claims to have unintentionally fallen into a lifeboat' (RHZ12/JAN.19177 Rhein-Zeitung, 19.01.2012)

In (41), the referring speaker is signalling that the subject of the sentence (*er* 'he') made a claim to the extent that he accidentally fell into a lifeboat. The referring speaker is thus attributing some information to the source, and is not trying to justify a statement of his own. Moreover, as in these constructions it is always the subject of the sentence containing *wollen* that is the source; the source is obligatorily mentioned and never absent. At the same time, though, the referring viewpoint is strongly present, as a de re reading is the only possible one. Moreover, the referred information (the sentence without *wollen*) is non-finite, so there is no real expression of a referred viewpoint, much like with SOLL and infinitival and nominal reported speech constructions. Where it diverges from quotatives is in the nature of its source marking. The present subjunctive (along with the pronominal shifts in direct speech) is a marker of deictic displacement, meaning that in terms of speaker-relation it relates primarily to the referred speaker. *Wollen* in (41), however, does not: the obligatory reference to the referred speaker (the source) is a case of lexical persistence from older (volitional) uses of *wollen*, where it expresses an intention, wish or desire of the sentential subject (*X wants Y*). Deictically it relates to the referring speaker, coding only his or her viewpoint, and only secondarily ("lexically") relating the subject to the referred information. This means *wollen* is deictic in the same way *sollen* is. At the same time, the referred information, being non-finite, has no illocutionary potential, and can thus not be considered a speech act. Rather, *wollen* has propositional scope: that the subject in (41) accidentally fell into a lifeboat may or may not be true. *Wollen* is an attributive construction, but it is a case of pure deixis (rather than displacement) and has propositional scope. Vanderbiesen (2014) labels this hybrid of quotative and reportive function 'quoportive', and it is this function that will henceforth be referred to as WILL.

WILL's hybridity is reflected in Table 4, which combines the source behaviour of quotatives with the behaviour of SOLL in the other parameters:

Table 4: Prototypical values of WILL

Parameter	Prototypical value	Number	Total
Source	overt (vs. absent)	200	(n = 200)
	concrete (vs. abstract)	182	(n = 200)
	implicit (vs. explicit vs. context)	199	(n = 200)
	clausal (vs. non-clausal)	200	(n = 200)
	main clause (vs. sub-clause)	200	(n = 200)
Referred information	deictic (vs. non-deictic vs. mixed)	200	(n = 200)
	clausal (vs. non-clausal)	200	(n = 200)
	non-finite (vs. finite)	200	(n = 200)
	main clause (vs. sub-clause)	N/A	N/A
	simple (vs. complex)	164	(n = 200)
Verb	3sg present indicative (vs. other)	151	(n = 200)
	in main clause (vs. in sub-clause)	154	(n = 200)
Syntax	N/A	N/A	N/A
Scope	proposition (vs. other)	200	(n = 200)
Viewpoint	referring (vs. referred vs. hybrid)	200	(n = 200)

Apart from the obligatory marking of the source as implicit (i.e. within the simple sentence containing the referred information), WILL seems to behave like a quotative in terms of the 'Source' parameter. In fact, it goes further in not allowing a source marking to be absent. Moreover, its insistence on concrete, singular, definite sources is atypical of deictically used modal verbs, and is reflective of the lexical persistence mentioned earlier, as only persons can wish or intend something. It behaves by and large like SOLL in terms of the other parameters, though it has a higher incidence of "complex" constructions (where the main verb itself has a clausal complement). Under 'Viewpoint' WILL is analyzed as reflecting mainly the referring viewpoint – though it does necessarily bring two conceptualizers on the scene (the referring speaker deictically through *wollen*, the referred speaker in the sentential subject), only one viewpoint is really expressed. In this sense WILL resembles infinitival and nominal reported speech constructions.

Nonetheless, because WILL inherently relates to a referred speaker, individual constructions may reinforce his or her viewpoint in various ways. In (42), for instance, WILL is combined with a quotation fragment, indicated by quotation marks, which is a clear indication of a referred viewpoint. In (43), a "complex" construction, *wollen* is almost used as a communication verb in a reported speech construction with an asyndetically hypotactic referred clause marked with a present subjunctive. Moreover, a parallel exists between *wollen wissen* 'claim to know' and the following genuine reported speech construction with the communication verb *verbreiten* 'disseminate'.

(42) *Die Grünen wollen nur „Alten Wein in jüngeren*
The-NOM Greens want-IND.PRS.3PL only old wine in younger
Schläuchen" geschmeckt haben […].
skins taste-PST.PTCP have-INF
'The Green Party claims to have only tasted "old wine in younger skins"' (FNP/12-09/15)

(43) *Die einen wollen wissen, der neue starke*
the-NOM ones want-IND.PRS.3PL know-INF the-NOM new strong
Mann laboriere an einer Rückenverletzung, andere
man suffer-SBJV.PRS.3SG from a-DAT back.injury others
verbreiten, er habe einen
disseminate-IND.PRS.3PL he have-SBJV.PRS.3SG a-ACC
leichten Herzinfarkt erlitten.
light heart.attack suffer-INF
'Some claim to know the new strong man is suffering from a back injury, others disseminate he has suffered a mild heart attack' (FAZ/12-09/7)

WILL can thus resemble either a SOLL- construction (as in [41]), or indirect speech (as in [42]), and though the former is decidedly more common in the sample, WILL itself seems to cover an overlap area between indirect speech and SOLL-constructions. Thus, it is subjected to the same type of viewpoint variation as the other quotative and reportive constructions. The behavior of WILL and the evidence adduced in the previous sections points to the existence of a cline that runs from direct speech over indirect speech and WILL- to SOLL-constructions, or, in other words, a cline that runs from quotative to reportive constructions. This cline is the subject of the next section.

4 The quotative-reportive cline

In Section 1 it was posited as a working assumption of this paper that viewpoint mixing is inherent in reported speech. This makes sense by the definition in Section 2.3, according to which reported speech brings at least two consciousnesses onto the scene (and these may each have their respective viewpoints). The data presented in Section 3 showed that on a quantitative basis a prototypical configuration of values can be posited both for direct and for indirect speech constructions, but that in both cases individual constructions may diverge from these values in different ways. These divergences, in turn, have an impact on the strength of the referred and referring viewpoints and thus on the degree to which both viewpoints are mixed. It became evident that the differences between these constructions show a progression from less to more referring orientation and more to less referred orientation. Though these findings underwrite the traditional analysis of reported speech as a cline of "types" between direct and indirect speech, they refine it by showing that mixing can be much more subtle, and occur along more parameters than simply syntax and deixis. Though the examples presented in 3.1 and 3.2 varied along all of the parameters introduced in Tables 1 and 2, even 'Scope' in the case of infinitival and nominal constructions, what remained unaltered was their quotative function of attributing information to a source. Reported speech can thus also be defined as a label applied to a range of quotative constructions that work with different quotative 'strategies' (such as quotation marks, mood, communication verbs, deictic shifts, sometimes even pragmatics).

Though in Section 1 reportives were assumed not to have the default viewpoint mixing of quotatives, they nonetheless can display a similar variation along the same parameters, as illustrated by the SOLL-constructions in Section 3.4. In addition to the quotative cline of reported speech forms, there thus seems to be a reportive cline of SOLL-forms in German. Section 3.4 revealed that what is a deviation from the typical quotative values (e.g. an absent source, a non-finite referred clause or a predominance of the referring viewpoint) is in fact often typical of reportives; both clines thus seem to be related, with the typical quotatives and typical reportives building the poles between which variation occurs. The existence of an intermediate domain between these poles is evident in the hybrid viewpoint of indirect speech constructions (where referred and referring viewpoints cannot be easily "disentangled") and also in WILL, where both the referring and the referred speaker are necessarily coded and whose prototypical values partly correspond with those of quotatives and partly with those of reportives.

	Quotative...Reportive
	Direct Speech...Indirect Speech ...WILL... SOLL
Function	Attribution...Justification
Viewpoint	Referred Viewpoint... Hybrid Viewpoint... Referring Viewpoint
	Full Reference Shift... Partial" Reference Shift ... ... No Reference Shift
Scope	Speech Act Scope ...Propositional Scope
Source	Source Concrete ... Source Abstract
	Source Marking Explicit... Source Marking Implicit
	Source Marking Clausal...Source Marking Non-Clausal
	Source Overt ... Source Absent
Referred Info.	i) Non-Deictic Marking... Deictic Marking ii) Deictic Displacement...Pure Deixis
	+Main Clause Phenomena ...Main Clause Phenomena
	Finite ... Non-Finite
	De Dicto ... De Re ...N/A
Syntax	i)–Embedding... +Embedding ...N/A ii) Juxtaposition ... Parataxis ... Hypotaxis ... Subordination...N/A

Fig. 1: The quotative-reportive cline

Figure 1 gives a representation of the quotative-reportive cline in German. This cline is in fact composed of multiple clines that each represent the possible variation of one of the values of the parameters that were introduced above. Ultimately, though, each of the parameters has an impact on viewpoint and is reflective of the function of the construction; thus the parameters of 'Function' and 'Viewpoint' are most important. If a given construction displays a constellation of values typical of quotatives, it may be said to have a high degree of 'quotativity', and if it displays more reportive traits, it has a higher degree of 'reportivity'. As a construction becomes more reportive, it becomes less quotative and vice versa. An infinitival reported speech construction on the whole has a rather high degree of reportivity, whereas a SOLL-construction with an overt source has a higher degree of quotativity than the typical SOLL-construction. Both constructions, however, still have their attributive or justificatory function and are thus still respectively quotatives and reportives.

As stated, the most important parameters are functional rather than structural. The parameter of 'Function' relates to the distinction between attribution and justification. Though these functions are different, they are nonetheless related in that they both mark relationships between non firsthand information, its sources, and those who experience or receive or refer to the information (Vanderbiesen [2014] calls this functional core 'Referral', and sees quotatives and reportives as different construals of it).

The parameter of 'Viewpoint' relates to the traditional question of whose viewpoint is dominant. It should be pointed out that in light of the data in Section 3 this parameter is to be taken as a generalization. The claim is not that all direct speech constructions, for example, reflect only the referred viewpoint, but rather that they are set up to relate this viewpoint, to make it the dominant one. In a typical direct speech construction great care is taken to separate both viewpoints and to indicate which is which, whereas a SOLL-construction may make no mention of a referred viewpoint at all. Moreover, both quotative and reportive constructions must be seen as having the 'potential' to express the opposing viewpoint. Even the most quotative constructions still rely fundamentally on the referring viewpoint (from where the indication of source happens), while reportive constructions rely crucially on the evocation of a source, whose viewpoint may be made explicit (but typically is not). The cline is thus not so much about "conjuring up" a viewpoint, but rather about reinforcing one that can already be present, however vaguely, fulfilling some 'potential'. It is clear, though, that quotatives more readily allow the expression of the referring viewpoint than reportives allow that of the referred viewpoint (one clear example is the very existence of indirect speech). This may be related to the egocentricity of speakers, i.e. their tendency to present things from their own point of view and to not normally take themselves out of the equation altogether. The values are also relative: whereas both WILL and SOLL are set up to reflect the referring viewpoint, WILL is clearly more closely related to the hybridity of indirect speech than SOLL is. A construction expresses a hybrid viewpoint when the prevalent viewpoint is a composite of the referred and referring viewpoints, usually in the sense that the form of the utterance reflects the referring viewpoint, whereas its content reflects the referred viewpoint.[17] Obviously, though, form and content are related, so that the way something is formulated may influence how it is understood.

'Reference Shift' is a parameter that relates to von Roncador's (1988) criterion for distinguishing direct speech from indirect speech. Direct speech has 'full reference shift' as all speaker-related elements no longer encode the referring viewpoint – the shift is marked from the referred viewpoint. 'No reference shift' refers to those cases where all speaker-related elements reflect the referring speaker. This is the case in SOLL and WILL and also in nominal or infinitival indirect speech or typically also indirect speech with no subjunctive marking. 'Partial shift' applies to subjunctive-marked indirect speech, as pronouns and other deictic elements are anchored in the referring speaker, but the present subjunctive also indicates a deictic link to the referred speaker. Here the shift is marked from the referring viewpoint.[18]

'Scope' is a straightforward parameter in that quotatives have speech act scope, whereas reportives have propositional scope. However, this parameter is also relative. Whereas it is clear that direct speech is concerned with embedded speech acts, it is more difficult for indirect speech constructions to represent them, though they still can (e.g. imperatives cannot be represented in direct speech directly as: *Mache das!* 'do that!' but as *Er sagte: "mache das!"* 'He said: "do that!"'; but in indirect speech it takes a modal substitution: *Er sagte, ich solle das machen* 'He said I had to do that').[19] It becomes even more difficult in infinitival constructions (which would resort to descriptions like *Er trug mich auf, das zu machen* 'He commanded me to do that') and impossible in nominal reported speech.

The values under the 'Source' parameter have been explained in Section 3, but a few of the values under the 'Referred information' parameter need clarification. First, the 'deictic' value of Tables 1–4 has been split up into two clines. The first one relates to whether it is possible to mark the function with non-deictic means. Section 3 showed that both direct and indirect speech can rely solely on the source marking itself, communication verbs or quotation marks to mark the

17 Fabricius-Hansen (2004: 120) says that in indirect speech the person deictics come from the referring speaker, while the content comes from another consciousness.

18 Berdychowska (2002: 124) speaks of a collision of two deictic systems in indirect speech.

19 Moreover, as pointed out by Mortelmans (2009: 178–179), in reference to Confais (1989), the present subjunctive itself is a "deperformative signal", i.e. it cannot be used to make a performative statement.

quotative function (there is no inherent reference to any speaker here), whereas *sollen* and *wollen* are themselves deictic modals and thus always presuppose deictic marking. The importance of this parameter is clear, as deictic elements are inherently anchored in a certain viewpoint. The second cline relates to the question of when deictic marking is possible, and what type of deictic marking this is. Both direct speech and most indirect speech constructions use markers of deictic displacement that are related to the referred viewpoint (shifts in, e.g., pronominal reference and the use of a present subjunctive), whereas both WILL- and SOLL-constructions rely on pure deictic markers (the verbs *wollen* and *sollen*) that relate only to the referring speaker. Second, the 'main clause phenomena' value captures whether the referred clause looks like a main clause. This criterion is gradual: whereas a direct speech referred clause is a full main clause, an indirect speech one may only look like one in terms of word order, but have the function of a sub-clause (e.g. the present subjunctive is not traditionally considered a main clause phenomenon). The other end of the scale is likewise gradual, as it encompasses constructions that have sub-clause word order, but also those that are non-finite or non-clausal. The relevance of the value lies in the fact that a main clause is best suited to express a viewpoint, whereas a non-finite or non-clausal construction can hardly express one at all. Third, the question of how strongly the referring speaker influences the portrayal of the referred information (the 'de dicto – de re' value) is only important for quotatives, as only they purport to express a referring viewpoint. Thus this cline ends with 'N/A' (Not Applicable) at the reportive end of the cline, because with reportives a speaker is not concerned with someone else's claim, but rather with his or her own.

The 'Syntax' criterion has likewise been divided into two clines. Section 3.1. showed that syntax is a less than straightforward criterion, and 3.2. illustrated how juxtaposition, parataxis and hypotaxis may all occur both in direct and indirect speech.[20] In Hopper and Traugott's (2003) terms, +dependent and –dependent forms occur on both sides. However, only indirect speech displays subordination (e.g. in constructions with the subordinator *dass* 'that, which' or in infinitival constructions), which is represented as +embedded in Hopper and Traugott's (2003) terms. This difference is what the first cline captures. The 'N/A' value on the right side of the cline encompasses constructions where there are no longer separate referring and referred clauses, i.e. where the source and the

20 While it is true that a hypotactic indirect speech referred clause is different from a direct speech one (e.g. Vliegen [2010: 220] speaks of a more clear type of hypotaxis in indirect speech), they are nonetheless both hypotactic. Seeing how there may be hypotactic direct speech constructions and juxtaposed indirect speech constructions, it cannot be said there is a steady progression towards more syntactic dependency in the transition from direct to indirect speech.

referred information are in the same simple sentence. The second cline is not related to the direct–indirect speech distinction, but to viewpoint. It does not imply that hypotaxis, for example, does not occur in direct speech, but rather that each type of sentential relation has an impact on the prevailing viewpoint. Plank (1986: 307) states that the looser the relation between referring and referred clause, the better for the expression of the referred viewpoint. Therefore juxtaposition seems most open to the referred viewpoint, whereas subordination and the 'N/A' value are least.

The quotative-reportive cline as represented in Figure 1 is not tied to specific, narrowly defined types of either reported speech or reportives that *as a whole* are reflective of a certain viewpoint. Rather, it allows for a more detailed analysis and comparison of individual constructions, and opens up possibilities for alternative classifications and "typing" (e.g. according to source behavior). Moreover, it allows for a satisfactory description of essentially hybrid constructions like WILL without needing to pidgeonhole them in existing categories that may not accommodate them fully.

5 Conclusion

The present paper has discussed viewpoint mixing in German reported speech and in WILL- and reportive SOLL-constructions. It analysed reported speech as a quotative domain, i.e. as a domain that has as its function the attribution of information to a source, and supported this analysis with a number of case studies on a sample of German newspaper texts. These case studies revealed that the formal and functional behaviour of reported speech and its markers (e.g. the present subjunctive) is reflective of their quotative function. At the same time, the case studies illustrated the extent to which viewpoint mixing may occur in reported speech by looking at a number of syntactic and semantic parameters and quantifying these. It was found that individual constructions may appear in any combinations of values of these parameters, and that these combinations each have a specific impact on the prevalence of either the referred or the referring viewpoint, and on the way in which they are mixed.

The paper then expanded its analysis to include non-reported-speech constructions with a comparable function. SOLL-constructions were defined as reportives, i.e. to have as their function the justification of some information by referring to its origin in a speaker-external source. Again, a number of case studies showed how SOLL's formal and functional behaviour is explained through a reportive analysis, and that SOLL behaves quite differently from reported speech.

This is to be expected if indeed its function is different. Nevertheless, it displays a viewpoint mixing comparable to that of reported speech by having different combinations of values of the same parameters that are of interest to quotatives. The last construction analysed was the WILL-construction, which appears to combine the traits and prototypical values of quotatives and reportives, and mixes viewpoints in much the same way.

A comparison of the results of the various case studies revealed that what is a deviation from the typical quotative values of reported speech is in fact typical of the reportive SOLL-constructions, and vice versa. Coupled to the existence of 'hybrid' constructions like WILL, this observation is indicative of a relation between the quotative and the reportive domain in terms of a cline, which was discussed in Section 4. The values (in Tables 1–4) that occur most in the constructions investigated (e.g. an overt, concrete, definite source vs. an absent source) seem to be their "optimal" values, i.e. those best suited to express quotative or reportive function. These prototypical values thus build the poles of the cline, and between them there is variation along a number of 'sub-'clines. Chief among these is a viewpoint cline that displays a gradual evolution from a focus on the referred viewpoint, over a hybrid viewpoint, towards constructions that centre around the referring viewpoint. Though quotatives and reportives have different functions, their clear relation in terms of a cline is evidence of a shared functional core between them.

List of abbreviations

1 = first person, 3= third person, ACC = accusative, DAT = dative, DET = determiner, EMPH = emphasis, ERG = ergative, F = feminine, GEN = genitive, IND = indicative, INF = infinitive, N = neuter, NOM = nominative, NPST = non-past, PART = particle, PL = plural, PRF = perfect, PRS = present, PST = past, PTCP = participle, QUOT = quotative, REFL = reflexive, REP = reportive, SBJV = subjunctive, SG = singular

References

Aikhenvald, Alexandra.2008. Semi-direct speech: Manambu and beyond. *Language Sciences* 30. 383–422.

Askedal, John Ole. 1996. Zur Regrammatikalisierung des Konjunktivs in der indirekten Rede im Deutschen. *Deutsche Sprache* 24(4): 289–304.

Askedal, John Ole. 1999. Satzarten und Satztypen in ‘berichteter Rede’. In Renate Freudenberg-Findeisen, *Ausdrucksgrammatik versus Inhaltsgrammatik. Linguistische und didaktische Aspekte der Grammatik,* 53–64.

Askedal, John Ole. 2000. Satzartendifferenzierung und Sprecherwechsel in ‘berichteter Rede’. *Studia Neophilologica* 72. 181–189.

Askedal, John Ole. 2007. Deutsche grammatische Terminologie: Latein oder Nummerierung? Zu den Termini „Partizip I, II“ und „Konjunktiv I, II“. In *Wahlverwandtschaften. Valenzen – Verben – Varietäten. Festschrift für Klaus Welke zum 70. Geburtstag*. 219–229.

Berdychowska, Zofia. 2002. Redewiedergabe und der personaldeiktische Verweis. In Daniel Baudot (ed.), *Redewiedergabe, Redeerwähnung: Formen und Funktionen des Zitierens und Reformulierens im Text,* 123–138. Tübingen, Germany: Stauffenburg.

Boye, Kasper & Peter Harder. 2009. Evidentiality. Linguistic categories and grammaticalization. In Lena Ekberg & Carita Paradis (eds.), Evidentiality in language and cognition. [Special issue]. *Functions of Language* 16(1). 9–43.

Boye, Kasper. 2010a. Semantic maps and the identification of cross-linguistic generic categories: Evidentiality and its relation to epistemic modality. *Linguistic Discovery* 8 (1). http://journals.dartmouth.edu (accessed 28/09/2015).

Boye, Kasper. 2010b. Evidence for what? Evidentiality and scope. *Sprachtypologie und Universalienforschung* [Language Typology and Universals] 63(4). 290–307.

Boye, Kasper. 2012. *Epistemic meaning: A crosslinguistic and functional-cognitive study* (Empirical Approaches to Language Typology 43).

Breslauer, Christine. 1996. *Formen der Redewiedergabe im Deutschen und Italienischen.* Heidelberg, Germany: Groos.

Bucalić, Tomislav. 2007. Ein typologischer Beitrag zu Formen der Redewiedergabe. In Elke Brendel, Jörg Meibauer & Markus Steinbach (eds.), *Zitat und Bedeutung* (Linguistische Berichte 15), 45–63. Hamburg, Germany: Buske.

Carlsen, Laila. 1994. Redewiedergebende Sätze mit präpositionalen Quellenangaben. *Neuphilologische Mitteilungen* 95 (4). 467–492.

Chojnicka, Joanna. 2012. Reportive evidentiality and reported speech: Is there a boundary? Evidence of the Latvian oblique. In Aurelija Usonienė, Nicole Nau & Ineta Daba’inskienė (eds.), *Multiple viewpoints in linguistic research on Baltic languages*, 170–192. Newcastle upon Tyne: Cambridge scholars publishing.

Cornillie, Bert. 2009. Evidentiality and epistemic modality: On the close relationship between two different categories. In Lena Ekberg & Carita Paradis (eds.), Evidentiality in language and cognition [Special Issue]. *Functions of Language* 16 (1). 44–62.

Coulmas, Florian. 1986. Reported Speech: Some general issues. In Florian Coulmas (ed.), *Direct and indirect speech* (Trends in linguistics. Studies and monographs 31), 1–28.

de Haan, Ferdinand. 1999. Evidentiality and epistemic modality: Setting boundaries. *Southwest Journal of Linguistics* 18. 83–101.

de Haan, Ferdinand. 2001. The relation between modality and evidentiality. In Marga Reis und Reimar Müller (eds.), *Modalität und Modalverben im Deutschen. Linguistische Berichte* (Sonderheft 9), 201–216. Hamburg: H. Buske.

Diewald, Gabriele. 1991. *Deixis und Textsorten im Deutschen* (Reihe germanistische Linguistik 118). Tübingen, Germany: Niemeyer.

Diewald, Gabriele. 1999. *Die Modalverben im Deutschen* (Reihe Germanistische Linguistik 208). Tübingen, Germany: De Gruyter.

Diewald, Gabriele & Elena Smirnova. 2010. *Evidentiality in German: Linguistic realization and regularities in grammaticalization*. Berlin: De Gruyter.

Diewald, Gabriele & Elena Smirnova. 2013. Kategorien der Redewiedergabe im Deutschen: Konjunktiv I versus *sollen*. *Zeitschrift für germanistische Linguistik* 41(3). 1–29.

Emberson, Jane. 1986. Reported speech in medieval German narratives. *Parergon: Bulletin of the Australian and New Zealand Association for Medieval and Renaissance Studies* 4. 103–116.

Fabricius-Hansen, Cathrine. 1997. Der Konjunktiv als Problem des Deutschen als Fremdsprache. In Friedhelm Debus & Oddleif Leirbukt (eds.), *Studien zu Deutsch als Fremdsprache III. Aspekte der Modalität im Deutschen – auch in kontrastiver Sicht* (Germanistische Linguistik 136), 17–36. Hildesheim, Germany: Olms.

Fabricius-Hansen, Cathrine. 2002. Nicht-direktes Referat im Deutschen – Typologie und Abrenzungsprobleme. In Cathrine Fabricius-Hansen, Oddleif Leirbukt & Ole Letnes (eds.), *Modus, Modalverben, Modalpartikeln*, 7–29. Trier: Wissenschaftlicher Verlag Trier.

Fabricius-Hansen, Cathrine. 2004. Wessen Redehintergrund? Indirektheitskontexte aus kontrastiver Sicht (Deutsch – Norwegisch – English). In Oddleif Leirbukt (ed.), *Tempus/Temporalität und Modus/Modalität im Deutschen – auch in kontrastiver Perspektive*, 119–155. Tübingen, Germany: Stauffenburg.

Güldemann, Tom. 2008. *Quotative indexes in African languages: a synchronic and diachronic survey* (Empirical Approaches to Language Typology 34). Berlin: Bod Third Party Titles.

Güldemann, Tom. 2012. Thetic speaker-instantiating quotative indexes as a cross-linguistic type. In Ingrid van Alphen & Isabelle Buchstaller (eds.), *Quotatives: Cross-linguistic and cross-disciplinary viewpoints* (Converging Evidence in Language and Communication Research 15), 117–142. Amsterdam: John Benjamins.

Güldemann, Tom & Manfred von Roncador (eds.). 2002. *Reported Discourse: A meeting ground for different linguistic domains* (Typological Studies in Language 52). Amsterdam & Philadelphia: Publisher.

Günthner, Susanne. 2000. Zwischen direkter und indirekter Rede. Formen der Redewiedergabe in Alltagsgesprächen. *Zeitschrift für germanistische Linguistik* 28. 1–22.

Helbig, Gerhard. 2007. Der Konjunktiv – und kein Ende. Zu einigen Kontroversen in der Beschreibung des Konjunktivs der deutschen Gegenwartssprache. *Deutsch als Fremdsprache* 44(3). 140–153.

Hopper, Paul & Elizabeth Closs Traugott. 2003 [1993]. *Grammaticalization*, 2nd edn. Cambridge: Cambridge University Press

Jäger, Siegfried. 1971. *Der Konjunktiv in der deutschen Sprache der Gegenwart. Untersuchungen an ausgewählten Texten* (Heutiges Deutsch I/1). Düsseldorf, Germany: Max Hueber.

Jäntti, Ahti. 2002. Zum Begriff des Zitats in der deutschen Presse. In Daniel Baudot (ed.), *Redewiedergabe, Redeerwähnung. Formen und Funktionen des Zitierens und Reformulierens im Text* (Eurogermanistik 17), 139–149. Tübingen, Germany: Stauffenburg.

Jendraschek, Gerd. 2003. *La modalité épistémique en basque*. München, Germany: LINCOM publishers.

Kaufmann, Gerhard. 1976. *Die indirekte Rede und mit ihr konkurrierende Formen der Redeerwähnung* (Heutiges Deutsch III/1). München, Germany: Max Hueber.

Leech, Geoffrey & Michael H. Short. 1981. *Style in Fiction: A Linguistic Introduction to English Fictional Prose*. London: Routledge.

Letnes, Ole. 1997. *Sollen* als Indikator für Redewiedergabe. In Friedhelm Debus & Oddleif Leirbukt (eds.), *Studien zu Deutsch als Fremdsprache III. Aspekte der Modalität im Deutschen – auch in kontrastiver Sicht* (Germanistische Linguistik 136),119–134. Hildesheim, Germany: Olms.

Letnes, Ole. 2008. Quotatives *sollen* und Sprecherhaltung. In Ole Letnes, Eva Maagerø & Heinz Vater (eds.), *Modalität und Grammatikalisierung* [Modality and grammaticalization] (FOKUS: Linguistisch-Philologische Studien 34), 23–37. Trier, Germany: Wissenschaftlicher Verlag Trier.

Li, Charles N. 1986. Direct speech and indirect speech: A functional study. In Florian Coulmas (ed.), *Direct speech and indirect speech* (Trends in Linguistics. Studies and Monographs 31), 29–46. Berlin: De Gruyter.

Marschall, Gottfried R. 2002. Ein Text oder zwei Texte? – Zur syntaktischen Integration zitierter Rede. In Daniel Baudot (ed.), *Redewiedergabe, Redeerwähnung. Formen und Funktionen des Zitierens und Reformulierens im Text* (Eurogermanistik 17), 97–109. Tübingen, Germany: Stauffenburg.

McCarthy, Michael. 1998. 'So Mary was saying': Speech reporting in everyday conversation. In Michael McCarthy (ed.), *Spoken language and applied linguistics*, 150–175. Cambridge: Cambridge University Press.

Mikame, Hirofumi. 1986. Die Einstellung des Sprechers zur Komplementsatzproposition und diesbezügliche syntaktische Phänomene bei Komplementsätzen mit DASS. *Deutsche Sprache* 14. 323–337.

Mortelmans, Tanja. 2009. *Erscheinungsformen der indirekten Rede im Niederländischen und Deutschen: zou-, soll(te)- und der Konjunktiv I.* In Werner Abraham und Elisabeth Leiss (eds.), *Modalität. Epistemik und Evidentialität bei Modalverb, Adverb, Modalpartikel und Modus* (Studien zur deutschen Grammatik 77), 171–187. Tübingen, Germany: Stauffenburg.

Mortelmans, Tanja & Jeroen Vanderbiesen. 2011. *Dies will ein Parlamentarier „aus zuverlässiger Quelle" erfahren haben.* Reportives *wollen* zwischen *sollen* und dem Konjunktiv I der indirekten Rede. In Gabriele Diewald & Elena Smirnova (eds.), *Modalität und Evidentialität* [Modality and evidentiality] (FOKUS. Linguistisch-Philologische Studien 37), 69–88. Trier, Germany: Wissenschaftlicher Verlag Trier.

Munzo, Pamela. 1982. On the transitivity of 'say'-verbs. In Paul J. Hopper & Sandra A. Thompson (eds.), *Studies in Transitivity* (Syntax and Semantics 15), 301–318. New York: Academic Press.

Plank, Frans. 1986. Über den Personenwechsel und den anderer deiktischer Kategorien in der wiedergegebenen Rede. *Zeitschrift für Germanistische Linguistik* 14(3). 284–308.

Plungian, Vladimir A. 2001. The place of evidentiality within the universal grammatical space. *Journal of Pragmatics* 33. 349–357.

Pütz, Herbert. 1989. Referat – vor allem Berichtete Rede – im Deutschen und Norwegischen. In Abraham, Werner & Theo Janssen (eds.), *Tempus – Aspekt – Modus. Die lexikalischen und grammatischen Formen in den germanischen Sprachen*, 183–223. Tübingen, Germany: Niemeyer

Reinhart, Tanya. 1975. Point of view in language – the use of parantheticals [sic]. In Gisa Rauh (ed.), *Essays on deixis* (Tübinger Beiträge zur Linguistik 188) 169–194. Tübingen, Germany: Gunter Narr.

Schecker, Michael. 2002. Über den Konjunktiv in der indirekten Rede. In Daniel Baudot (ed.), *Redewiedergabe, Redeerwähnung: Formen und Funktionen des Zitierens und Reformulierens im Text*, 1–14. Tübingen, Germany: Stauffenburg.

Smirnova, Elena & Gabriele Diewald. 2011. Indirekte Rede zwischen Modus, Modalität und Evidentialität. In Gabriele Diewald & Elena Smirnova (eds.), *Modalität und Evidentialität* [Modality and evidentiality] (FOKUS: Linguistisch-Philologische Studien 37), 89–108. Trier, Germany: Wissenschaftlicher Verlag Trier.

Squartini, Mario. 2001. The internal structure of evidentiality in Romance. *Studies in Language* 25(2). 297–334.

Squartini, Mario. 2004. Disentangling evidentiality and epistemic modality in Romance. *Lingua* (114). 873–895.

Sridhar, Shikaripur N. 1990. *Kannada*. London: Routledge.

Steube, Anita. 1986. Kontext und mögliche Welt (Eine Untersuchung der indirekten Rede). In Jacob L. Mey (ed.), *Language and discourse: Test and protest*, 327–372. Amsterdam: John Benjamins.

ten Cate, Abraham P. 1996. Modality of verb forms in German reported speech. In Theo A. J. M. Janssen & Wim van der Wurff (eds.), *Reported Speech: Forms and Functions of the Verb*, 189–211. Amsterdam: John Benjamins.

Thompson, Geoff. 1994. *Collins COBUILD English Guides 5: Reporting*. London: Collins CoBUILD.

Vanderbiesen, Jeroen. 2014. *Wollen*: On the verge between quotative and reportive evidential. *Yearbook of the German Cognitive Linguistics Association* 2. 167–189.

Vanderbiesen, Jeroen. 2015. The grounding functions of German reportives and quotatives. *Studies van de BKL* 9. http://uahost.uantwerpen.be/linguist/SBKL/Vol9.htm (accessed 28-09-2015).

Vanderbiesen, Jeroen (to appear). Reportive *sollen* as evidence for a functional view of evidentiality.

Vliegen, Maurice. 2010. Verbbezogene Redewiedergabe: Subjektivität, Verknüpfung und Verbbedeutung. *Deutsche Sprache* 38(3). 210–233.

von Roncador, Manfred. 1988. *Zwischen direkter und indirekter Rede. Nichtwörtliche direkte Rede, erlebte Rede, logophorische Konstruktionen und Verwandtes* (Linguistische Arbeiten 192). Tübingen, Germany: De Gruyter.

Wiesemann, Ursula. 1990. Researching quote styles. *Notes on Linguistics* 51. 31–35.

Willett, Thomas. 1988. A cross-linguistic survey of the grammaticization of evidentiality. *Studies in Language* 12(1). 51–97.

Zifonun, Gisela, Ludger Hoffman & Bruno Strecker. 1997. *Grammatik der deutschen Sprache* 3. Berlin: Mouton de Gruyter.

Katsunobu Izutsu and Mitsuko Narita Izutsu

Viewpoint fusion for realism enhancement in Ainu and Japanese narratives

Abstract: This paper analyzes narrative devices of Ainu and Japanese folktales in terms of how multiple viewpoints are fused and integrated in discourse. Folktales in both languages manifest themselves in multiple reported discourses, which usually presuppose nested "mental spaces" (Fauconnier 1994), one being embedded in the next: (Episode Space <) Tale Space < Narration Space < Speech-act Space; and they involve different levels of speech-event participants (Characters, Narrator/audience, Speaker/Addressee). Ainu folktales largely divide into tales of humans and tales of gods. The human and the divine. The Narrator's self-reference is made with the inclusive and the exclusive 'we' affixes, respectively, on the basis of whether the human audience is the Narrator's in-group or out-group. The clusivity distinction encourages the Addressee to compare the human or divine Narrator with the human audience, whereby the Addressee, originally situated in the Speech-act Space, is merged with the audience and conceptually juxtaposed with the Narrator in the Narration Space. In Japanese, the alternate use and non-use of quasi-dialectal/archaic hearsay evidentials fuse the Speaker's and the Narrator's voices or viewpoints, thereby blurring the boundary between the Speech-act Space and the Narration Space and allowing the Addressee to be conceptually juxtaposed with the Narrator. These are all describable as narrative devices for enhancing "realism" (Leech and Short 1981) by placing the Addressee conceptually in the Narrator's vicinity.

1 Introduction

This paper analyses narrative devices of Ainu and Japanese folktales in terms of multiple viewpoints. In Ainu, an indigenous language of Japan, folktales are mostly autobiographical spoken narratives of gods or humans, and can be broadly divided into three categories: tales of gods (mostly concerning animals and plants), tales of humans (often ancient people), and epics of human heroes. They are recited in the form of first-person retellings. As these narratives are multiple reported discourses by nature, they typically presuppose four major "mental spaces" (Fauconnier 1994, 1997), one being embedded in the next: Episode Space (ES) < Tale Space (TS) < Narration Space (NS) < Speech-act Space (SS).[1] For instance, $_{\text{(SS)}}$an old woman performs $_{\text{(NS)}}$a male god who narrates a tale in which $_{\text{(TS)}}$he travels around as well as thinks of or says $_{\text{(ES)}}$something of lasting importance, while $_{\text{(TS)}}$a dream often gives him important $_{\text{(ES)}}$knowledge or information. Although this kind of Narrator is always a single god or person, their self-reference is made in different first-person plural forms: the exclusive 'we' occurs in tales of gods as in (1a) but the inclusive 'we' occurs in tales of humans as in (1b) (Chiri 1973b: 492–494).[2] This usage can be analysed in terms of whether the audience (human) is the Narrator's out-group or in-group, which is one manifestation of multiple viewpoints (of the Narrator and the audience). The performer usually gets back to their viewpoint in a "coda" (Labov 1972) with formulaic phrases like *sekor...yayeisoitak* [*yayetuitak*] '...said so,' as in (1a–b).[3]

[BEGINNING OF THE TALE]

(1) a. *piskan ta tatni unarpe or ta sap=**as**...*
surroundings at birch aunt place at go.out=**1.PL.EXCL.**
'I went to the neighbor, where was a goddess of birch...'

[END OF THE TALE]

*...kusu paye=**as** sekor eper katkemat **yayeisoitak.***
because go.PL=**1.PL.EXCL.** QUOT bear lady **tell.about.oneself**
'... so, I (often) go (there), the lady god of bear said so.'
(Sugimura and Otsuka 1969; our gloss and translation)

---

1 The original version of the present paper used "Narrative Space" to refer to what is termed "Narration Space" in the present version. As one reviewer points out, Dancygier's (2012: Ch.3 inter alia) concept of "narrative space" would apply to any level of narrative structure; it could include Narration Space, Episode Space, and Tale Space in the present discussion.

2 Tales of gods are assumed to be autobiographical narratives of *kamuy* (gods, animals, plants, or spirits), while tales of humans are understood to be human heroes' and ancestors' life stories (typically called *yukar* and *oyna*, respectively), or folks' accounts of their experiences (named *uwepeker*, *tuytak*, etc.).

3 Abbreviations used in this paper include the following: 1: first person; ACC: accusative; CP: connective particle; COMP: complementizer; EVD: evidential; EXCL: exclusive; FP: final particle; GEN: genitive; INCL: inclusive; NOM: nominative; PAST: preterit; PL: plural; POL: polite; PROG: progressive; SG: singular; QUOT: quotative.

[BEGINNING OF THE TALE]

(1) b. *ranma* *kane* *okay=**an*** *kesto* *kesto* *kemeiki*
usually CP be.PL=**1.PL.INCL.** everyday everyday sewing
ikarkar *patek* *an= eyaynewsarka* *wa*
embroidery only **1.PL.INCL.**=do.in.one's.spare.time and
*okay=**an...***
be.PL=**1.PL.INCL.**
'I lived a life of routine, killing time by doing nothing but needlework and embroidery every day...'

[END OF THE TALE]

... sekor *Otasutun* *mat* ***yayetuitak.***
QUOT in.Otasut woman **tell.about.oneself**
'..., the woman of Otasut said so.'

(Asai 1972; our gloss and translation)

Japanese old tales presuppose at least a Tale Space, Narration Space, and Speech-act Space. However, the Narrator is typically human and does not refer to himself/herself within the narrative. The Performer often uses dialectal or archaic hearsay evidentials like *to(sa)/soona* 'it is [or *'tis*] said that...' or *nozyatta* 'it was [or *'twas*] that...,' as illustrated in (2). The use of such evidentials indicates that he or she is using the Narrator's wording, not his or her own, and that the description comes from the Narrator's viewpoint. However, this viewpoint distinction is usually blurred because the evidentials occur on and off in the course of narrative; the Performer's and the Narrator's voices are thus "intertwined" (Sanders 2010). This is another manifestation of multiple viewpoints. The intertwined voices are sometimes disentangled by a coda cliché like *oɜimai/owari* '(that's) the end,' as the narrative moves from the Narrator to the Performer speaking there in front of the rapt faces of Ainu and/or Japanese listeners. With the use of this language device, a figurative curtain closes on the imagined world.

[BEGINNING OF THE TALE]

(2) *mukasi,* *Sagami-no* *kuni* *Kunezaki* *mura,* *ima-no* *Kawasaki-ni*
old.days Sagami-GEN country Kunezaki village now-GEN Kawasaki-at
rippana *tera-ga* *atta-**to**. (...)*
splendid temple-NOM was-**it.is.said**
'(It is said that) there was a splendid temple in Kunezaki village, what is now called Kawasaki. (...)'

[END OF THE TALE]

(...) sore-irai	*kono*	*ike-no*	*kani-no*	*senaka-wa,*	*hinoko-o*
... that-since	this	pond-GEN	crab-GEN	back-TOP	spark.of.fire-ACC

kabutta-yooni	*akakunatta-**soona**.*	*kon-de*	***osimai***	*tyon tyon.*
was.covered-as.if	became.red-**it.is.said**	this-with	end	snip-snip

'(...) Since then, the crabs in this pond have had red backs as if they had sparks of fire on, they say. That is all about it. The end'

Senakano Akai Kani (Retold by Noboru Hagisaka; our gloss and translation)[4]

These Ainu and Japanese grammatical constructions, which are based on multiple viewpoints, can be best described as narrative devices for enhancing "realism" (Leech and Short 1981) by placing the Addressee conceptually in the Narrator's vicinity. As schematically represented in (3a), the Addressee (A) is normally located next to the Performer (P) in the Speech-act Space, while the Narrator (N) and other Tale-Participants/Characters (C) are in an embedded space (Narration Space, Tale Space, or Episode Space).[5] In Ainu, the use of the exclusive or inclusive 'we' promotes a comparison of the Narrator (human or divine) with the Addressee (human), whereby the Addressee's viewpoint is projected onto the Narration Space and conceptually juxtaposed with the Narrator's viewpoint, as roughly described in (3b). In Japanese, the alternate use and non-use of dialectal/archaic hearsay evidentials serves to blur the boundaries of Narration Spaces and to fuse the Performer's and Narrator's viewpoints.[6] This fusion allows the Addressee to sit side by side with the Narrator as well as the Performer, as sketched in (3c).

(3) a. $[_{(SS)}$P, A $[_{(NS)}$N $[_{(TS)}$C ... $[_{(ES)}$...]]]]
    b. $[_{(SS)}$P $[_{(NS)}$N, A $[_{(TS)}$C ... $[_{(ES)}$...]]]]
    c. $[_{(SS)}$P, A $[_{(NS)}$N $[_{(TS)}$C ... $[_{(ES)}$...]]]]

"Free indirect speech" is known to represent the viewpoint fusion of the Narrator and a Character in English narratives.[7] In contrast, the Ainu narrative devices serve to realize the viewpoint fusion between the Addressee and narrative audi-

4 http://minwa.fujipan.co.jp/hagukumu/minwa/kantou/k_026/

5 Although unrelated to, and different in many respects from, the present analysis, comparable descriptions and notations of multiple viewpoints in Quechua oral narratives are found in Howard (2012: 253).

6 Of course, there are also old tales told consistently with dialectal and/or archaic hearsay evidentials.

7 Dancygier (2012: §3.2) discusses "viewpoint compression" (p. 67), "Ego-viewpoint blends" (p. 73) or the way "the narrator's viewpoint alternatively blends with the character-viewpoint" (p. 69) in free indirect discourse.

ence (or "narratee"), and in the case of the Japanese narratives, between the Performer and Narrator.

The folktales analysed in the present discussion are "recited narratives"; their linguistic content as well as their story lines are more or less established and stored in the Performer's memory or through some other form of documentation, and they are supposed to be presented as oral performances.[8] In these respects, they cannot be categorically distinguished from cases when an actual speech-event participant recites a biographical fiction or historical novel. Section 2 gives a more in-depth explanation of the role of the Performer and Narrator in the relevant narratives. Section 3 analyses the discourse conceptualizations of Japanese folktales and Section 4 deals with those of Ainu folktales with more complicated structures and mechanisms.

2 Multiple mental spaces and viewpoints

2.1 Multiple reported discourses and their participants

As in many other languages, folktales in both Ainu and Japanese usually manifest themselves through multiple reported discourses, or, in Dancygier's (2012: 108) terms, "represented speech and thought, represented perception, or some variety of narration". Such discourses, by nature, presuppose nested or embedded structures of "mental spaces" (Fauconnier 1994, 1997).[9] Since these conceptual structures can readily occur in non-narratives as well as narratives other than folktales, we will first give a brief sketch of how multiple reported discourses and their participants are conceptualized in everyday speech. As diagrammed in Figure 1, in every utterance, each speech-event participant as a physical entity consciously or unconsciously conceptualizes the Speech-act Space in which the conception of himself or herself and his or her Addressee is located.[10] When one participant hears another talking about a past event, they envision a Past Space in which the relevant event unfolds itself. The relationships that hold between the Speech-act

8 One reviewer informs us that the term "textualized orature" has been used in the study of indigenous narratives in their printed form.

9 Dancygier (2012: Ch.2) demonstrates that narrative spaces develop comparable nested structures.

10 An elusive fact is that our understanding of the speech event that we are currently engaging in is usually a "blend" of a number of spaces (cf. Sweetser 2012): the Speech-act Space (mental space) and some perceptual representations that the participant gains while speaking or listening (visual, auditory, and sensorimotor spaces).

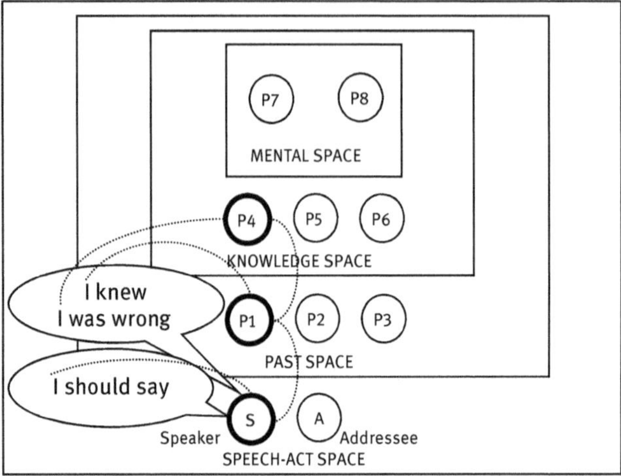

Figure 1: Speaker's conception involved in *I should say I knew I was wrong*

Space and the envisioned space as well as between the participants and other elements of each space form what Verhagen (2005: 7) calls the "construal configuration".

As in the above example, if the speech-event participant utters *I should say I knew I was wrong*, the *I* of *I should say* refers to the participant's self-conception in the Speech-act Space, represented by the circle labelled S in the diagram. The speaker in the Speech-act Space entertains the Past Space, in which one participant, P1, is identified with the Speaker. The *I* of *I knew* refers to P1, who within that further evokes a Knowledge Space with its self-conception, P4. The *I* of *I was wrong* indicates P4.

Likewise, narratives – including folktales – usually presuppose further multiple levels of speakers. Here we will distinguish between three levels of speakers: Speaker, Narrator, and Character.[11] In recited narratives, the Speaker is equivalent with the Performer, an active participant in the Speech-act Space equated with the relevant physical speech event. The Addressee is another speech-event participant, one who listens to the Speaker in the Speech-act Space. It is convenient to distinguish the Addressee from those who listen to the story told in Narration Space. The latter will be referred to as the audience.[12]

11 For multiple levels of speaker and hearer, see Labov (1972), Goffman (1981: Ch.3), and Dancygier (2012: Ch.3).

12 The distinction between the Addressee and the audience seems far more important in understanding Ainu narratives than the Speaker-Narrator distinction, as will be shown in Section 4.

Speaker: a speech-event participant's self-conception in Speech-act Space
Narrator: a sentient entity that recounts a story in Narration Space
Character: a sentient entity in a further nested mental space
Addressee: a speech-event participant's conception of another person in Speech-act Space who listens to Speaker
audience: sentient entities that listen to the story told in Narration Space

As will be discussed in Sections 3 and 4, it is important to make a clear distinction between the Speaker (Performer) and the Narrator in recited narratives. The former refers to the physical entity that physically (re)produces the relevant narrative as a whole, while the latter indicates the entity, existent or non-existent, that is supposed to speak (or narrate) in the Narration Space. The two might be viewed as overlapping in cases when one is giving an account of their own experience or life story. Even in such cases, they may still be distinct in that the person who now speaks in the relevant physical speech event that corresponds to Speech-act Space is temporally and spatially separable (thus differs in viewpoint and mental space) from the person who created the narrative content or texts some time before the speech event. The Speaker (Performer) can recite autobiographical discourses that he or she previously produced (e.g., diary, autobiography). When improvising such a discourse (talking about one's own experience or life story with no preparation), the Narrator might maximally approach or almost overlap with the Speaker in conceptual terms. In Ainu and Japanese folktales, the Narrator is distinguished from the Speaker by linguistic means. This Speaker/Narrator distinction seems to underlie one of the major narrative effects argued below: realism enhancement.

2.2 Multiple reported discourses in recited narratives

In order to demonstrate how discourse conceptualizations work in recited narratives, we will start our discussion with a somewhat complicated but familiar bedtime story situation in which a child cuddles up and becomes immersed in his or her mother's reading of, in this case, an English translation of *Le Petit Prince* (de Saint Exupéry 1943). *The Little Prince* opens with the passage below. Suppose that the child knows, from the book cover, that it was written by a person named "Antoine de Saint Exupéry". As his or her mother recites the first line (below), the child may consider this person to be talking about a picture the person saw as a six year-old.[13]

13 Here we do not argue that *The Little Prince* is an autobiography but only assume that some people, such as children, can conceive of the story as such when they hear it read aloud.

> *Once when I was six years old I saw a magnificent picture in a book, called* True Stories from Nature, *about the primeval forest.*
>
> *The Little Prince* (de Saint Exupéry 1943; translated by Woods: 3)

The discourse conceptualization of the recited narrative can be diagrammed as in Figure 2, where the balloon conveys the passage first recited. If this passage is assumed to reflect Antoine de Saint Exupéry's voice as supposed above, the Speaker, a circle labelled S in the diagram, corresponds to his self-conception in Speech-act Space. The S evokes a Past Space, in which the S's self-conception, P1, is six years old. The first-person pronoun *I* in the passage refers to P1. The thick line indicates the pronominal referent, while the dotted lines represent the referential relations and the correspondence between the referents.

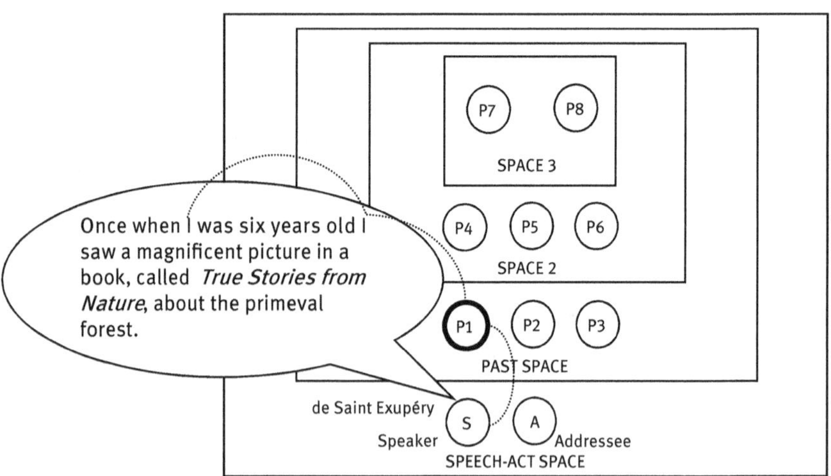

Figure 2: Narrative setting of a passage from *The Little Prince* (1)

However, the original text is written in French and Antoine de Saint Exupéry is no longer alive. If the child listening to the story knows this, de Saint Exupéry could hardly be viewed as the Speaker in the Speech-act Space; he is more likely to be interpreted as the the Narrator in the Narration Space, i.e., P1, as diagrammed in Figure 3. The mother who reads aloud or recites the story will be conceived of as the Speaker in the Speech-act Space. In this interpretation, the pronoun *I* refers to P4 in the Past Space, which corresponds to the Narrator.

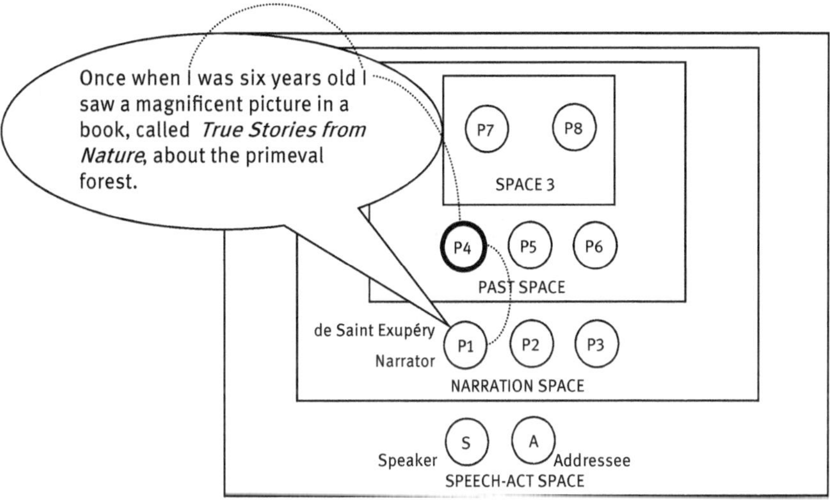

Figure 3: Narrative setting of a passage from *The Little Prince* (2)

Some children may assume that the story is not from Antoine de Saint Exupéry's experience but someone else who recounts his autobiography. Under this assumption, de Saint Exupéry can be understood to have written down the story that he heard from that someone or, as many adults instinctively presume, to have created a fiction with that someone as a first-person Narrator as well as a Character. In these cases, de Saint Exupéry might still be in a narrating role but may serve rather as the creator of the narrative content; he is no longer located in the Narration Space, let alone the Speech-act Space.[14] If he were somehow subsumed into the overall narrative discourse, he would be situated in another mental space such as the Creation Space, as diagrammed in Figure 4. However, by and large, it is safe to say that children are unlikely to conceive of such a creator during the time they are drawn into and become absorbed in the story; that conception would be nothing but an implication. In the present analysis, the passage is understood to represent the voice of the Narrator in the Narration Space, namely P4, as diagrammed in Figure 4. The pronoun *I* refers to P7, which stands for P4's self-reference in the Past Space.

14 As one reviewer indicates, the role of the creator or author is not entirely equivalent to that of the Speaker. One could even imagine someone other than Antoine de Saint Exupéry to be an author (cf. the notion of the "implied author").

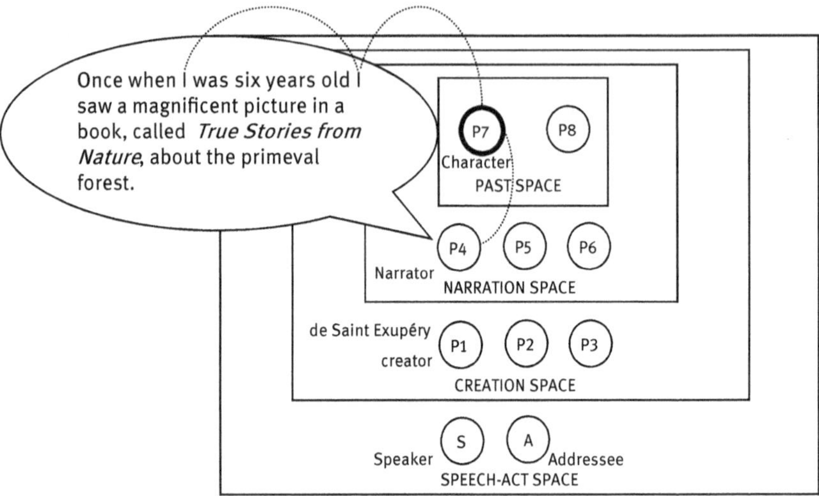

Figure 4: Narrative setting of a passage from *The Little Prince* (3)

In the folktales analysed below, the creators (authors) are in most cases unknown; the audiences of such narratives do not usually create a mental image of any of the originators of age-old tales. Therefore, neither the Creation Space nor the creator intervenes between the Speech-act Space and the Narration Space in the relevant conceptualization of a narrative discourse. On the other hand, novels and other fictions tend to involve those elements because the readers almost always know something of the creators, the authors who wrote the works. Diverse positions of literary criticism bear different conceptions of creators or authors in the narrative structures of the fictions, which the present discussion will not go into any further. It is one advantage of the narratives analysed below that their analysis may permit the avoidance of such complications.

3 Narrative conceptualization in Japanese folktales

3.1 Self-allusion by the use and non-use of dialectal and archaic evidentials

Japanese folktales are typically equipped with established sentence-final expressions which, rather than making a clear mention of, merely allude to, the Speaker and the Narrator. (4a-b) are the first two paragraphs of a Japanese old tale, *The Gratitude of the Crane*. Suppose that the Speaker is a woman, who reads aloud or recites the story performing the Narrator's voice. As in (4a), she begins with a cliché like *a long, long time ago* or *once upon a time* and adorns her first utterance with a dialectal and/or archaic form of hearsay-evidentiality, an expression like *-soona*, *-soozya*, or *-to(sa)*.[15] Those expressions correspond to *-sooda(yo)*, *-soodesu(yo)*, or *-ndatte(sa)* in present-day Standard Japanese.

(4) a. *Mukasi mukasi, aru tokoro-ni, kokoro-no yasasii oziisan-to*
antiquity antiquity one place-at heart-GEN kind old.man-and
*obaasan-ga sun-deori-masita-**soona**.*
old.woman-NOM live-PROG-POL:PAST-EVD
'Once upon a time a kind-hearted old man lived with his wife in a little house deep in the woods.'

b. *Aru hi no koto, oziisan-ga yama-de sibakari-o*
one day-GEN thing old.man-NOM mountain-in firewood.gathering-ACC
site-no kaerimiti numa-no atari-de turu-no
doing-GEN way.back marsh-GEN surrounding-in crane-GEN
*nakisakebu koe-ga kikoe-**masita**.*
cry voice-NOM be.heard-POL:PAST
'One day, as usual, the old man went out to gather firewood in the mountains near his home. He was on his way back that evening when he heard what sounded like a cry for help.'

The Gratitude of the Crane (Kawauchi 1998: 10–11; our gloss)

Generally, the basic operative assumption in this type of discourse is that the Speaker's voice does not use dialectal and archaic evidentials while the Narrator's voice does. At the very beginning, the Addressee assumes that the phrase *Mukasi mukasi, aru tokoro-ni kokoro-no yasasii oziisan-to obaasan-ga sun-deori-masita-* is being told in the Speaker's voice and from her point of view, as in Figure 5. On encountering the use of the dialectal/archaic evidential *-soona* in the sentence-final position, however, the Addressee can understand that the phrase is being recounted by another person, the Narrator, represented by a circle labelled P1, as shown in Figure 6. Here the shift in voice and viewpoint from the Speaker to the

15 In a strict sense, it may be more appropriate to call these expressions "quasi-dialectal" or "quasi-archaic" rather than dialectal or archaic forms because one does not ordinarily assume any specific dialect or period of time in which they are or were actually used. The present discussion, however, refers to them as dialectal or archaic forms for convenience's sake. For hearsay evidentiality, see Chafe and Nichols (1986).

Narrator helps to activate the Narration Space, in which the relevant narrative act unfolds. Other things being equal, the Addressee tends to assume that the Narrator rather than the Speaker continues to relate the second paragraph given in (4b): *Aru hi-no koto, oziisan-ga yama-de sibakari-o site-no kaerimiti...*

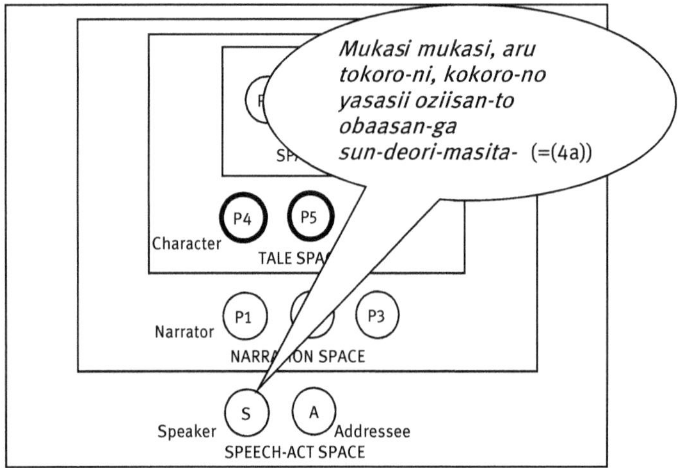

Figure 5: Narrative setting of Japanese folktale (1)

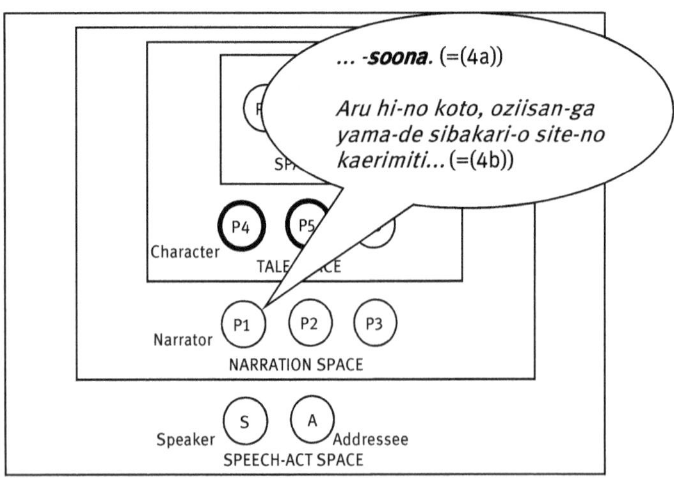

Figure 6: Narrative setting of Japanese folktale (2)

Nevertheless, the sentence in (4b) is concluded with the non-dialectal and non-archaic expression *-masita*. Since the narrating voice here shifts back to the non-use of a dialectal/archaic evidential, it can thereby inform the Addressee that the story is being told by the Speaker herself rather than the Narrator, as in Figure 7. Citing an autobiographical travel narrative by Jonathan Raban, a travel writer, Dancygier (2004: 366) argues that different names for the writer's self-reference in the text reflect two narrative viewpoints and that they "can also coexist in the same narrative context and alternate in their role of the main character". In the Japanese folktale narratives seen above, the Speaker's non-use and the Narrator's use of dialectal/archaic hearsay evidentials reflect their respective viewpoints as they alternate in their roles as the storyteller.

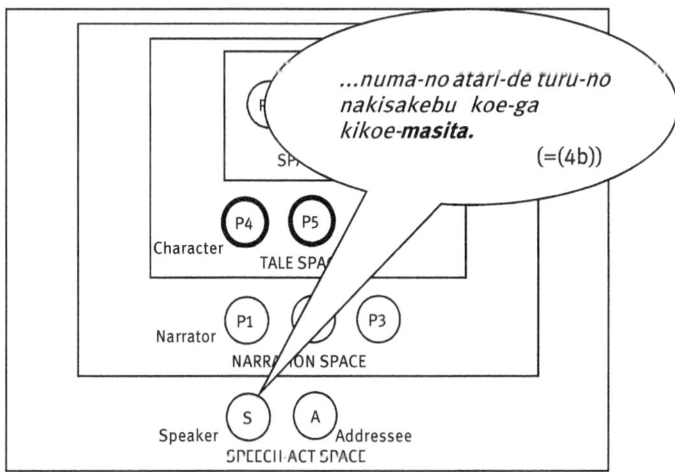

Figure 7: Narrative setting of Japanese folktale (3)

Japanese has a canonical sentence structure that ends with a main verb, optionally followed by auxiliaries (modals and evidentials) as well as final particles (attitudinals) (Izutsu and Izutsu 2013: 226). Because these sentence-final elements often reflect dialectal or historical variations of the language, they can readily reveal the linguistic background of their user. The use and the non-use of dialectal/archaic evidentials in narratives like (4) thus serve as the Narrator's and the Speaker's self-allusion, respectively; the use implies the Narrator's viewpoint as well as voice, while the non-use hints at the Speaker's. As argued in the following subsection, they usually alternate through the progression of the narrative and thereby effect viewpoint fusion between the Speaker and the Narrator.

3.2 A merger between the Speaker and the Narrator

In typical Japanese folktales such as (4), sentences are occasionally recited with hearsay evidentials, the use and the non-use of which add the Narrator's and the Speaker's voice to each sentence, as shown above. The narrative content is not supposed to be what the Speaker herself heard, let alone experienced; rather it is supposed to be what the Narrator heard. Nevertheless, the non-dialectal and non-archaic utterance-final wording indexed with modern, standard Japanese *-masita*, as in (4b), strikes the Addressee as the Speaker's rather than the Narrator's voice. This is because the Speaker's voice is assumed not to use such dialectal and archaic evidentials as used by the Narrator's voice, as noted in Section 3.1.

Moreover, the non-dialectal and non-archaic utterance-final wording with no hearsay evidentials gives the Addressee the impression that the Speaker is talking as if she had directly heard it or possibly experienced it in one way or another. As Mushin (2001: 169) demonstrates, Japanese "retellers" consistently prefer to adopt a "reportive epistemological stance" linguistically coded in hearsay or inferential evidentials. They are, as she infers, motivated by certain norms of the speech community to represent the story they retell as derived from someone else's experience. The absence of such evidentials thus implies that the narrative is a report of the Speaker's own experience or "the reteller's own experience of hearing the story" (Mushin 2001: 116). The use and the non-use of hearsay evidentials in narratives like (4) allude separately to the Narrator's and the Speaker's voices, respectively, while these voices are both recounting the same narrative content. This duality of the narrating voice with the same narrative content enables the Speaker and the Narrator to overlap, as depicted in Figure 8.

The Speaker-Narrator overlap can further blur the boundary between the Speech-act Space and the Narration Space, which in turn induces the merger between the Speaker and the Narrator or the fusion of their viewpoints, as in Figure 9. This can be easily accompanied by a merger of the Addressee with P2, which supposedly stands in the position of the Narrator's intended audience in the Narration Space in Figure 8. This conceptual overlap and merger are essentially identical with "intertwined voices" (Sanders 2010) and "viewpoint compression" (Dancygier 2012).

This alternate use and non-use of dialectal and archaic evidentials observed in Japanese folktales can be characterized as a narrative device which, in Leech and Short's (1981) terms, enhances "realism". The induced fusion of the Speaker's and the Narrator's viewpoints serves to place the Addressee conceptually in the vicinity of the Narrator so that the Addressee can feel himself or herself to be listening directly to the Narrator telling about her experience in the Narration Space.

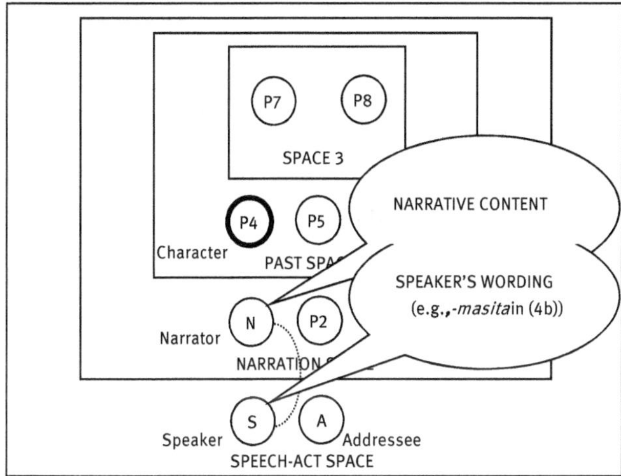

Figure 8: Speaker-Narrator overlap

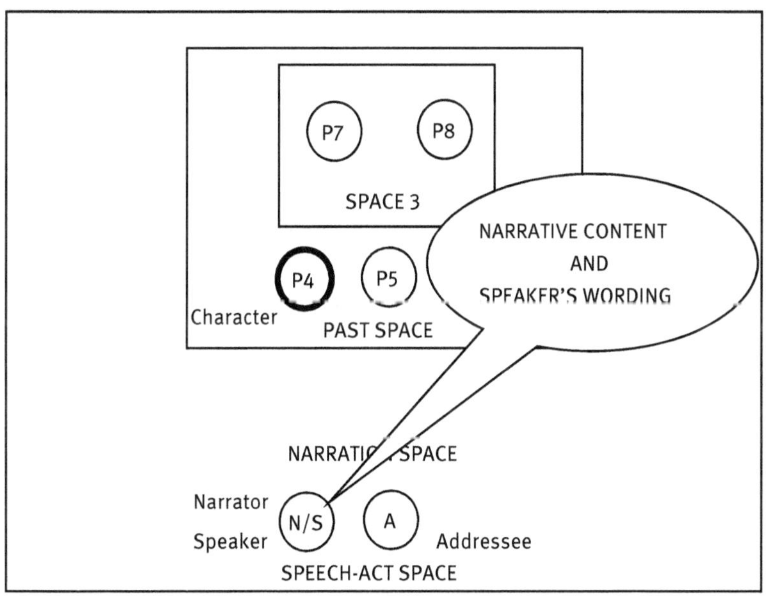

Figure 9: Speaker-Narrator merger

4 Narrative conceptualization in Ainu folktales

4.1 First-person marking in the Speech-act Space

A narrative device that enhances "realism" is also found in Ainu, an indigenous language of Northern Japan. Unlike Japanese, this language exploits its inclusive/exclusive distinction in first-person plurals. Before proceeding to the discussion of their narrative uses, we will show how first-person marking operates in Colloquial Ainu. Table 1 shows the pronominal affixes of the first-person distinct in two major dialectal groups, the north-eastern and south-western Hokkaido dialects. Verbs are notably marked with subjective and objective cases in the first and second person. Colloquial Ainu distinguishes between singular and plural, and the plural is further divided into the so-called inclusive and exclusive, that is, the 'we' that includes the Addressee and the 'we' that does not (Chiri 1973b; Asai 1969; Tamura 1988; Izutsu and Izutsu 2012, among others), as illustrated in (5).

Table 1: First-person pronominal affixes in Colloquial Ainu (based on Chiri 1973b: 494)

	First person		
Northeastern dialect	sg.	*ku*=(V) (subjective) *en*=(Vt) (objective)	
	pl.	excl.	*ci*=(Vt), (Vi)=*as* (subjective) *un*=(Vt) (objective)
		incl.	*an*=(Vt), (Vi)=*an* (subjective) *i*=(Vt) (objective)
Southwestern dialect	sg.	*k(u)*=(V) (subjective) *en*=(Vt) (objective)	
	pl.	excl.	*c(i)*=(Vt), (Vi)=*as* (subjective) *un*=(Vt) (objective)
		incl.	*a(n)*=(Vt), (Vi)=*an* (subjective) *i*=(Vt) (objective)

Colloquial and non-narrative speech uses the subjective *ku*= and the objective *en*= for first-person singular marking as illustrated in (5a). As specified in Figure 10, the set of affixes for singular (*ku*= and *en*=), instantiated in (5a), refers to a single Speaker in the Speech-act Space.

(5) a. ***ku***=*ye kusune na*. (***en***=*nu wa* ***en***=*kore*).
I=say will FP me=listen.to and me=give
'I will tell it. (Listen to me.)'

b. ***an***=*ye kusune na*. (***i***=*nu wa* ***i***=*korpare yan*).
we.INCL=say will FP us.INCL=listen.to and us.INCL.PL=give FP
We will tell it. (Please listen to us.)'

c. ***ci***=*ye kusune na*. (***en***=*nu wa* ***un***=*kore*).
we.EXCL=say will FP us.EXCL=listen.to and us.EXCL=give
We will tell it. (Listen to us.)'

(Our constructed sentences)

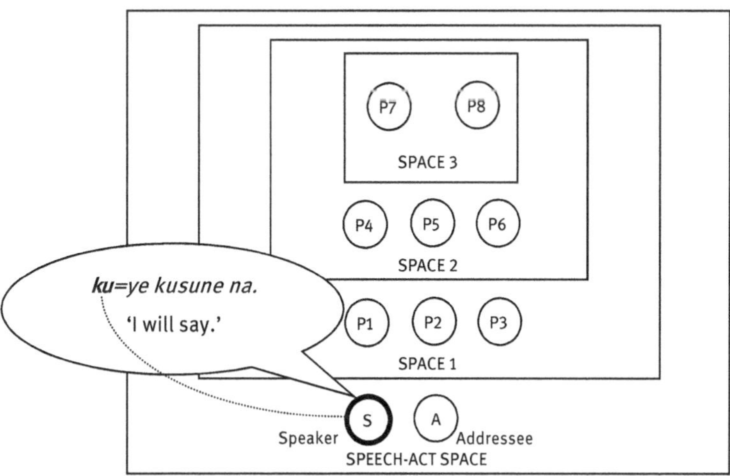

Figure 10: Speech-event conception of *ku=ye kusune na*

The set of affixes for inclusive 'we' (*an*=, =*an*, and *i*=), exemplified in (5b), indicates that a group of people represented by the Speaker include the Addressee, as diagrammed in Figure 11. This function can be termed "addressee inclusion". On the other hand, the affix set for exclusive 'we'' (*ci*=, =*as*, and *un*=), illustrated in (5c), conveys that people grouped together with the Speaker do not include the Addressee, as shown in Figure 12. This function can be dubbed "addressee exclusion".

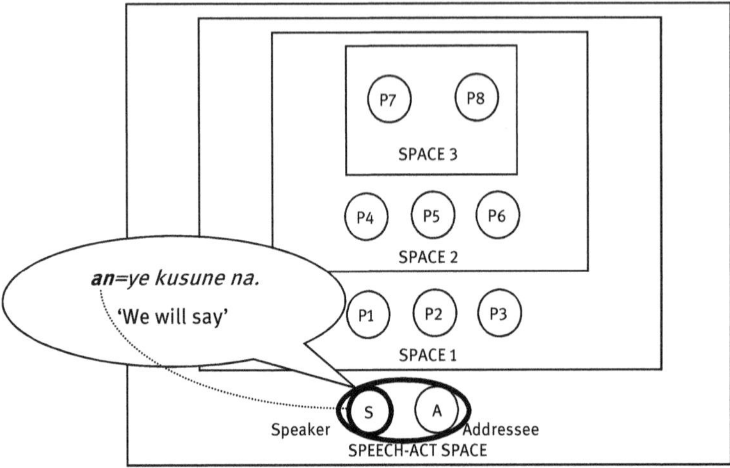

Figure 11: Speech-event conception of *an=ye kusune na*

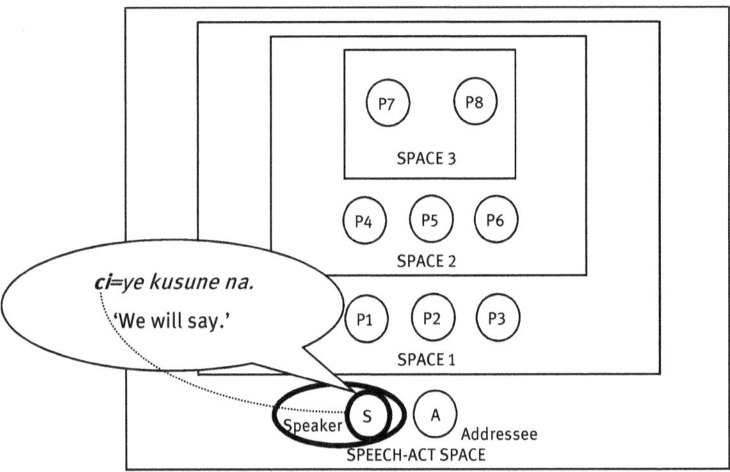

Figure 12: Speech-event conception of *ci=ye kusune na*

4.2 First-person marking in narrative spaces

The first-person marking in narratives differs from that in the colloquial speech outlined above (Nakagawa 1997: 217). In many Ainu dialects, narratives adopt first-person PLURAL forms for first-person singular reference. Ainu folktales broadly divide into autobiographical narratives recounted by gods or humans as performed by the Speaker, who can also be dubbed the Performer or Reciter. Tales of gods typically use the exclusive 'we' set of first-person plural affixes, while human tales employ the inclusive 'we' set of first-person plural affixes (Chiri 1973b: 492–494).

> Tales of gods (mostly autobiographical narratives of animals or plants) are characterised by:
>
> *ci*=Vt, Vi=*as*, *un*=Vt (exclusive 'we')
>
> Human (heroic) tales (mostly human autobiographical narratives) are characterised by:
>
> *an*=Vt, Vi=*an*, *i*=Vt (inclusive 'we')

Although the Narrator is mostly a single god or person taking on the persona of a human, his or her self-reference is made with the exclusive 'we' in tales of gods as in (6) and with the inclusive 'we' in human tales like example (7). The first portions of (6a) and (7a), for instance, do not convey 'we went to the neighbourhood...' and 'we lived a life of routine...' but 'I (a single divine Narrator) went to the neighbourhood' and 'I (a single human Narrator) lived a life of routine,' respectively.

(6) a. *piskan ta tatni unarpe or ta sap=**as**...*
surroundings at birch aunt place at go.out=**1.PL.EXCL**
'I went to the neighborhood, where was a goddess of birch...'
(Sugimura and Otsuka 1969; our gloss and translation)

b. "*... hoskino aynu kotan **ci**=wente kusu*
long.ago man village **1.PL.EXCL**=destroy because
*unci=epanakte kusu makayo ne okay=**as**.*
1.PL.PASS=punish.for because butterbur.bud as be.PL=**1.PL.EXCL**
tane wano okay sipase kamuy, ecikki aynu kotan wente
now from be.PL weighty god don't man village destroy
na" sekor Oyna kamuy pon turesi yayeisoitak hawan.
FP QUOT myth god little 's.sister recount.oneself EVD
' "...Long ago I destroyed a human village and was punished for that, and thus I am now a butterbur bud. Weighty gods hereafter, don't destroy a human village," it is said that God of Myth's little sister told so about herself. '
(Hokkaido Board of Education 1994: 292; our gloss and translation)

(7) a. *ranma kane okay=**an** kesto kesto kemeiki ikarkar*
usually CP be.PL=**1.PL.INCL** everyday everyday sewing embroidery
*patek **an**=eyaynewsarka wa okay=**an**...*
only **1.PL.INCL**=do.in.one's.spare.time and be.PL=**1.PL.INCL**
'I lived a life of routine, killing time by doing nothing but needlework and embroidery every day...'
(Asai 1972: 2; our gloss and translation)

b. "... *menoko raunkut **i**=kore keray kusu siknu=**an***
woman loincloth **1.PL.INCL**=give favor for survive=**1.PL.INCL**
*pe ne kusu tap **an**=eucasikuma hawan na"*
COMP be.SG because thus **1.PL.INCL**=recount EVD FP
ari Otasutun hekaci yayeisoitak.
QUOT in.Otasut child recount.oneself
"... She gave me a loincloth and it later helped me survive," a child from Otasut told so about himself.'
(Ainu Mukei Bunka Densho Hozonkai 1982: 223; our gloss and translation)

Nakagawa (1997: 224) suggests that the use of plural rather than singular forms for first-person reference in tales of gods could be attributed to the "integration" of a natural deity "main character" and a human "reciter," which will be analysed as a first-person divine Narrator in the Narration Space and a human Speaker in the Speech-act Space, respectively, below. Nakagawa provides a possible interpretation of the exclusive plural forms (*ci*=, =*as*, and *un*=) in tales of gods: "...the person of 'we' is used because epic songs are not the type of narratives in which a human recounts a god's experience in place of the god but the type in which a god as a main character possesses a human as reciter, and the two integrate themselves into one and talk together" (1997: 224; our translation).[16]

As Nakagawa (1997: 223) points out, Chiri (1973a) suggests that the use of the exclusive-'we' type of pronominal affixes and pronouns in tales of gods can be ascribed to the assumption that gods speak a different language than humans to distinguish themselves from humans.[17]

---

16 Nakagawa (1997: 225) acknowledges that the use of plural rather than singular forms for the Narrator's self reference in these narratives has not been fully accounted for in Ainu linguistics.
17 One reviewer remarks that there is not enough evidence for such a strong claim; gods do speak the language humans can understand. Another interpretation suggested by the reviewer is that the space from which a god can speak is separate from the world inhabited by humans. This seems compatible with Sato's (2004: 181–183) hypothesis about the channels of communication between this (human) world and the other (divine) world in Ainu culture.

> The characteristic of this person system [the system in tales of gods] is that only [the] first person uses special pronominals [*ci*=, =*as*, and *un*=], which seems to stem from the intention that gods should speak a different language from men's to distinguish themselves from men. (Chiri 1973a: 164; our translation)

Nakagawa's interpretation can account for the plurality of but not for the distinction between exclusives in tales of gods and inclusives in human tales. Chiri's account can accommodate the clusivity distinction, although it does not give a sufficient explanation of the plurality.

Basically following Chiri's line of explanation, the present discussion assumes that Ainu narratives employ the grammatical distinction between the singular and the plural of first person to differentiate the Speaker in the Speech-act Space from the Narrator in the Narration Space and exploit the exclusive/inclusive distinction of the plural to differentiate Narrators as gods from Narrators as humans. The analysis below will demonstrate how the exclusive/inclusive-'we' distinction serves the differentiated marking of the divine Narrator's and human Narrator's self-reference. We will further argue that the clusivity distinction in folktales can be analysed as another narrative device for enhancing realism.

4.3 Clusivity distinction and its narrative effect

The conceptual analysis of multiple reported discourses presented above can help readers to understand why the addressee-inclusion/exclusion functions serve to distinguish between Narrators as gods and humans. It can also explain the unique narrative effect that the functions produce in Ainu folktales. Grammatical marking of the inclusive/exclusive distinction of first-person Narrators constantly alludes to the human audience included as the Narrator's in-groups or excluded as out-groups. The Addressee can easily self-identify as the audience because they are both equally engaged in listening to the story. As Dancygier (2004: 369) succinctly points out, the inclusive and exclusive 'we' both "assume the speaker to be the deictic anchor, but the scope of the reference varies". Ainu narratives seemingly exploit this function of evoking the scope of reference for the effect of realism enhancement as well as the human/god-Narrator distinction. See Dancygier (2004: 369–372) for the viewpoint-marking function of the pronoun 'we' beyond the simple inclusive/exclusive distinction.

As noted above, Ainu folktales utilize the singular/plural distinction of first-person marking for differentiating between the Speaker in the Speech-act Space and the Narrator in the Narration Space. In the customary oral tradition, when someone is to sit and begin a story in front of someone else, she will use the singular affix *ku=* as in *tuytak* ***ku****=ye kusune na* 'I will tell an old story' or in (5a). The first-person singular affixes (*ku=* and *en=*) serve to single out the Speaker in the Speech-act Space," as diagrammed in Figure 13. This is essentially the same as the ordinary first-person singular usage in Colloquial Ainu, depicted in Figure 10 above.

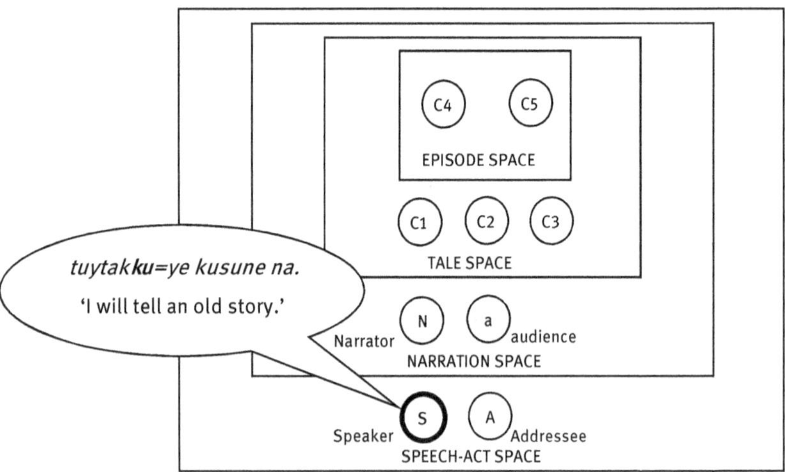

Figure 13: Speaker singling out

And then, once she starts a narrative, the Speaker shifts to another set of first-person affixes for self-reference: the inclusive or exclusive 'we' outlined in Sections 4.1 and 4.2. As noted above, human tales are typically human life accounts (autobiographical narratives), in which the Narrator's self-reference is made with inclusive-'we' affixes like *an=*, *=an*, and *i=*, as illustrated in (7). The shift from the affix set of *ku=* and *en=* to the set of *an=*, *=an*, and *i=* informs the Addressee that the tale is being recounted by the Narrator rather than the Speaker (cf. Nakagawa 1997: 222). At the same time, the affixes serve addressee inclusion as diagrammed in Figure 14.[18] They suggest that the Narrator's group includes a human audience, represented by a circle labelled "a"; the Narrator is thereby imagined as a human living somewhere else, probably some time ago. Both the Addressee in the

18 Note that the present discussion uses the uncapitalized word "addressee" as a cover term for narrative listeners including both the Addressee in the Speech-act Space and the audience in the Narration Space. The "addressees" relevant to addressee inclusion in human tales amount to the audience in the first place and to the Addressee in the second place.

Speech-act Space and the audience in the Narration Space are in the same relation to the Speaker and the Narrator: they both listen to the story. Being remarkably similar to the listener of the story, the Addressee can easily identify or confuse himself or herself with the audience.[19] The confusion creates the impression that the Addressee is next to the Narrator in the Narration Space, an effect that can be termed "Addressee-audience overlap".

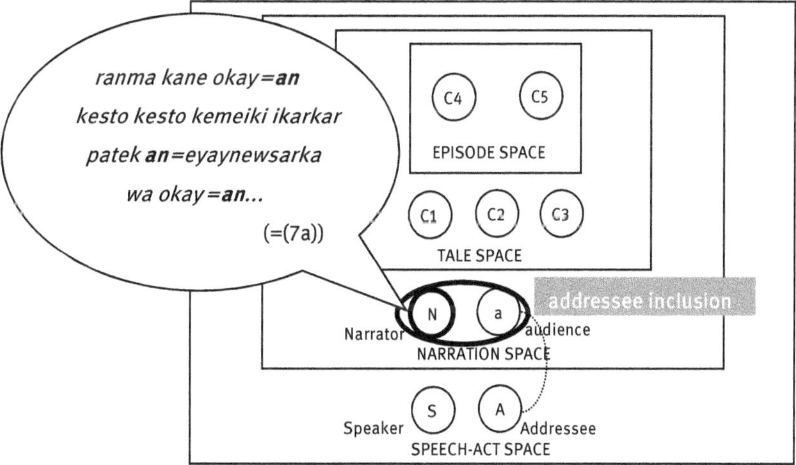

Figure 14: Addressee (audience) inclusion in human tales (*an*=, =*an*, and *i*=)

However, in tales of gods the Speaker typically adopts exclusive-'we' affixes like *ci*=, =*as*, and *un*=, as exemplified in (6). Here again the use of these affixes instead of the singular affixes (*ku*= and *en*=) informs the audience that the tale is being told in the Narrator's voice, not the Speaker's. In this case, the affixes that

19 There are at least three motivations for this confusion. Firstly, the effect is likely in first-person narratives where the Narrator's self-reference, 'I,' strongly suggests the presence of someone being addressed, "you". Secondly, both the Addressee and the audience are supposed to be human and can therefore be equated easily. Finally, the obligatory marking of addressee inclusion/exclusion encourages the Addressee to look for and eventually self-identify as the relevant addressees (audience) treated as being either included in or excluded from the Narrator's group. Although there might be a conceivable audience in the Narration Space, it is never referred to except in that it can be addressed with second-person pronominals or vocative expressions at the very end of narratives.

serve addressee exclusion suggest that the Narrator's group does not include the human audience, as diagrammed in Figure 15.[20]

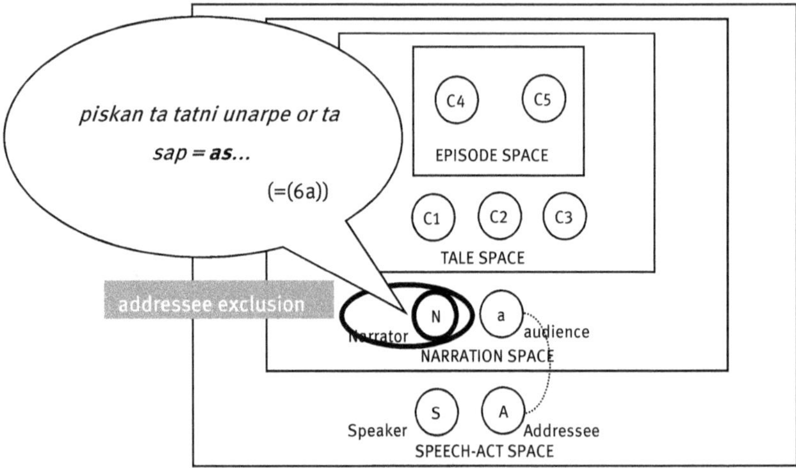

Figure 15: Addressee (audience) exclusion in tales of gods (*ci=*, *=as*, and *un=*)

The indication of exclusion entails implicit reference to the excluded human audience. Being the same listening entities, not only the audience but also the Addressee feels as if they were excluded from the Narrator's group. This leads the Addressee to the understanding that the Narrator is a god, distinct from both the human audience and the Addressee. Like addressee inclusion, addressee exclusion alludes to narrative addressees, firstly to the audience (the Narrator's addressees) in the Narration Space and secondly to the Addressee in the Speech-act Space. This indirect reference can readily effect the Addressee-audience overlap, which in turn creates the impression that the Addressee is listening directly to the Narrator in the Narration Space.

4.4 The Addressee-audience merger for realism enhancement

As demonstrated above, the clusivity marking in Ainu folktales effects the Addressee-audience overlap regardless of the difference between the addressee in-

20 Here as well, the "addressees" pertinent to the addressee exclusion in tales of gods correspond to the audience in the first place and to the Addressee in the second place.

clusion and exclusion. Such conceptual overlap can further result in Addressee-audience merger, as depicted in Figure 16. The essential part of the clusivity conceptualization does not lie in the inclusive/exclusive distinction but in the repeated allusion to the human audience (narrative addressees) in that conceptualization, whether they are the human Narrator's in-groups (addressee inclusion) or, in the case of a god, the divine Narrator's out-groups (addressee exclusion).

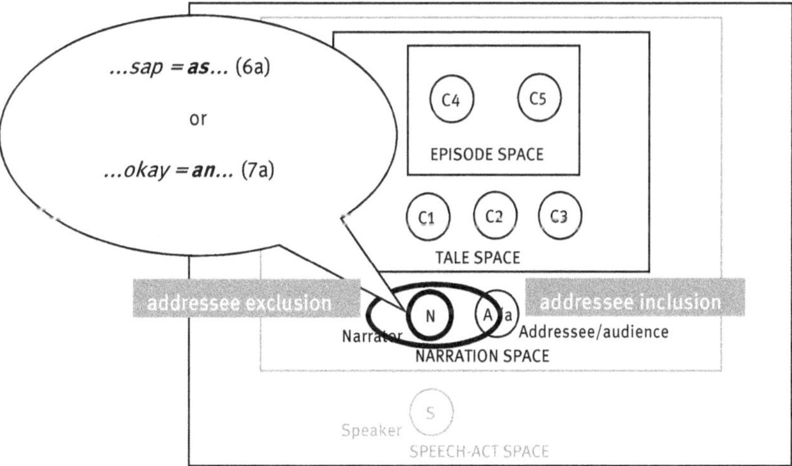

Figure 16: Addressee-audience merger driven by addressee inclusion/exclusion

In tales of humans and gods alike, the narrating voice and point of view are located in the Narration Space rather than the Speech-act Space by means of the first-person plural (whether inclusive or exclusive) rather than first-person singular affixes. As demonstrated in Section 4.3, the inclusive affix set is employed for the human Narrator's self-reference, while the exclusive set is adopted for the divine Narrator's self-reference. In either tale, the plural affixes invariably allude to narrative addressees in terms of the addressee inclusion or exclusion; the Narrators are supposed to judge whether the addressees (humans) are included in their group (humans) or excluded from their group (gods). The narrative addressees are primarily the audience in the Narration Space, but the Addressee in the Speech-act Space can easily self-identify as this audience. This is because there is a substantial overlap between the roles of the Addressee and the audience in the overall narrative; they both serve to listen to the narrative.

The conceptual overlap between the Addressee and the audience creates an Addressee-audience merger, which brings about a conceptual juxtaposition of the

Addressee with the Narrator, as depicted in Figure 16. The viewpoint fusion that results from the Addressee-audience merger can be analysed as another narrative device that enhances "realism". What differs remarkably from a similar Japanese device discussed in Section 3.2 is that the conceptual juxtaposition of the Addressee with the Narrator is realized by the viewpoint fusion of the Addressee and the audience rather than the Speaker and the Narrator.

There is one piece of evidence that supports the present analysis of the clusivity distinction in Ainu folktale narratives: its narrative function is grammaticalized in some dialects. Unlike the instances cited above, some dialects adopt an inclusive set of first-person plurals (*a=*, *=an*, and *i=*) for the Narrator's self-reference in tales of both gods and humans, as illustrated in (8). In the Saru and Chitose dialects, verbs with a singular Narrator subject, marked with those affixes, take singular forms (e.g., *an=an* 'I am' and *arpa=an* 'I go') instead of plural forms (e.g., *oka=an* 'we are' and *paye=an* 'we go'); moreover, such dialects have uniquely developed the singular pronoun, *asinuma* (Narrator 'I') besides the plural pronoun, *aoka* (inclusive 'we'), both of which correspond to the inclusive affix set (Nakagawa 1997: 220–221).

(8) a. *upascironnup uirwakikor wa, sukup orusipe, uwepeker ne a=ye*
weasel be.siblings and grow story tale as PASS=say
*hi, tane **ku**=ye oasi hawe tapan na.*
COMP now **1.SG** =say start voice be FP
'I will tell a story of weasel brothers, told as a tale.'

b. *upascironnup kamuy **a**=ne hine oka=**an** hike,*
weasel god **1.PL.INCL**=be and be.PL=**1.PL.INCL** and
***a**=yupihi an wa, tun **a**=ne wa,*
1.PL.INCL=brother be and two **1.PL.INCL**=be and
*uheturaste=**an** wa oka=**an** hike,*
live.together=**1.PL.INCL** and be.PL=**1.PL.INCL** when
***i**=panake ta ka inne kotan an.*
1.PL.INCL=downstream at too crowded village be
'I am a weasel god. I have an older brother and we live together. There is another village with a large population downstream from our village.'
(Tamura 1985: 58; our gloss and translation)

The narrative discourse starts with (8a), in which the Speaker informs the Addressee that she is going to tell a story of weasel brothers, referring to the representation of herself in the Speech-act Space with the first-person singular set of pronominal affixes (*ku=* and *en=*). Then she moves on to (8b), in which she switches to the first-person plural set (*a*=, =*an*, and *i*=) for self-reference as the younger brother weasel.

Nakagawa (1997: 225) infers that tales of gods in these dialects, like those in other dialects, must have originally been recounted with the use of exclusive plurals for the Narrator's self-reference. This inference suggests that the inclusive plurals in the dialects previously served solely for a human Narrator's self-reference but were later extended to subsume a divine Narrator's self-reference as well. This generalized use of inclusive marking for both human and divine Narrators is analysable as an instantiation of "semantic bleaching" (Sweetser 1988) as well as "functional extension" (Heine and Kuteva 2002: 2). In this particular use, the set of inclusive affixes loses the plurality and inclusive/exclusive distinction but retains the function of allusion to addressees (Addressee and audience). The use of the inclusive forms (vis-a-vis the colloquial first-person singular forms *ku*= and *en*=) serves to invoke the Narration Space and the Narrator therein. The loss of plurality and clusivity distinction implies that the main function of inclusive/exclusive forms in Ainu narratives is not plurality marking but tacit reference to narrative addressees, whether they are included in the Narrator's group or not. In the relevant dialects, this function has later been grammaticalized as a special system of first-person marking that refers to Narrators in folktales in general (cf. Nakagawa 1997: 222).

The extension of inclusive affixes from the human Narrator's to the divine Narrator's self-reference in the Saru and Chitose dialects might also be motivated by some newly developed conceptions in which a divine Narrator is envisioned as being more like a human audience and an Addressee and is thus felt to be all the more familiar or emotively closer to the Addressee. This could also be viewed as enhancing realism in terms of familiarity and hominess. At the same time, the generalized use of inclusive affixes for the Narrator's self-reference in tales of both humans and gods can also be understood to serve the same function as the inclusive and exclusive sets of affixes used separately for human and divine Narrators in many other dialects.

As noted above, the essential function of clusivity marking in Ainu narratives consists in the repeated allusion to the audience and the Addressee that produces realism enhancement. The Saru and Chitose dialects have nearly lost the clusivity distinction for the Narrator's self-reference and have extended the inclusive set of affixes to the divine Narrator's as well as the human Narrator's self-reference. However, the generalized use of these inclusive affixes for the Narrator maintains the function of allusion to the audience and the Addressee, which effects an Addressee-audience merger and creates the impression that the Addressee is listening directly to the Narrator in the Narration Space.

5 Conclusion

The present paper has demonstrated the following three major points. First, the alternate use and non-use of quasi-dialectal/archaic hearsay evidentials in Japanese fuse the Speaker's and the Narrator's voices or viewpoints. This fusion also blurs the boundary between the Speech-act Space and the Narration Space, thereby allowing the Addressee to be next to the Narrator. Second, the inclusive/exclusive-'we' affixes in Ainu introduce a human/divine Narrator's voice or viewpoint. The clusivity helps to contrast the Narrator with the human audience, whereby the Addressee is merged with the audience and conceptually juxtaposed with the Narrator in the Narration Space. Third, the Japanese dialectal/archaic evidentials and the Ainu clusivity marking in folktale narratives are best described as narrative devices for realism enhancement, based on multiple viewpoints (of Speaker, Addressee, Narrator, audience, and Character) and the evoked multiple mental spaces (Speech-act, Narration, Tale, and Episode Spaces).

The conceptualization of narrative discourses with multiple viewpoints and mental spaces can be schematically represented in (9a). The Speaker (S) and the Addressee (A) are juxtaposed in the Speech-act Space, while the Narrator (N) and the Characters (C), respectively, occupy the Narration Space (NS) and the Tale Space (TS) (or further embedded spaces like the Episode Space [ES]). The Narration Space could accommodate a narrative audience (a). In Ainu, the distinction between the exclusive and inclusive "we" promotes the comparison of the Narrator (human or divine) with the Addressee (human) as well as with the narrative audience (a), whereby the Addressee's viewpoint is projected onto the audience's in the Narration Space and is conceptually juxtaposed with the Narrator's, as in (9b). The Addressee's and audience's viewpoints are fused into one. In Japanese, the (quasi-)dialectal/archaic evidentials distinguish the Narrator's from the Speaker's viewpoint, but the alternate use and non-use of such evidentials serve to fuse the two viewpoints together. This fusion blurs the boundary of the Narration Space and allows the Addressee to sit side by side with the Narrator as well as the Speaker, as schematized in (9c).

(9) a. $[_{(SS)}$S, A $[_{(NS)}$N, (a) $[_{(TS)}$C ... $[_{(ES)}$...]]]]
b. $[_{(SS)}$S $[_{(NS)}$N, A/a $[_{(TS)}$C ... $[_{(ES)}$...]]]]
c. $[_{(SS)}$S/N, A $[_{(NS)}$ $[_{(TS)}$C ... $[_{(ES)}$...]]]]

Unlike free indirect speech, which is known to represent the viewpoint fusion of the Narrator and Character in English narratives, the Japanese narrative device serves to achieve the viewpoint fusion of the Speaker and the Narrator. On the other hand, the Ainu narrative device serves to realize the viewpoint fusion of the

Addressee and the audience. Free indirect speech helps to obscure the boundaries of the Tale Space or further embedded spaces like the Episode Space, while the Japanese device blurs the boundaries of the Narration Space. The Ainu device does not exhibit such an effect but brings the Addressee into the Narration Space or possibly further embedded spaces.

These kinds of recited narratives in Ainu and Japanese as well as in English presuppose multiply embedded mental spaces. The Narration Space and other narrative-related spaces may thus be fairly similar structures across languages, but the model conception of narrative setting could differ from one language to another. In languages like English and Japanese, embedded mental spaces are conceptualized primarily on the basis of a stage setting like Langacker's (1991: 284) "stage model," in which spectators observe an embedded space of on-stage play.

In Ainu, mental spaces may be modelled on a dream setting in which someone asleep entertains an embedded space of a dream. While mental spaces are comparable nested structures with one structure embedded in another, a Tale or Episode Space established as a dream can play an important role in the way Ainu narrative discourse unfolds. As noted in the introduction, for example, an old woman in the Speech-act Space performs a male god in the Narration Space, who narrates a tale in which he travels around, thinks, and speaks. In this Tale Space, a dream – also conceived of as a further embedded space – often gives him important knowledge or information. Sato (2004: 184; our translation) argues that "... it is the most convincing hypothesis to consider that the first-person narrative style in Ainu literature was originally put to use based on the scene setting of 'oracles in dreams'".

One advantage of the present analysis is that it can offer a motivated account of the use of different sets of first-person pronominal affixes in Ainu folktales. They serve as "space builders," specifically Narration Space builders. They also help to specify whether the Narrator is human or god, or occasionally to make the Narrator's identity ambivalent as in heroic tales or epics. Another advantage is that the analysis can give a consistent account of the recently observed fact that the exclusive – and inclusive – 'we' set of pronominal affixes can alternate in a number of tales of gods (Nakagawa 2011). The more humanlike a divine Narrator is assumed to be, the more likely it is that the inclusive-'we' set is adopted for the Narrator's self-reference. Such a shift encourages the Addressee to feel the Narrator's godlike status all the more familiar or emotively closer to the Addressee. Finally, the analysis reveals that apparently different linguistic devices in geographically related but genealogically unrelated languages like Japanese and Ainu serve to bring about a very similar narrative effect. The devices help to enhance the realism of recited narratives by the viewpoint fusion of the Speaker and the Narrator, as in Japanese folktales, or that of the Addressee and audience, as in Ainu folktales.

This paper analysed recited folktale narratives and substantiated the importance of the distinction between the Narrator in the Narration Space and the Speaker (or Performer) in the Speech-act Space. Whereas narratives of this type are supposed to be orally presented or performed on a speech-act basis, they can also be discussed more or less from the perspective of their printed form. Similar narratives are referred to as "textualized orature" in the study of indigenous stories, in which an accurate discussion of the 'teller' in the narratives has not been provided.[21] We hope that the present discussion will also contribute to the very much needed future work in this direction.

Acknowledgements

We would like to thank Nicholas Evans, Barbara Dancygier, and other participants in the 12th ICLC theme session "Linguistic manifestations of mixed points of view in narratives" for helpful questions and comments. In revising the paper, we are most indebted to two anonymous reviewers, whose insightful comments and suggestions contributed a lot to improvements in this article. We are also very grateful to Martin J. Murphy for editorial, stylistic, and technical advice on the final draft.

References

Ainu Mukei Bunka Densho Hozonkai. 1982. *Eiyuu no Monogatari* [Heroic stories]. Sapporo: Ainu Mukei Bunka Densho Hozonkai.

Asai, Toru. 1969. Ainugo no bunpoo: Ainugo Ishikari hoogen bunpoo no gairyaku [An Ainu grammar: A grammatical overview of the Ishikari dialect]. Ainu Bunka Hozon Taisaku Kyogikai (ed.), *Ainu Minzokushi*, 771–800. Tokyo: Daiichi Hoki.

Asai, Toru. 1972. *Ainu no Mukashi Banashi* [Ainu folktales]. Tokyo: Nihon Hoso Shuppan Kyokai.

Chafe, Wallace & Johanna Nichols. 1986. *Evidentiality: The linguistic coding of epistemology*. Norwood, NJ: Ablex.

Chiri, Mashiho. 1973a. Ainu no shinyoo (ichi) [Ainu tales of gods (1)]. *Chiri Mashiho Chosakushuu 1: Setsuwa shinyoo hen*. Tokyo: Heibonsha.

Chiri, Mashiho. 1973b. Ainu gohoo kenkyuu: Karafuto hoogen o chuushin toshite [A Study of Ainu Grammar: With special reference to the Sakhlin dialect]. *Chiri Mashiho Chosakushuu 3: Seikatsushi minzokugaku hen*. Tokyo: Heibonsha.

21 We are indebted to one reviewer for the points made in this final paragraph.

Dancygier, Barbara. 2004. Identity and perspective: The Jekyll-and-Hyde effect in narrative discourse. In Michel Achard & Suzanne Kemmer (eds.), *Language, culture, and mind*, 363–376. Stanford: CSLI Publications.

Dancygier, Barbara. 2012. *The language of stories: A cognitive approach*. Cambridge: Cambridge University Press.

De Saint Exupéry, Antoine. 1943. *Le Petit Prince* [The little prince] (translated by Katherine Woods). San Diego: Harcourt Brace Jovanovich.

Fauconnier, Gilles. 1994 [1985]. *Mental spaces: Aspects of meaning construction in natural language*. Cambridge: Cambridge University Press.

Fauconnier, Gilles. 1997. *Mappings in thought and language*. Cambridge: Cambridge University Press.

Goffman, Erving. 1981. *Forms of Talk*. Philadelphia: University of Pennsylvania Press.

Heine, Bernd & Tania Kuteva. 2002. *World Lexicon of grammaticalization*. Cambridge: Cambridge University Press.

Hokkaido Board of Education. 1994. *Oina 3*. Sapporo: Hokkaido Board of Education.

Howard, Rosaleen. 2012. Shifting voices, shifting worlds: Evidentiality, epistemic modality and speaker perspective in Quechua oral narrative. *Pragmatics and Society* 3. 243–269.

Izutsu, Katsunobu & Mitsuko Narita Izutsu. 2013. From discourse markers to modal/final particles: What the position reveals about the continuum. In Liesbeth Degand, Bert Cornillie, and Paola Pietrandrea (eds.), *Discourse markers and modal particles: Categorization and description*. Amsterdam: John Benjamins.

Izutsu, Mitsuko Narita and Katsunobu Izutsu. 2012. Inclusivity and non-solidarity: Honorific pronominals in Ainu. *Pragmatics and Society* 3. 149–166.

Kawauchi, Sayumi. 1998. *Once upon a time in* Ghostly *Japan*. Tokyo: Kodansha

Labov, William. 1972. *Language in the inner city*. Philadelphia: University of Pennsylvania Press.

Langacker, Ronald W. 1991. *Foundations of cognitive grammar, volume II: Descriptive application*. Stanford: Stanford University Press.

Leech, Geoffrey N. & Michael H. Short. 1981. *Style in fiction: A linguistic introduction to English fictional prose*. London: Longman.

Mushin, Ilana. 2001. *Evidentiality and epistemological stance: Narrative retelling*. Amsterdam: John Benjamins.

Nakagawa, Hiroshi. 1997. *Ainu no Monogatari Sekai* [Ainu narrative world]. Tokyo: Heibonsha.

Nakagawa, Hiroshi. 2011. Ainu no shinyoo niokeru Jojutsusha no ninshoo [On the person for narrators in Ainu epic songs]. *Hoppo Gengo Kenkyuu* 1. 139–156.

Sanders, José. 2010. Intertwined voices: Journalists' modes of representing source information in journalistic subgenres. *English Text Construction* 3. 226–249.

Sato, Tomomi. 2004. Ainu bungaku niokeru ichininshootai no mondai [Notes on the "first person narrative style" in the Ainu oral literature]. *The Annual Report on Cultural Science* 112. 171–185. Hokkaido University.

Sugimura, Kinarabuk & Kazuyoshi Otsuka. 1969. *Kinarabukku Yuukara Shuu* [A Kinarabuk anthology of Ainu songs and stories]. Asahikawa: Asahikawa Sosho Henshu Iinkai.

Sweetser, Eve E. 1988. Grammaticalization and semantic bleaching. *Proceedings of the fourteenth annual meeting of the Berkeley Linguistics Society* 14. 389–405.

Sweetser, Eve. 2012. Introduction: Viewpoint and perspective in language and gesture, from the Ground down. In Barbara Dancygier and Eve Sweetser (eds.), *Viewpoint in language: A multimodal perspective*, 1–22. Cambridge: Cambridge University Press.

Tamura, Suzuko (ed.). 1985. *Ainugo Onsei Shiryoo* 2 [Ainu language audio recording material 2]. Tokyo: Institute of Language Teaching, Waseda University.

Tamura, Suzuko. 1988. Ainugo [The Ainu language]. Takashi Kamei, Rokuro Kono, and Eiichi Chino (eds.), *Nihon Rettoo no Gengo*, 1–88. Tokyo: Sanseido.

Verhagen, Arie. 2005. *Constructions of intersubjectivity: Discourse, syntax, and cognition*. Oxford: Oxford University Press.

Elisabeth Engberg-Pedersen and Ditte Boeg Thomsen

The socio-cognitive foundation of Danish perspective-mixing dialogue particles

Abstract: Danish dialogue particles are nine optional, non-focusable monomorphemic words which point to intersubjective configurations of shared knowledge, conflicting perspectives, or different balances in knowledge states. Acquisition of the particles requires sophisticated perspective-taking skills as children must be able to represent a proposition from both their own and another person's perspective simultaneously.

A comparison of results from 164 Danish children and 60 adults on a gap-filling test with three of the particles suggests that most 11-to-14-year-olds follow adult-like usage norms for these three particles. The children demonstrated understanding of the complex meaning of each individual particle and sensitivity to the ways in which constellations of character perspectives shifted in the narratives. A comparison with the performance of Danish same-age, verbal children with autism, known to have difficulties with taking others' perspective, showed that the children with autism chose the most appropriate dialogue particle in the test significantly less often than the typically developing children. The results confirm the semantic analysis of the particles and the cognitive-functional view of language as reflecting cognitive predispositions and communicative requirements.

1 Introduction

Danish dialogue particles allow speakers to signal the relationship between their own and the addressee's understanding of a state of affairs. They are positioned close to the finite form of the verb and have scope over the entire clause. The group of dialogue particles is usually said to consist of nine particles (Davidsen-Nielsen 1996; Hansen and Heltoft 2011) that can be singled out as a special group phonologically, semantically and syntactically. They are optional, monomorphemic, cannot be focused, and they point to intersubjective configurations of shared knowledge, conflicting viewpoints or different balances in access to information (Davidsen-Nielsen 1996). Examples of the particles are *jo* (shared knowledge, presupposed agreement), *da* (shared knowledge, opposing perspectives) and *vel* (speaker uncertainty, privileged recipient knowledge). Acquiring dialogue particles requires sophisticated perspective-taking skills as children must be able to entertain a state of affairs, taking into account both their own mental state and another person's mental state simultaneously. Furthermore, the acquisition of dialogue particles may be especially taxing because of their perceptual inconspicuousness: the particles are unstressed monosyllables in non-salient, utterance-medial position.

Cognitive linguistics assumes that linguistic viewpoint-marking depends on general socio-cognitive skills of attending to others' perspectives (Evans 2010, Ch. 4; Verhagen 2005). The purely intersubjective function of dialogue particles makes them particularly useful for investigating the relationship between linguistic viewpoint constructions and social cognition. They allow us to examine whether individuals with and without the prerequisite perspective-taking skills differ in their command of linguistic expression of viewpoint. If we find that individuals with age-appropriate general language skills but impaired sensitivity to others' mental states have difficulties using dialogue particles in an appropriate manner, this will constitute independent empirical evidence for the hypothesis of a socio-cognitive foundation for linguistic viewpoint constructions. In this study we examine the socio-cognitive foundation of Danish dialogue particles by testing the command of them in two populations with different cognitive profiles: typically developing children and children with Autism Spectrum Disorders.

Typically developing children develop perspective-taking skills gradually over the first four years of life. Hobson (1991, 2002, 2010) emphasizes infants' emotional engagement with others in the early months of life as the foundation for their developing understanding of others as experiencing beings like themselves. Tomasello and his collaborators set "the first major ontogenetic step in human social recognition" (Tomasello and Carpenter 2005: 2) to about one year of age when infants begin to perceive the intention behind others' actions and perception and to share attention with others (Carpenter, Nagell, and Tomasello 1998). In the second year of life, children develop the ability to create joint intentions and joint commitments in cooperation (Tomasello et al. 2005; Tomasello and Carpenter 2007). Wimmer and Perner (1983) see children's ability to reason about others' false belief about a situation around the age of four as the decisive step in their socio-cognitive development. At this age, children are said to acquire a theory of mind (Premack and Woodruff 1978) or a metarepresentation, i.e., the ability to understand that a mental state is a representation and not reality *per se* (Leslie 1987; Perner 1991). Regardless of these differences in defining the key ontogenetic step in typical socio-cognitive development, the common finding is that typically developing children have sophisticated perspective-taking skills already at kindergarten age.

Theories about what fundamentally characterizes autism focus on different points in the socio-cognitive development. According to Hobson (1993, 2002), infants with autism do not engage with others emotionally in the early months of life, they do not understand others as experiencing beings, and this is the reason for their subsequent failure on tests of theory of mind (Baron-Cohen, Leslie, and Frith 1985, 1986; Happé 1994). Tomasello et al. (2005) find that some children with autism are capable of perceiving the intention behind others' actions (as evidenced, for instance, by their use of modal verbs [Baron-Cohen, Leslie, and Frith 1985]), but they fail to share the intentions of others and to engage in collaboration with them. The theory of impaired theory of mind in autism sees an inability to represent beliefs as mental representations as the foundation of autism (Baron-Cohen 1995).

No matter the exact theoretical explanation, the important point in this context is that children and adults with autism do not intuitively understand and relate to others' grasp of a situation, or do so to a smaller degree than typically developing individuals. We may therefore expect individuals with autism not to use or to fail to understand perspective mixing dialogue particles as these require the user to keep track of the interlocutor's knowledge state and involvement in communication.

In testing differences in dialogue-particle command in typically developing children and children with autism we look for independent empirical support for a relationship between language and conceptual systems. Thereby we evade the risk of circularity in semantic analyses in cognitive linguistics pointed out by, for instance, Evans and Green (2006). These authors distinguish cognitive semanticists and cognitive grammarians by their primary interest. Cognitive semanticists are said to be primarily concerned with finding out what linguistic meaning "can reveal about the nature of the human conceptual system" (Evans and Green 2006: 170), while cognitive grammarians are "concerned with studying the language system itself, and with describing that system, and our knowledge of that system, on the basis of the properties of the conceptual system" (Evans and Green 2006: 170). Evans and Green describe the two approaches as "two sides of the same coin":

> cognitive semanticists rely on language to help them understand how the conceptual system works, while cognitive grammarians rely on what is known about the conceptual system to help them understand how language works. (Evans and Green 2006: 170)

That is, cognitive semanticists study language to find out about the human conceptual system, and cognitive grammarians draw on the conceptual system to find out about language. What is needed, as also highlighted by Evans and Green, is converging evidence for linguistic analyses.

The need for converging evidence is also emphasized by Langacker (1999), who declares "converging evidence from multiple sources" to be "the most fundamental methodological principle" (1999: 26) of Cognitive Grammar. Langacker demonstrates how he seeks converging evidence from what he describes as three different sources. The first source is descriptive constructs "necessary for the adequate semantic description of multiple phenomena in various languages" (Langacker 1999: 27). The second source, Langacker argues, is "independently observable cognitive abilities": in the second step he examines whether the constructs are "commensurate with (if not identical to) independently observable cognitive abilities" (Langacker 1999: 27). Finally, he demonstrates that "the same constructs – psychologically natural and semantically necessary – are critical for the explicit characterization of varied grammatical phenomena" (Langacker 1999: 27). An example is *profiling*, which is a construct needed to describe a substructure denoted by a particular word within a conceptual *base*, a base being a context necessary for understanding the word's meaning. For instance, *hypotenuse* evokes a right-angled triangle as its base and profiles the side opposite the right angle as its substructure. We necessarily understand the meaning of *hypotenuse* in the context of a right-angled triangle, but the word only denotes a substructure of a right-angled triangle. Langacker then claims that "profiling represents a kind of focusing of attention, obviously a basic and well-established cognitive ability" (1999: 28). This may be so, but it is clearly desirable to substantiate the last claim about attention with empirically based evidence if we wish to draw on cognitive abilities as converging evidence for linguistic analyses.

In this paper we want to demonstrate that finding differences in the command of dialogue particles in individuals with different perspective-taking skills can constitute converging evidence for semantic analyses of the particles as perspective-mixing linguistic constructions. Our hypothesis is that children with autism, who can be expected to have impaired sensitivity to others' perspectives, will have difficulties acquiring dialogue particles and using them in an appropriate manner compared to typically developing children, who can be expected to be sensitive to others' mental states. We compare children with autism and typically developing children who do not differ on vocabulary and grammar comprehension, written word recognition, and chronological age and nonverbal cognitive ability. We measure the command of dialogue particles by means of a gap-filling test with a forced choice between the three Danish dialogue particles *jo, da* and *vel*, the *JDV-test*. The test was piloted with Danish adults and children. The high degree of consensus among these users of Danish serves in itself as empirical verification of the analyses of the dialogue particles' perspective-mixing meaning.

The dialogue particles are unbound morphemes. The three particles *jo, da*, and *vel* can be combined with each other and with other dialogue particles in typical but varying orders (e.g., *da nu vel, jo nu da, sgu da vel*), and they may occur right after the finite verb but also after the finite verb plus the subject or a light pronominal object or, in some cases, clause-finally (cf. Section 2 and note 2). Their grammatical status may thus be disputed. Boye and Harder (2012: 13) propose that grammatical meaning is "by convention discursively secondary". One criterion of grammatical status is thus an inability to occur in focused position. As this is exactly true of the dialogue particles, their status is grammatical, according to Boye and Harder's theory. In this study we give independent empirical evidence for the grammatical status of the dialogue particles.

The paper is structured as follows. In the next section we will present the Danish dialogue particles, focusing on the three particles used in the empirical study. Section three presents the results from the study of the degree of consensus in adults' and children's responses to the gap-filling test used for measuring the understanding of the particles. Section four presents the comparison of the understanding of the perspective-mixing particles by means of the test in children with autism and typically developing children. Finally, in section five we discuss the implications of the study for both our understanding of autism and of methodology in Cognitive Linguistics.

2 Danish dialogue particles

Danish has a series of particles that require a finite verb and have scope over the entire clause (Davidsen-Nielsen 1996; Christensen 2006; Hansen and Heltoft 2011). They all include the speaker's perspective, and most of them also include one more perspective, that of the addressee or another position in the context. By means of the choice of particle, speakers specify their understanding of the interaction in relation to the propositional content. For this reason we call them *dialogue particles*, but they are also known as *discourse particles* (Davidsen-Nielsen 1996), *modal particles* (Christensen 2006) and, inspired by Bakhtin, *dialogic particles* (Hansen and Heltoft 2011). Nine of the particles are monosyllabic and monomorphemic, and may be seen as a special group (Davidsen-Nielsen 1996). They are never obligatory, never take stress, and they occur in clause-medial position right after the finite verb or another dialogue particle following the verb unless the subject or a light pronominal object takes up this position, in which case they occur after the argument.[1]

1 The presentation of the meaning of the dialogue particles in the translations should only be seen as approximative. Their meaning is explained in the text. DP in the glossing stands for *dialogue particle*, INF for the Danish infinitive marker *at*.

(1) *Peter forstod* ***jo*** *argumentet.*
Peter understood DP the argument
'Peter understood the argument, you know.'

(2) a. *Så forstod Peter* ***jo*** *argumentet.*
Then understood Peter DP the argument
'Then Peter understood the argument, you know.'
b. *Peter forstod det* ***jo.***
Peter understood it DP
'Peter understood it, you know.'

If there is no complement or other adverbial besides the dialogue particle following the finite verb and/or subject, the dialogue particle may occur clause-finally:[2]

(3) *Det er det* ***jo!***
That is it DP
'So it is indeed.'

The particles' inconspicuous form – one syllable, no stress – and their usually medial position make them easy to overlook.

In this paper we will concentrate on three of the particles that include an extra perspective which is in agreement or in conflict with the speaker's perspective, *jo, da*, and *vel*. *Jo* indicates that the addressee's perspective is presupposed or expected to be in agreement with the speaker's perspective presented in the clause. *Jo* can thus be paraphrased as 'I expect you to agree with me' or 'you know and I know, and we agree'. *Peter forstod jo argumentet* in (1) is thus meant as a claim about something that the speaker expects the addressee to agree on.

In contrast to *jo*, *vel* signals the speaker's uncertainty and appeal to the addressee for confirmation. *Vel* can be paraphrased as 'I am uncertain, and you probably know better'. The two perspectives are again presupposed or expected to be in agreement, as can be seen from the following abbreviated example from the test that we developed for this study (see Section 3).

---

2 A full description of the possible positions of the dialogue particles is beyond the scope of this paper (see Hansen and Heltoft 2011). For instance, occasionally, examples of sentence-final position can be heard:

Nu skal vi have frokost ***jo.***
Now shall we have lunch DP.
'Now we are going to have lunch, as a matter of fact.'

Context: Two children, Julie and Signe, have planned to go to a swimming bath, but Julie gets sick. The two friends talk on the phone, and Signe says:

(4) *Du når* **vel** *at blive rask til på lørdag.*
you are-in-time-for DP INF get well for Saturday
'You'll get well in time for Saturday, won't you?'

Here Signe indicates her expectation, but also signals uncertainty, and she appeals to Julie as the expert on her health to confirm Signe's expectation.

Da, in contrast to the other two particles, signals a possible conflict between the speaker's and some other perspective, possibly the addressee's, and, at the same time, the speaker's claim that the proper understanding is already known to the addressee. An example from the test:

Context: Julie and Signe are discussing their plans for the weekend. Julie says: I can't bother to go to Mia's birthday. She's just so annoying. Signe says:

(5) *I plejer* **da** *at være gode venner gør I ikke?*
you use-to DP INF be good friends do you not?
'I believe you are usually good friends, aren't you'

Signe expresses her surprise at Julie's attitude to Mia, given the fact that Julie and Mia are good friends, a fact that Julie is otherwise supposed to agree on. An overview of the semantic dimensions along which the three particles diverge is given in Table 1.

Table 1: The meaning of the three dialogue particles presented schematically

	jo	*da*	*vel*
shared knowledge	yes	yes	no
conflict	no	yes	no
speaker uncertainty	no	no	yes

As word forms, *jo, da* and *vel* are all homographs, though not precise homophones. Besides being a dialogue particle, *jo* (with stress and frequently with a different vowel quality) is an interjection used to affirm a negated question. *Da* (with stress) is a temporal adverb ('then') and (stressless) a subordinating conjunction ('when', 'since'). And *vel* (with stress) represents a noun meaning 'welfare, well-being', as well as an adjective meaning 'in good health', an adverb meaning 'well', and it can be used in tag questions after a negative clause. Furthermore, as dialogue particles, all three have derived functions. *Jo* can be used in clauses with propositions on which the interlocutors clearly do not agree, as an attempt to persuade the addressee to take over the speaker's view, and it has a mirative use when speakers express their surprise at an unexpected fact (Engberg-Pedersen 2009). *Da* has a derived use in polite evaluations of something expressed by the addressee in the preceding turn: *Det var da skønt!* 'That was wonderful indeed!' Boeg Thomsen (2012) suggests that this derived use may be a way of doing away with potential and feigned disagreement, and thereby expressing an even stronger support for the addressee's point. Especially in children's competitive language, *da* is used to defy claims of uniqueness that have not even been expressed: A: *Look, I can draw a star*, B: *Det kan jeg* ***da*** *også* 'So can DP I!'. Finally, *vel* is used as a mitigator in polite language in cases where the speaker is more informed; the use of *vel* indicates that the speaker acknowledges the situation as one in which there might be doubt.

The dialogue particles, and in particular *jo, da,* and *vel,* are very frequent in spoken Danish. With their subtle meanings that require the ability to track shared knowledge and potential agreement and disagreement, we expect them to be difficult to acquire for children with autism whereas their meanings should not present typically developing children with problems after a certain age. However, given their inconspicuous form, their facultative status, their clause-medial position, the many forms that are more or less homophonic, and the derived uses, there is a possibility that even typically developing children struggle to achieve adult-like command of the dialogue particles. Before comparing children with and without autism, it is therefore important to establish two things: on the one hand, that Danish adults do indeed concur on the meanings suggested by previous semantic analyses, and on the other hand, that typically developing Danish schoolchildren have adult-like or close to adult-like command of the particles. In the following section, we present a test developed to study consensus on the meaning of the particles and schoolchildren's understanding of *jo, da,* and *vel.*

3 A test of the consensus on the meaning of *jo, da*, and *vel*: the JDV-test

In order to test the semantic analysis of the dialogue particles *jo, da* and *vel*, we developed a gap-filling test which required participants to read small stories with open slots for inserting what they considered the most appropriate dialogue particle (*jo, da*, or *vel*) (Engberg-Pedersen 2008; Boeg Thomsen 2012). The contexts were constructed to present configurations of perspectives which contrasted the core differences between the three particles: shared knowledge (presence: *jo, da*, absence: *vel*), conflict (presence: *da*, absence: *jo, vel*) and privileged recipient knowledge (presence: *vel*, absence: *jo, da*). Each context was supposed to present the prototypical configuration of perspectives for one dialogue particle only and to exclude both use of the other particles and derived uses (such as persuasive *jo* or polite *vel*). Adequate gap-filling requires attribution of mental states to two fictive characters simultaneously and choice of the appropriate perspective-mixing particle. Example 6 presents a (partly translated) test item with a gap for *jo*:

Signe has just been to Mia's birthday.
Signe asks Mia: Wasn't it a nice present we had found for your birthday?
Mia answers:

(6) *Helt klart! Jeg elsker tegneserier.*
Completely clearly I love DP comics
'Definitely! I love comics.'

This is a prototypical context for *jo* because it presents shared knowledge and agreement between the speaker and the addressee, who have been introduced as close friends in previous items, and who can therefore be expected to be aware of each other's taste. There is no opposing viewpoint to motivate *da* (shared knowledge and conflict), and the speaker obviously knows more about her own taste than the addressee, thus excluding *vel* (speaker uncertainty and privileged recipient knowledge). Examples (4) and (5) in section 2 above present two of the test items with *vel* and *da*, respectively.

The first version of the gap-filling test contained 24 items (8 per particle), and it was piloted with 60 adults (30 males, 30 females). In scoring the test responses, one point was given per item where a participant gave the expected answer. Overall, the test showed a very high consensus among mature Danish language users on the different usage potentials of the three dialogue particles in contexts with mixed perspectives: out of 24 possible points, the mean score for participants was 22.8 (variance 1.2; SD 1.1). This supports prior semantic analyses of the perspective-mixing meanings of *jo, da,* and *vel*. Looking at the adequacy of items for eliciting agreement on particle use, the contexts with their different constellations of perspectives appeared to work very well in general, the mean score per item being 57 (out of 60 possible; variance 11.9; SD 3.4). For 7 items, 60 adults all chose the same particle; for 5 items, 59 adults did so.

This shows that the test format works, and that it is possible to create contexts with configurations of perspectives that make only one perspective-mixing particle appropriate for mature language users. A few items, however, turned out to be too open to interpretation to be useful for particle-use comparisons. They appeared to allow participants to attribute different mental states to the fictive characters, thus making more dialogue particles appropriate (the two most open items had 22 % and 17 % unexpected answers). In our second version of the test, a shortened 15-item version, we removed the three most open items per particle, keeping only the strongest items with 92–100 % agreement on particle appropriateness among mature language users. Counting only responses to these remaining 15 items, the average score for the 60 adult participants was 14.7 (variance 0.3; SD 0.6), and all participant scores fell within the range of 13–15 points. The test was illustrated with drawings from Picto Selector to make it more appetizing to children.

To examine typically developing children's grasp of perspective-mixing meanings of dialogue particles, we administered the 15-item version of the JDV test to 164 monolingual schoolchildren (age range 11; 2–14; 7 years; 74 girls, 89 boys, 1 anonymous). The children took the test in their classrooms following instruction and training. Again, one point was given for each appropriate gap-filling, and each participant could thus score 0–15 points. Like adults, 11-to-14-year-olds demonstrated a high degree of consensus on the usage potentials of the three particles, on average scoring 13.2 out of 15 possible points (variance 3.2; SD 1.8). The most frequent result was the maximum score (15 points: 44 children, 27 %), and the scores of 72 % of the children (118 of 164) fell within the same range as the adults' (13–15 points). These results indicate that most Danish 11-to-14-year-olds follow adult-like usage norms for *jo, da,* and *vel*, being aware of their perspective-mixing functions. This proficiency is also what we would expect given previous findings of typically developing children's sensitivity to others' perspectives from early in ontogeny (e.g., Hobson 2002, Tomasello et al. 2005, Wimmer and Perner 1983). Potential hindrances such as inconspicuous form and position do not seem to impede development of adult-like proficiency in typically developing schoolchildren (see, however, Section 4 on attention to non-focused information).

The average score for the 164 schoolchildren (13.2, SD 1.8) was, however, lower than for the adults (14.7, SD 0.6), and the scores spread out more. Figure 1 shows the numbers of children achieving each possible score (from 0 to 15). It is probable that some typically developing children are still in a phase of stabilizing their understanding of dialogue particles at this age, and it is also possible that children, taking the test together in their classrooms, had more concentration lapses than the adults. Moreover, there may have been children with cognitive impairments or reading problems in the classrooms. However, the generally high homogeneity in typically developing schoolchildren's responses to the test makes the test a promising tool for comparing understanding of dialogue particles in children with different cognitive profiles.

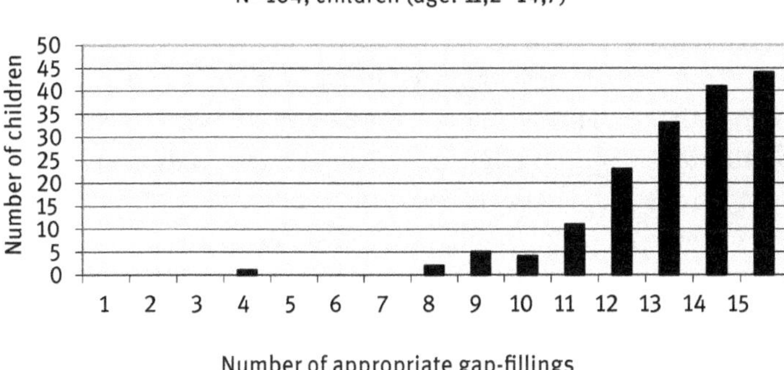

Figure 1: The number of children who achieved each possible score (0–15) on the JDV-test

4 *Jo*, *da*, and *vel* and children with autism

A study of Danish preschoolers' spontaneous use of the three particles *jo*, *da*, and *vel* (Boeg Thomsen 2012) showed that the particles rarely occur until the fourth year of age when typically developing children begin to pass classical false-belief tasks. Comprehension of shared or diverging understanding of a situation recurs in the use of the dialogue particles. The JDV-test is even more demanding than most false-belief tasks as it requires a different type of mental state understanding than the traditional so-called first-order false-belief tasks. In order to choose the most appropriate dialogue particles, the children need to understand a story character's understanding of a different story character's perspective. This task is equivalent to the so-called second-order false-belief tasks, ones that typically developing children pass around the age of six (Perner and Wimmer 1985). As children with autism have been shown to fail or be delayed in passing false-belief tasks of both first and second order compared with typically developing children (Baron-Cohen, Leslie, and Frith 1985; Happé 1994; Steele, Joseph and Tager-Flusberg 2003), we may expect these children not to understand the dialogue particles or to be delayed at understanding them.

We used the JDV-test to compare a group of 28 children with autism (ASD, 24 boys, 4 girls) with a group of 29 typically developing children (TD, 16 boys, 13 girls). The children with autism were all in special schools in the greater Copenhagen area. An admission criterion of these schools is a diagnosis within the autism spectrum. We asked the parents to fill in the Children's Communication Checklist-2 (Bishop 2003), and according to the parents' reports, twenty of the children with autism had communication profiles symptomatic of autism, three children had positive, but very low values on the Index of Social Interaction, and for five children, the parents either did not return the questionnaire or it was not completed. The typically developing children were contacted in general public schools in Copenhagen. For all children, the parents gave informed written consent. The typically developing children in this comparative study are not identical to the ones used for developing the JDV-test, but the test results from the two groups of typically developing children did not differ significantly.

The children with autism and the typically developing children in the comparative study were matched for chronological age, nonverbal cognitive ability as measured by the Matrices subtest of the Wechsler Nonverbal Scale of Abilities (Wechsler and Naglieri 2006),[3] vocabulary comprehension as measured by a Danish version of the Peabody Picture Vocabulary Test (Dunn and Dunn 2007; Bremer Nielsen 2008), and grammar comprehension as measured by a Danish version of TROG-2 (Bishop 2010) (see Table 2). The children were also given two false-belief tests, one of location change and one of unexpected contents with altogether three questions about beliefs (Wellman and Liu 2004). Four children with autism answered two out of three questions correctly, one child did not want to give one of the answers in the second test, and twenty-three children with autism had three correct answers. Two typically developing children answered two of three questions correctly (one child did not get the last question), and all others had three correct answers. Table 2 shows that the children with autism are very competent with age-equivalent linguistic and nonverbal cognitive abilities as measured by standard tests. Any deviance on the JDV-test is thus likely to be due to the specific socio-cognitive problems of children with autism, not other cognitive or linguistic problems.

The difference between the two groups of children on the JDV-test is statistically significant (ASD: range 4–15, mean 10.5, SD 3.16; TD: range 9–15, mean 12.8, SD 1.68; $t(40.89) = 3.35$, $p < 0.005$). As a group, the children with autism did not choose the most appropriate dialogue particle for each story as often as the typically developing children. We also found a significant correlation with a strong effect between the children's scores on the JDV-test and their scores on the test for grammar comprehension (TROG-2) within each group (ASD: $r = .65$, $p = .0002$; TD: $r = .52$, $p = .004$, one child left out of the TD group because he did not take the

3 On the subtest of WNV there was an outlier in each group (ASD: 23, TD: 16). When the outliers were left out, the groups still did not differ significantly on nonverbal cognitive ability (ASD: range of T-scores 40–71, mean 50.04, SD 8.22, TD: range of T-scores 38–76, mean 52.64, SD 8.46). The two outliers had scores between 40 and 46 on other subtests of WNV and were, therefore, included in the study.

Table 2: Mean scores (SD) and range for chronological age, nonverbal cognitive ability (T-scores), and vocabulary and grammar comprehension. None of the variables differed significantly.

	ASD (N = 28)	TD (N = 29)
Chronological age (months), mean	143.14 (SD 7.94)	144.51 (SD 8.43)
Range (years; months)	10;5–13;6	10;6–13;3
Nonverbal cognitive ability, mean	49.07 (SD 9.54)	51.38 (SD 10.74)
Range	23–71	16–76
Vocabulary comprehension, mean	93.39 (SD 12.38)	97.90 (SD 13.59)
Range	70–121	85–130
Grammar comprehension, mean	53.14 (SD 29.53)	56.71 (SD 23.10)
Range	3–86	10–86

grammar test) and between the JDV-test and the test for vocabulary comprehension within the autism group, but only a trend towards such a correlation within the group of children with typical development (ASD: r = .52, p = .005; TD: r = .33, p = .08). For the children with autism, better grammar and vocabulary comprehension was associated with better comprehension of the dialogue particles, for the typically developing children, only better grammar comprehension was associated with better understanding of the particles. Moreover, within the group of children with autism only, there was a significant correlation between the children's scores on the test for nonverbal cognitive abilities and their scores on the JDV-test (ASD: r = .45, p = .02; TD: r = .12, p = ns). For the children with autism only, better nonverbal cognitive ability was associated with better comprehension of the dialogue particles. The children's scores on the JDV-test and the test for written word recognition did not correlate significantly for either group. Thus, the children's literary decoding skills did not influence the results.

5 Discussion

The facts that all 60 adults agreed on 13–15 items, and that 141 out of 164 11- to 14-year-olds agreed on 12–15 items of the JDV-test, support the semantic analysis of the particles' meaning, and we consider the test a valid tool for measuring the understanding of the three dialogue particles. In the comparison of the typically developing children and the children with autism, our prediction was born out: as a group, the children with autism scored significantly lower than the typically developing children on the JDV-test. This result supports semantic analyses of the particles as perspective-mixing, and, in a wider perspective, constitutes converging evidence in the sense of Langacker (1999) for cognitive-linguistics analyses of linguistic viewpoint-marking as depending on the basic human preoccupation with others' minds (Evans 2010: 70–79; Verhagen 2005: 210–216).

As can be seen from examples (4)–(6), each narrative of the JDV-test was very short, and the contents closely related to children's everyday life. Nevertheless, children with autism are known to have difficulty forming a centrally coherent context out of several pieces of information and to have a tendency to focus on details (Happé and Frith 2006). Therefore, the possibility exists that the children with autism had trouble integrating the information of each short narrative to a whole that would enable them to make a decision as to the most appropriate particle.[4] However, twenty-one of the children with autism also took a test of their ability to infer the most likely sequel, out of three, to a cartoon of three pictures of, for instance, a man digging a hole, placing a tree in the hole and looking at the tree (the most likely sequel is a picture of the same man watering the tree). This test can be said to tap the children's ability to infer a coherent intentional action out of a sequence of possibly disparate actions. The correlation between the scores on this test and the JDV-test for the twenty-one children with autism was not significant.

In the comparison study, we found that the scores on the JDV-test correlated with the scores on the test of grammar comprehension for the children in both socio-cognitive groups. The test for grammar comprehension tests comprehension of, among other features, passive clauses, clauses with case-marked pronominal subject and object, word order by means of reversible clauses, and clauses with different types of relative clauses. In the test situation the children are asked to point to the correct picture out of four when they hear, for instance, a passive clause said in isolation. The pictures are such that the child has to depend on grammar to figure out which picture is the correct one. As pointed out in the introduction, the dialogue particles are grammatical (in the sense of 'non-lexical') by the theory proposed by Boye and Harder (2012): they are obligatorily unstressed and cannot be focused in any other way, for instance in a cleft sentence. Furthermore, the particles are optional and probably used to different degrees by different people. In contrast to many other grammatical features, they can be avoided. If Boye and Harder's theory of grammatical status is right, we would expect dia-

4 This objection could be rejected by giving the children a similar insertion test with a choice between a different semantic type of adverbs, e.g., temporal adverbs. Such a test would also exclude the possibility that the children with autism who scored low on the JDV-test did so for other reasons than that they did not understand the dialogue particles, for instance, because they failed to understand what they were supposed to do in the test. This must, however, be left for future research.

logue particles to group psycholinguistically with other grammatical features, which is exactly what was found in this study, thereby substantiating Boye and Harder's theory of what is grammatical.

Surprisingly, the study also showed that some children with autism (9 out of 28) scored at the same level as the typically developing children (12–15 most appropriate answers). This result may be interpreted in the light of the finding that the scores on the JDV-test and on the test for nonverbal cognitive ability correlated only for the children with autism. All children with autism in our study passed either one or both of two false-belief tasks, which is to be expected since children with autism on average pass the tests at a verbal mental age of 9;2 (Happé 1995), and for the children in our study their verbal ability is approximately equivalent to their chronological age (10;5–13;6). But as mentioned, the JDV-test requires second-order false-belief understanding. Other studies have shown that few children with autism pass second-order false-belief tasks (e.g., 12 % of 57 children between the ages of 4 and 14 in a study by Steele, Joseph and Tager-Flusberg 2003). It is debated whether the children with autism are delayed in their acquisition of mental-state understanding, or whether their development differs from typical development (Bowler 2007: 220–224). A possible explanation for the correlation between the scores on the JDV-test and on the nonverbal cognitive measure in only the children with autism may be that these children use different strategies to manage the second-order false belief requirements necessary for managing the JDV-test.

It might be argued that the reason why there is no correlation between the JDV scores and the measure of nonverbal cognitive abilities in the typically developing children is that they are almost at the ceiling in the JDV-test. But if that was the only reason for the lack of correlation between their scores on the JDV test and on the nonverbal cognitive test, their JDV-scores could not correlate with their scores on the test for grammar comprehension either, which they do.

We set out to develop the JDV-test in order to test consensus on the meaning of the three Danish dialogue particles among adults and children, and to compare data from children with autism with typically developing children in order to find converging evidence for the socio-cognitive analysis of the meaning of the three Danish dialogue particles. We have supported the semantic analysis of the particles as perspective-mixing particles by showing the high degree of consensus on the choice of a particle in distinct contexts among typically developing children and adults, and the problems encountered by some, if not all, children with autism, a group of children with reduced socio-cognitive abilities. We suggest that the fact that scores on the JDV-test correlate significantly with scores on a test for grammar comprehension for all children substantiate Boye and Harder's (2012) definition of what is grammatical, in the sense of non-lexical, as the dialogue particles are truly grammatical in this sense by not being focusable. Finally, we suggest that the reason why some children with autism get a high score on the JDV-test is due to other cognitive abilities than the typically developing children since only the scores on the test for nonverbal cognitive abilities by the children with autism correlated significantly with the scores on the JDV-test.

Acknowledgements

Part of the research behind this paper was undertaken in the project *Language and Cognition – Perspectives from Impairment* (LaCPI) 2011–2014, supported by a grant to Elisabeth Engberg-Pedersen from The Danish Council for Independent Research | Humanities, by The Faculty of Humanities, University of Copenhagen, and The Department of Scandinavian Studies and Linguistics, University of Copenhagen. The other members of the research group are Rikke Vang Christensen and Hanne Trebbien Daugaard. Boeg Thomsen has the main responsibility for Section 3, Engberg-Pedersen for the other sections.

The studies behind the paper were presented at the International Cognitive Linguistics Conference 12, Edmonton, Alberta 2013 and at an open workshop in LaCPI (Language and Cognition – Perspectives from Impairment) in April 2014.

We would like to thank two anonymous reviewers for comments on an earlier version of the paper, Mikkel Hansen for helping with the statistical analyses, and the other members of LaCPI as well as all the children, their parents, the schools, and the adult participants who made the development of the test and the comparative study possible.

References

Baron-Cohen, Simon. 1995. *Mindblindness: Essay on autism and the Theory of Mind*. Boston, MA: The MIT Press.

Baron-Cohen, Simon, Alan M. Leslie & Uta Frith. 1985. Does the autistic child have a "theory of mind"? *Cognition* 21. 37–46.

Baron-Cohen, Simon, Alan M. Leslie & Uta Frith. 1986. Mechanical, behavioural and intentional understanding of picture stories in autistic children. *British Journal of Developmental Psychology* 4. 113–125.

Bishop, Dorothy. 2003. *The children's communication checklist: CCC-2*, 2nd edn. London: Psychological Corporation. (Danish version 2012)

Bishop, Dorothy. 2010 [2003]. *Test for reception of grammar: TROG-2*, 2nd edn. Danish version developed by Kristine Jensen de Lopez, Ane Knüppel and Lone Sundahl Olsen. Bromma, Sweden: Pearson Assessment.

Boeg Thomsen, Ditte. 2012. *Viet til vinkler, viernes vinkler: typisk udviklede danske børns beherskelse af synsvinkelmarkerende diskurspartikler* [Typically developing Danish children's mastery of perspective-marking discourse particles]. Copenhagen, Denmark: University of Copenhagen MA Thesis.

Bowler, Dermot M. 2007. *Autism Spectrum Disorders: Psychological theory and research*. Chichester, UK: John Wiley & Sons, Boye, Kasper & Peter Harder. 2012. A usage-based theory of grammatical status and grammaticalizazion. *Language* 88(1). 1–44.

Bremer Nielsen, Jeanette. 2008. *Det mentale leksikon og testning af receptivt ordforråd: ændring af Peabody-testen* [The mental lexicon and testing of receptive vocabulary: changes to the Peabody test]. Copenhagen, Denmark: University of Copenhagen MA Thesis.

Carpenter, Malinda, Katherine Nagell & Michael Tomasello. 1998. Social cognition, joint attention, and communicative competence from 9 to 15 months of age. *Monographs of the Society for Research in Child Development* 63(4).

Christensen, Tanya Karoli. 2006. Hyperparadigmer: en undersøgelse af paradigmatiske samspil i danske modussystemer [Hyperparadigms: an investigation of the paradigmatic interplays in Danish mood patterns]. Roskilde, Denmark: Roskilde University PhD Thesis.

Davidsen-Nielsen, Niels. 1996. Discourse particles in Danish. In Elisabeth Engberg-Pedersen, Michael Fortescue, Peter Harder, Lars Heltoft & Lisbeth Falster Jakobsen (eds.), *Content, expression and structure: studies in Danish functional grammar*, 283–314. Amsterdam, The Netherlands: John Benjamins.

Dunn, Lloyd M. & Douglas M. Dunn. 2007. *Peabody picture vocabulary test*-IV, 4th edn. Bloomington, MN: Pearson.

Engberg-Pedersen, Elisabeth. 2008. Comprehension of the Danish perspective-expressing discourse particle *jo*. Paper presented at The Danish Royal Society Symposium on Empirical Methods in Investigating Linguistic Perspective, Copenhagen, 26 – 28 November.

Engberg-Pedersen, Elisabeth. 2009. Det er *jo* Lisbeths fødselsdag! Om nytten af instrukssemantik [It is *jo* Lisbeth's birthday! On the use of instructional semantics]. In Ken Farø, Alexandra Holsting, Niels-Erik Larsen, Jens Erik Mogensen & Thora Vinther (eds.), *Sprogvidenskab i glimt: 70 tekster om sprog i teori og praksis* [Linguistic glimpses: Text on language theory and language use], 225–229. Odense, Denmark: Syddansk (University of Southern Denmark).

Evans, Nicholas. 2010. *Dying words: Endangered languages and what they have to tell us*. Chichester, UK: Wiley-Blackwell.

Evans, Vyvyan & Melanie Green. 2006. *Cognitive linguistics: An introduction*. Edinburgh, Scotland: Edinburgh University Press.

Hansen, Erik & Lars Heltoft. 2011. *Grammatik over det danske sprog: Syntaktiske og semantiske helheder* [Grammar of Danish: syntactic and semantic units]. Copenhagen, Denmark: Det Danske Sprog- og Litteraturselskab [The Danish Language and Literature Society].

Happé, Francesca. 1994. An advanced test of theory of mind: Understanding of story characters' thoughts and feelings by able autistic, mentally handicapped, and normal children and adults. *Journal of Autism and Developmental Disorders* 24(2). 129–154.

Happé, Francesca. 1995. The role of age and verbal ability in the Theory of Mind task performance of subjects with autism. *Child Development* 66(3), 843–855.

Happé, Francesca & Uta Frith. 2006. The weak coherence account: Detail-focused cognitive style in autism spectrum disorders. *Journal of Autism and Developmental Disorders,* 36(1). 5–25.

Hobson, R. Peter. 1991. Against the theory of 'Theory of Mind'. *British Journal of Developmental Psychology* 9(1). 33–51.

Hobson, R. Peter. 1993. Understanding persons: The role of affect. In Simon Baron-Cohen, Helen Tager-Flusberg & Donald J. Cohen (eds.), *Understanding other minds: Perspectives from autism,* 204–227. Oxford, UK: Oxford University Press.

Hobson, R. Peter. 2002. *The cradle of thought: Exploring the origins of thinking.* London, UK: Pan Macmillan.

Hobson, R. Peter. 2010. Explaining autism: Ten reasons to focus on the developing self. *Autism* 14(5). 391–407.

Langacker, Ronald W. 1999. Assessing the cognitive linguistic enterprise. In Theo Janssen & Gisela Redeker (eds.), *Cognitive linguistics: Foundations, scope, and methodology,* 13–59. Berlin, Germany: De Gruyter Mouton.

Leslie, Alan M. 1987. Pretense and representation: The origins of "Theory of Mind". *Psychological Review* 94(4). 412–426.

Perner, Josef. 1991. *Understanding the representational mind.* Cambridge, MA: The MIT Press.

Perner, Josef & Heinz Wimmer. 1985. "John *thinks* that Mary *thinks* that...": Attribution of second-order beliefs by 5- to 10-year-old children. *Journal of Experimental Child Psychology* 39(3). 437–471.

Premack, David & Guy Woodruff. 1978. Does the chimpanzee have a theory of mind? *The Behavioral and Brain Sciences* 1(4). 515–526.

Steele, Shelly, Robert M. Joseph & Helen Tager-Flusberg. 2003. Brief report: Developmental change in Theory of Mind abilities in children with autism. *Journal of Autism and Developmental Disorders* 33(4). 461–467.

Tomasello, Michael & Malinda Carpenter. 2005. *The emergence of social cognition in three young chimpanzees.* Boston, MA & Oxford, UK: Blackwell Publishing.

Tomasello, Michael & Malinda Carpenter. 2007. Shared intentionality. *Developmental Sciences* 10. 121–125.

Tomasello, Michael, Malinda Carpenter, Josep Call, Tanya Behne & Henrike Moll. 2005. Understanding and sharing intentions: The origins of cultural cognition. *Behavioral and Brain Sciences* 28(5). 675–735.

Verhagen, Arie. 2005. *Constructions of intersubjectivity: Discourse, syntax, and cognition.* Oxford, UK: Oxford University Press.

Wechsler, David & Jack A. Naglieri. 2006. *WNV_{TM}: Wechsler nonverbal scale of ability.* Bloomington, MN: Pearson.

Wellman, Henry M. & David Liu. 2004. Scaling of Theory-of-Mind tasks. *Child Development* 75(2). 523–541.

Wimmer, Heinz & Josef Perner. 1983. Beliefs about beliefs: Representations and constraining function of wrong beliefs in young children's understanding of deception. *Cognition* 13(1). 103–128.

Part II: **Across languages**

Kobie van Krieken, José Sanders, Hans Hoeken

Blended viewpoints, mediated witnesses: A cognitive linguistic approach to news narratives

Abstract: This study identifies the linguistic strategies used in news narratives to represent the viewpoints of eyewitnesses to shocking news events and describes how these strategies invite readers to vicariously experience these events as mediated witnesses. A cognitive linguistic model for the analysis of narrative news discourse is developed and then applied to two news narratives of (different) mass shootings (Dutch and American). The analysis shows how verbs of perception and cognition are used to describe the events from the viewpoints of eyewitnesses. To blend the viewpoints of eyewitnesses with the journalist's viewpoint, Free Indirect Discourse is used in the American narrative whereas present tense narration of cognition and perception is used in the Dutch narrative. The analysis furthermore reveals that reported discourse may serve two different functions in news narratives: (1) a dramatizing function, by accessing a Narrative-Internal Discourse Space which represents what news sources were saying and thinking while the news events took place and (2) a legitimizing function, by accessing a Narrative-External Discourse Space which represents the information exchange between news sources and the journalist after the events took place. The present study thus clarifies the sophisticated relation between the form and function of news narratives.

1 Introduction

On July 20, 2012, a gunman killed twelve people and wounded another seventy in a movie theatre in Aurora, Colorado. The next day, *The Washington Post* published an article about the shooting of which the intro is presented below.

Excerpt 1
There was a thump, the emergency-exit door swinging open. Then a flood of light pouring into the darkness. A figure wearing a gas mask and black body armour stepped into the theatre. The man paused. In the second row, Jennifer Seeger thought he might have stood there a full minute. "Maybe he's just dressing up and being silly," she thought. After all, this was a midnight showing of "The Dark Knight Rises," Hollywood's latest Batman movie. (*Washington Post* 2012, July 21)

Remarkably, these sentences do not provide the reader with any newsworthy information: they do not answer the questions that are by convention addressed in the lead paragraph of news reports about what happened, when it happened, where it happened, and who was responsible (Bell, 1991: 175–185). A narrative format is employed instead to elucidate *how* the shooting happened, which is indicated by the chronological ordering of events and the description of these events from the perspective of an eyewitness.

According to Peelo (2006), news narratives about high-impact criminal acts serve a specific function: they allow readers to engage emotionally with the people involved and invite them to virtually experience the news events as *mediated witnesses*. The present study aims to identify and describe the linguistic strategies that are used in news narratives to fulfil this function. Building on the cognitive linguistic theory of Mental Spaces (Fauconnier 1985), we will build upon models for the analysis of narrative discourse (Dancygier 2012; Sanders, Sanders and Sweetser 2012) to develop a model for the analysis of these journalistic stories. This model will then be applied to two news narratives about mass shootings in order to examine how language is used in these narratives to turn readers into mediated witnesses to the shootings.

1.1 Journalistic narratives: reconstructing reality

As opposed to fictional narratives, journalistic narratives do not construct realities but (are supposed to) reconstruct "the" reality. The relationship between reality and journalistic reports about that reality is by nature a problematic one, and it is compromised even further when journalists attempt to engage their readers by employing fictionalizing literary techniques to report upon facts (see Bird & Dardenne 1988; Roeh 1989 for discussions).

One of the key issues in discussions about the ethics and aesthetics of journalistic narratives revolves around the *absent reporter*. Journalists usually do not witness news events themselves but recount these events in a detailed and vivid way that suggests their presence at the scene (Frank 1999). In addition, they provide compelling narrative accounts of what happened by describing the events from the viewpoints of people involved, thus simulating a certain degree of omniscience (Frank 1999). These strategies are powerful means to engage readers (Van Krieken, Hoeken, and Sanders 2015), but may also raise questions about the veracity of the report.

That is why, as Greenberg (2014: 529) puts it, journalistic narratives set "the double constraints of aesthetic persuasiveness through concrete detail, and ethical persuasiveness through the attempt to test details against an external reference point; an 'other'". Precisely these constraints make it relevant to study the relationship between the form and function of journalistic narratives, as they force journalists to carefully balance between the use of strategies to engage readers on the one hand and the use of source attribution strategies to meet the genre's demand of factuality on the other hand. Analysing these linguistic strategies should clarify how journalistic narratives function as mediators of experience within the boundaries of nonfiction.

To analyse the strategies journalists use to turn readers into mediated witnesses to shocking news events, we build on the cognitive linguistic approach of Mental Space Theory (Fauconnier 1985; Sweetser and Fauconnier 1996) and its derivative Blending Theory (Fauconnier & Turner 2002). The integrated concepts of *embedded mental spaces* and *blended mental spaces* have proved essential in the understanding of text-linguistic phenomena at the level of clauses and smaller stretches of discourse (Fauconnier 1985; Sanders et al. 2012; Sweetser and Fauconnier 1996). Crucially, they are equally applicable to the analysis of larger discourse entities such as news stories (Sanders 2010) and even complete fictional novels (Dancygier 2012). In this paper, we specifically want to argue that the notions of space embedding and space blending help explain how experience can be mediated by journalistic narratives: space embedding entails the representation of news events through the viewpoint of a person other than the journalist, while space blending strategically merges the viewpoint of a news actor into the viewpoint of the journalist, with the effect that the news events are related through this blended viewpoint (Sanders 2010). These strategies, we will argue, enable the journalist to attribute information to sources in order to legitimize the narrative reconstructions, while simultaneously enabling the public to vicariously experience distant news events from up close, as mediated witnesses.

1.2 Narrative discourse: constructing realities

Information in narrative discourse that is valid from the perspective of a particular character is not necessarily valid from the perspective of other characters or the narrator; it is not necessarily "true" or "real" but may be restricted to a person or situation, or it may be shared by a particular character and the narrator (Sanders and Redeker 1996). Mental Spaces Theory offers a framework to account for such restrictions in terms of embedded viewpoint spaces and blended viewpoint spaces (Fauconnier 1985; Sweetser and Fauconnier 1996). Elaborating these basic notions, Dancygier (2012: 183) argues that narrative realities are constructed and become meaningful by an ongoing process of the negotiation of such viewpoints.

In any given communicative discourse, a Basic Space can be assumed that represents the viewpoint of the Speaker. From this Basic Space, embedded spaces can be opened up by linguistic elements that function as space builders. What follows from the use of a space builder is an embedded space that represents a space of restricted validity: a piece of content that is possibly true, not true, true in another time or place, or true for some person other than the Speaker (Sanders and Redeker 1996). In narrative discourse, the first embedded space is the Narrative Space in which all narrative events take place (Main Narrative Space in terms of Dancygier 2012; Content Domain in terms of Sanders et al. 2012). Within the Narrative Space, characters can be selected as (embedded) narrators, a phenomenon described as Ego-Viewpoint by Dancygier (2012).

Importantly, the conceptual distance between the Narrative Space and the Basic Space varies between stories and often even within stories. Parameters affecting this distance include choice of grammatical person (first versus third), verb tense (present versus past), and the profiling of one or several character viewpoints (or not). The distance between the Narrative Space and the Basic Space is responsible for the negotiation of viewpoints in narrative discourse. In written narratives, third person past tense narration is the default, which represents considerable epistemic and temporal distance between the Basic Space and the Narrative Space. In this case, the role of characters' viewpoints is reduced, while there is ample room for the narrator to intervene, comment, and reflect. Deviating from this default by choosing other linguistic options strategically reduces this distance, as we will show in the following sections.

1.3 A model for the cognitive linguistic analysis of journalistic narratives

In journalistic narratives, the negotiation of viewpoints is more complex than in fictional narratives. Two fundamental issues, both pertaining to journalism's unique relation with reality, underlie this complexity. First, the Basic Space in journalistic narratives always represents the viewpoint of the journalist who, by definition, coincides with the "real-life" author of the narrative. The Basic Space of journalistic narratives thus represents the here-and-now of reality. Second, journalistic narratives should only represent content in the Narrative Space that is factually true in the Basic Space as well. These two issues have consequences for the basic set-up of spaces and the negotiation of viewpoints. We therefore present an extended model for the cognitive linguistic analysis of journalistic narratives. The basic configuration of spaces is displayed in Figure 1.

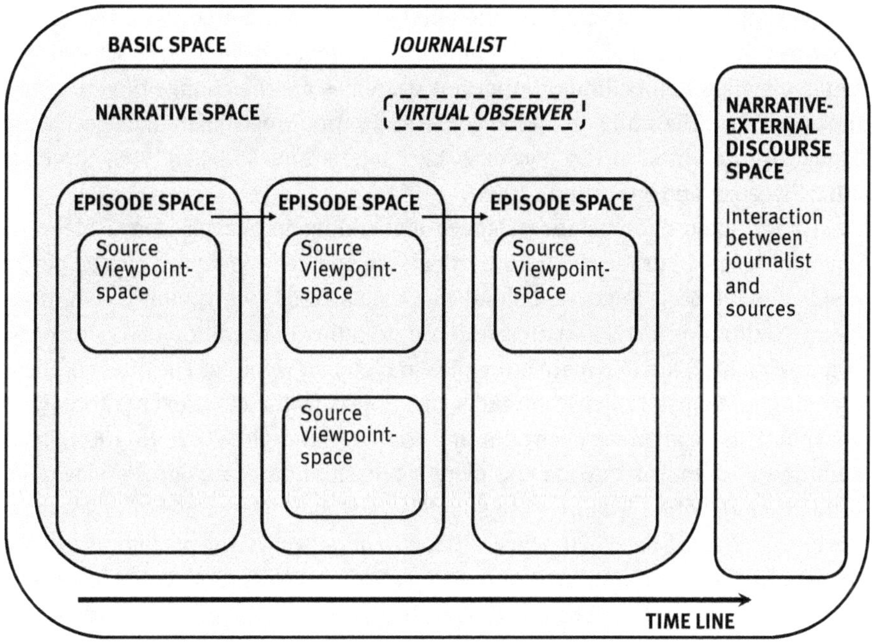

Figure 1: Basic configuration of spaces in journalistic narratives

The Basic Space represents the deictic here-and-now viewpoint of the actual journalistic narrator in the present. Embedded in the Basic Space is the Narrative Space, which represents the viewpoint of a Virtual Observer: a derivative of the narrator projected into the narrative who observes the different narrative events as they unfold and mediates them. The presence of a Virtual Observer in the Narrative Space has to be assumed in order to account for the absent reporter.

Within the Narrative Space, Episode Spaces represent the subsequent narrative episodes on the time line which the Virtual Observer experiences. Each Episode Space has a distinct topology in terms of time, space, and characters involved. Transfer from one Episode Space to another is typically constructed by one or more of the following linguistic signals: full noun reference to a main character, indication of place, or a temporal adverb (Sanders 1990).

Since embedding in narrative discourse is a recursive mechanism (cf. Sanders et al. 2012), Episode Spaces may in turn include the viewpoints of characters (news sources) that play a role in it; for within each Episode Space, embedded Source Viewpoint-spaces can be opened up that represent the thoughts, perceptions, or utterances of a particular person. These Source Viewpoint-spaces are thus filled with information that is valid from the point of view of this particular person, but not necessarily from the point of view of other sources, the Virtual Observer, or the journalist. Several linguistic strategies have been described that signal viewpoint embedding. Important strategies are the change of verb tense, the use of cognitive and perception verbs, and various instruments of speech and thought representation (Dancygier 2012; Sanders and Redeker 1996; Sweetser 2012; Sweetser and Fauconnier 1996).

Under some circumstances, space embedding implicates space blending (Fauconnier and Turner 2002). In particular, a source's viewpoint can be percolated up to the Basic Space and blend with the narrator's viewpoint. Free Indirect Mode (Nikiforidou 2012) and present tense narration of cognition and perception (Dancygier 2012) are two main strategies to blend viewpoints. The effect of these blending strategies is that the reader has access to the story events through a viewpoint space shared by narrator and source (Dancygier 2012: 96–100). Space blending thus moves beyond the mere representation of a source's viewpoint through embedding; it allows the source's viewpoint to (temporarily) structure the narrative at the level of the Basic Space. In other words, the narrator draws the reader close to specific sources or even inside their heads, thus guiding readers' identification with these persons (Cohen 2001; Oatley 1999) and facilitating their transformation into mediated witnesses to news events.

In doing so, journalists have to attribute information to the sources in order to guarantee the truthfulness of their narratives. Such attributions, which often take the form of quotations (Vis, Sanders and Spooren 2015), take the reader temporarily outside the narrative in order to demonstrate that the journalist and the eyewitness exchanged information about the news events, somewhere between the occurrence of these events and the journalistic narrating of these events. In terms of Mental Space structures, attributions give access to a Narrative-External Discourse Space. As can be seen in Figure 2, this Discourse Space is positioned outside of the Narrative Space to indicate that the interaction between journalist and source is not part of the narrative itself. As such, the Narrative-External Discourse Space establishes the crucial link between reality and the narrative reconstruction of that reality.

In the following, we will apply our framework to two journalistic narratives about mass shootings. It will be demonstrated how the linguistic strategies employed by the journalists lead to embedding and blending in these narratives which aim to turn readers into mediated witnesses to these events within the boundaries of the genre.

2 Materials

An American and a Dutch news narrative, both covering a (different) spree killing, were selected. The American narrative was taken from *The Washington Post* (2007, April 19).[1] This article covers the spree killing on the Virginia Tech campus on April 16, 2007 and was published three days after the shooting. The article can be characterized as a relatively long narrative (5,385 words) which covers the entire day on which the spree killing took place, from the morning rituals of the perpetrator and his roommates up to the investigation of the perpetrator's room by the police that evening. Of particular interest for this study is a section headed "Popping sounds in the hallway". Since this part of the narrative describes the actual attacks on the students and teachers who were gathered in the lecture rooms of Virginia Tech, it is the best-suited section to study the linguistic elements that are used to transform readers into mediated witnesses. The analysis of the *Washington Post* article was therefore restricted to this section (1,538 words).

The second narrative was taken from the Dutch quality newspaper *NRC Handelsblad* (2011, April 11). This narrative covers a spree killing in a shopping mall in Alphen aan den Rijn, a town in the western Netherlands, on April 9, 2011. The Alphen aan den Rijn and Virginia Tech shootings are of a comparable nature and impact: in both cases, the perpetrator was a lone wolf who went on a rampage in a crowded place, and in both cases, the rampage resulted in the deadliest spree killing caused by an individual in the history of each nation. The Dutch narrative was published two days after the spree killing took place.[2] It covers the spree killing from its beginning, when the perpetrator parked his car near the shopping mall, until the end of the day, when the police were investigating the perpetrator's home and the crime scene. The narrative focuses mainly on the attacks inside the shopping mall and was therefore analyzed in its entirety (1,238 words).

3 Analyses

First, the narratives are examined in terms of Episode Spaces and the embedding of Source Viewpoint-spaces. The analysis then moves on to the blending of viewpoints and the construction of Narrative-External Discourse Spaces.

1 This article is part of a series of articles about the Virginia Tech Shooting for which *The Washington Post* won the 2008 Pulitzer Prize in the category 'Breaking News Reporting'.

2 Since the spree killing took place on a Saturday and no newspapers are issued on Sunday in the Netherlands, this narrative was one of the first articles about the event to be published.

3.1 Episode analysis and embedding of Source Viewpoint-spaces

From the episode analysis of the *Washington Post* article, an overall pattern of space building emerges which can be summarized as follows: from the journalist's Basic Space, six different Episode Spaces are opened up within the Narrative Space. The first Episode Space introduces the viewpoint of the Virtual Observer. In the subsequent five Episode Spaces, the Virtual Observer presents a generic viewpoint on the students and teachers inside the lecture rooms. From these generic viewpoint spaces, embedded Source Viewpoint-spaces are opened up by the Virtual Observer representing the particular viewpoints of individual eyewitnesses. Throughout the narrative, the Virtual Observer moves through time from space to space, chronologically following the perpetrator's route through the building. Excerpt 2 below illustrates the recursive process of embedding in the *Washington Post* article.

Excerpt 2
(1) *The first attack came in Room 206, advanced hydrology taught by Loganathan. There were 13 graduate students in the class, all from the civil engineering department. There was no warning, no foreboding sounds down the hallway.* (...)
(2) *In Jamie Bishop's German class, they could hear the popping sounds. What was that? Some kind of joke? Construction noises? More pops.* (...) (3) *Trey Perkins knocked over a couple of desks and tried to take cover.* (4) *No way I can survive this, he thought.*

From the Basic Space, a Narrative Space is construed in which all narrative events are represented. In (1), an Episode Space is opened up by the location marker "*in Room 2006*". The following clauses introduce the viewpoint of the Virtual Observer: "*There was no warning, no foreboding sounds down the hallway*". Only the Virtual Observer has access to the future episodes and is therefore able to "notice" the absence of foreboding sounds. After the Virtual Observer's viewpoint is constructed, a new Episode Space is opened up in (2) by the location marker "*In Jamie Bishop's German class*". This is followed by a representation of the class's thoughts from a generic viewpoint: "*What was that? Some kind of joke? Construction noises? More pops*". In (3) and (4), embedding to a deeper level takes place: an eyewitness is introduced in (3), whose Source Viewpoint-space is opened up by the direct thought in (4): "*No way I can survive this*".

Note that the Episode Spaces have subsequent positions on the time line but can also partly overlap. This is the case in the following Excerpt.

Excerpt 3
(1) *The scene in the [German] classroom "was brutal," Perkins recalled. Most of the students were dead. He saw a few who were bleeding but conscious and tried to save them. He took off his gray hoodie sweat shirt and wrapped it around a male student's leg.*
(2) *The French class next door was also devastated by then. Couture-Nowak, whose husband was a horticulture professor at Tech, was dead. Most of Kristina Heeger's classmates were dead.* (...)
(3) *Like those in other classes, the French students had heard the banging, or pops.*

The German classroom Episode ends in (1) with observations and acts by a witness after the shooter has left the room; (2) marks a new Episode, transferring from the German to the French classroom by the place indication *"The French class next door"*. The temporal expression *"by then"* indicates what the shooter has caused in another classroom by this particular point in time. The Virtual Observer did not immediately follow the perpetrator to the class next door but lingered in the German classroom to observe a young man's attempts to save his classmates. Thus, the Virtual Observer has stayed a little too long in the German classroom-space to observe the shooting in the French room next door and can only observe the results upon arrival there.

Then, in (3), a remarkable shift back in time to the actual shooting takes place, described from the generic viewpoint of the French class students. This interpretation is motivated by the past perfect *"had heard"*, which takes the reader back to an earlier moment on the time line to signify what the French students were hearing at that point. This perception takes place in Episode Space 3 at the moment the shooting takes place in Episode Space 2. The use of the past perfect in (3) thus shows how the Virtual Observer has access to (multiple) Episode Spaces at any moment during the events, much like an omniscient narrator. While the journalist determines at which point in time we access an Episode Space, the Virtual Observer fills in the gaps caused by the linear linkage of events.

The analysis furthermore reveals that verbs of perception and cognition are the journalist's main instruments to embed spaces that represent the viewpoints of eyewitnesses. Consider, for example, Excerpt 4 below:

Excerpt 4
(1) *After every shot, Violand thought, "Okay, the next one is me."*
(2) *But shot after shot, and he felt nothing. He played dead.*

In (1), the cognitive verb *thought* opens up an embedded Source Viewpoint-space. This embedded space represents event-related information from the point of view of an eyewitness, with the implication that the validity of the information is restricted to this person (Sanders and Redeker 1996). In this case, the information is conveyed through a direct thought (*"Okay, the next one is me"*). The direct thought expresses the impact of the events on the eyewitness by pointing out the stark contrast between the life threatening situation on the one hand and the witness's submissive, apathetic state of mind on the other hand. In (2), the perception verb *felt* is used to continue the representation of events from the viewpoint of the eyewitness.

Figure 2 represents the configuration of Episode Spaces and Source Viewpoint-spaces in the *Washington Post* article.

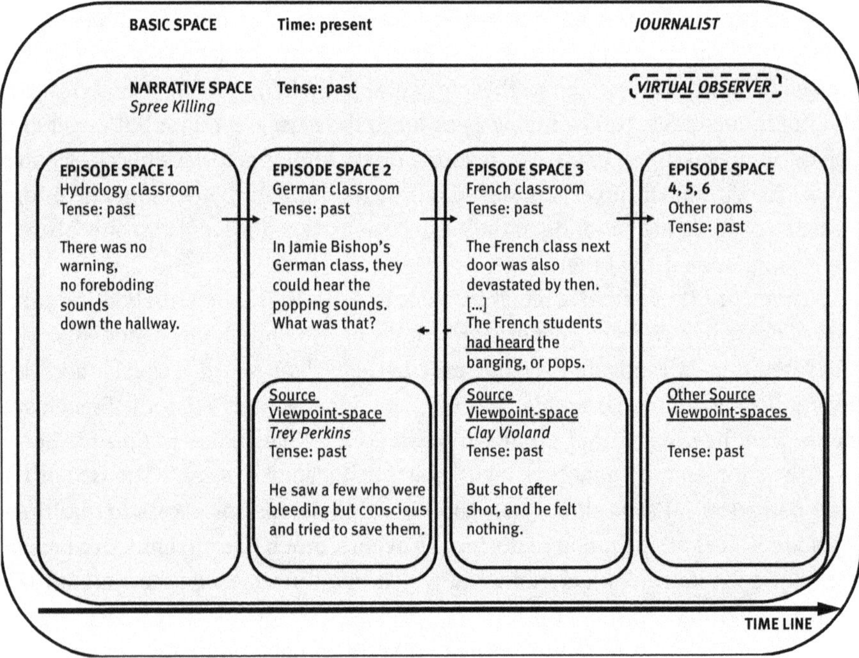

Figure 2: Configuration of Episode Spaces and Source Viewpoint-spaces in the *Washington Post* narrative

Note that Episode Spaces 1, 2, and 3 represent the Episode Spaces discussed so far. For reasons of clarity, the Episode Spaces that are not discussed (4, 5, and 6) are not elaborated in the figure. The dashed arrow signifies the shift back in time as an effect of the past perfect.

From the episode analysis of the *NRC Handelsblad* narrative, a similar overall pattern of space building emerges: from the journalist's Basic Space, seven different Episode Spaces are opened up. However, in contrast to the *Washington Post* article, these spaces are not elaborated in much detail and, with the exception of one Episode Space, do not structure generic viewpoints of groups of persons. Instead, they function primarily as spatial and temporal anchors of the narrative that help the reader to form a mental image of the perpetrator's path through the shopping mall. Excerpt 5 below illustrates the embedding of spaces in the *NRC Handelsblad* article (see the Appendix for the original Excerpts in Dutch).

Excerpt 5
(1) *Tristan van der V. parks his black Mercedes at the Carmen square near shopping mall De Ridderhof around twelve o'clock Saturday afternoon. He carries three guns with him. He gets out and shoots someone. He then ascends a staircase of stone and enters the shopping mall through a door.*
(2) *In his car, which is later being investigated by the Bomb Squad, is a note. It states that there are explosives in three other shopping malls in Alphen aan den Rijn.*
(3) *The indoor shopping mall is crowded. Van der V. calmly passes het Kruidvat, de Zeeman, de Hubo. Shooting. Glass flies around. People fall, run away, duck away. He walks on.*
(4) *An older man escapes in front of him and ducks into de Hubo.*
(5) *He was just with his granddaughter, but he has now lost her. Quickly he gets up again.*
(6) *He sees a man and a woman lying on the ground, bathed in blood. He sees fear, panic.*

In (1), an Episode Space is opened up by the location marker *"at the Carmen square"*. Note that (2) interrupts the chronological ordering of events by describing an observation made by the Virtual Observer in a subsequent Episode Space (*"which is later being investigated"*). This shift indicates that in the Dutch article, too, the Virtual Observer has access to (multiple) Episode Spaces at any moment during the events. In (3), the reader is taken inside the shopping mall at the moment the shooting begins. An eyewitness is introduced in (4). The tense shift from present to past in (5) combined with the temporal adverb *"just"* signals the embedding of the eyewitness's viewpoint (see Sanders 2010). In (6), the narration is continued from the Source Viewpoint-space of this man, as indicated by the perception verb *sees*.

3.2 Viewpoint blending

The embedding of Episode Spaces and Source Viewpoint-spaces facilitates imagination, and this imagination is in turn dramatized when the eyewitnesses' viewpoints are integrated in the journalist's viewpoint through space blending. In the Dutch narrative, present tense narration of cognition and perception is used as a strategy to blend viewpoints.

Similar to the American narrative, the Dutch narrative frequently uses verbs of perception and cognition to represent the viewpoints of eyewitnesses. Although all perceptions and cognitions took place in the past, they are being narrated in the present tense, which is atypical for printed news stories (Bell 1991: 202) and must be interpreted as the *historical present* (Fleischman 1985, 1990). The historical present compresses the temporal distance between the Basic Space and the Narrative Space. As a result, the use of verbs of cognition and perception provides an account of the events through the actual, *online* thoughts and perceptions of the eyewitnesses (Dancygier 2012: 70). Consider, for example, Excerpt 6 below.

Excerpt 6
(1) *In the C1000 stockroom, on the second floor, Lennart Schellinghout is working.*
(2) *He hears cracks.*

In (2), the present tense verb *hears* percolates a past perception of the eyewitness introduced in (1) into the journalist's here-and-now; in other words: their viewpoints are blended. The events inside the shopping mall are in great part narrated through such mixed viewpoints, which adds a strong sense of immediacy to the narrative and invites the reader to vicariously observe the events from up close.

In the American narrative, similar effects are achieved through the use of a different blending technique. Excerpt 7 below provides an example.

Excerpt 7
(1) *The small group of 10 in Haiyan Cheng's computer class heard the loud banging outside.*
(2) *She thought it was construction noise at first, but it distracted her.*
(3) *No, they were pops. Then silence, then more pops.*

From the generic viewpoint in (1), a Source Viewpoint-space is opened up by the cognitive verb *thought* in (2). Although the tense in (3) is past (and thus related to the journalist's deictic coordinates), the combination with a speech element (*no*) and informal lexicon (*pops*) indicates that the viewpoint of the eyewitness is blended with the journalist's viewpoint in a case of Free Indirect Thought: the speech and informal lexicon represent the eyewitness's viewpoint, whereas the past tense represents the journalist's viewpoint. The Free Indirect Mode "shift[s] the perspective to a vantage point close to or inside the narrated events, with an effect of zooming in on the events" (Nikiforidou 2012: 180). Without going so far as to represent past events in the journalist's present, the Free Indirect Mode allows for the representation of other persons' inner states (Toolan 1990: 73). In the Dutch article, Free Indirect Mode was not found, while several occurrences were found throughout the *Washington Post* article. Thus, it appears that two distinct types of viewpoint blending explain different ways in which the reader is drawn close to the news events through the consciousness of eyewitnesses.

3.3 Narrative-External Discourse Space

The representation of eyewitnesses' viewpoints through space embedding and blending dramatizes the narratives. As argued above, in the genre of journalism, the use of such strategies calls for attribution. Consider Excerpt 4 of the *Washington Post* article again, repeated and extended below as Excerpt 8:

Excerpt 8
(1) *After every shot, Violand thought, "Okay, the next one is me."*
(2) *But shot after shot, and he felt nothing. He played dead.*
(3) *"The room was silent except for the haunting sound of moans, some quiet crying, and someone muttering: It's okay. 'It's going to be okay. They will be here soon,'" he recalled.*
(4) *The gunman circled again and seemed to be unloading a second round into the wounded.*
(5) *Violand thought he heard the gunman reload three times. He could not hold back odd thoughts: "I wonder what a gun wound feels like. I hope it doesn't hurt. I wonder if I'll die slow or fast."*

Parts (1) and (2) might raise suspicions among readers about the truthfulness of the article. It is, after all, impossible for the journalist to enter the mind of the eyewitness, but the direct thought suggests the opposite holds true. The succeeding sentence affirms the factual status of the narrative: the direct speech followed by the attribution *"he recalled"* in (3) indicates that the journalist and the eyewitness exchanged information about the events at a later point in time, somewhere between the shooting and the here-and-now of the journalistic narrating. This quotation thus gives access to a Narrative-External Discourse Space representing what was said *after* the events took place. The attribution *"he recalled"* clearly

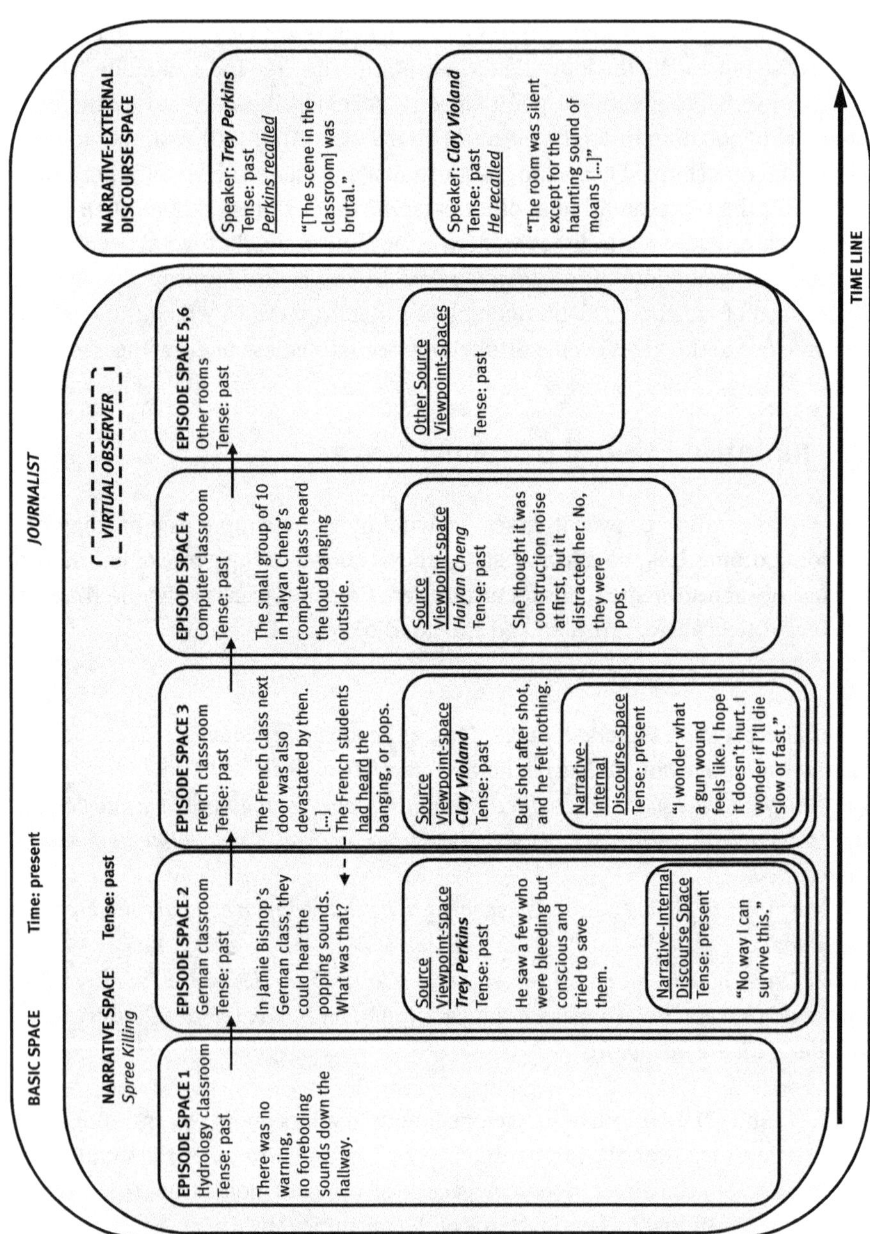

Figure 3: Configuration of Episode Spaces, Source Viewpoint-spaces, and Discourse Spaces in the *Washington Post* narrative

indicates that the eyewitness is recollecting what has happened and shifts his role of narrative character to that of news source. Throughout the article, the Narrative-External Discourse Space is accessed multiple times.

Sentence (4) of Excerpt 8 takes the reader back into the Narrative Space. In (5), the cognitive verb *thought* is used to re-access the viewpoint of the eyewitness, who now returns to his role of narrative character. Again, direct thought is used to represent his mental state during the attack.

Note that in Excerpt 8 as well as in the other Excerpts of the *Washington Post* article, the journalist also employs present tense direct speech and thoughts (e.g., *"I wonder what a gun wound feels like"*). These representations evoke a complete deictic shift such that the time of the utterance or thought is "fictively current" (Davidse and Vandelanotte 2011: 248). Hence, present tense direct speech and thoughts give access to Narrative-*Internal* Discourse Spaces that represent what a person inside the narrative says or thinks *while the events take place*. Tense, in the American narrative, is thus used strategically to represent events in Narrative-External as well as Narrative-Internal Discourse Spaces. The configuration of Discourse Spaces in the *Washington Post* article is visually represented in Figure 3 (again, Episode Spaces that are not discussed are not elaborated in the figure).

In the *NRC Handelsblad* article, too, direct quotations are used to access the Narrative-External Discourse Space. Consider, for example, the following Excerpt:

Excerpt 9
(1) *The shooter arrives at the Albert Heijn, where Ramon Vleerlaag is getting groceries.*
(2) *He hears something "like a cap gun".*
(3) *Employees direct the customers to the back of the shop. For about two minutes Vleerlaag hears shots, at irregular intervals. Then he sees the perpetrator.*
(4) *"He walked along the shop, at the checkouts. He looked into the shop, exactly the aisle at the end of which I stood. Then he kneeled, put the gun against the side of his head and fired. He immediately fell down."*

In this fragment, the Episode Space "Albert Heijn" is represented with Ramon Vleerlaag as a central eyewitness. In (2), the Source Viewpoint-space of this eyewitness is accessed by the perception verb *hears*. The partial quotation *"like a cap gun"* quickly accesses the Narrative-External Discourse Space. In (4), this Discourse Space is accessed again by the direct representation of the eyewitness's speech. Note that the shift from the present tense to the past tense clearly indicates that the eyewitness reflects upon the news events from a later point in time. The Narrative-External Discourse Space thus firmly grounds the reconstruction of events through the viewpoint of the eyewitness. Contrary to the *Washington Post*

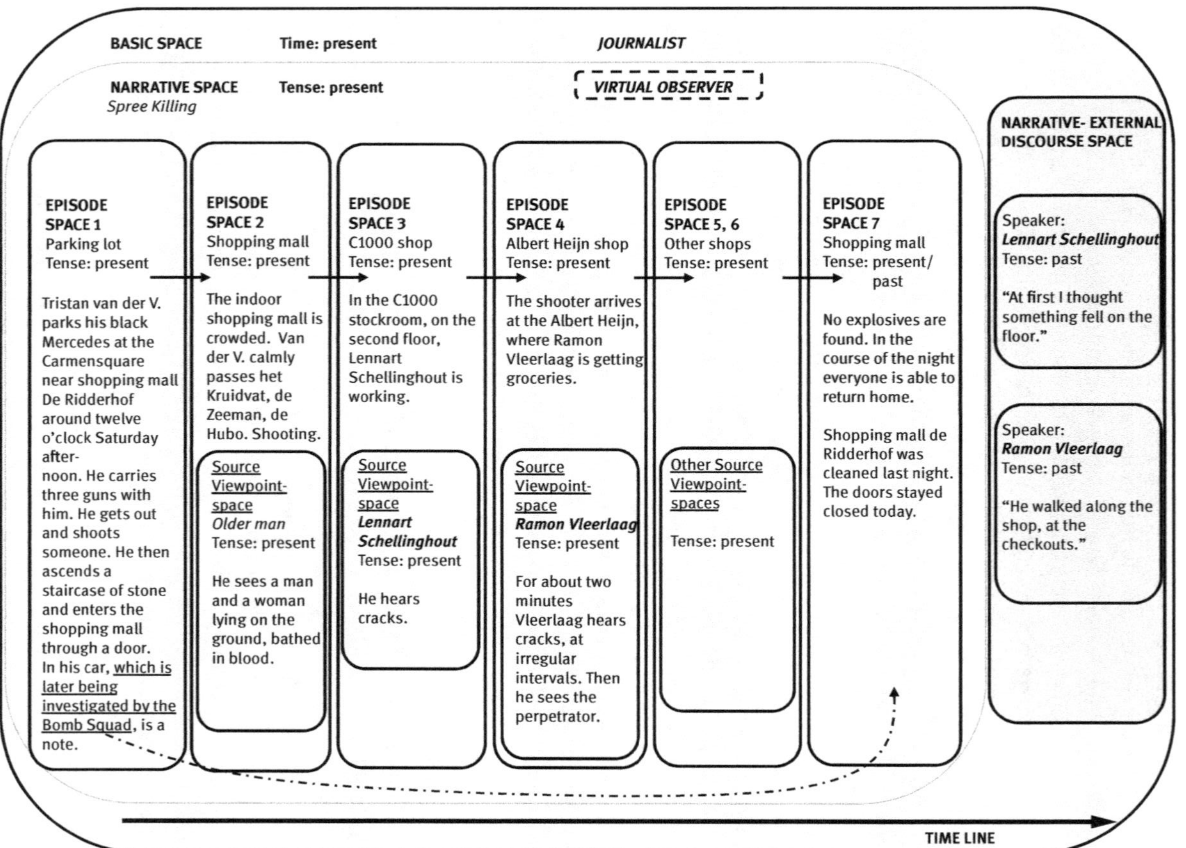

Figure 4: Configuration of Episode Spaces, Source Viewpoint-spaces, and Discourse Space in the *NRC Handelsblad* narrative

article, no Narrative-Internal Discourse Spaces are set up in the *NRC Handelsblad* article to represent utterances or thoughts of eyewitnesses during the shooting.

Figure 4 provides a visual representation of the configuration of spaces in the *NRC Handelsblad* narrative (Episode Spaces not discussed in the analysis are not elaborated in the figure).

Note that the dashed arrow indicates a shift forward in time. The thin dashed line between the Basic Space and the Narrative Space denotes the temporal compression between these spaces as an effect of the historical present used throughout the narration (Dancygier 2012: 75). The conceptual distance between the Basic Space and the Narrative Space is thus less profound in the Dutch article compared to the American article. In the final sentences of the Dutch article, however, a remarkable shift from the present tense to the past tense takes place, as can be seen in Excerpt 10:

Excerpt 10
(1) *No explosives are found. In the course of the night everyone is able to return home.*
(2) *Shopping mall de Ridderhof was cleaned last night. The doors stayed closed today.*

In part (1), the events are narrated from the final Episode Space of the narrative, from the viewpoint of the Virtual Observer. The shift to the past tense in part (2) signals a transition from the Narrative Space to the journalist's here-and-now Basic Space and solidly locks the shooting events in the past. This tense shift thus quite literally concludes the narrative by terminating the viewpoint blend and *decompressing* the Narrative Space and the Basic Space into separate spaces (cf. Dancygier 2012): the Basic Space, present for journalist and reader, is placed at a safe distance from the shooting.

4 Discussion and conclusion

This study underscores the value of Mental Spaces Theory and its elaborations in the study of narratives. Taking this framework as a starting point, we extended cognitive linguistic models for the analysis of narrative discourse (Dancygier 2012; Sanders et al. 2012) and developed a model that accounts for the genre-specific conventions of journalistic narratives. The application of our extended model to two news narratives about high-impact shootings clarified the sophisticated relation between the form and function of these narratives. First, verbs of perception and cognition are used to access the viewpoints of eyewitnesses to the events. In the American narrative, embedding to a deeper level takes place through the use of direct speech and thoughts in the present tense to express the emotional state of eyewitnesses during the attack. In addition, present tense narration of cognition and perception (in the Dutch narrative) and Free Indirect Mode (in the American narrative) are employed to blend the viewpoints of eyewitnesses with the journalist's viewpoint.

Together, these linguistic strategies provide a highly experiential account of shocking criminal acts. Through processes of embedding and mixing viewpoints, journalistic narratives invite readers to vicariously experience otherwise distant news events from up close, as mediated witnesses (Peelo 2006). This virtual experience is thought to help a society to recover from high-impact crimes that can be seen as "threats to sacred centres" of that society (Katz 1987: 68). The present study adds to our understanding of this process by identifying the linguistic strategies that are used in news narratives to transmit the experiences of people affected by crimes to other members of society. This transmission creates a communal sense of right and wrong, thereby both restoring and reinforcing society's moral and cultural values.

An important conclusion from this study is that reported discourse may serve two different functions in news narratives. First, it can serve a dramatizing function by accessing a Narrative-Internal Discourse Space which represents what was said or thought while the news events took place. Second, it can serve a legitimizing function by accessing a Narrative-External Discourse Space which represents the information exchange between the source and the journalist after the events took place. The Narrative-External Discourse Space should be considered a distinctive feature of news narratives as it identifies the narrative events and characters as real world events and people. It represents realistic speech in order to demonstrate, rather than describe, what was actually said by news sources (Clark and Gerrig 1990) and thus to indicate their trustworthiness. As such, this Discourse Space legitimizes the narrative reconstruction of real world events through the viewpoints of these sources. The Narrative-External Discourse Space is, in other words, what distinguishes non-fictional news narratives from fictional narratives.

The relevance of this External Discourse Space for the genre of news narratives calls for further investigations. Do different types of news narratives, for instance, use similar strategies to construct a Narrative-External Discourse Space? And has this Discourse Space always been a characteristic of news narratives or has it developed under pressure of the objectivity ideal which spread across America and Europe in the early twentieth century? In a follow-up study, we apply our model to a large corpus of historical and contemporary news narratives to answer these and other questions (Van Krieken and Sanders in press).

Our analysis furthermore revealed some noteworthy differences between the news narratives in their configuration and negotiation of viewpoints. We therefore propose that there are at least two structurally different basic types of viewpoint configuration and suggest that this difference in configuration explains the different ways in which viewpoint blends are established. Figure 5 below visualizes the first type of viewpoint configuration: *present tense narration* such as in the *NRC Handelsblad* text on the mall shooting.

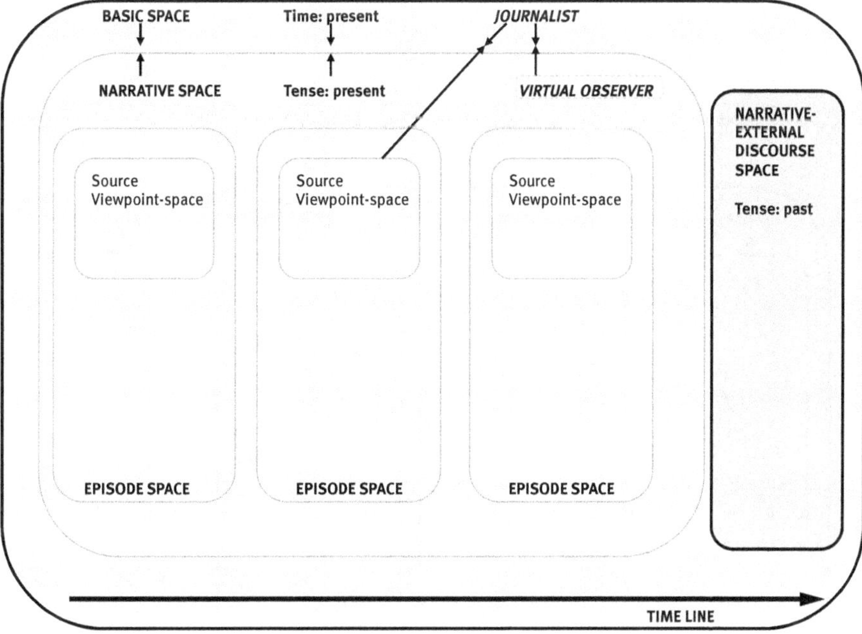

Figure 5: Configuration and blending of viewpoints in news narratives (type 1)

Figure 5 depicts – by means of thin dotted lines and colour agreement – a high degree of compression of the Basic Space, Narrative Space, and Episode Spaces as an effect of the present tense in the Narrative Space. This implies that the conceptual distance between the viewpoints of the journalist and the news sources is much reduced, which facilitates the process of viewpoint blending. In the standard narrative situation, the viewpoint of the journalist blends with the viewpoint of the Virtual Observer such that the observations made by the latter coincide with the narration thereof by the former. If, however, a Source Viewpoint-space is accessed, this source's viewpoint is directly percolated up to the journalist's Basic Space, culminating in a viewpoint blend of the source and the journalist. In this case, the observations and cognitions of the news source coincide with the narration thereof by the journalist. Hence, in this configuration, the journalist minimizes the role of his own viewpoint by narrating the news events through a viewpoint shared with those who have direct access to the events. Note that the Narrative-External Discourse Space, by the use of past tense, is placed at a larger distance from the Basic Space, which is depicted in Figure 5 by a solid line and darker colour.

Now compare Figure 6 below, which visualizes the second type of viewpoint configuration such as that found in the *Washington Post* text on the school shooting.

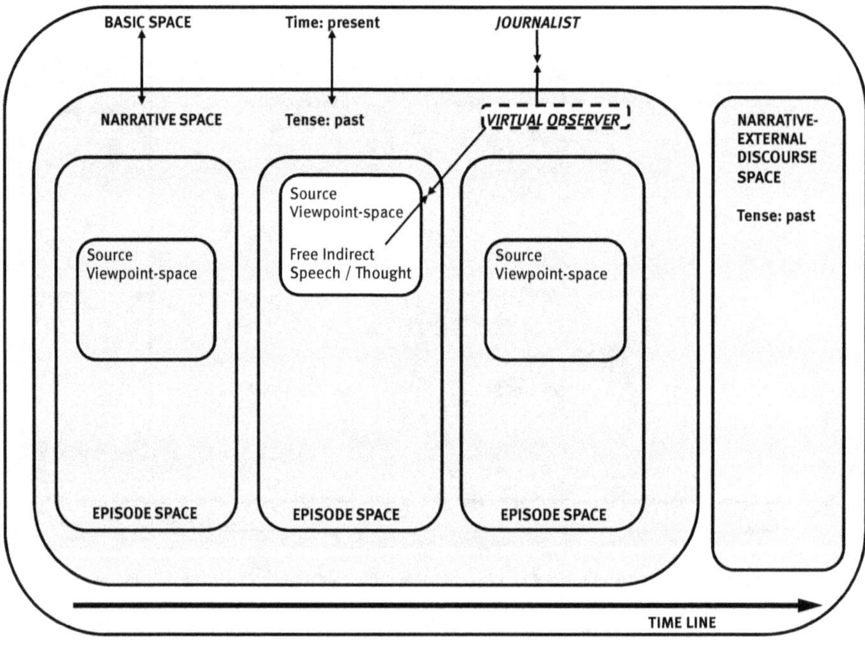

Figure 6: Configuration and blending of viewpoints in news narratives (type 2)

Figure 6 illustrates the default configuration of viewpoints in *past tense narrations*. The past tense in the Narrative Space creates distance between the Basic Space, Narrative Space, and Episode Spaces. As a result, there is considerable conceptual distance between the viewpoints of the journalist, Virtual Observer, and news sources. In this configuration, the Virtual Observer functions as a mediator between the viewpoints of the news source and the journalist. In using the Free Indirect Mode to represent news sources' speech and thought, the Virtual Observer reduces the distance between the source and the journalist by collapsing their viewpoints, thus creating drama in the narrative.

Our analysis exposed a difference in viewpoint configuration between the Dutch narrative (type 1) and the American narrative (type 2). An interesting question is whether this difference and the corresponding difference in viewpoint blending should be interpreted as language-specific conventions. Such a structural difference may be in line with Verhagen (2012), who identifies fundamental differences between Dutch Free Indirect Discourse and English Free Indirect Discourse and argues that, by consequence, the natures of these representation modes differ between the two languages. Verhagen (2012) further argues that there is no *a priori*, language-independent concept of Free Indirect Discourse which is realized differently across languages; rather, this representation mode is dependent on the linguistic tools used by narrators to create mixed viewpoints (see also Lu and Verhagen, this volume). Accordingly, if we want to understand cross-linguistic conventions for blending viewpoints in (news) narratives, we need to start our analyses from the ground up by identifying the linguistic strategies that prompt the process of viewpoint blending rather than solely identifying the resulting blended viewpoint space. The present study provides a sound framework to perform such analyses in a larger corpus (Van Krieken and Sanders in press).

A final direction for future research lies in the domain of the audience's reception of the strategies journalists use to describe news events from the viewpoints of eyewitnesses. Of particular interest are the strategies used to blend viewpoints, since these strategies unequivocally violate journalistic genre conventions: Free Indirect Discourse implies that the journalist has access to the minds of others, while present tense narration of cognition and perception fictively situates past experiences in the present. At the same time, viewpoint blending should facilitate a mediated witness experience, as blending provides *direct* access to another person's consciousness (e.g., Dancygier 2012; Oatley 1999). Important questions are whether the journalistic violations caused by viewpoint blending are noted as such by the audience and how blending affects readers' engagement with news narratives. Sanders and Redeker (1993) found that readers appreciate the suspense evoked by viewpoint blending techniques, but consider their use in hard news texts as less appropriate. Future experimental research should determine whether these findings still hold two decades later, in a time when the publication of newspaper narratives is on the rise (Hartsock 2007; Singer 2010).

References

Bell, Allan. 1991. *The Language of News Media*. Oxford: Blackwell.

Bird, Elizabeth S. & Robert W. Dardenne. 1988. Myth, chronicle, and story. In Daniel A. Berkowitz (ed.), *Social meanings of news: A text-reader*. London: Sage. 67–86

Clark, Herbert H.&Richard J. Gerrig. 1990. Quotations as demonstrations. *Language* 66 (4). 764–805.

Cohen, Jonathan. 2001. Defining identification: A theoretical look at the identification of audiences with media characters. *Mass Communication & Society* 4 (3). 245–264.

Dancygier, Barbara. 2012. *The language of stories: A cognitive approach*. Cambridge: Cambridge University Press.

Davidse, Kristin & Lieven Vandelanotte. 2011. Tense use in direct and indirect speech in English. *Journal of Pragmatics* 43 (1). 236–250.

Fauconnier, Gilles. 1985. *Mental spaces: Aspects of meaning construction in natural language*. Cambridge: Cambridge University Press.

Fauconnier, Gilles & Mark Turner. 2002. *The way we think: Conceptual blending and the mind's hidden complexities*. New York: Basic Books.

Fleischman, Suzanne. 1985. Discourse functions of tense-aspect oppositions in narrative: Toward a theory of grounding. *Linguistics* 23 (6). 851–882.

Fleischman, Suzanne. 1990. *Tense and Narrativity: From Medieval Performance to Modern Fiction*. Texas: University of Texas Press.

Frank, Russell. 1999. "You had to be there" (and they weren't): The problem with reporter reconstructions. *Journal of Mass Media Ethics* 14 (3). 146–158.

Greenberg, Susan. 2014. The ethics of the narrative: A return to the source. *Journalism* 15 (5). 517–532.

Hartsock, John C. 2007. "It was a dark and stormy night": Newspaper reporters rediscover the art of narrative literary journalism and their own epistemological heritage. *Prose Studies* 29 (2). 257–284.

Katz, Jack. 1987. What makes crime news. *Media, Culture and Society* 9 (1). 47–75.

Lu, Wei-lun & Arie Verhagen (this volume), Shifting viewpoints: How does that actually work across languages? An exercise in parallel text analysis.

Nikiforidou, Kiki. 2012. The constructional underpinnings of viewpoint blends: The *Past + now* in language and literature. In Barbara Dancygier & Eve Sweetser (eds.), *Viewpoint in language: A multimodal perspective*, 177–198. Cambridge: Cambridge University Press.

Oatley, Keith. 1999. Meetings of minds: Dialogue, sympathy, and identification, in reading fiction. *Poetics* 26 (5). 439–454.

Peelo, Moira. 2006. Framing homicide narratives in newspapers: Mediated witness and the construction of virtual victimhood. *Crime, Media, Culture* 2 (2). 159–175.

Roeh, Itzhak. 1989. Journalism as storytelling, coverage as narrative. *American Behavioral Scientist* 33(2). 162–168.

Sanders, José. 1990. Expliciet of niet? Referentie-bepalende factoren bij personen in nieuwsberichten. [Explicit or not? Reference determining factors for persons in news texts.]. *Interdisciplinair Tijdschrift voor Taal- en Tekstwetenschap 9* (3). 159–180.

Sanders, José. 2010. Intertwined voices: Journalists' modes of representing source information in journalistic subgenres. *English Text Construction* 3 (2). 226–249.

Sanders, José & Gisela Redeker. 1993. Linguistic perspective in short news stories. *Poetics* 22 (1). 69–87.
Sanders, José & Gisela Redeker. 1996. Perspective and the representation of speech and thought in narrative discourse. In Gilles Fauconnier & Eve Sweetser (eds.), *Spaces, worlds and grammar*, 290–317. Chicago/London: University of Chicago Press.
Sanders, José, Ted Sanders & Eve Sweetser. 2012. Responsible subjects and discourse causality: How mental spaces and perspective help identifying subjectivity in Dutch backward causal connectives. *Journal of Pragmatics* 44 (2). 191–213.
Singer, Jane B. 2010. Journalism ethics amid structural change. *Daedalus* 139 (2). 89–99.
Sweetser, Eve. 2012. Introduction: Viewpoint and perspective in language and gesture, from the Ground down. In Barbara Dancygier & Eve Sweetser (eds.), *Viewpoint in language: A multimodal perspective*, 1–25. Cambridge: Cambridge University Press.
Sweetser, Eve & Gilles Fauconnier. 1996. Cognitive links and domains: Basic aspects of mental space theory. In Gilles Fauconnier & Eve Sweetser (eds.), *Spaces, worlds, and grammar*, 1–28. Chicago: University of Chicago Press.
Toolan, Michael J. 1990. *The Stylistics of Fiction: A Literary-linguistic Approach*. London: Routledge.
Van Krieken, Kobie, Hans Hoeken & José Sanders. 2015. From reader to mediated witness: The engaging effects of journalistic crime narratives. *Journalism & Mass Communication Quarterly* 92 (3). 580–596.
Van Krieken, Kobie & José Sanders (in press). Diachronic changes in forms and functions of reported discourse in news narratives. *Journal of Pragmatics*. http://dx.doi.org/10.1016/j.pragma.2015.11.002
Verhagen, Arie. 2012. *Construal and Stylistics – within a language, across contexts, across languages*. Paper presented at the Stylistics across Disciplines conference, Leiden University.
Vis, Kirsten, José Sanders & Wilbert Spooren. 2015. Quoted discourse in Dutch news narratives. In André Lardinois, Sophie Levie, Hans Hoeken & Christoph Lüthy (eds.), *Texts, transmissions, receptions: Modern approaches to narrative texts*, 152–172. Leiden: Brill.

Appendix

Original Dutch Excerpts of the *NRC Handelsblad* narrative

Excerpt 5

Tristan van der V. parkeert zaterdagmiddag rond twaalf uur zijn zwarte Mercedes op het Carmenplein bij winkelcentrum de Ridderhof. Hij heeft drie wapens bij zich. Hij stapt uit en schiet iemand neer. Dan gaat hij een stenen zijtrap op en door een deur het winkelcentrum in. In zijn auto, die later door de Explosieven Opruimingsdienst wordt onderzocht, ligt een briefje. Daarop staat dat er explosieven liggen in drie andere winkelcentra in Alphen aan den Rijn.

Het is druk in het overdekte winkelcentrum. Rustig loopt Van der V. langs het Kruidvat, de Zeeman, de Hubo. Schietend. Glas vliegt in het rond. Mensen vallen neer, rennen weg, duiken weg. Hij loopt door.

Een oudere man vlucht voor hem uit en duikt de Hubo in. Hij was net nog met zijn kleindochter, maar die is hij kwijt. Al snel staat hij weer op. Hij ziet een man en een vrouw op de grond liggen, badend in het bloed. Hij ziet angst, paniek.

Excerpt 6

In het magazijn van de C1000, op de tweede verdieping, is Lennart Schellinghout aan het werk. Hij hoort knallen.

Excerpt 9

De schutter komt aan bij de Albert Heijn, waar Ramon Vleerlaag boodschappen doet. Hij hoort iets wat "lijkt op een klapperpistool". Medewerkers dirigeren de klanten naar achter in de winkel. Ongeveer twee minuten hoort Vleerlaag schoten, met onregelmatige tussenpozen.

Dan ziet hij de dader. "Hij liep voor de winkel langs, bij de kassa's. Hij keek de winkel in, precies het gangpad aan het eind waarvan ik stond. Toen knielde hij, zette het wapen tegen de zijkant van zijn hoofd en schoot. Hij viel meteen om."

Excerpt 10

Er worden geen explosieven gevonden. In de loop van de nacht kan iedereen weer naar huis.

Winkelcentrum de Ridderhof werd afgelopen nacht schoongemaakt. De deuren bleven vandaag gesloten.

Wei-lun Lu and Arie Verhagen

Shifting viewpoints: How does that actually work across languages? An exercise in parallel text analysis

Abstract: This chapter provides a parallel-text-based analysis of shifting viewpoints in English and Chinese. The data come from *Alice in Wonderland* and its four published Chinese translations, and from *Jiu Guo* and its published English translation. We observe that the English text systematically utilizes a specific combination of conventional constructional tools (including punctuation, letter case and connectives) for the purpose of constructing a gradual shift from one viewpoint to another. These elements are however partially missing in Chinese, which results in the translators' difficulty in adopting the entire constructional complex from the source language and forces them to use a variety of constructions available to them, sometimes losing the stylistic effect of the English original. A comparison of the Chinese original with its English translation reveals a similar result. The productivity of deictic verbs in Chinese resultative constructions allows the Chinese text to easily mix viewpoints using deictic verbs, whereas the English text does not exhibit such a tendency. We conclude by discussing how the study of parallel texts reveals the radically conventional nature of grammar and provides a powerful addition to research tools in cognitive linguistics.

1 Introduction

The questions that comparative stylistic research is dealing with are simultaneously quite concrete and quite general. On the one hand, we are interested in a very concrete question of cross-linguistic comparison: How exactly is a specific discourse pattern in English – one in which the dominant viewpoint shifts from the narrator to a character in a story rather smoothly – rendered in Chinese, a lan-

Note: Parts of this study were presented at the 12th International Cognitive Linguistics Conference (ICLC-12) and the 2014 Conference on Language, Discourse and Cognition (CLDC 2014). We thank the conference participants for suggestions. We also thank two reviewers for insightful comments on a previous version, with the usual disclaimers applying. The completion of this paper was partially supported by the project "Employment of Best Young Scientists for International Cooperation Empowerment" (CZ.1.07/2.3.00/30.0037) co-financed by the European Social Fund and the Czech Republic.

guage that does not have direct parallels of the linguistic features that constitute the English pattern? On the other hand, and at the same time, we are interested in a much more general theoretical and methodological question, namely, how precisely this *type* of question may and should be investigated: What procedures and what kind of data are appropriate, and especially: What is the status of concepts that we use in such a comparative study? The main goal of this paper is to address these general methodological and conceptual questions. We will do so by means of a detailed comparison of a small number of highly significant text fragments involving mixed viewpoints, using parallel texts: four translations from an English original to Chinese, and one from Chinese to English.

2 Method, data and research question

The use of parallel texts – putting an original alongside its translation(s) and comparing them for the purpose of semantic and grammatical analysis – already has some history and some systematic reflection in linguistics in general (Barlow 2008; Chamonikolasova 2007; Cysouw and Wälchli 2007; Van der Auwera et. al 2005). The use of parallel texts is highly beneficial, as by seeing the author and the translators as sensible text producers that try to get across the same conceptual contents in different languages, it allows us to compare how a usage-event is verbalized by the speakers of different languages, i.e. with different sets of linguistic tools available to each text producer.[1] Moreover, it allows us to compare languages in a more time-efficient way than experimental methods would, if the researcher has adequate knowledge of all or most of the languages involved.[2]

The method has also gained interest in cognitive linguistics in recent years; witness Rojo and Ibarretxe-Antuñano (2013), Slobin (1996, 2003), Tabakowska (1993, 2014), Verkerk (2014), among others. However, in the study of viewpoint phenomena, the parallel-corpus-based approach is still almost new, Tabakowska (2014) being the only study, as far as we know. Tabakowska investigates viewpoint manifestations in *Alice in Wonderland* in terms of the theoretical framework

1 The method also has its own specific limitations, as translational discourse may be different from natural discourse. See Xiao (2010), for instance, for how translational Chinese is different from Chinese discourse that is spontaneously produced by native speakers. Another issue taken with parallel texts is that translations are largely confined to the written genre (Verkerk 2014:34). But in spite of the above constraints, the parallel text is still a powerful tool for contrastive linguistic research.

2 For a more comprehensive overview of use of parallel texts in linguistics research, see Verkerk (2014) and Wälchli (2007).

of Cognitive Grammar (Langacker 1987, 2008), using the original and five different Polish translations. Most extensively, she discusses reference (in view of the fact that Polish, unlike English, lacks the systematic distinction into definite and indefinite articles), and then more briefly the use of aspect (involving differences between the Polish imperfective and the English progressive), epistemic modality, de-idiomatization and iconicity, as tools for viewpoint construction in *Alice* and its Polish translations. They function as signals for different aspects of common ground shared by Alice, the narrator and the reader, and thus as indicators of a particular point of view in a clause or text fragment. However, although Tabakowska mentions the classical narratological and stylistic phenomenon of Speech and Thought Representation (STR), and especially that of viewpoint mixture in so-called Free Indirect Discourse (FID), she does not include these in her analysis. Given their importance and pervasiveness, we consider it useful to focus on these in this study. Our goal, moreover, goes beyond a demonstration of the usefulness of a cognitive semantic approach to translation studies: We will argue that the detailed study of translations (in this case in English and Mandarin Chinese) of STR fragments provides evidence for the radically language-specific nature of the grammatical tools for 'implementing' viewpoints.[3]

Given that verbalizations of the same usage event are largely aligned sentence by sentence in parallel texts, the special organization of such texts creates a methodological opportunity that allows us to look into this research issue: How may grammatical constructions involved in viewpoint management be compared cross-linguistically? To put it more precisely, when we see a viewpoint construction of Language A in a certain stretch of discourse, do we also systematically find some counterpart or translation equivalent in its translation in Language B? If not, what do we find in Language B and what does that tell us about viewpoint management cross-linguistically?

To answer this query, we also begin, like Tabakowska, with a study of *Alice in Wonderland* by Lewis Carroll, now alongside its Chinese translations published in Taiwan. *Alice in Wonderland* is well known for its juxtaposition of the narrator's voice with the protagonist's voice that reflects the author's split personality (see Tabakowska 2014 for a review and for further references). We use four Chinese translations, done by Yuan-ren Chao, by Li-fang Chen, by Hui-hsien Wang, and by Wenhao Jia and Wenyuan Jia. We focus on a special, highly significant pattern of STR in the original, and the different ways in which the translators have dealt with it in the Mandarin translations, constrained by the conventional grammatical patterns of that language.

3 As we will see, grounding predications of the type that Tabakowska focuses on, will ultimately turn out to be important in our analysis as well, especially in the section on *Jiu Guo*.

To counterbalance the possible impression that English would provide a 'richer' toolkit for viewpoint management than Mandarin, we also present a brief case study of translation in the opposite direction: from Mandarin to English; the original text is *Jiu Guo (The Republic of Wine)*, a Chinese masterpiece written by Mo Yan, Nobel laureate in 2012, and the translation into English, done by Howard Goldblatt. Our choice of *Jiu Guo* was motivated by the hallucinatory realism of Mo Yan's writing, which was one of the main reasons for Mo Yan's receiving the Nobel Prize for Literature.

3 Mixing viewpoints in *Alice in Wonderland* and its four Chinese translations

First we will demonstrate a recurrent textual patterns of mixing viewpoints used by Lewis Carroll. Our examples all come from the first chapter, but readers can easily verify that it is in fact characteristic of, and occurs throughout, the whole book. In section 3.1, we identify the grammatical patterns which allow the author to construct this specific pattern. As we will show, at least part of this pattern is specific to the grammar of English – it is based on an English *convention* for connecting a reported clause to a reporting one, a convention that does not as such exist in Mandarin. In section 3.2, we present the corresponding passages in the Mandarin versions to demonstrate and evaluate different strategies employed in the translations.

3.1 Analysis of the English text

The very first sentence (and paragraph) of *Alice in Wonderland* reads as follows:

(1) a. *Alice was beginning to get very tired of sitting by her sister on the bank, and of having nothing to do: once or twice she had peeped into the book her sister was reading, but it had no pictures or conversations in it, 'and what is the use of a book,' thought Alice 'without pictures or conversations?'*

The fragment appears to start with an outsider's view of Alice sitting on the bank (though with some *hint* of an internal mental state: experiencing boredom), and ends clearly and unambiguously with a *direct* evocation of a highly specific thought of Alice, in her own words ("direct thought"). It is worthwhile to consider in some detail how exactly the point of view progresses from (almost) completely outside to completely internal to Alice. At least the following elements, and their specific combination, play a role. One is the coordinating conjunction *and*[4] at the beginning of Alice's direct thought, and the fact that *and* is in lower case (preceded by a comma). The use of the coordinating conjunction *and*, in lower case, presents Alice's *direct* thought as a straightforward continuation of the text segment preceding it – so this preceding segment must at least to *some* extent also represent Alice's thought; put differently, in terms of content: The (rhetorical) question in quotation marks is Alice's thought; it must be based on some consideration presented in the text preceding it (*but it had no pictures or conversations in it*); so this must also to some extent contain Alice's thought; the combination of the comma, conjunction, and lower case marks the direct thought as part of a *train* of thoughts. But up until the first quotation mark, this train of thoughts is not presented as a *direct* representation, in Alice's own words, so here it is partly the narrator who is responsible for the wording and the presentation of Alice's thought: in this sense, this segment – the first conjunct of *and* – shows a mixture of viewpoints: the content primarily gives Alice's point of view (what she perceives as a result of her 'peeping' into her sister's book), but it is presented to us in the narrator's voice.

Another element is the combination of the contrastive conjunction *but* and the negation (*no pictures or conversations*) in the fragment itself. As these evoke a configuration of mental spaces with different epistemic stances towards the same object of conceptualization (Verhagen 2005, ch.2, and references cited there), they in fact invite the reader to imagine some mental agent who might be looking for or expecting to see pictures or conversations. In the present context, the best candidate is of course Alice (an expectation that is quickly fulfilled with the repetition of the words *pictures or conversations* in Alice's direct thought); this makes the use of *and* at the start of the direct thought as natural as it is. So the contrastive conjunction and the negation are linguistic cues pointing to Alice's viewpoint, her world view and expectations, even though the narrator is (co-)responsible for the wording;[5] this also contributes to this fragment creating

4 Strictly speaking, the element *and* may also function as a discourse marker. In this context, however, its status as a conjunction seems clear. Moreover, as we will see, there are other instances of the same pattern in which the place of *and* is taken by an element that is unambiguously a conjunction.

5 One might want to take this as a basis for labelling this clause as Free Indirect Discourse (FID), but it does not show the linguistic characteristics traditionally associated with it, especially not a mixture of past tense with proximal adverbs (such sentences do occur elsewhere in the the text, e.g. *she was now only ten inches high*). On the other hand, this observation could be a starting point for a criticism of the traditional conception of FID, but we will not pursue that issue here.

a ‘smooth’ transition between the initially external (narrator) viewpoint and the final internal (Alice) viewpoint.

Thirdly, there is the relative ordering of the reported and the reporting clause, i.e. the medial placement of the reporting clause, *between* two parts of the reported clause.[6] In order for the gradual shift in viewpoint to work, the reporting clause must not be placed before the reported clause (as in prototypical direct discourse). Compare (1a) with the constructed example (1b) below.

(1) b. ... *but it had no pictures or conversations in it, and/so Alice thought: ‘(and) what is the use of a book without pictures or conversations?’*

The stylistic effect of a smooth transition between external and internal viewpoints no longer exists in (1b), where the full clause in the narrator’s discourse is now structurally severed from Alice’s direct thought. As a consequence, the use of a coordinating conjunction at the beginning of this direct thought is also less felicitous (*and* would have to be interpreted differently here, perhaps as a discourse marker; hence the parentheses): it cannot immediately connect to a relevant piece of information in the preceding context. The structural independence of the two text segments in the narration thus has important consequences for the management of the viewpoints in the text. As stated above, the thought that the book contains no pictures or conversations is primarily Alice’s (though filtered through the narrator’s voice); in (1b), by contrast, we are now pushed towards reading the *but*-clause as an explanation of Alice’s (naïve) response to the book by the *narrator*.

Sentence (1a) is definitely not the only one exhibiting this particular effect of a very gradual transition from narrator’s to Alice’s viewpoint, dependent on precisely this combination of linguistic items. Example (2) is another instance, which we will explain in a bit less detail.

(2) ... *but she could not even get her head through the doorway; ‘and even if my head would go through,’ thought poor Alice, ‘it would be of very little use without my shoulders. [...]’*

As we can see, (2) is structurally highly similar to (1a). Both excerpts comprise a full narrative clause followed by a secondary boundary mark[7], a lower case coor-

---

6 According to Quirk et al. (1985: 1022) “[m]edial position is very frequent”; see also McGregor (1990) and Vandelanotte (2009).

7 Secondary boundary marks include the comma, the semicolon and the colon, as opposed to terminal marks, which include the full stop, the question mark and the exclamation mark (Huddleston and Pullum 2002).

dinating conjunction that starts the direct thought of the character (containing a repetition of an element in the first conjunct: here *head*), with a medial reporting clause. The only difference is the use of a semicolon at the end of the full clause in the narration. A semicolon also indicates interdependency of the conjoined clauses, so it still contributes to the slow shifting of the viewpoint when used in this position, like the comma in (1a).

As the narrative unfolds, the next passage that shares the same pattern, now with the coordinating conjunction *for*, is (3).

(3) *... she felt a little nervous about this; 'for it might end, you know,' said Alice to herself, 'in my going out altogether, like a candle...*

In (3), the combination of structural tools that creates a shifting viewpoint mixture is almost identical to (1a) and (2), including the full clause in the narrator's discourse, followed by a semicolon and Alice's subsequent self-oriented direct speech, interrupted by a reporting clause.[8] All of the examples above stem, as we said, from the first chapter of *Alice in Wonderland*, but the pattern occurs throughout the entire story: 21 of the 26 cases of the phrase *thought Alice* occur in precisely this pattern (in only 5 cases is the formula sentence final), and the same holds for about half of the 115 cases of the phrase *said Alice* (the difference between *thought* and *said* is mostly due to the fact that the latter also occurs in descriptions of conversations, with another participants taking the turn after Alice has said something).

Based on these observations, we can formulate a general pattern for a recurrent stylistic strategy in *Alice in Wonderland*, a schematic viewpoint construction for constructing a gradually shifting mixture from the narrator's to the protagonist's viewpoint:

(4) [CL] – [SecBound Mark] – "[CoorConj] – [Frag1]" – [Reporting CL] – "[Frag2]"

In this schema, [CL] stands for a Full Clause, [SecBound Mark] for a Secondary Boundary Mark, [CoorConj] for a Coordinating Conjunction, and [FragX] for Fragment-of-a-sentence.

Below, we will first examine whether the translators have a consistent strategy for expressing the view-pointing effect in the Chinese passages corresponding to the English ones that are characterized by (4). As we have seen, the view-pointing effect in the English text is achieved through a consistent and recurrent

8 Notice that the element *for*, playing a crucial role in the gradual transition from the narrator's to (100 %) Alice's discourse, is unambiguously a coordinating conjunction (cf. note 5).

constructional complex, and we would like to see whether the translators, in the same context, are similarly able to craft a (more or less) consistent constructional means for the same stylistic end of mixing viewpoints.

3.2 Analysis of the four Chinese translations

In this section, we will first discuss the commonalities of the four translations to describe how Chinese can accommodate the shifting viewpoint mixture in the original, and then we will further explore whether and how such recurring choices are capable of rendering the shifting viewpoint effect of the original text.

However, the very first observation that we can make about the four translations is that no consistent set of structural tools is used to produce the stylistic effect of a shifting mixture of viewpoints.

The absence of such a consistent set of structural tools may be surprising at first sight, but the reasons quickly become clear when we consider some properties of the grammar of Chinese, especially with regard to the ordering of clauses: Chinese does not have a conventional pattern for a medial reporting clause (though such an arrangement does not sound completely intolerable); the preferred convention clearly is to place a reporting clause before the reported one. The four translations of (3a) adhere to this convention by consistently placing the reporting clause before Alice's direct thought; (5) and (6) are typical examples.

(5) …她 有時候 偷偷 地 瞧 她 姊姊 看 的 是 什麼
ta youshihou tou-tou di qiao ta jie-jie kan de shi sheme
she sometimes secret-RED LK see she sister read LK PRT what
書， 可是 書 裡 又 沒有 畫兒， 又 沒有
shu, keshi shu li you meiyou hua-er, you meiyou
book but book in also NEG picture-DIM also NEG
說話， 她 就 想道， 「一本書 裏 又 沒有
shuohua, ta jiu xiang-dao, “yi-ben-shu li you meiyou
speech she PRT think-COMP one-CL-book in PRT NEG
畫兒， 又 沒有 說話， 那樣書
hua-er, you meiyou shuohua, na-yang-shu
picture-DIM also NEG speech that-kind-book
要 牠 幹什麼 呢？」 (Chao)
yao ta gansheme ne?”
want it what for PRT
‘... She sometimes secretly looked what book her sister was reading, but the book did not have any picture, nor did it have any conversation, so she thought “A book that does not have any picture, nor any conversation, why would one want a book like that?”’

(6) 雖然 她 也 曾 在 一旁 窺視 姊姊 所
suiran ta ye ceng zai yipang kuishi jie-jie suo
although she also at one point LOC next to peep sister REL
閱讀 的 書籍， 卻 因 書 中 無 圖 也
yuedu de shuji, que yin shu zhong wu tu ye
read LK book but because book in NEG picture also
無 對話 的 內容 而 覺得 索然無味。 愛麗思
wu duihua de neirong er juede suoranwuwei. ailisi
NEG conversation LK content CONJ feel bored stiff Alice
心 想： 「沒有 圖案 也 沒有 對話 的
xin xiang: “meiyou tuaan ye meiyou duihua de
heart think NEG picture also NEG conversation LK
書 有 什麼 用處 呢？」 (Wang)
shu you sheme yongchu ne?”
book have what use PRT
‘Although she at one point peeped at the book that her sister was reading, she felt bored from the content of the book that contained no picture and no conversation. Alice thought: “What is the use of a book that contains no picture and no conversation?”’

The consequence of this grammatical convention of Chinese is that it deprives translators of the possibility of exploiting the same structural tools that are used throughout the original, i.e. a medial reporting clause, for the same stylistic purpose; as a result, translators seem to be forced to find other linguistic tools available to them, or to abandon the attempt to render the shifting of viewpoints in the Chinese translation.

However, when we look at the translations of (2), it turns out that three out of four actually have the reporting clause in medial position; (7) and (8) are examples.

(7) 但是 她 連 頭 都 擠不進 那扇門。 「就算
danshi ta lian tou dou ji-bu-jin na-shan-men. “jiusuan
but she PRT head PRT squeeze-NEG-in that-CL-door even if
我 的 頭 擠得進，」 可憐 的 愛麗絲 心想，
wo de tou ji-de-jin,” kelian de ailisi xin-xiang,
I LK head squeeze-PFV-in poor LK Alice heart-think
「肩膀 也 擠不進去⋯ (Chen)
“jianbang ye ji-bu-jin-qu...
shoulder also squeeze-NEG-in-go
‘But she could not squeeze her head into that door. “Even if my head could be squeezed in,” poor Alice thought, “my shoulder would not go through...”’

(8) 但 她 連 頭部 都 鑽不進 門口： 「就算 我
dan ta lian tou-bu dou zuan-bu-jin menkou: “jishi wo
but she PRT head-part PRT squeeze-NEG-in entrance even if I
的 頭 能 勉強 塞進 門口，」 愛麗絲
de tou neng mianqiang sai-jin menkou,” ailisi
LK head AUX with force squeeze-in entrance Alice
悲傷 地 想， 「我 的 肩膀 擠不進去⋯ (Wang)
beishang di xiang, “wo de jianbang ji-bu-jin-qu...
sad LK think I LK shoulder squeeze-NEG-in-go
‘But she could not even get her head through the door: “Even if my head could be forced into the door,” Alice thought sadly, “my shoulder would not go through...”’

The inconsistency among the translations of (1a) and (2) is striking, which raises a question: What is Chinese language usage really like in this respect, in natural (not translated) discourse? One possibility is that Chinese, unlike English, does not allow a nominal head and a post-modifier to be split (as in (1a)), but does allow splitting the two clauses of a conditional (as in (2)). So the question is: Does a medial reporting clause occur in natural (written) discourse of Chinese at all? In order to answer this question, we consulted the Sinica Corpus of Modern Chinese. We looked up all instances of *xin-xiang* ('heart-think', used in Chen's translation) and *pansuan* ('calculate', used in Jia & Jia's translation), and determined the position of the reporting clauses headed by one of these verbs relative to the associated reported clause. There were 127 reporting clauses with *xin-xiang*, all of which preceded their reported clause; there were 12 reporting clauses with *pansuan*, 9 of which occurred initially relative to the reported clause, and 3 finally. In other words, the overwhelming majority of reporting clauses occurs initially, and none of them are medial, in the corpus. Thus, we may safely conclude that the conventional ordering patterns for reporting and reported clauses in English and in Chinese are different. As recognized in the comprehensive Quirk et al. (1985: 1022), English has three conventionalized patterns – initial ('reporting-reported'), final ('reported-reporting'), and medial ('reported1-reporting-reported2') – the last of which can be used in the construction of gradual viewpoint shift.[9] Chinese, on the other hand, has at most two conventional patterns, initial and final, possibly with a preference for the former.[10]

Thus, there is a tension between the grammatical conventions of Chinese and the 'local' communicative goal of construing a shift in viewpoint from narrator to character. In three out of the four translations of (2), translators have chosen to use a non-conventional pattern, allowing them to follow the order of clauses in the original English text and thereby to try to construct the view-pointing effect in the original, but not, of course, undoing the tension. The unconventional clause ordering seems to some extent tolerable (also according to the first author's intuitions). Thus, it is not expected to block an average Mandarin reader's understanding of the situation being described; at the same time, its effect, as a non-standard device, is not that of a *smooth* shift from the narrator's viewpoint to Alice's, as in English. Notice that neither (7) nor (8) has a coordinating conjunction at the beginning of Alice's direct thought (the original, see (2), has *and*); recall that we argued that this use of a coordinating conjunction is integral to the construal of a smooth transition between viewpoints in the English narrative, which thus clearly cannot be straightforwardly constructed in Chinese.

In fact, in the Chinese translations of these three passages, coordinating conjunctions are missing at the beginning of Alice's direct thought in all cases but

---

9 Conceivably, there may also be functional differences between initial and final position of the reporting clause, but we do not discuss that possibility any further here.

10 But this might also be dependent on the reporting verbs (witness the difference between *xin-xiang* and *pansuan*). Again, we leave this issue for future research.

one. Of the twelve translated passages involved, only one (the translation of (3) by Chen) has a coordinating conjunction: *yinwei* in (9):

(9)

	她	有一點	擔心，	「因為，」	愛麗絲	自言自語：	「再
…	ta	youyidian	danxin,	“yinwei,”	ailisi	ziyanziyu:	“zai
	she	a little	worry	because	Alice	talk to oneself	further

縮下去	的	結果，	有可能	是	我	整個	人
suo-xiaqu	de	jieguo,	youkeneng	shi	wo	zhengge	ren
shrink-IPFV	LK	result	possible	PRT	I	entire	person

就	像	一個	蠟燭	般… (Chen)
jiu	xiang	yi-gen	lazhu	ban…
PRT	like	one-CL	candle	PRT

‘She was a little worried, “because,” Alice spoke to herself: “the result of my going even smaller could be my going out like a candle…”’

The systematic absence (compared to the English original) of coordinating conjunctions in this significant position points to another difference in the relevant grammatical constructions available in English and in Chinese. In Chinese, the coordinating conjunction that is semantically closest to English *and* is *erqie*, but this is typically not used for temporal or causal relations, while the relations in fragments of the type characterized in (4) precisely do have some causal (viz. inferential) aspect (it is the absence of pictures that makes Alice draw a conclusion about the book’s function, etc.). The distribution of *erqie* is in fact quite different from that of English *and*. In particular, *erqie* does not typically occur utterance initially in direct discourse; in the Sinica Corpus of Modern Chinese, we find no tokens of *erqie* introducing direct discourse, in a total of 2,637 tokens in the corpus. The only initial conjunction we find is in the translation by Chen in (9), where the English original in fact has a causal conjunction (*for* in [3]): *yinwei* ‘because’. Interestingly, this conjunction has a distributional profile that is actually more similar to English *and* than *erqie*, in particular in direct discourse: In the Sinica Corpus, we find four tokens of *yinwei* opening direct discourse, in a total of 5,000 in the whole corpus.

Finally, a closer look at the remaining translations of (3) reveals the possibility of yet another strategy, which comes down to an attempt to follow the English original and adhere to the conventions of Chinese at the same time. Consider Wang’s translation in (10):

(10) 愛麗絲 有點兒 緊張 地 想：「再 繼續 縮下去，
ailisi youdianer jinzhang di xiang: “zai jixu suo-xiaqu,
Alice a little nervous LK think further continue shrink-IPFV
可能 會 完蛋 的，」 又 對 自己 說，「如果
keneng hui wandan de,” you dui ziji shuo, “ruguo
AUX AUX doomed PRT again to self say if
全 身 的 皮膚 都 不見 了，像 隻 蠟燭
quan shen de pifu dou bujian le, xiang zhi lazhu
whole body LK skin all gone CRS like CL candle
般⋯ (Wang)
ban...
PRT
‘Alice thought a little nervously: “(If I) keep going smaller, I am doomed,” again (she) spoke to herself, “if my skin is gone, like a candle...”’

The first clause in the original is *she felt a little nervous about this*, a description of Alice’s mental state, but not a reporting clause. The translator turned this clause about nervousness into a reporting clause, with the proper name *Alice* as the subject, and then further on inserts another (subjectless) reporting clause, in medial position. While the latter splits the direct thought in two and thus more or less directly reflects the English original, the first intervention makes Alice’s viewpoint explicit (more so than in the original) in the first clause, thereby preventing it from being read as the narrator’s explanation for her state of mind, and it conforms to the conventions of the Chinese language (moreover, as the first part of the direct thought in [10] constitutes a full sentence, the second reporting clause might also be taken as initial, introducing a new thought; notice the element *you*, “again”). There is a tension between the attempt to preserve a stylistic effect by respecting the author’s practice of placing the reporting clause medially and the conventions of the target language (that the reporting clause preferably precedes the reported one); (10) shows a compromise between these two competing forces.

We have now looked at 12 translations of a single consistent linguistic pattern of viewpoint mixing and shifting in *Alice in Wonderland*. Looking closely at the translations, the first thing that we observe is that there does not seem to be a single consistent linguistic pattern to evoke this mixture and shifting in Chinese, and that this is certainly due, at least to a very large extent, to differences in conventionalized grammatical patterns for relating reported to reporting clauses. Table 1 below summarizes the four translators’ choices.

Table 1: Position of the reporting clause with respect to the direct discourse

	Translation of (1a)	Translation of (2)	Translation of (3)
Y.R. Chao	Initial	Initial	Initial
L.F. Chen	Initial	Medial	Medial
H.H. Wang	Initial	Medial	Initial (10)
W. Jia & W. Jia	Initial	Medial	Medial

Among the four translations, there is one (by Y.R. Chao) that sticks strictly to the preferred pattern of Chinese grammar. In his translations of all three fragments, he places the reporting clause before Alice's direct thought. This translator chooses to render the viewpoint effect by combining less schematic, lexical constructions and reporting Alice's thought verbatim in the narration, instead of trying to use a general constructional schema as in the English text. For instance, in (5), the Chinese expression *you* is an emphatic negation marker, and also a part of the larger composite construction *you... you...* (functioning somewhat similarly to *neither... nor...* in English). The narration in (5) contains *you meiyou hua-er, you meiyou shuo hua*, which is repeated verbatim in Alice's direct thought. This full and literal repetition aligns Alice's viewpoint at the end of the fragment with that reported by the narrator and thus helps make the transition less abrupt, which is functionally similar to the structural pattern in the English text – in fact, it is an 'enhanced' version of the lexical repetitions present in the English text (cf. above). But the other three translators choose to partially follow the clausal order of the English text more closely, while also selectively adopting other constructions, such as *lian... dou...* in (7) and (8), to embed Alice's viewpoint in the narration.[11]

The specific mixing and shifting of viewpoints in Lewis Carroll's text is a result of the author's strategic exploitation of the conventional tools available to him in his language, with the medial placement of the reporting clause being an indispensable element of the stylistic schema. Since this medial placement is not a conventionalized pattern in the grammar of Chinese (although it is not totally impossible either), this language does not provide its users with a consistent way of rendering a consistent pattern of viewpoint construction in the English original, as we see reflected in the variety of different translation strategies.

The crucial term here is "conventional". The relevant differences do not only involve grammatical rules in the traditional sense, i.e. regular patterns for combining words and phrases into sentences, but also typographic factors, which

11 Readers are referred to Lai (2008) and Wang and Su (2012) for a thorough analysis of the *lian... dou...* construction.

are equally conventional tools stemming from a specific cultural development, according to usage-based principles. Given the logographic writing system of Chinese, the distinction between upper case and lower case is meaningless, as opposed to the segmental writing system of English. So as a number of important constitutive elements in a relevant constructional complex in the source language is missing in the target language, any adoption of the constructional schema in the target language is necessarily going to be only partial, and will not do the same job as it does in the source language.

A difference between languages in the conventional tools available for viewpoint management does not entail that the ultimate viewpoint relations constructed by readers in interpreting a text are going to be radically different as well. After all, different sets of tools may serve to create similar products. Linguistically mediated meaning construction always combines the use of words and constructions with inferences based on common ground. The relative proportion of what comes from explicit signals and what from inferencing may differ between languages, while the combined results for particular texts may well be similar. Parallel texts provide an excellent basis for investigating precisely the question in what ways and in what dimensions the explicit, conventionalized tools for viewpoint management in languages differ or coincide, and thus ultimately also: how the *general* conceptual space of viewpoint management is and can be structured. We will return to this issue at the end of the next section and in our conclusion.

4 Mixing viewpoints through deixis in *Jiu Guo* and its English translation

We will now reverse the perspective, and briefly look at the way viewpoint is managed in an original Chinese text and how this comes out in its translation. As we have seen, English has quite a rich set of clause combining tools that may be used in viewpoint management, while Chinese has a comparatively less elaborate set of such tools. However, Chinese may well have more elaborate tools than English in some other domain. A case in point is constituted by the occurrence of the morphemes *lai* 'come' and *qu* 'go' in verbal resultative constructions (cf. Lu et al., in preparation).[12] Consider (11a), (11b), (12a) and (12b), where examples (a)

12 The term "resultative" as used in Chinese linguistics is different from that in English. The latter denotes an argument structure construction with two participants, the second of which reaches a specified state as a result of the process described by the verb ([NP-V-NP-Result-state], as in *He cried his eyes red*; cf. Goldberg and Jackendoff 2004). The former denotes a verbal con-

are taken from the narration of the Chinese original, and examples (b) are their counterparts in the published English translation.

(11) a.

丁钩儿	接过	酒瓶子，	晃晃，	蝎子	在
dinggouer	jie-guo	jiuping-zi	huang-huang	xiezi	zai
Ding Gou’er	take-over	wine bottle	shake-RED	scorpion	LOC

参须	间	游泳，	怪	味道	从	瓶口
sen-xu	jian	youyong	guai	weidao	cong	ping-kou
ginseng root	LOC	swim	strange	odor	LOC	bottle mouth

冲出来。
chong-chu-lai
rush-out-come

‘Ding Gou’er took over the bottle, shook it, scorpions swimming among the ginseng roots, with a strange odor rushing out (coming [towards ORIGO]) from the mouth of the bottle.’

(11) b. *He shook the bottle, and the scorpions swam in the ginseng-enhanced liquid. A strange odor emanated from the bottle.*

(12) a.

他	感到	乏味、	无趣，	便	把	她	推开。	她
ta	gan-dao	fawei	wuqu	bian	ba	ta	tui-kai	ta
he	feel-PFV	bland	uninteresting	then	PRT	she	push-aside	she

却	像	一只	凶猛的	小豹子	一样，
que	xiang	yi-zhi	xiongmeng-de	xiao baozi	yiyang
nevertheless	like	one-CL	fierce-LINK	leopard cub	same

不断地	扑上来...
buduandi	pu-shang-lai
relentlessly	pounce-up-come

‘He felt uninterested and then pushed her away. But she was like a fierce leopard cub and relentlessly threw herself (upon him) – coming [towards ORIGO].’

(12) b. *That was a turn-off, it killed his desire, and he pushed her away. But, like a plucky fighting cock, she sprang back at him hard, catching him off guard and making resistance all but impossible.*

---

struction indicating a verbal process leading to some result associated with the meaning of the verb, i.e. a kind of ‘intrinsic’ result (cf. certain particle constructions in English like *come in*, *jump up*, where the particles also indicate resultant states of the verbal process, and thus turn the verbal expression as a whole into one of achievement, not just a process. Readers are referred to Chao (1968) or Li and Thompson (1981) for a detailed description of these resultative constructions in Chinese.

We can observe that the way viewpoints are constructed in the Chinese original and in the English translations differ, due to the occurrence of *lai* in the verbal complex of the sentences in the Chinese version of the story. In (11a), the viewpoint presented in the narration is a mixture of the narrator's and the protagonist's (Ding Gou'er's). The way Ding Gou'er is referred to, by his full name, is an indication of the narrator's perspective; the resultative verbal construction presents the manner and the end-state of the movement (rushing out), while the combination with *lai* invites the reader to take the point of view of the one perceiving the odor, i.e. the character. This kind of mixture can be produced straightforwardly in Mandarin, due to the fact that there is a conventional way of marking deixis on a verb (here by adding *lai*). Since English lacks such a tool, the mixing of viewpoints cannot be represented so easily; the choice of the verb *emanate* by Goldblatt makes the movement explicit and leaves the character's viewpoint implicit.

Fragment (12a) shows the same mixture of viewpoints. Ding Gou'er is referred to by a third person pronoun *he*, so the deictic center is the narrator. On the other hand, with *lai* in the verbal complex, the event of her throwing herself at him is explicitly and effortlessly presented as perceived from the protagonist's point of view, in the Chinese version. In the English translation, the latter point of view is much more left to inference, for example through the addition of lexical elements suggestive of his attitude (*off guard*, *resistance*).

There is a lexical construction in English that can be considered a translation equivalent of the deictic verbal element *lai* in Chinese, viz. the lexeme *come*. But what is crucial here is the difference between the conventional combinatorial properties of these elements in the two languages. In the original Chinese version of the story, the stylistic effect of mixed viewpoints is achieved through a combination of an objective reference to the protagonist, presentation of the protagonist's perceptual content, and the use of a deictic verbal morpheme. The stylistic 'recipe' is different in the English version, as the constructional possibility of the deictic verbal morpheme is missing, so the translator has to resort to linguistic means available in the target language, such as the lexical items mentioned above, or, more subtly, the spatial preposition *at* in (12b).[13] Note that the

13 It was suggested to us that *at* might have a strong association with *come*, stronger than with *go*, and because of that it might represent (deictic) viewpoint. However, a Google search for both *came at him* and *went at him* returned numbers of results in the same order of magnitude, and *went back at him* in fact occurred considerably more frequently than *came back at him*, so that a connection between *at* and deictic viewpoint must at least involve more than association with *come*. Still, looking at possible viewpoint effects of the use of spatial prepositions in English is a valuable direction of investigation (in this context, the use of *came* would work better than *went*, while another preposition (e.g. *to*, *after*) would not have that effect).

construals created by the use of a deictic verb and by a preposition are bound to be different, as different parts of a conceptual scene are profiled (Langacker 1987). Therefore, although the difference in linguistic conventions does not make translation impossible, the ways viewpoint mixture can be linguistically *achieved* (and conceptually appreciated) in the two languages remain irreducibly different. As we mentioned at the end of section 3, different 'compositional pathways' may well lead to comparable overall interpretations of viewpoint relations, but the pathways are as much a factor in the style of a text as the overall interpretation. Creating a complex mixing of viewpoints for the same usage event in another language at least involves an irreducibly different constructional composition of the mixed viewpoints.

Again, this analysis demonstrates the methodological advantages of using parallel texts in cross-linguistic viewpoint research. First of all, the method shows us that the distribution of viewpoint constructions – in this case, the translation equivalents *lai* and *come* – varies according to the conventions of the languages involved. Therefore, although English also has viewpoint expressions like *come see for yourself*, *go figure* that may create a construal similar to one that involves *lai* and *qu* 'go' in Chinese, the linguistic manifestation of mixing viewpoints *in the same usage event* is bound to be constrained by the relevant conventions of a specific language. Second, on this basis, the method provides a methodological cutting edge for investigating the relation between the general conceptual space of viewpoint and the dimensions in which languages may differ in their explicitly coded, conventionalized tools for viewpoint management.

5 Conclusion

In sections 3 and 4, we considered very different linguistic phenomena and translation samples of different directions, which we believe point to the same methodological and theoretical significance.

First of all, we see an important *methodological* advantage: Putting parallel passages in different languages side by side, especially when the languages involved are not at all related, focuses the investigator's attention on elements that would otherwise easily remain below the level of conscious awareness. Indeed, some of the details of the shifting viewpoint pattern in *Alice in Wonderland*, such as the role of the coordinating conjunction and that of lower case, only became apparent to us in the comparison with the Chinese translations.

Secondly, there is a fundamental *theoretical* consequence of the approach we implemented here. Ultimately, all management of viewpoints in discourse, especially of viewpoint mixing, depends not only on general cognitive abilities (empathy, Theory of Mind), but crucially also on the linguistic tools for viewpoint management that language users have at their disposal, and what we can now clearly appreciate is that these are language and culture specific, having been transmitted (with slight modifications) to present day language users over the generations. Thus, although the necessary cognitive infrastructure is presumably universal, there will not be universal *linguistic patterns* of viewpoint management. The systematic possibility of shifting smoothly from mainly-narrator-viewpoint to mainly-character-viewpoint in *Alice in Wonderland* is dependent on certain conventions of the English language, and the systematic possibility to effortlessly combine manner of movement and viewpoint in *Jiu Guo* is dependent on certain conventions of the Chinese language. That is, we can establish a conclusion about categories of viewpoint organization in discourse that parallels Croft's (2001) conclusion about syntactic categories: As such categories can only be defined in terms of properties of constructions, and the latter are necessarily language specific, the categories are of necessity also language specific. Similarly, as linguistic patterns of viewpoint mixing can only be defined (in a way that allows instances of them to be identified in texts) by reference to conventional linguistic items, with all their language specific properties, they are also of necessity language specific (van Krieken, Sanders & Hoeken, this volume, come to a similar conclusion). The generality suggested by terms like "direct" and "indirect discourse" for certain patterns of viewpoint organization may thus be misleading. It induces investigators to ask questions like: "How is FID expressed in Language X?" (cf. Hagenaar 1992), while these are in fact unanswerable, as the presuppositional condition (that a language independent way of identifying different types of STR exists) cannot be met as a matter of principle. This is not to say that attempts to answer such a question have not produced interesting and insightful results (as Hagenaar [1992] in fact demonstrates). But to the extent that they have, we conclude that they should be 'reconceptualized' as insights about the variability in the possible conventional coding of different aspects of viewpoint management.

What exactly the properties of the items involved in viewpoint management in a specific language are will have to be established by a large scale investigation of actual language use. Thus, our characterizations of the English and Chinese phenomena discussed here, may in some respects be inaccurate or incomplete. For example, in section 3, we did not look at a large number of verbs of communication and cognition, so there might be different ordering patterns associated with different semantic types of verbs in Mandarin, or in English, or in both. But our theoretical point is not weakened by this kind of uncertainty, because of the method of studying parallel text fragments: The conclusion *that* viewpoint construction in discourse is language specific can already be drawn on the basis of careful analysis of specific parallel instances of language use, precisely because they are parallel.

Finally, the use of parallel texts has a high potential in helping set a research agenda for cross-linguistic viewpoint research, especially if the scope can be extended to cover a representative sample of languages, and preferably also discourse types (there are limitations here; we do not foresee parallel day-to-day conversations in the near future, for example). It will allow a better understanding of how various languages represent viewpoint and what aspects of viewpoint construction are systematically distinguished in the grammars of many different languages and which only in a few. The methodology of parallel text analysis can contribute significantly to a solid empirical foundation for answering this intriguing and important question.

References

Barlow, Michael. 2008. Parallel texts and corpus-based contrastive analysis. In María de los Ángeles Gómez González, J. Lachlan Mackenzie & Elsa M. González Álvarez (eds.), *Current trends in contrastive linguistics: Functional and cognitive perspectives*, 101–121. Amsterdam/Philadelphia: John Benjamins Publishing Company.

Chamonikolasová, Jana. 2007. *Intonation in English and Czech dialogues*. Brno: Masaryk University Press.

Chao, Yuan Ren. 1968. *The grammar of spoken Chinese*. Berkeley: University of California Press.

Croft, William. 2001. *Radical construction grammar*. Oxford: Oxford University Press.

Cysouw, Michael & Bernhard Wälchli (eds.). 2007. Parallel texts. Using translational equivalents in linguistic typology. [Special issue]. *Sprachtypologie & Universalienforschung STUF* 60(2).

Goldberg, Adele E. & Ray Jackendoff. 2004. The English resultative as a family of constructions. *Language* 80. 532–568.

Goldblatt, Howard. 2011. *The Republic of wine*. New York: Arcade Publishing.

Hagenaar, Elly. 1992. *Stream of consciousness and free indirect discourse in modern Chinese literature*. Leiden: Center for Non-Western Studies.

Huddleston, Rodney & Geoffrey K. Pullum. 2002. *The Cambridge grammar of the English language*. Cambridge: Cambridge University Press.

van Krieken, Kobie, José Sanders, Hans Hoeken (this volume). Blended viewpoints, mediated witnesses: A cognitive linguistic approach to news narratives.

Lai, Huei-ling. 2008. Using constructions as information management devices: Analysis of Hakka lien5...ya3/du3 constructions. *Bulletin of the Institute of History and Philology Academia Sinica* 79. 343–376.

Langacker, Ronald W. 1987. *Foundations of cognitive grammar: Vol I. Theoretical prerequisites*. Stanford: Stanford University Press.

Langacker, Ronald W. 2008. *Cognitive grammar: A basic introduction*. New York: Basic Books.

Li, Charles N. & Sandra Thompson. 1981. *Mandarin Chinese: A functional reference grammar*. Berkeley: University of California Press.
Lu, Wei-lun, I-wen Su & Arie Verhagen. In preparation. Constructions as cultural tools of viewpoint operation: A case study of deictic verbs in Chinese-English parallel texts.
McGregor, William B. 1990. The metafunctional hypothesis and syntagmatic relations. *Occasional Papers in Systemic Linguistics* 4. 5–50.
Quirk, Randolph, Sydney Greenbaum, Geoffrey Leech & Jan Svartvik. 1985. *A comprehensive grammar of the English language*. London/New York: Longman.
Rojo, Ana & Iraide Ibarretxe-Antuñano (eds.). 2013. *Cognitive linguistics and translation advances in some theoretical models and applications*. Berlin: De Gruyter.
Slobin, Dan I. 1996. Two ways to travel: Verbs of motion in English and Spanish. In Masayoshi Shibatani & Sandra A. Thompson (eds.), *Grammatical constructions: Their form and meaning*, 195–220. Oxford: Clarendon Press.
Slobin, Dan I. 2003. Language and thought online: Cognitive consequences of linguistic relativity. In Dedre Gentner & Susan Goldin-Meadow (eds.), *Language in mind: Advances in the study of language and thought*, 157–192. Cambridge, MA: MIT Press.
Tabakowska, Elżbieta. 1993. *Cognitive linguistics and poetics of translation*. Tübingen, Germany: Gunter Narr Verlag.
Tabakowska, Elżbieta. 2014. Lewis Carroll's *Alice* in grammatical wonderlands. In Chloe Harrison, Louise Nuttall, Peter Stockwell & Wenjuan Yuan (eds.), *Cognitive grammar in literature*, 101–116. Amsterdam: John Benjamin.
Vandelanotte, Leiven. 2009. *Speech and thought representation in English: A cognitive-functional approach*. Berlin: De Gruyter.
Van der Auwera, Johan, E. Schalley & Jan Nuyts. 2005. Epistemic possibility in a Slavonic parallel corpus – a pilot study. In Björn Hansen & Petr Karlik (eds.), *Modality in Slavonic languages. New perspectives*, 201–217. München: Sagner.
Verkerk, Annemarie. 2014. *The evolutionary dynamics of motion event encoding*. Nijmegen: MPI Series in Psycholinguistics.
Wang, Chueh-chen & Lily I-wen Su. 2012. Distinguishing synonymous constructions: A corpus-based study of Mandarin *lian...dou* and *lian ...ye* constructions. *Journal of Chinese Linguistics* 40(1). 84–101.
Xiao, Richard. 2010. How different is translated Chinese from native Chinese? *International Journal of Corpus Linguistics*. 15(1). 5–35.
Xiao, Richard, & Dai Guangrong. 2014. Lexical and grammatical properties of Translational Chinese: Translation universal hypotheses reevaluated from the Chinese perspective. *Corpus Linguistics and Linguistic Theory* 10(1). 11–55.

Research materials used

Carroll, Lewis. 2014 [1865]. *Alice's adventures in Wonderland*. http://www.gutenberg.org/ebooks/11(accessed 28 September 2015).
Carroll, Lewis. 1939. *Alisi Manyou Qijing Ji* (Alice's adventures in Wonderland, Trans. Yuan Ren Chao). Shanghai: The Commercial Press.
Carroll, Lewis. 2005. *Ailisi Mengyou Xianjing* (Alice's adventures in Wonderland, Trans. Wenhao Jia and Wenyuan Jia). Taipei: Shangzhou Publishing.

Carroll, Lewis. 2006. *Ailisi Mengyou Xianjing* (Alice's adventures in Wonderland, Trans. Li-fang Chen). Taipei: Gaobao Publishing.

Carroll, Lewis. 2011. *Ailisi Manyou Qijing* (Alice's adventures in Wonderland, Trans. Hui-hsien Wang). Taipei: Licun Culture Publishing.

Mo, Yan. 2008. *Jiu Guo* [The Republic of wine]. Shanghai: Shanghai Wenyi Publishing.

Mo, Yan. 2011. *The Republic of wine* (Trans. Howard Goldblatt). New York: Arcade Publishing.

Sinica Corpus of Modern Chinese
http://app.sinica.edu.tw/kiwi/mkiwi

Ad Foolen and Toshiko Yamaguchi

Perspective: Kawabata's *Beauty and Sadness* and its translations into English, German, and Dutch

Abstract: It has been pointed out that Japanese culture, including literature, has a preference for a special type of subjective construal, with an experiencing subject embedded in the experienced situation (see, for example, Ikegami 2005, 2008). At the same time, it is often claimed that Western culture and literature prefer a more objective, distanced, perspective. In the present paper, this assumed contrast is tested by analyzing the opening scene of *Beauty and Sadness*, a novel by the Japanese author Yasunari Kawabata and its translations in English, German, and Dutch. The four versions differ with respect to the way perspective is handled. In our analysis, we show that the original author and the translators recruit a variety of linguistic means (adverbs, pragmatic markers, negation, and constructions on the sentence level) to express perspective and guide perspectival shifts. We did not find, however, a systematic contrast in perspective taking between the Japanese original and its translations in Western languages. Instead, we found variation among the three translations, sometimes coming closer to the original, sometimes deviating from it substantially. We conclude that perspective in literary texts is a challenge for translators, which deserves more attention in translation theory and practice.

1 Introduction

The central question in cognitive linguistics is how languages conceptualize the world, or better, how *people* conceptualize the world in their language, or, even better, how they conceptualize *experience* (of the world) in their language. Whichever version one prefers, conceptualization remains the central notion. Conceptualization takes place with the help of cognitive processes like categorization, image schemas, metaphor, metonymy, etc. (see for example, the different chapters in Part I of Geeraerts and Cuyckens [eds., 2007] *Oxford Handbook of Cognitive Linguistics*).

The central aspect of conceptualization is 'construal', a cover term for "non-objective facets of meaning" (Verhagen 2007: 48). In general, construal can be defined as "the relationship between a speaker (or hearer) and a situation that he conceptualizes and portrays" (Langacker 1987: 487–488). With objective conceptualization, the relation between the speaker and the situation stays in the background, but when the conceptualization is "nonobjective", or "subjective", it becomes part of the portrayed situation. It is as if the conceptualizer brings the conceptualization relation itself into the picture.

Within construal, different aspects can be distinguished, such as the degree of detail in the conceptualization of a situation ("granularity") or the degree of prominence of different parts of the situation ("figure" versus "ground"). Another aspect of construal, the one that will be central to this chapter, is "perspective", or the phenomenon where the same situation can be viewed from different perspectives. In Cognitive Grammar, perspective has been part of the model from the beginning (cf. Langacker [1987: 120], where he defines perspective as "the way in which a scene is viewed"). The overall relationship between the "viewer" and the situation being viewed is called the "viewing arrangement" (Langacker 2008: 73).

A standard example of perspective taking is the difference expressed by the deictic verbs *come* and *go*, as used in *John came into the house* and *John went into the house*. In the first example, the conceptualizer perceives the situation from inside the house and in the second example from outside. How central or widespread perspective as an aspect of the conceptualization process is, is a question that will be on the research agenda of Cognitive Linguistics for some time to come. The present chapter intends to contribute to answering this question by exploring perspective phenomena in a Japanese novel and its translations into English, German, and Dutch.

Perspective is not an important notion only in Cognitive Linguistics; it has played a central role in theorizing literary narrative for several decades already. In section 2, we will pay attention to this line of research. Section 3 is devoted to a presumed Japanese preference for subjective construal. In section 4, we will consider perspective as a specific challenge for translators. We chose translations into English, German, and Dutch to avoid analyzing solely the choices of one translator and to see whether these closely related languages nevertheless show subtle differences based on, for example, word order patterns. In section 5, we will present our data, which will be analyzed in section 6. The analysis will make use of the notions and distinctions we have introduced in section 2, 3 and 4, with special attention to the passages where multiple perspectives seem to play a role simultaneously, as this is the central topic of the present volume. Section 7 concludes this chapter.

2 Perspective in literary texts

Niederhoff (2013) gives an overview of perspective research in literary theory. He points out that terminology varies: *perspective*, *point of view*, *vantage point*, *voice*, and *focalization*. There are certain subtle theoretical differences between these notions, but for the present purpose, we can consider them to be more or less equivalent.

The perspective in a literary text can vary. The "viewer" can be the character ("protagonist") who plays a central role in the story (this is typically the case in first person narratives) or it can be a narrator who does not play a role himself except being the narrator, typically leading to third person narratives. In the latter case, the narrator often shifts perspective to different characters, which makes the narrative more lively and easier to identify with.

2.1 Multiple perspectives

In a third person narrative, the perspective of the narrator is the unmarked perspective. If the narrator shifts the perspective to that of a character, he can mention the character explicitly and state what he/she perceived, thought or felt. There are, however, more implicit means to indicate perspective shift, like the use of adverbs or particles that evoke a subjective perspective. Analyzing the use of the German particle *wohl*, which indicates epistemic uncertainty, Eckardt points out that "uncertainty often only makes sense for a protagonist, not for the narrator. Hence, *wohl* can be a reliable clue for a shift in context." (Eckardt 2012: 11). Harris and Potts (2009) discuss epithets like *the idiot*, which can easily lead to what they call "pragmatically-mediated perspective shifting" (p. 524). More research into other linguistic techniques that can be used for implicit or explicit perspective shifting is still necessary.

The narrator can also explicitly switch the perspective to him/herself. Chafe (2010: 57) gives examples of what he calls "interpolated narrator comments" from George Eliot's *Middlemarch* (1871). Similar examples can be observed in *The Luminaries*, the Man Booker Prize winning novel of 2013 by Eleanor Catton, who uses the explicit narrative perspective as one of the ways to imitate 19th century novelistic style. Some of these narrator comments relate to the actual wording chosen, as in *[T]he benefit of the doubt, to take the common phrase, ...* (p. 125); others refer to an earlier passage, as in *Mannering, as has been already observed, was a very fat man* (p. 178); or bring in a reflection by the narrator on a specific observation, as in *Clinch's efforts in love were always of a mothering sort, for it is a feature of human nature to give what we most wish to receive, and it was a mother that Edgar Clinch most craved – his own having died in infancy* ... The narrator even uses the explicit personal pronoun *we* to refer to himself when he makes a discourse organizational remark in reaction to the very elaborate style of one of the characters: *We shall therefore intervene, and render Sook Yongsheng's story in a way that is accurate to the events he wished to disclose, rather than to the style of his narration* (p. 262).

Up till now, we have seen that the unmarked narrative perspective can shift to an explicit perspective of a character or to that of the narrator. These shifts lead to a sequence of different perspectives, which, together, constitute multiple perspectives in a stretch of discourse. This type of sequential multiperspectivity can fulfill a broad range of functions, such as "creating suspense, as a self-reflective way of foregrounding the process of narration, or as a method of endorsing a thematic aspect of a moral within the narrative by, for example, presenting it repeatedly from different standpoints" (Hartner 2014: section 2).

In the context of the present paper and volume, the relevant question is, however, whether it is also possible to express different perspectives at the same time, in situations of simultaneous perspectives or mixed points of view. There are indeed techniques to bring different perspectives in even closer contact than just presenting them sequentially. Cui (2014) shows how Virginia Woolf uses parentheticals to insert a different perspective within one that is created in the main clause: "the consciousness presented in a parenthetical works collaboratively with the consciousness presented in the host to depict a whole picture for a certain scene. The text no longer revolves around a single source of consciousness; simultaneity and multiplicity have become the new mode." (Cui 2014: 184).

The simultaneous presence of multiple perspectives is strongest when linguistic elements (words or constructions) encode two or more perspectives at the same time. Evans (2005) presents fascinating examples from different languages, for example demonstrative pronouns which locate referents with respect to both the speaker and the hearer, or particles like Italian *mica*, which indicates that the speaker assumes that the proposition is believed by the hearer, at the same time asserting himself that the proposition does not hold. In this way, the speaker presents his perspective against the background of the assumed perspective of the hearer.

In narrative theory, free indirect discourse is the best known and most studied technique for creating mixed points of view, combining the perspective of the narrator with that of a character (Vandelanotte 2009). This is a relatively new technique, which fully developed in the context of writing in the 20th century. In our data, we find a clear example of this technique (see section 6 for further discussion).

2.2 On-line experience

One aspect of perspective concerns the distance between the viewer and what is viewed, which also typically correlates with granularity: with decreasing distance, granularity typically increases. If the distance is very small, the distinction between the viewer and the viewed can get blurred, the viewer becoming the experiencer, the viewed experience "involved experience". The viewer is not at a distance from the experience anymore but in the middle of it. What we mean here is not simply that the viewer is "on stage" in Langacker's sense, but rather that the distinction between the experiencer and the experience dissolves.[1]

Several researchers have tried to capture this type of "involved perspective" from different theoretical backgrounds. MacWhinney (2005) distinguishes between the depictive and enactive mode in perspective taking, the latter being the involved one. Dancygier (2012: 102ff) distinguishes "on-line conceptualization" as one type of perspective taking, which seems to come close to what MacWhinney calls the enactive mode. Dancygier writes (2012: 103–104): "there is a difference between thoughts and experiential conceptualizations (...) [which] allow the reader to *experience* the narrated reality through the eyes of the narrating Ego... The fictive vision here is a simulation of experiential on-line conceptualization (as opposed to stable categorization)". As Dancygier points out, the progressive is one of the grammatical means that can help to implement this experiential viewpoint (cf. her example on p. 104: *We were shrinking; at the rate I was going* ...). Techniques like these contribute to one of the main characteristics of narratives, namely their "experientiality", as Garrod and Emmott (2012: 6) call it: "the importance of embodiment and emotion as a basis for experiencing narrative". Chafe (2010: 54) contrasts displaced and immediate consciousness. The first type is often discontinuous (island-like), with low resolution (attenuated detail) and distal (there, then), the second is continuous, with high resolution (granularity) and proximal. We are not claiming that MacWhinney, Dancygier, and Chafe are aiming at exactly the same concepts and distinctions, but, in our view, they come close to each other. In particular the notions of enactive mode, on-line experience, and immediate consciousness are meant to capture a type of perspective where the viewer is "in the middle of" the viewed situation, which then becomes involved, direct experience.

1 Sheets-Johnstone (2009: 34) points out that a similar kind of experience can occur in dance. She calls it "thinking in movement", which is "an experience in which all movements blend into an ongoing kinetic happening; a singular kinetic density evolves. (...) My experience of an ongoing present exists only in virtue of an immediate moment, that is, the actual here-now creating of this gesture or movement".

3 Perspective in Japanese

3.1 Subjective construal in Japanese

In section 2.1, we have pointed out that different historical periods have different literary preferences for certain types of perspectives (interventions with explicit narrator perspective in the 19th century, mixed point of view in free indirect discourse in the 20th century). Perspectival preferences seem to exist between different cultures as well. As has been argued by Japanese scholars in particular, Japanese narrative shows a preference for a type of perspective that comes close to what has been characterized above as enactive perspective, narrating on-line experience, and immediate consciousness.

Starting from Langacker's notion of subjective construal, Yoshihiko Ikegami has explored this Japanese preference (Ikegami 2005, 2008). In Ikegami (2008: 230), for example, he characterizes it as follows: "The maximally subjective construal is one in which the conceptualizer is totally embedded in the environment which s/he is to construe and encode. In other words, the conceptualizer is on the very scene, verbalizing what s/he directly perceives and experiences". Another term Ikegami uses for this specific perspectival arrangement is "subject-object merger" (p. 239).

Ikegami and other authors (for example Maynard 2002; Ide and Uemo 2011) link this preference for subjective construal to other preferences in Japanese culture. One of these preferences is associated with the notion of *ba*, which means 'field' or 'context' (cf. Ide and Ueno 2011: 458 ff.; Maynard 2002: Ch. 4) and which indicates that the individual should make a coherent whole with the context. There are two other notions that have to do with the relation between individual and context. The first one is *wakimae* (cf. Ide & Ueno 2011; Ide 2012), which indicates the position of the self in the contextual relation with others. The other is *mono no aware*, 'the sense of things', the emotion one feels for things and the awareness of their temporal existence, which often leads to sadness and melancholy (cf. Maynard 2002). The combination of *wakimae* and *mono no aware* characterizes a situation in which someone is coherently and emotionally connected with the environment.

Reflections of these social-cognitive characteristics of Japanese culture can be found in Japanese art. As Ikegami (2008: 240) points out: "the technique of 'perspective' was generally not practiced in Japanese painting until its introduction from the West". Similarly, reflections of this ethos can be found in the language. Ide (2012: 121) points out that "the Japanese language has abundant modal expressions from the morpheme level to the discourse level that index the context in order to show the speaker's attitude toward the contextual elements involved". The sensitivity to context also shows up in politeness phenomena and in particles that indicate awareness of "territories of knowledge" (cf. Hayano 2013). The recurring theme is that subjects of conception are embedded in the context and that this implies a non-distanced perspective.

Another linguistic phenomenon which can be interpreted from the perspective of embeddedness in the context and avoiding a distanced perspective is that of pro-drop. Japanese is a pro-drop language, which means that pronouns, in particular subject pronouns, referring to referents that can be inferred from the context, can be left out. This property occurs in other languages as well. Generally, linguistic theory assumes that sentences with and without explicit pronouns have the same meaning. In their experimental work, Sato and Bergen (2013) have shown that for Japanese speakers this meaning equivalence indeed holds on the level of pure propositional content. But when it comes to perspective, they found that utterances without pronouns lead to "viewpoint-invariant representations" (p. 372), The specific meaning of such viewpoint-invariant, pronoun-less utterances fits the characterization of the Japanese subjective construal as given by Ikegami (cf. also Uehara 2006, 2011).

3.2 A possible explanation for the Japanese construal preference

There is an increasing body of research showing that Japanese language and culture display construal preferences that are different from Western preferences. Often, this difference is attributed to the difference between "East Asians" and "Westerners", as is done in Nisbett and Masuda (2003: 11169): "We have shown that East Asians attend to the field more than do Westerners and that Westerners pay more attention to focal objects". However, Tajima and Duffield (2012: 706) provide evidence for their claim that "the notion of a homogeneous Asian culture, and a concomitant uniform Asian bias, is too wide-sweeping a construct to explain observed cultural variation... Japanese speakers attend more to the Ground, primarily because they *need* to do so in Thinking for Speaking: because they are speakers of Japanese, not because they are Asian".

One does not have to go with this Neo-Whorfian view of Tajima and Duffield to accept their finding that the *Chinese* subjects who participated in their experiments attended more to the Figure, like the English (UK) speakers. Unfortunately, they do not make explicit which part of China their Chinese subjects come from. Region might, however, be an important variable. Talhelm et al. (2014: 607) claim that the main regional difference is that between rice and wheat agriculture: "This study shows that China's wheat and rice regions have different cultures. China's rice regions have several markers of East Asian culture: more holistic thought, more interdependent self-construals, and lower divorce rates. The wheat-growing north looked more culturally similar to the West, with more analytic thought, individualism, and divorce". In their view, collectivism and attention to the ground has its primary explanation in a type of agriculture that requires collaboration, implying more holistic thinking. Now, if we may link "collectivism" with a psychological tendency to pay strong attention to the context, then we have the start of an answer why Japanese people (and, expectedly, other rice-growing cultures) have a strong preference for a perspective in which the perceiver is embedded in the context.

4 Perspectives in translation

If, as we have suggested before, languages and cultures differ in their preferences for perspective taking, then this will lead to challenges for the translator. Bernaerts et al. (2014: 204) point out that "narrative theorists often assume that, even though the act of translation is never neutral and may involve significant alterations (...), the translation process does not affect the narrative structure of texts". By "narrative structure", they mean "place and time, perspective and narrative voice". They argue, however, that these aspects *are* affected, without getting sufficient attention in the translation process. Empirical research is scarce, but there are a few studies, which we will summarize here.

Data-Bukowska (2007: 308) analyzed translations from Swedish into Polish and found that "in Swedish conceptualizations... the reality described in the story is seen from afar and it presupposes a distant vantage point. By contrast, in Polish it is consistently brought closer. These ways of viewing reality seem to be encoded within the two languages". This difference results in the choice of demonstrative pronouns and specificity of verbs. For example, the Swedish verb *dra* 'pull' corresponds to a variety of more specific Polish verbs, implying a higher granularity.

Tabakowska (2014) analyzed translations of *Alice in Wonderland* into Polish and observed several challenges on the level of perspective. One example is the progressive which can be used for the "internal perspective" of a character, as in the opening passage of Alice: *Alice was beginning to get very tired.* Because in Polish a construction parallel to the English progressive is missing, "the Polish translations choose either the objective POV [point of view] of the narrator ... or a more subjective construal with the imperfective" (p. 111). Another example, discussed by Tabakowska, has to do with epistemic modality. English *seem* is translated with a variety of Polish epistemic adverbs like *prawdopodobnie* and *chyba*, both meaning 'probably', but conveying a subjective and objective construal respectively.

Against the background of these examples from translations between 'Western' languages, and the difference, pointed out before, between Japanese and Western preferences for perspective taking, the question is how perspective phenomena in Japanese literature are rendered in translations into Western languages like English, Dutch, and German.

In publications on subjective construal in Japanese, passages from novels by Kawabata are often given as illustrative examples. For instance, Maynard (2002: 396) compares the original and the English translation of the first sentence of *Snow Country* (1948 [1955]). The translation takes an "outside" perspective: *The train came out of the long tunnel into the snow country*, whereas a literal translation of the original would be: 'Coming out of a long tunnel at the border (of provinces), it was snow country'. Maynard comments: "The self presented in [the original] is the self who witnesses what happens in the context of a locale, a place, and describes it from a personal perspective. ... The English translation takes the 'agent-does' structure; the 'train' as an agent of action (i.e., came out) surfaces, although in the original Japanese, there is no mention of it [the train]". In the Japanese text "this self is the 'feeling self' who describes the event on the basis of one's personal experience, from a personal point of view".

In a similar vein, Ide and Ueno (2011: 440) analyze a passage from *The Izu Dancer* (1926). Two girls observe a passing boy and the one girl whispers to the other girl, in a respectful manner: *He is a high school boy*, as the English translation says. In the Japanese original, there is no subject or copula, the phrase *high school boy* is accompanied by the honorific form –*san* and the utterance contains the final particle *yo*. With this type of utterance "Japanese speakers ... situate themselves in the context while speaking, whereas English speakers take an objective perspective on the speech event". One could comment that the translations are of low quality, but both novels were translated by Edward Seidensticker (1921–2007), well known for his landmark translations of Yasunari Kawabata.[2]

Inspired by these examples, we would like to explore this topic further by comparing passages from another novel by Kawabata, namely *Utsukushisa to Kanashimi to*, *Beauty and Sadness*, from 1964, with its translations into English, Dutch and German.

2 http://en.wikipedia.org/wiki/Edward_Seidensticker

5 The analyzed text and its author

5.1 Yasunari Kawabata (1899–1972)

Ikegami (2008: 239–240) points out that Kawabata explicitly positioned himself as a "neo-subjectivist" writer, in opposition to the naturalistic approach in literature. Kawabata (1925) states that there are three possible types of construal in describing a lily: (i) 'I am inside the lily', (ii) 'The lily is inside me', and (iii) 'The lily and I exist independently of each other'. According to Kawabata, and Ikegami, there is ultimately no difference between (i) and (ii). They involve a merger between subject and object, which is typical for the Japanese type of subjective construal, which Kawabata advocates in his neo-subjectivist approach to writing.

In Kawabata's own view, the neo-subjectivist approach of literature fits Japanese culture. In his Nobel Prize address (1968), he reflects on qualities of the wisteria plant: "Disappearing and then appearing again in the early summer greenery, they have in them that feeling for the poignant beauty of things long characterized by the Japanese as *mono no aware*". The title of the novel he wrote four years earlier, *Beauty and Sadness*, also expresses this feeling of "poignant beauty."[3]

5.2 *Beauty and Sadness*

In chapter 1, the main character Oki Toshio travels by train from Tokyo to Kyoto on the 29th of December. The official goal of Oki's trip is to hear the New Year's Eve bells in Kyoto (that is what he told his wife and son), but his personal, and rather primary goal, is seeing Otoko again. Otoko is the woman he had an affair with 24 years ago, when she was 15 and he was 30 and married (16 and 31 in the Dutch translation). Otoko got pregnant, the baby was born prematurely and died soon after birth. Otoko never married, probably because of this scandalous affair in her youth and moved from Tokyo to Kyoto. After his arrival in Kyoto, Oki goes

---

3 In fact, instead of speaking of "the feeling of poignant beauty", singular, it might be better to speak of feelings in the plural, as it is a typical case of mixed emotions. Research on mixed emotions is a growing field in psychology, cf. Larsen and McGraw (2014: 263), who point out that there is "a growing body of evidence that people can feel happy and sad at the same time while watching films, listening to music, and experiencing meaningful endings. We also review evidence that people sometimes experience other types of mixed emotions, including disgust accompanied by amusement and fear by enjoyment".

to his hotel and makes a telephone call to Otoko. She agrees to meet him on New Year's Eve, to hear the bells together. Oki had hoped to spend the evening alone with Otoko, but she organized company, a protégée of Otoko and two geisha's.

We focus here on the first four paragraphs of the novel. Below, the English translation is copied, divided up in fragments, mostly consisting of sentences, numbered 'S1' to 'S13'.

S1. Five swivel chairs were ranged along the other side of the observation car of the Kyoto express. Oki Toshio noticed that the one on the end was quietly revolving with the movement of the train. **S2.** He could not take his eyes from it. **S3.** The low armchairs on his side of the car did not swivel.

S4. Oki was alone in the observation car. **S5.** Slouched deep in his armchair, he watched the end chair turn. **S6.** Not that it kept turning in the same direction, at the same speed: **S7.** sometimes it went a little faster, or a little slower, or even stopped and began turning in the opposite direction. **S8.** To look at that one revolving chair, wheeling before him in the empty car, made him feel lonely. Thoughts of the past began flickering through his mind.

S9. It was the twenty-ninth of December. **S10.** Oki was going to Kyoto to hear the New Year's Eve Bells.

S11. For how many years had he heard the tolling of those bells over the radio? **S12.** How long ago had the broadcast begun? **S13.** Probably he had listened to them every year since then.

6 Comparison of the Japanese, English, German, and Dutch versions

In this section, we will have a closer look at most of the first thirteen sentences, presenting the original version in transliterated form, accompanied by English glosses and followed by the translations in English, German, and Dutch.

First paragraph

(1) *Tōkaidō-sen, tokubetsu-kyūkō-ressha“hato” no tenbōsha ni wa*
Tokaido-line special-express train “Hato” GEN observation car LOC TOP
katagawa no madogiwa ni sotte, itsutsu no kaitenisu ga
one.side GEN side.of.the.window LOC along five GEN swivel.chair NOM
naran-deiru, sono hashi no hitotsu dake ga, ressha no ugoki ni
be.arranged-ASP that edge GEN one only NOM train GEN movement LOC
tsurete, hitorideni sizukani mawat-teiru-no-ni, Oki wa kizui-ta
following by.itself quietly swivel-ASP-NMLZ-LOC Oki TOP notice-PAST

E: Five swivel chairs were ranged along the other side of the observation car of the Kyoto express. Oki Toshio noticed that the one on the end was quietly revolving with the movement of the train.
G: Im Aussichtswagen des Expresszuges >>Hato<< der Tokaido-Linie standen an einer Fensterseite fünf Drehsessel in einer Reihe. Toshio Oki bemerkte, dass sich der letzte Sessel in dieser Reihe durch die Bewegungen des Zuges geräuschlos hin- und herdrehte.
D: Vijf draaistoelen stonden op een rij langs het raam in het panoramarijtuig van de Hato-expres op de Tokado-lijn. Het viel Toshio Oki op dat alleen de verste rustig ronddraaide op het ritme van de trein.

Our first observation has to do with the order in which the Figure, the five chairs, and the Ground, the observation car, are presented. The Japanese version displays the Ground-Figure order, in accordance with the preference that Tajima and Duffield (2012) pointed out: first the context, then the Figure. Starting with the Ground and then zooming in on the Figure fits the Japanese preference for taking the whole situation into perspective and situating the Figure in this context. In the English and Dutch translation, this order is reversed, but the German version follows the Japanese order. German is known for its flexibility regarding the constituents that can be put in the initial position; it is even more flexible than Dutch, which might explain the choice that the translator has made for German. With this choice, the translator stays closer to the Japanese way of portraying the situation.

If we turn to perspective now, we observe that in the Japanese original, the sentence ends with *Oki wa kizui-ta* ‘Oki noticed’, which places the foregoing content in Oki’s perspective. The reader thus receives this perspectival information only after the content itself. In all three translations, the sentence is split up in two. In the first sentence, the arrangement of the five swivel chairs in the observation car is described from a neutral narrator perspective. At the beginning of the second sentence, Oki’s perspective is introduced (*Oki Toshio noticed, Toshio*

Oki bemerkte, Het viel Toshio Oki op). Probably, this leads the reader to incorporate, in retrospect, what has been described in the first sentence into Oki's perspective. A foreshadowing of this incorporation-in-retrospect can be seen in the English version, which has *on the other side* in the first sentence, which implicitly already evokes a vantage point which is situated "on this side". The other versions, including the original, present the placement of the chairs from a neutral perspective: *katagawa* 'one side', *an einer Fensterseite* 'at one window side', *op een rij langs het raam* 'at a row along the window'. Only later is the personalized perspective of Oki introduced.

Already in this first fragment, we have observed a subtle interplay between the perspectives of the narrator and the character. The two perspectives are distinguishable but smoothly merge and separate.

(2) sore *ni* *me* *o* *hika-reru-to* *hanase-nakat-ta.*
it DIR eye ACC attract-PASS-as depart-NEG-PAST

E: He could not take his eyes from it.
G: Er starrte gebannt darauf.
D: Nu dit zijn aandacht had getrokken, kon hij er zijn ogen niet meer van afhouden.

In the Japanese original of S2, the observed situation (represented by the pronoun *sore*) is the point of departure of the sentence. From there, the attention of the reader moves to the fascination in the eye and mind of Oki. The same "direction" is taken in the Dutch translation (with the pronoun *dit* 'this'), whereas the English and German translations depart from Oki. It is hard to decide which of the two perspectives is the more subjective one. The English and German versions are ambiguous: on the one hand, they allow a separate narrator's perspective, observing Oki and seeing that he is fascinated and keeps on looking at the one revolving chair. The alternative interpretation is that starting with *he/er* allows the reader to take Oki's perspective directly and follow the fascination from his eyes to the situation. The German verb *starren* 'stare' captures the fascinated view early on in the sentence in a compact way. The Japanese and Dutch versions proceed stepwise, from the observed situation to the more subjective perceptual process itself, stating that Oki could not give up his involved perception.

(3) *Oki no koshikake-teiru-gawa no hikui hijikakeisu wa ugoka-nu-mono*
Oki GEN sit-ASP-side GEN low arm.chair TOP move-NEG-NMLZ
de korera wa mochiron kaiten deki-nai.
as these TOP certainly swivel can.do-NEG

E: The low armchairs on his side of the car did not swivel.
G: Die niedrigen Sitze mit Armlehne auf der Seite, wo er saß, waren fest und unbeweglich.
D: De lage armstoelen aan Oki's kant zaten vast, en konden *uiteraard* niet om hun as draaien.

The aspect we want to comment upon in this sentence is the modal adverb *mochiron* 'certainly' in the Japanese version, translated in Dutch as *uiteraard*, 'of course, as everybody will understand'. Note that an equivalent of this modal meaning is totally lacking in the English and German versions.

In section 2.1, we referred to Eckardt (2012: 110), who pointed out that a marker of uncertainty "often only makes sense for a protagonist, not for the narrator. Hence, *wohl* can be a reliable clue for a shift in context". In a footnote, Eckardt notes that narrators too can indicate their uncertainty, although this is rather exceptional. In the present text, we have a marker of *certainty*. To whom should this be ascribed? Is it the narrator who indicates that the non-swiveling property of the chairs is evident or is it rather to be ascribed to Oki, meaning that he realizes that the chairs on his side are fixed?

Mochiron and *uiteraard* evoke an implicit dialogic, intersubjective context for the actual utterance (cf. Engberg-Pedersen & Boeg Thomsen, this volume, on dialogue particles). The possibility of the alternative (swiveling chairs) is evoked as a possible option, proposed by another voice and then strongly rejected. But who, then, is the other voice in the dialogue? If the modal marker is ascribed to the narrator, then the reader comes into the picture as the partner addressed. In this interpretation, we have to do with an "intrusive narrator", commenting on the observation of the non-swiveling and sharing it with the reader, who is treated as someone who has the same knowledge about chairs in Japanese observation cars. Nuyts (2012) would call this "intersubjective modality", where the attitude of certainty is shared (between the narrator and the reader). An extra effect that occurs under this interpretation is that of taking a certain distance from the character: we, the narrator and the reader, see poor Oki, sitting in his chair, "stuck", as his chair can't move.

The alternative interpretation would be that the modal certainty is ascribed to Oki and only to Oki. In that case, we have a strong subjective perspective. An inner dialogue of Oki is suggested, wherein he talks to himself. In the end Oki realizes that he is "stuck", as his type of chair is not of the moving type.

We find it hard to reach a final decision about which interpretation is the right one. Given the fact that Japanese, and Kawabata in particular, opts for a subjective perspective, Japanese *mochiron* can very well be interpreted as a means to intensify Oki's subjective perspective ('I am stuck, no doubt about it'). Dutch *uiteraard* is a rather formal word, which invites the ascription to the narrator. The ascription problem might have been the reason for the English and German translators simply to neglect the modal marker.

Second paragraph

(4)	*tenbōsha*	*ni*	*Oki*	*hitoride*	*at-ta.*
	observation.car	LOC	Oki	alone	be-PAST

E: Oki was alone in the observation car.
G: Oki war der einzige Reisende im Aussichtswagen.
D: Oki was de enige passagier in de wagen.

Note first that in the Japanese original the order is again Ground-Figure, whereas all three translations take the reverse order. With regard to perspective, it can be observed that German and Dutch use the predicate *Reisende, passagier* 'passenger', which rather suggests an objective, outside perspective, as if someone counted the number of passengers, with the outcome "one". Japanese *hitoride* and English *alone* can also mean 'feeling alone', which makes the text more ambiguous. Besides the narrator's perspective, Oki's feelings or even his perspective come into the picture. If we accept both perspectives holding at the same time, then we have a case of mixed perspectives here.

(5) *Oki wa hijikakeisu ni fukaku motare-te, mukō-gawa no*
Oki TOP arm.chair LOC deep lean-CONJP over.there-side GEN
kaitenisu no hitotsu ga mawaru-no o nagame-tei-ta.
swivel.chair GEN one NOM swivel-NMLZ ACC observe-ASP-PAST

E: Slouched deep in his armchair, he watched the end chair turn.
G: Tief in seinem Sitz zurückgelehnt, beobachtete er den sich hin-und herdrehenden Sessel *auf der anderen Seite.*
D: Diep achterovergeleund staarde hij naar die ene stoel *aan de overkant.*

S5 has two parts. In the first clause, it is observed that Oki is slouched deep in his armchair. This evokes primarily the narrator's perspective. But in the second clause, the perspective switches to Oki's, who observes the turning of the chair. Note that the Japanese, German and Dutch versions refer to 'the other side', which had been done in the English version already in S1. This 'other side' phrasing strengthens the subjective perspective. We conclude that in all four versions the two perspectives easily flow from one to the other.

(6) *kimatta hōhō-ni kimatta sokudo de mawat-teiru to*
fixed direction-DIR fixed speed at turn-ASP QUOTE
iu-no-de-wa nakat-ta.
say-NMLZ-CONJP-TOP non.existent-PAST

E: *Not that* it kept turning in the same direction, at the same speed:
G: *Nicht dass* dieser sich immer in dieselbe Richtung mit immer derselben Geschwindigkeit bewegte,
D: Hij draaide niet in een bepaalde richting of met een constante snelheid.

In the Dutch translation, there is no main clause–subordinate clause division, and the negation is simply embedded in the one main clause. The English and German versions have a special construction here: *not that* ..., with an elliptical main clause containing a negation, and an embedded clause without negation. It seems that in Japanese, the construction is similar in this respect: there is a main clause at the end, *iu-no-de-wa nakka-ta*, with a negation in *nakat*. Dancygier (2012b) discusses the neg-raising controversy and claims that the presence of negation in an embedding main clause often relates to an epistemic stance. This seems to be the case here too. The Japanese, English and German versions suggest a deliberating subject, who wonders why the chair is not simply swiveling in one and the same direction and at the same speed. This inner dialogue can be seen as a mixing of points of view within one person. In the Dutch version, the construction is not subjective; the observation of the varying swiveling could as well be ascribed to the narrator, although in the context of the previous sentence, the ascription to the protagonist is the more plausible one. One could say that the ascription to Oki is more strongly prompted by the construction in Japanese, English and German, while it is left to the reader in the Dutch version.

(7) *sukoshi hayaku nat-tari, yuruyakani nat-tari, tokidoki*
little fast become-and slow become-and sometimes
tomat-tari, mata gyaku no hō e mawaru-koto mo at-ta.
stop-and again opposite GEN direction DIR turn-NMLZ too be-PAST

E: Sometimes it went a little faster, or a little slower, or even stopped and began turning in the opposite direction.
G: Er drehte sich mal etwas schneller, mal etwas langsamer, stand zuweilen still und schwenkte dann wieder in die entgegengesetzte Richtung.
D: Nu eens ging hij snel, dan wat trager, en soms stopte hij eventjes, om vervolgens weer de tegengestelde richting uit te gaan.

In S7, the swiveling movements of the chair are observed in on-line sequential detail, with high resolution. According to Chafe (2010: 54), such passages evoke "immediate consciousness", this time Oki's. We see no differences between the four languages here. This immediate consciousness of the details in the movement easily affects the inner motions of the perceiver, and that is indeed what happens in the next passage.

(8)

tonikaku	*shikashi*	*kyakusha*	*ni*	*Oki*	*hitori-dake*	*no*	*mae*	*de,*
anyway	but	passenger.car	LOC	Oki	alone-only	GEN	front	at

kaitenisu	*no*	*hitotsu-dake*	*ga*	*hitorideni*	*mawaru-no*	*o*
swivel.chair	GEN	one-only	NOM	by.itself	turn-NMLZ	ACC

mi-teiru-no	*wa,*	*Oki*	*no*	*kokoro*	*no*	*uchi*	*no*	*sabishisa*
see-ASP-NMLZ	TOP	Oki	GEN	heart	GEN	inside	GEN	loneliness

o	*sasoi-dashi,*	*ironna*	*omoi*	*o*	*yurameka-se-ta*
ACC	invite-begin	various	thought	ACC	flicker-CAUS-PAST

E: To look at that one revolving chair, wheeling before him in the empty car, made him feel lonely. Thoughts of the past began flickering through his mind.
G: Der Anblick dieses einen sich im Aussichtswagen hin-und herdrehenden Sessels weckte ein Gefühl der Einsamkeit in ihm. Die verschiedensten Gedanken gingen ihm durch den Kopf.
D: *Hoe dan ook*, het tafereel van de stoel die als enige rondtolde in het bijzijn van één enkele passagier, deed Oki in eenzame gedachten verzinken.

As opposed to S7, S8 shows differences between the four versions. In the Japanese and Dutch versions, the sentence starts with a marker which is absent in the English and German versions. In Japanese, it is *tonikaku shikasi*, in Dutch *hoe dan ook*, 'however that may be, anyway', marking a rather abrupt transition, in this case from describing the swiveling of the chair to the feelings of Oki caused by it. Such discourse markers are typical for a narrator's voice, but what precedes and what follows the discourse marker represents content from Oki's perspective. The sentence is about Oki's attention, which shifts from his outward oriented observation to his inside feeling. There is a natural connection between the two, as the observed swiveling chair evokes the lonely feeling. Connections between observation and feeling are a favorite "topos" in Japanese literature, and in the translations, the link does not look strange either. So maybe the right interpretation of the discourse markers in the Japanese and Dutch versions is that they are meant to indicate Oki's rather sudden realization that he feels lonely. However, Dutch *hoe dan ook* sounds rather formal, and the same holds for *uiteraard* in S3. Whereas the English and German translators decided to leave out a direct translation in both cases, the Dutch translator tried to stay close to the original, with a non-optimal result.

Third paragraph

(9) *kure* *no* *nijuku-nichi* *de* *ar-u.*
year.end. GEN twenty.nine-day LOC be-PRES

E: It was the twenty-ninth of December.
G: Es war der 29. Dezember.
D: Het was 29 december.

(10) *Oki* *wa* *Kyoto* *e* *joya* *no* *kane* *o* *kiki-ni*
Oki TOP Kyoto DIR New.Year's.Eve GEN bell ACC listen.to-PURPOSE
iku-nodat-ta.
go-EXPLAIN-PAST

E: Oki was going to Kyoto to hear the New Year's Eve bells.
G: Oki war auf dem Weg nach Kyoto, um dort das Neujahrglockenläuten mitzuerleben.
D: Oki was op weg naar Kyoto, om er te luisteren naar de nieuwjaarsklokken van de tempels.

The second paragraph ends in a very subjective way: Oki's feeling of loneliness, strengthened by the one revolving chair, whirling up memories of the past. In contrast to this, the third paragraph strikes the reader as a sharp break, back to the perspective of the narrator, who gives some background information on time and place. This information sounds "objective", but in fact, both time and place are strongly loaded with emotion: the change of place from Tokyo, where Oki's family resides, to Kyoto, where Otoko lives. And New Year's Eve has a strong emotional meaning for Oki, as the next paragraph makes clear. From the narrator's objective informational perspective in the present paragraph, there is a shift to a mixed perspective in the next paragraph.

Paragraph 4

(11) *Oki* *ga* *ōmisoka* *no* *yoru* *rajio* *de* *joya* *no* *kane*
Oki NOM Silvester GEN night radio LOC New.Year's.Eve GEN bell
o *kiku* *narawashi* *wa* *mō* *ikunen*
ACC listen.to custom TOP already many.years
tuzui-ta-daro-ka
continue-PAST-ASSUM-QUEST

E: For how many years had he heard the tolling of those bells over the radio?
G: Wie viele Jahre mochte er es *wohl schon* in der Silvesternacht im Radio gehört haben?
D: Hoe lang had hij *nu al* de gewoonte om op oudejaarsavond via de radio naar het luiden van de klokken te luisteren?

(12) *kono hōsō ga nannen-mae kara hajimat-ta-ka*
this broadcast NOM how.many.years-before from begin-PAST-QUEST
osorakuwa sore irai, kakasazuni
probably that since continuously
kii-ta-no-de-wa-nakaro-ka
listen.to-PAST-NMLZ-CONJP-TOP-ASSUM-QUEST

E: How long ago had the broadcast begun? *Probably* he had listened to them every year since then, ...
G: Wie viel Jahre gab es diese Sendung schon? Hatte er überhaupt je versäumt, sie zu hören?
D: De uitzending ervan was jaren geleden begonnen, en *ongetwijfeld* had hij er sindsdien geen enkele gemist.

(13) *Nihon no achirakochira no furudera no meisho no oto*
Japan GEN here.and.there GEN old.temple GEN attraction GEN
o kiki-nagara, anaunsā no kaisetu ga kuwawar-u.
ACC listen.to-as announcer GEN commentary NOM be.added-PRES

E: ... and to the commentary by various announcers, as they picked up the sound of famous old bells from temples all around the country.
G: Während das Geläut berühmter Glocken alter Tempel aus allen Teilen Japans erklang, sprach der Ansager seinen Kommentar.
D: Men liet het gelui van beroemde oude tempelklokken van over heel Japan horen, voorzien van enige toelichting door verslaggevers.

S11, 12, and 13
These sentences represent free indirect discourse, the paradigmatic case of mixed point of view in narrative discourse. One indication can be found in the Dutch translation of S11, where *nu* 'now' is combined with past tense *had* 'had' (cf. Nikiforidou 2012). S11, 12, 13 present in more detail the 'thoughts of the past', which were indicated already in S9. Oki is not sure about the number of years he has listened to the bells over the radio. The questions in S11 and 12 represent a clear example of "inner dialogue in which self-knowledge is achieved through the

posing of questions, to which answers are provided" (Pascual 2014: 6, referring to the ideas of Bakhtin). In S11, the Japanese particle *mō* 'already, by this time', German *wohl schon*, and Dutch *nu al* contribute to the subjective perspective (cf. Eckardt 2012). The prototypical epistemic marker *probably* in S12 also indicates a subjective perspective. It is remarkable that the Dutch version has *ongetwijfeld* 'without doubt' here. We have no idea why the translator shifted the modality, but it is quite possible to interpret it from Oki's perspective as an answer to his self-question about whether there had been a year when he had missed the broadcast. His answer is "certainly not".

7 Conclusion

The opening fragment of *Beauty and Sadness* is full of motion and emotion. The time moves to a new year, the train moves from one city to another, Oki leaves his family behind and looks forward to seeing his lover again, his thoughts move to memories of the past. The perspective is also "floating". We as readers look with the narrator at Oki. Oki looks at the revolving chair. But the narrator's perspective easily merges with Oki's, and the perceived object, the revolving chair, easily merges with Oki's revolving feelings and memories. The smooth transitions and mergers can be interpreted as an implementation of Kawabata's intention to write in a subjectivist way.

We had expected to find a uniform pattern in which the Japanese text differs in a systematic way from its European translations. Besides finding some support for the expected Japanese preferences (Ground-Figure presentation, subjective perspective), we also found quite a lot of variation in the translations. Aspects of perspective and subjectivity varied quite a lot between the different versions. The least we can say is that the translators seem to have had some problems with finding the right perspective and degree of subjectivity and intersubjectivity. In general, perspective is an aspect of a literary text that provides a challenge for translators, but this challenge is even greater when it comes to (certain) Japanese texts, as we hope to have shown.

Perspective is primarily a cognitive dimension, but we have seen that linguistic cues of different kinds (adverbs, pragmatic markers, constructions) play a role in guiding the perspective in the direction of the narrator or the character, or into a mix of these two perspectives. We hope that linguistic analyses of perspective phenomena will find their way into translation training programs and yield more consistent translations.

Besides the practical use of studies like the present one, we agree with Chafe (2010: 52) when he suggests that "studying the language of literature should be seen not only as a valid branch of linguistics, but as having the potential to shed unique light on the nature of human consciousness and thought." Studying the *translation* of literature can add another dimension to this potential in that it shows us that human consciousness and thought has cultural specific preferences. These preferences also show in perspective taking. Realizing this can contribute to a stronger awareness of what is involved in intercultural communication.

Acknowledgements

We thank the editors of this volume and two anonymous reviewers for their constructive feedback. We also thank the participants of the theme session Linguistic Manifestations of Mixed Points of View in Narratives at the ICLC12 conference in Edmonton (June 26–27, 2013), where we presented an earlier version of this paper.

References

Bernaerts, Lars, Liesbeth De Bleeker, & July De Wilde. 2014. Narration and translation. *Language and Literature* 23(3). 203–212.

Catton, Eleanor. 2013. *The luminaries*. London: Granta.

Chafe, Wallace. 2010. Literature as a window to the mind. *Acta Linguistica Hafniensia* 42(1). 51–63.

Cui, Yaxiao. 2014. Parentheticals and the presentation of multipersonal consciousness: A stylistic analysis of *Mrs Dalloway*. *Language and Literature* 23(2). 175–187.

Dancygier, Barbara. 2012a. *The language of stories. A cognitive approach.* Cambridge: Cambridge University Press.

Dancygier, Barbara. 2012b. Negation, stance verbs, and intersubjectivity. In: Barbara Dancygier & Eve Sweetser (eds.), *Viewpoint in language. A multimodal perspective.* Cambridge: Cambridge University Press. 69–93.

Data-Bukowska, Ewa. 2007. The world from afar – the world in close-up. Some thoughts on manifestations of viewing in translations of Swedish texts into Polish. In: Władysław Chłopicki, Andrzej Pawelec & Agnieszka Pokojska (eds.), *Cognition in language. Volume in honour of Professor Elżbieta Tabakowska*. Kraków: Tertium. 290–311.

Eckardt, Regine. 2012. Particles as speaker indexicals in free indirect discourse. *Sprache und Datenverarbeitung* 35(2) & 36(1). 109–119.

Engberg-Pedersen, Elisabeth & Ditte Boeg Thomsen. This volume. The socio-cognitive foundation of Danish perspective-mixing dialogue particles.

Evans, Nicholas. 2005. View with a view: Towards a typology of multiple perspective constructions. *BLS* 31(1). 93–120.
Harris, Jesse A. and Christopher Potts. 2009. Perspective shifting with appositives and expressives. *Linguistics and Philosophy* 32(6). 523–552.
Hartner, Marcus. 2014. Multiperspectivity. In: Peter Hühn et al. (eds.), *The living handbook of narratology*. Hamburg: Hamburg University, http://www.lhn.uni-hamburg.de/article/multiperspectivity (accessed 17 August 2014).
Hayano, Kaoru. 2013. *Territories of knowledge in Japanese conversation*. PhD Nijmegen, MPI.
Ide, Sachiko. 2012. Roots of the *wakimae* aspect of linguistic politeness. Modal expressions and Japanese sense of self. In: Michael Meeuwis & Jan-Ola Östman (eds.), *Pragmaticizing understanding. Studies for Jef Verschueren*. Amsterdam: Benjamins. 121–138.
Ide, Sachiko & Kishiko Uemo. 2011. Honorifics and address terms. In Gisle Andersen & Karin Aijmer (eds.), *Pragmatics of society* (Handbook of Pragmatics 5). Berlin: de Gruyter Mouton. 439–470.
Ikegami, Yoshihiko. 2005. Indices of a subjectivity-prominent language: Between cognitive linguistics and linguistic typology. *Annual Review of Cognitive Linguistics* 3. 132–164.
Ikegami, Yoshihiko. 2008. Subjective construal as a 'fashion of speaking' in Japanese. In: María de los Ángeles Gómez Gonzaléz, J. Lachlan Mackenzie & Elsa M. González Álvare (eds.), *Current trends in contrastive linguistics. Functional and cognitive perspectives.* Amsterdam: Benjamins. 229–250.
Kawabata, Yasunari. 1925 [1999]. Shinshin sakka no shinkeiko kaisetsu. [Commentaries on the new trends of the latest authors]. In *Kawabata Yasunari Zenshu* [Collected works of Kawabata Yasunari] 30. 172–183. Tokyo: Shinchosha.
Kawabata, Yasunari. 1998. *The Izu dancer and other stories*. North Clarendon, VT: Tuttle Publishing. [Original Japanese version 1926, *Izu no odoriko*].
Kawabata, Yasunari. 1956. *Snow country*. New York: Knopf. [Original Japanese version 1948, *Yukiguni*].
Kawabata, Yasunari. 1975. *Beauty and Sadness*. London: Penguin Books. [Original Japanese version 1964, *Utsukushisa to kanashimi to*].
Kawabata, Yasunari. 1990. *Schönheit und trauer*. Munich: dtv 1990. [Original Japanese version 1964, *Utsukushisa to kanashimi to*].
Kawabata, Yasunari. 2006. *Schoonheid en verdriet*. Amsterdam: Meulenhoff. [Original Japanese version 1964, *Utsukushisa to kanashimi to*].
Kawabata, Yasunari. 1968. Nobel Lecture: "Japan, the Beautiful and Myself", http://www.nobelprize.org/nobel_prizes/literature/laureates/1968/kawabata-lecture.html.
Langacker, Ronald W. 1987. *Foundations of Cognitive Grammar, vol. 1, Theoretical prerequisites*. Stanford: Stanford University Press.
Langacker, Ronald W. 2008. *Cognitive grammar: A basic introduction*. New York: Oxford University Press.
Larsen, Jeff T. & A. Peter McGraw. 2014. The case for mixed emotions. *Social and Personality Psychology Compass* 8. 263–274.
Maynard, Senko K. 2002. *Linguistic emotivity. Centrality of place, the topic-comment dynamic, and an ideology of* pathos *in Japanese discourse*. Amsterdam: Benjamins.
MacWhinney, Brian. 2005. The emergence of grammar from perspective. In: D. Pecher & R. Zwaan (eds.), *Grounding cognition*. Cambridge: Cambridge University Press, 198–223.
Niederhoff, Burkhard. 2013. Perspective – Point of view. In: Peter Hühn, John Pier, Wolf Schmid & Jörg Schönert (eds.), *The living handbook of narratology*. Hamburg: Hamburg University,

http://www.lhn.uni-hamburg.de/article/perspective-%E2%80%93-point-view. (Accessed 17 August 2014).

Nikiforidou, Kiki. 2012. The constructional underpinnings of viewpoint blends: The Past + now in language and literature. In: B. Dancygier & E. Sweetser (eds.), *Viewpoint and perspective in language and gesture*. Cambridge: Cambridge University Press. 177–197.

Nisbett, Richard E. & Takashiko Masuda. 2003. Culture and point of view. *PNAS* 100(19). 11163–11170.

Nuyts, Jan. 2012. Notions of (inter)subjectivity. *English Text Construction* 5(1), Special issue 'Intersections of intersubjectivity'. 53–76.

Pascual, Esther. 2014. *Fictive interaction. The conversation frame in thought, language, and discourse*. Amsterdam: Benjamins.

Sanford, Anthony J. & Catherine Emmott. 2012. *Mind, brain and narrative*. Cambridge: Cambridge University Press.

Sato, Manami & Benjamin K. Bergen. 2013. The case of missing pronouns: Does mentally simulated perspective play a functional role in the comprehension of person? *Cognition* 127. 361–374.

Sheets Johnstone, Maxine. 2009. *The corporeal turn. An interdisciplinary reader*. Exeter: Imprint Academic.

Tabakowska, Elżbieta. 2014. Point of view in translation. Lewis Carroll's *Alice* in grammatical wonderlands. In: Chloe Harrison, Louise Nuttall, Peter Stockwell & Wenjuan Yuan (eds.), *Cognitive Grammar in literature*. Amsterdam: Benjamins. 101–116.

Tajima, Yajoi & Nigel Duffield. 2012. Linguistic versus cultural relativity: On Japanese-Chinese differences in picture description and recall. *Cognitive Linguistics* 23(4). 675–709.

Talhelm, T., X. Zhang, S. Oishi, C. Shimin, D. Duan, X. Lan, & S. Kitayama. 2014. Large-scale psychological differences within China explained by rice versus wheat agriculture. *Science* 344. 603–608.

Uehara, Satoshi. 2006. Internal state predicates in Japanese: A cognitive approach. In: June Luchjenbroers (ed.), *Cognitive linguistics investigations across languages, fields, and philosophical boundaries*. Amsterdam: Benjamins. 271–291.

Uehara, Satoshi. 2011. *The cognitive theory of subjectivity in a cross-linguistic perspective: Zero 1st person pronouns in English, Thai and Japanese*. Paper, ICLC11, Xi'an.

Vandelanotte, Lieven. 2009. *Speech and thought representation in English: A Cognitive-Functional approach*. Berlin: Mouton de Gruyter.

Verhagen, Arie. 2007. Construal and perspectivization. In: Dirk Geeraerts and Hubert Cuyckens (eds.), *The Oxford handbook of Cognitive Linguistics*. Oxford: Oxford University Press. 48–81.

Part III: **Across modalities**

Chie Fukada

The dynamic interplay between words and pictures in picture storybooks: How visual and verbal information interact and affect the readers' viewpoint and understanding

Abstract: Like language, visual images have a "grammar", a set of elements and rules for producing and understanding meanings when they are used in social communication (Kress and van Leewen 2006). Stories can therefore appear not only in narrative forms but also in visual forms, and their combination can afford a better understanding of the story represented. Picture storybooks present fictive worlds through this combination, but the viewpoint reflected in verbal narratives, which is relatively stable and objective (Matsuoka 1987), is not always consistent with that of the visuals, producing "mixed" points of view. However, readers can create consistent stories by employing their everyday experiences and prior knowledge to adjust these different viewpoints. The current study conducts an in-depth analysis of a picture storybook at both verbal and visual levels of representation, and discusses how the three types of viewpoints, i.e. the viewpoints in the narrative and the visuals and that of the readers, are integrated to produce a coherent story in the readers' minds. It elucidates the mechanisms of how picture storybooks prompt readers to set up, understand, and become involved in the fictive worlds expressed in them.

Note: This study is an expansion and explication of Fukada (2011). It was partially supported by the Ministry of Education, Science, Sports and Culture, Grant-in-Aid for Scientific Research (C), 2011–2014 (24520541, Kazumi Taniguchi). I would like to thank the anonymous reviewer for their comments and suggestions for improving my paper. I would also like to express my gratitude to Takatsugu Kojima, Haruhiko Yamaguchi, José Sanders, Eve Sweetser, Wei-lun Lu, Sandra Healy and Yasushi Tsubota for their insightful comments and suggestions and to Kathleen Yamane for her careful reading of my first draft. I am also indebted to Ryoma Nishizawa, Fumiko Kishimoto, Yuko Suzaki and Ami Tsukamoto for their assistance. All remaining errors are, of course, my own.

1 Introduction

Picture storybooks present fictive worlds through the interplay between two different modes of representation: visual and verbal. The readers integrate these two kinds of information into a coherent story by associating them with their own knowledge and everyday experience. Here, two questions arise: (i) In what ways do these two different sources of information merge to create a coherent story? and (ii) What kinds of words and/or pictures evoke the readers' everyday experiences and enable them to understand the story?

Although there is extensive literature on picture books in the fields of children's literature and literacy education, much of the work deals with questions of literacy such as "What ways of reading are effective for children to understand the story more deeply?" (e.g., Nakamura 1995) or "How are the verbal, visual, oral performance, and instructional cues intertwined to promote children's interpretation of the story?" (e.g., Golden and Gerber 1990). Nikolajeva and Scott (2001) provide one of the few exceptions in that their study addresses the dynamics between words and images in the genre of picture books, but their claims need to be validated or supported by experimental evidence. Another exception is the work of Johnston (2012), which contains an analysis of a picture storybook with no words. However, she mainly focuses on how the story grows out of the images.

Furthermore, a number of studies within the framework of mental spaces have provided a detailed account of our mental processes of understanding literary texts or visual information like gestures and sign language (e.g., Fauconnier and Sweetser 1996 and Dancygier and Sweetser 2012), but no research has been conducted on picture books in this field so far. As for the interplay between visual and verbal information, some studies in cognitive science and artificial intelligence have addressed the issue of how both types of information are processed and integrated in learning language (e.g., Oka et al. 2013), but very few have dealt with the dynamics of text, images and the reader's understanding process of picture books.

In this study, therefore, I conduct an in-depth and practical analysis of the picture storybook *Shiroi Usagi to Kuroi Usagi* (hereinafter, simply *Usagi*) at each level of representation, i.e. the visual and the verbal, and explore what kind of pictures and/or words affect the reader's viewpoint, understanding, or even involvement, and how they do this. Section 2 provides a brief commentary on *Usagi*, and Section 3 investigates the illustrations and text of the book in detail, revealing how they differ and how they combine. Section 4 presents an extended discussion of the results of our experimental pilot study conducted in 2013. Finally, Section 5 gives some concluding remarks and addresses remaining issues.

2 The Object of investigation: *Usagi*

The picture book treated in this study, *Usagi*, is the Japanese version of *The Rabbits' Wedding* (hereinafter, *TRW*), a popular illustrated children's book by Garth Williams published in America in 1958. The book has been read in Japan for over 50 years, and thus it has become familiar to Japanese people of many ages.[1] Matsuoka (1987: 51–56) proposes that the picture storybooks which have been read for over 25 years should be classified as outstanding (although she does not mention what characteristics those books share), and so by this standard the book *Usagi* certainly deserves deeper investigation.

Although the title is not a direct translation of *TRW* and some names of the games and plants were changed to those that Japanese readers can easily imagine, the story develops in the same way as in the original English version.[2] A synopsis of *TRW* is as follows:

> Two little rabbits, one white and the other black, played together happily in the forest. But in between the games of Hop Skip And Jump Me and Race Around The Blackberry Bush the black rabbit stopped and sighed. "I'm just thinking," he would say, when the white rabbit asked him what was the matter. But he finally admitted he was wishing – wishing that he and the white rabbit could be together forever and always. And after he had wished a little harder his wish came true.
>
> (quoted from the jacket of *TRW*)

As with the vast majority of picture books, the relationship between words and pictures is, at least at first glance, symmetrical, consonant, or complementary, although upon closer examination even books of this kind contain some interesting contrasts or discrepancies between them (see discussion in Nikolajeva and Scott 2001: 14). The next sections, in conducting an in-depth analysis of the picture book *Usagi* at both the visual and verbal levels of information, not only show such contrasts but also discuss how they are adjusted by the reader to create a coherent single story.

---

1 I am also very familiar with the book *Usagi*. When I was a child, I repeatedly read this book with my father and by myself; furthermore, I personally experienced the feeling of gradually coming to understand the feelings of the two rabbits, thus becoming more involved in this fictive world.

2 The following differences in bookmaking can also be observed between the English and Japanese versions: (i) only the English version has a double-spread title page with no picture after the flyleaf; and (ii) the closing remarks are written on the back flyleaf with no pictures in the English version, while they are incorporated into the final page of the story in the Japanese version.

3 An analysis of *Usagi*: Contrasts and harmonies between pictures and words

3.1 What the pictures represent

In this section, I analyse the pictures in *Usagi* with special attention to the colours used in this book, the size of the two characters, their facial expressions, and their eye (or face or body) orientations. Although Kress and van Leeuwen (2006) have concentrated on explicating the grammar in visual communication in

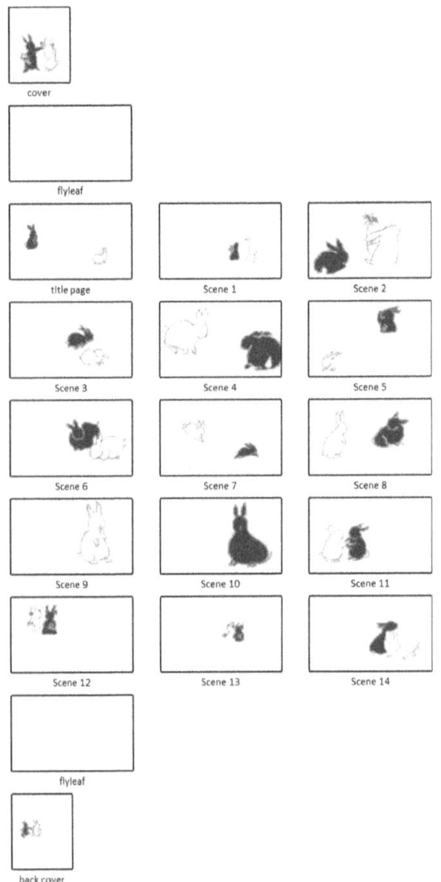

Figure 1: Line drawings of the picture storybook *Usagi*

western cultures, not in non-western cultures including Japan, and they have not dealt with the sequence of pictures in picture books, the analysis in this paper is based largely on their findings of how the depicted elements and their structures (colour, size, framing, etc.) of visual design are combined into meaningful wholes. Before analysing the pictures in *Usagi*, I will show how the story is depicted in its entirety in Figure 1. Figure 1 presents rough line drawings of the two rabbits in all of the pictures in the book *Usagi*, created for the discussion below.

3.1.1 The use of colour

The colours used in *Usagi* are white (mostly for the white rabbit), black (mostly for the black rabbit), and yellow (mostly for the background including plants). The yellow in most scenes is subdued and greenish, although a pure yellow is used for the flowers, and the background of Scene 9. Combined with the soft feel of the brush, this subdued or low-saturation colour throughout the book gives the story a tranquil, calm atmosphere. The colour can also be viewed as representing the subtle or tender characteristics of the black rabbit (see discussions in Kress and van Leeuwen 2006: 234), while the pure yellow in Scene 9 can be seen as reflecting the feeling of the white rabbit, namely a complete but delightful surprise at the words of the black rabbit.

3.1.2 Changes in the size of the characters

As shown in Figure 1, the sizes of the characters depicted change from scene to scene. The repetition of large and small sizes can be seen in the scenes leading up to the climax (i.e., Scenes 9 and 10) of the story.[3] At the climax, the two rabbits are depicted largest, and after that (more precisely, from Scenes 11 to 13) they get smaller. As Kress and van Leeuwen (2006: 124–129) argue, the choice between close-up, medium shot, long shot, etc. indicates, by analogy with everyday social interaction, the distance of the represented participants from the viewers: at intimate distance we only see the face or head of the other person, at close personal distance we see his or her head and shoulders, at far personal distance we see him or her from the waist up, at close social distance we see his or her whole figure, at far social distance we can see the whole figure with space around it, and at public

3 Strictly speaking, at the text level, the climax begins with the second dialogue between the protagonists in Scene 8 and ends in Scene 11 with the white rabbit's acceptance of the black rabbit's marriage proposal.

distance we can see his or her whole body with a lot of space around him or her. Although this distinction is not perfectly applied in the case of *Usagi* (because the protagonists are two rabbits with short legs), it can be assumed that the size of the rabbits changes the feeling of the distance between them and their readers and that this leads to a change in the readers' viewpoint and their involvement in the fictive world of the picture book. For instance, the repetition of large and small sizes of the protagonists from Scenes 1 to 8 places the readers repeatedly at the locations of "far social" and "close social", which gradually leads them into the fictive world of the two rabbits. The close-ups of each rabbit in Scenes 9 and 10 put the readers at "far personal" distance, thus involving them more deeply in this fictive world, and the diminishing sizes of the protagonists from Scenes 11 to 13 gradually change the readers' position from "close social" to "far social" and even to "public", which would detach the readers from the world of the two rabbits.

3.1.3 Facial expression and eye direction of the characters

On all pages of the picture book *Usagi*, the characters' facial expressions (and their behaviours) are illustrated in realistic detail (see Figure 2). Since we have the ability to recognize and produce current emotions through facial expressions, such detailed facial expressions of the two rabbits can draw the readers' immediate attention and allow them to imagine how each character feels.[4]

As for the gaze or face (or sometimes body) direction of the characters, Nikolajeva and Scott (2001: ch. 5) have argued that a right-looking picture of a character shows that the character is going into the next stage of the story.[5] In the picture book *Usagi*, the face (or body) direction of the characters (especially that of the black rabbit) is closely linked to the speed of the progression of the relationship between the two rabbits. For instance, in Scenes 1, 2, 3 and 7, where the black rabbit directs his eyes (Scenes 1, 2 and 7) or his body (Scene 3) to the right (i.e. the same direction of reading), the text shows that the black rabbit enjoys playing

4 It is well known that even newborn babies prefer to look at face-like configurations over non face-like ones. Snowden et al. (2012: ch.10) report that infants of 12 days old can recognize and respond to certain facial expressions and that by the first year infants can use the facial expressions of others as a guide to how one should behave in various situations.

5 Nikolajeva and Scott (2001: ch.5) also discuss the relationship between the left and the right pages in double-page spreads. They argue that the left page means "home" or "secure" while the right portrays "away" or "adventure."

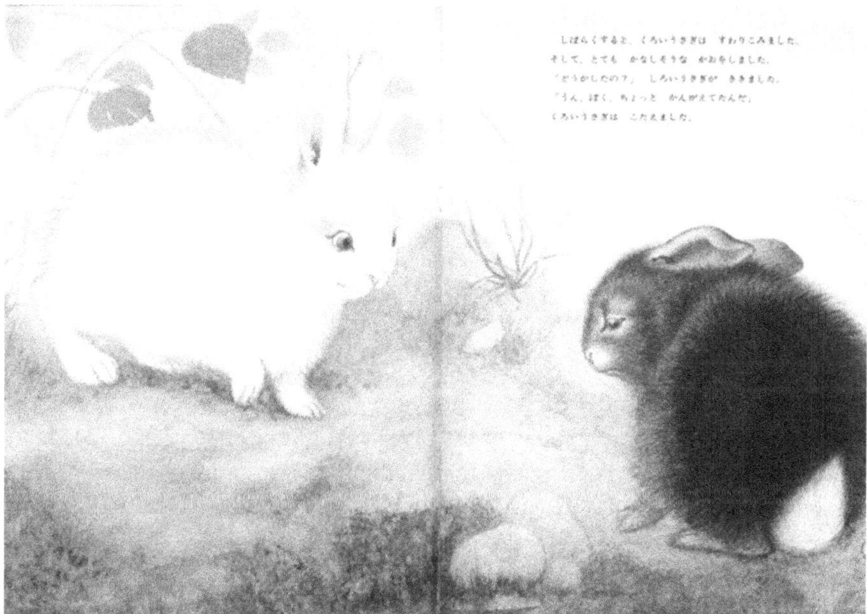

Figure 2: Scene 4 in *Usagi* (reproduced with permission)

with the white rabbit.[6] In these scenes, therefore, we can say that their relationship gradually deepens. In contrast, in Scenes 4, 5, 6 and 8, where the black rabbit directs his face or body to the left (i.e. the opposite direction of reading), the black rabbit cannot tell his wish to the white rabbit.[7] This means that their relationship does not progress in these scenes. In Scenes 9 and 10, the rabbits are shown alone in each scene for the first and only time, and this signifies a dramatic change in their relationship. As the text shows, in Scene 9 (where only the white rabbit is depicted with not only her eyes but also her face and body to the right), the white rabbit, who for the first time heard the black rabbit's wish in Scene 8, responds to his wish encouragingly, and, in Scene 10 (where only the black rabbit is illustrated with not only his eyes but also his face and body to the

6 Nikolajeva and Scott (2001: ch.5) and Johnston (2012) have pointed out that picture book readers normally "read pictures" from left to right in accordance with their western reading conventions and that picture book authors draw pictures while taking this tendency for granted.

7 A discrepancy can be found between the eye (or face) direction and the body direction in Scenes 6 and 8. In Scene 6, the black rabbit turns to the right with his body to the left, and in Scene 8 he turns to the left with his body to the right. Which of the two directions is more directly linked to the progression of the relationship between the two rabbits will be the subject of future work.

front), the black rabbit prays harder for his wish to come true. After these scenes, in Scene 11 onwards, the two rabbits are depicted close together, which signifies that the black rabbit's wish has come true. The directions of the black rabbit's face in Scenes 11 to 13 seem to suggest that the relationship between the two rabbits has become stable, because in Scenes 11 and 13 he looks to the left and in Scene 12 to the front. The illustration in Scene 14, in which the rabbits are facing to the right, shows that they have started living together in harmony in the forest into which the readers cannot set foot any longer.[8] This is more clearly shown on the back cover by the image of two rabbits walking away from the readers deeper into the forest. *Usagi*, therefore, conveys the story by effectively employing the correlations between eye (or face or body) direction of the characters, the speed of the story, and the readers' left-to-right movement across the pages.

In addition, the frontal view of the black rabbit in Scenes 10 and 12 is noteworthy. Since "the frontal angle is the angle of maximum involvement" of the viewers (Kress and van Leeuwen 2006: 145) and the gaze of the character depicted "demands something from the viewer, demands that the viewer enter into some kind of imaginary relation with him or her" (Kress and van Leeuwen 2006: 118), the frontal view of the black rabbit in these scenes, especially in Scene 10 in which the black rabbit is illustrated at the biggest size, would make the readers feel as if they were involved in the world of this picture book as participants.

3.2 What the text represents

Matsuoka (1987: 76–90), as an author, translator, and oral performer of picture books, has argued that the text of picture books is easy to understand when it contains some repetitions at regular intervals and consists of expressions from an objective point of view. In this section, therefore, I analyse the text of *Usagi* with special reference to the following expressions: (i) repetitions of a particular word/phrase/clause/paragraph; (ii) direct speech or direct quotation, which "evokes the original speech situation and conveys, or claims to convey, the exact words of the original speaker in direct discourse" (Coulmas 1986a: 2), (iii) deictic expressions like *kuru* ('come'), which are generally considered to reflect the speaker's viewpoint, and (iv) expressions which describe the characters' behaviours and/or facial expressions objectively. Expressions (i–iii) can be assumed to affect or determine the viewpoint of the readers, and expression (iv) evokes the readers' sensorimotor experience.

8 The two rabbits in Scene 14 are no longer anthropomorphic. This signifies that the two rabbits have returned to the animal kingdom which we are not allowed to enter easily.

3.2.1 Repetitions

The text of *Usagi* exhibits repetitions of a particular phrase or clause, or even a particular paragraph.[9] A paragraph similar to that shown in (1) below, for instance, appears four times in this picture book, in Scenes 4, 5, 6 and from 7 to 8, although some changes are made in the second, third, and fourth repetitions; for example, the first and second sentences are conjoined like "... suwarikonde, totemo kanashisoona kao o shimashita" ('squatted down and showed a sad face') in the second and third repetitions and "kanashisoona kao o shite, suwarikonde shimaimashita" ('showed a sad face and squatted down') in the fourth repetition; the phrase "Dooka shita no?" is changed to "Doo shita no?" in the second, third, and fourth repetitions; and the Japanese quotative marker *to* is added to the utterance of the black rabbit only in the fourth repetition.

(1) *Shibarakusuru to kuroi usagi wa suwarikomimashita.*
while.pass when black rabbit TOP squat.down.POL.PAST[10]
'After a while, the black rabbit squatted down.'
Soshite totemo kanashisoona kao o shimashita.
and very sad.look.ADN face ACC do.POL.PAST
'And he showed a very sad face.'
"Dooka shita no?" Shiroi usagi ga kikimashita.
what happen.PAST SFP white rabbit NOM ask.POL.PAST
'"What's happened?" asked the white rabbit.'
"Un boku, chotto kangaeteta n da." Kuroi usagi wa kotaemashita
mm I little think.STAT.PAST NMZ COP black rabbit TOP answer.POL.PAST
'"Mm, I'm just thinking," answered the black rabbit.' [Scene 4]

The phrase "kanashisoona kao o suru" also appears in the final scene, Scene 14, although it changes into the negative form. The form of [quoted sentence – reporting clause] in a direct quote is repeatedly used throughout the text (see also discussion of direct speech in 3.2.2), and in the conversation in Scene 11, the black rabbit repeats what the white rabbit says about their commitment to a shared

9 For more on repetitions in picture books, including *Usagi*, see also Kasanuki (2010).
10 The following abbreviations are used in the glosses: ACC = accusative, AND = adnominal, COM = complementizer, COP = copula, GEN = genitive, GER = gerundive, NEG = negative, NMZ = nominalizer, NOM = nominative, PAST = past, POL = polite, SFP = sentence-final particle, STAT = stative, TOP = topic.

future, using different intonation (shown by the different orthographical cues, "?" and "." or "!") to indicate an increasingly firm commitment. In addition, the phrase "me o manmaruku shite" ('with perfectly round eyes') appears twice, once in Scene 9 and again in Scene 10 (for more details of this expression, see Section 3.2.4), and the word "yattekuru" ('come') is used once in Scene 12 and once again in Scene 13 (see also 3.2.3 below).

Matsuoka (1987: 84–90) emphasizes that repetitions help the readers frame or set up the world described in a given narrative. Since *Usagi* shows many repetitions from the beginning of the story, it is reasonable to assume that this book makes it easy for readers to frame and understand the world of the two rabbits.

3.2.2 Direct speech

As Coulmas (1986b) and Yamaguchi (2009) have shown, the speech and thought representation (hereinafter, STR) in Japanese is quite different from that in English. Unlike English, which has several grammatically distinguishable types such as direct, indirect, and free indirect speech/thought (cf. Vandelanotte 2009), Japanese has no specialized grammatical forms which automatically distinguish direct and indirect discourse (see, for example, Yamaguchi 2009), although "there is a great variety of means indicating speaker perspective: directional and respectful or humble verbs, other lexical and morphological honorific personal pronouns, deictic demonstratives" (Coulmas 1986b: 172). In addition, Yamaguchi (2009 and personal communication) argues that the Japanese STR system reflects the reporter's psychological distance from the content of the quoted speech or even from the reported speaker rather than the difference in perspective or viewpoint. Yamaguchi (2009) has pointed out, in discussing the differences between the quotative markers *to* and *tte* in Japanese (both of which are categorized as complementizers), that while the quotative marker *to* shows a neutral attitude by the reporter toward the speech reported, *tte* indicates that the reporter is detaching himself from the quoted speech or has no empathy with the speaker. Thus, while most of the research on English STR focuses on the ways in which different viewpoints (especially the narrator's and the character's viewpoints) are expressed and mixed (see, for instance, Rubba 1996; Sanders and Redeker 1996; Dancygier 2008; Vandelanotte 2009), the research on Japanese STR should be conducted with respect to the reporter's psychological distance from the reported speech or from the reported speaker.

In *Usagi*, all of the utterances by the two main characters (22 utterances in total) are represented with quotation marks, i.e., are direct quotes, as shown in (1) above. Of these 22 utterances 5 appear with the quotative marker *to* and 17 appear with no quotative marker, neither *to* nor *tte*.[11] The fact that the quotative marker *to* is used shows that the narrator is reporting the conversations between the two rabbits as he hears them, taking and maintaining a psychologically neutral stance to the contents or even to the two rabbits. As for the direct quotes with no quotative marker in Japanese, it has not been discussed even in Coulmas (1986b) and Yamaguchi (2009), but Yamaguchi (personal communication) suggests that the form adds a rhythm to the story and lets the readers read it smoothly. It seems to me that the frequent use of direct speech with no quotative marker in *Usagi* serves to take the readers effortlessly into the world of the two rabbits. The direct quotes in *Usagi* thus not only place the readers in a position where the conversation between the two rabbits can be heard, but also allow them to adopt and maintain a psychologically neutral stance to the protagonists and their utterances.[12]

Such a position, however, does not match the position reflected in the pictures. In 3.1.2, I argued that the readers' position could be assumed to change in accordance with the change in the size of the characters depicted. Section 4 below presents an investigation of which position is predominant when reading this picture book.

The book *Usagi* employs the quotative marker *tte* only once, as seen in (2):

(2) *Sorekara* *to* *iu* *mono,* *kuroi* *usagi* *wa* *moo* *kesshite*
after.that COM say thing black rabbit TOP no.longer never
kanashisoona *kao* *o* *shimasen* *deshita* *tte.*
sad.look.ADN face ACC do.POL.NEG COP.POL.PAST COM
'And then, the black rabbit never showed a sad face, I heard.' [Scene 14]

This is the final sentence of the story. Given that *tte* shows the narrator's psychological detachment or remoteness from the content of the quoted speech, it is assumed that this *tte* serves as a prompt to make the readers detach themselves from the world of the two rabbits and return to the real world.

11 Direct speech with no quotative marker is quite common in Japanese picture books.

12 The polite form *masu* is consistently used in the narrative part of *Usagi*, and all of the verbs in the part, except *tobi-koeru* ('jump over') in Scene 3, appear in the past tense form *ta*. These facts also indicate that the narrator consistently adopts a neutral, objective stance toward the two rabbits and even the fictive world of the picture book.

3.2.3 Deictic expressions

In *Usagi*, only two deictic expressions, the demonstrative pronoun *kono* ('this') and the compound verb *yattekuru*, which consists of two verbs *yaru* ('send') and *kuru* ('come') but conveys almost the same meaning as the single verb *kuru* ('come'), appear in its narrative. These expressions indicate that the narrator's viewpoint is located close to the two rabbits. As shown in (3) and (4), both expressions are used in Scenes 12 and 13, i.e. in the scenes after the climax. Given that the direct quotes place the readers in a position where they can hear the two rabbits' conversation (see 3.2.2) and that the illustrations in the climax have the power to involve the readers in the fictive world of *Usagi* as participants (see 3.1.2 and 3.1.3), it can be reasonably assumed that readers would place themselves in the position very close to the protagonists (especially the white rabbit) in the climax and keep their position close to the protagonists after the climax. The use of the two deictic expressions in Scenes 12 and 13 is, therefore, quite natural, despite the two rabbits in the illustrations being depicted at a "far social" (Scene 12) or "public" (Scene 13) distance.

(3) *Nihiki no kono shiawasena yoosu o mini, hoka no*
two.animal GEN this happy.ADN state ACC see.to other GEN
chiisana usagi ga oozei yattekismashita
small.ADN rabbit NOM many send.come.POL.PAST
'Many little rabbits came out to see how happy these two rabbits were.'
[Scene 12, my underlining]

(4) *Mori ni sumu hoka no doobutsutachi mo dansu o*
forest in live other GEN animals also dance ACC
oozei yattekimashita.
many send.come.POL.PAST
'Other animals living in the forest also came out to see the dance'
[Scene 13, my underlining]

3.2.4 Onomatopoeia and other expressions

The text of *Usagi* describes the world of the two rabbits objectively, i.e. it mainly consists of descriptions of the actions and facial expressions of the two rabbits. The following sentence from Scene 9, for instance, perfectly describes the state of the white rabbit depicted in the picture of this scene.

(5) *Shiroi Usagi wa me o manmaruku shite jitto*
white rabbit TOP eyes ACC perfectly.round do.GER steadily
kangaemashita
think.POL.PAST
'The white rabbit steadily thought (about what the black rabbit said to her) with her eyes perfectly round.' [Scene 9]

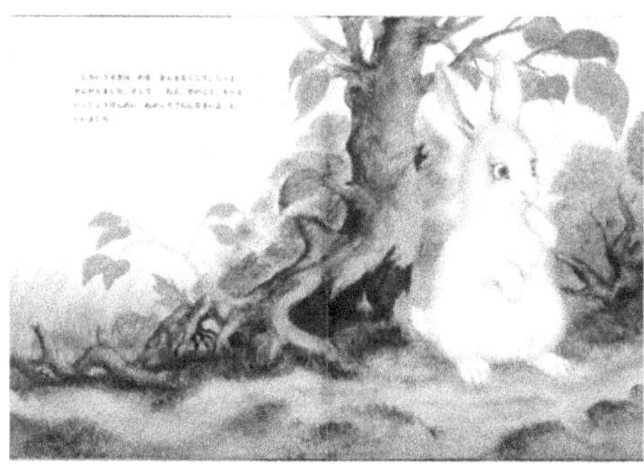

Figure 3: Scene 9 in *Usagi* (reproduced with permission)

The expression "me o manmaruku shite" completely matches the picture in this scene. The Japanese expression "me o maruku suru" (which literally means 'make one's eyes round') is commonly used as an idiom to express great surprise, and the prefix *man-* ('perfectly') attached to *maruku* stresses the magnitude of surprise. Therefore, by connecting what is said in the text and the image in Scene 9 to their own experience, the readers can easily understand how surprised the white rabbit was at what the black rabbit said to her. As for the word *jitto* (which is an example of onomatopoeia, although most Japanese people might not recognize the word as such), it shows that the white rabbit is frozen with surprise, in harmony with the picture of the white rabbit with her left hand placed in front of her mouth. Combining the text in (5) with the picture thus helps readers to understand more deeply the feelings of the white rabbit.

Onomatopoeia also serves as a prompt to arouse the reader's sensorimotor experience. As Fukada (2008) has argued, Japanese people use a variety of onomatopoeia in accordance with their own sensorimotor experience from the early stages of language acquisition.[13] Although *TRW*, the original English version of *Usagi*, has no onomatopoeia in it, the Japanese version contains several cases,

13 For a detailed discussion of Japanese onomatopoeia, see Kita (1997) and Tamori & Schourup (1999).

as listed under (6). The word *pyon* represents the jump of a small animal like a rabbit, *pyon pyon* the repetition of this action, and *pyoon* the act of jumping even higher and/or longer. The word *guruguru* expresses the repeated action of going around, *jitto* means 'steadily,' and *sotto* implies 'gently.'

(6) a. pyon pyon no pyoon [Scene 3, twice, 'no' is used as a linker here.]
b. pyon pyon [Scene 6, once]
c. guruguru [Scene 6, once]
d. jitto [Scene 9, once]
e. sotto [Scene 11, once]

4 Tension between words and pictures and how their contrasts are adjusted

As explained in Section 3, the illustrations and the text in the picture book *Usagi* show some discrepancies between them, especially in the viewpoint from which the world of the two rabbits is represented: while the illustrations show that the point of view is changing from scene to scene, the text presents a rather stable, objective viewpoint toward the world of the two rabbits. How can the readers deal with such discrepancies? The experiment conducted by Kojima et al. (2013) and its results can provide some answers to this question.[14]

4.1 An overview of the experiment by Kojima et al. (2013)

Kojima et al. (2013) performed an experiment to examine the effect of the text of *Usagi* on the viewpoint and gaze of the readers and their comprehension. In all, 22 undergraduate and graduate students at Kyoto University participated in this study (9 males and 13 females, M=20.91 years, SD=1.98 years). The participants were seated in front of a computer screen with their heads resting on a chin rest so that their eye movements could be measured. Each participant first performed a practice trial, and then two experimental trials. Two different types of stimulus sets were prepared for the experimental trials, both of which were based on the reduced scanned images of the double-spread pages of *Usagi* from the title page

14 For a more detailed description of the method, see Kojima et al. (2013). Kojima et al. (2013), however, only gave a brief discussion of the results of the experiment. This paper analyses the data in more detail from a cognitive point of view.

to Scene 14 (15 images in total). The stimulus set used in the first experimental trial was a series of images with all of the words removed from the scanned data (hereinafter, "no-text condition"), and in the second set the images included both the text and illustrations (hereinafter, "text condition"). In both experimental trials, the stimuli were presented on the computer screen in the same order as in the actual picture book.

The participants were instructed to look at each stimulus for as long as they wanted and then to choose one of multiple choice statements on the screen describing their viewing experience and feelings. All of the statements were presented in Japanese. Throughout the experiment, the eye movements of the participants were recorded.

English translations of the statements we presented are shown in (7) below, although only those in (7b–d) are relevant to this paper. The statement in (7b) concerns the participants' sense of distance from the two rabbits, and the statements in (7c–d) involve the relative locations of the two rabbits.

(7) English translations of the presented statements:
  a. [Title page] "You first looked at {the white rabbit/the black rabbit}".
  b. [Scenes 1–8 and 11–13] "You feel as if {you are closer to the two rabbits/you are more distant from the two rabbits/you are staying at the same position}".
  c. [Scene 9] "The black rabbit is {in front of/behind/to the left of/to the right of} the white rabbit".
  d. [Scene 10] "The white rabbit is {in front of/behind/to the left of/to the right of} the black rabbit".
  e. [Scene 14] "You feel that the two rabbits are {anthropomorphic/not anthropomorphic}".

We expected that in the no-text condition the participants' sense of distance would be affected only by the size of the characters (e.g., if the character is depicted as being larger than in the preceding scene, the participants would feel as if they were closer to the two rabbits), as discussed in 3.1.2; on the other hand, in the text condition we expected that the sense of distance would be greatly influenced by the text and that the participants would adopt a rather stable viewpoint, the same as that of the narrator (see discussion in 3.2.2). As for the relative positions between the two rabbits, the text shows that the white rabbit looking to the right in Scene 9 directs her eyes to the black rabbit (Figure 3) and that the black rabbit facing the front in Scene 10 looks at the white rabbit (Figure 4). If participants answered "front" in both scenes, it would indicate that the participants adopted a fictive position very close to the white rabbit, or even the same position as the white rabbit's, and had deeper involvement in the two rabbits' world. We expected that in the text condition participants could correctly identify the position of each rabbit, while they could not in the no-text condition.

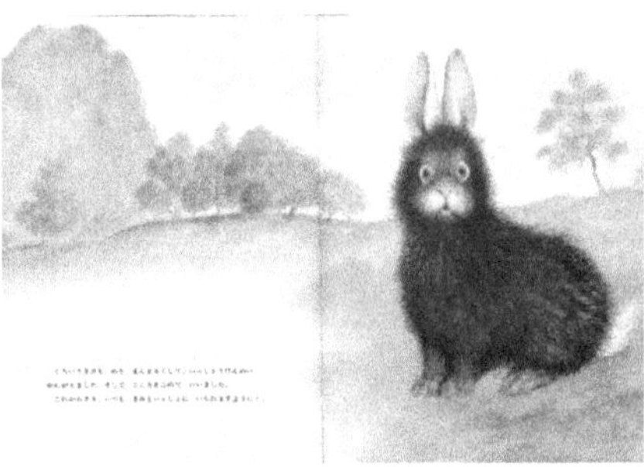

Figure 4: Scene 10 in *Usagi* (reproduced with permission)

4.2 The results of the experiment and discussion

4.2.1 The participants' sense of distance from the two rabbits

As Table 1 shows, statistically significant differences can only be observed in Scenes 1 and 6 between the no-text and the text conditions, but when focusing on the number of answers given as "the same", the number increases in Scenes 1, 3, 4, 5, 6, 8, 12 and 13 in the text condition. In particular, the increase in this answer and the decrease in the answer "more distant" in Scenes 3 and 5 deserve to be discussed, since the picture shows a viewpoint shift from "close social" to "far social" in these two scenes (see 3.1.2). In Scene 3, the text starts describing the two rabbits' conversation in the form of a direct quote, and in Scene 5, nearly the same conversation as in Scene 4 appears in the text (see 3.2.1). Assuming that being able to hear the conversation of others indicates physical proximity to them, the results in Scenes 3 and 5 would show that the direct quotations of the characters' utterances made some of the participants feel "not distant" from the two rabbits. The increase in "the same" and the decrease in "closer" responses in Scene 6 can also be explained in the same way. Since nearly the same conversation as in Scene 4 or 5 appears in this scene (see discussion in 3.2.1), the viewpoint of the text, i.e. the viewpoint fixed at the location at which the conversation between the two rabbits can be heard, overrides the viewpoint shift from "far social" to "close social" represented in the illustration. In Scenes 12 and 13, the increase in the number of "the same" responses in the text condition is slight and the

Table 1: Number of responses for each possible answer to the question about the participants' sense of distance

Condition	Scene	1	2	3	4	5	6	7	8	11	12	13
no-text	closer	15	16	8	14	5	18	2	15	12	9	5
	the same	3	3	3	3	2	4	6	2	3	2	2
	more distant	4	3	11	5	15	0	14	5	7	11	15
text	closer	4	18	9	14	4	9	3	18	13	7	5
	the same	6	3	8	4	8	8	4	4	2	4	4
	more distant	12	1	5	4	10	5	15	0	7	11	13
significance		*$p < .01$	*ns*	*ns*	*ns*	*ns*	*$p < .01$	*ns*	*ns*	*ns*	*ns*	*ns*

number of "more distant" is almost the same as that in the no-text condition. Since these scenes are the ones toward the end of the story, the participants who could understand the flow of the story from the text might feel as if they were gradually becoming distant from the world of the two rabbits, stimulated by the illustrations, even though the deictic expressions *kono* and *yattekuru*, both of which indicate that the narrator's viewpoint is close to the two rabbits (see 3.2.3), are used in these two scenes. The results show that when some conflict arises in the viewpoint between the text and the pictures, the text generally affects the readers' viewpoint more strongly than the pictures.

The results in Scene 1 under both conditions – 15 participants answered "closer" in the no-text condition and 12 answered "more distant" in the text condition – are surprising because the rabbits in this scene are depicted at almost the same size as those on the preceding title page. The results in the no-text condition might be attributed to the fact that the rabbits are depicted with detailed facial expressions (see discussion in 3.1.3). Since such facial expressions can be recognized at close range in everyday interaction, the participants might feel closer to the two rabbits despite the smallness of their size. In contrast, one plausible factor to explain the results in the text condition is that the participants recognized Scene 1 as the first page where the story begins. Since we know that the fictive world shown in picture books is not the same as the real world, the two rabbits, the citizens of the fictive world of *Usagi*, may have been regarded as distant.

4.2.2 Relative locations of the two rabbits

Tables 2 and 3 show the responses to the questions about the relative locations of the two rabbits. The number of participants who said "front" in both scenes, Scenes 9 and 10, in the no-text condition was 8, but 17 in the text condition. The results indicate that the combination of text and pictures afforded a better understanding of these two scenes.[15] From Scene 1 to Scene 8, the pictures and the text, which portray matching and mismatching viewpoints, gradually lead the readers into the world of the two rabbits (see discussion in 3.1.2), and in the climax scenes, in Scenes 9 and 10, the text presents detailed descriptions of the protagonists which completely match the pictures depicted (see discussion in 3.2.4), and the combination between the words and the pictures enhances the readers' involvement in the two rabbits' world. The participants who read the text with pictures, therefore, were more easily involved in the world of the two rabbits in Scenes 9 and 10, as the illustrations induce them to do so (see discussion of the close-ups in 3.1.2 and the frontal view in 3.1.3), and correctly identified the relative locations of the two rabbits. Scenes 9 and 10 make good use of the dynamic interplay between words and illustrations.

Table 2: Number of responses for each possible answer to the question about the location of the black rabbit in Scene 9

Condition	front	behind	left	right
no-text	9	10	1	2
text	17	0	0	5

Table 3: Number of responses for each possible answer to the question about the location of the white rabbit in Scene 10

Condition	front	behind	left	right
no-text	15	3	1	3
text	21	0	1	0

15 Before conducting the experiment, we had predicted that no participant would answer "behind" or "left" in these scenes; however, as the results show, some participants answered "behind" or "left" in the no-text condition in both scenes and one "left" even in the text condition in Scene 10. Although various plausible factors can be considered, a discussion of this is beyond the scope of the current paper.

5 Concluding remarks

Picture storybooks employ various strategies to prompt the readers to set up and understand the fictive worlds expressed within them. The current study has shown some of the strategies the picture book *Usagi* adopts, highlighting the dynamic interplay between the words, pictures and our everyday (social and physical) experiences. This study has also discussed in detail how the readers adjust the discrepancies between the words and the pictures in this picture book, based on the results of our experimental pilot study in 2013. However, there remain many issues to be solved: (i) undertaking a more detailed analysis of the experiment described in Section 4; (ii) conducting experiments on the effect of oral narratives on the (young) reader's viewpoint and understanding; (iii) exploring the differences in the readers' processing or understanding of the story based on the differences between the narrative styles of English and Japanese picture books; and (iv) modelling the process of understanding and/or engaging in the story. All of these issues will be addressed in future studies.

References

Coulmas, Florian. 1986a. Reported speech: Some general issues. In Florian Coulmas (ed.), *Direct and indirect speech*, 1–28. Berlin: Mouton de Gruyter.

Coulmas, Florian. 1986b. Direct and indirect speech in Japanese. In Florian Coulmas (ed.), *Direct and indirect speech*, 161–178. Berlin: Mouton de Gruyter.

Dancygier, Barbara. 2008. Personal pronouns, blending, and narrative viewpoint. In Andrea Tyler, Yiyoung Kim & Mari Takada (eds.), *Language in the context of use: Discourse and cognitive approaches to language*, 167–182. Berlin: Mouton de Gruyter.

Dancygier, Barbara & Eve Sweetser (eds.). 2012. *Viewpoint in language: A multimodal perspective*. Cambridge: Cambridge University Press.

Fauconnier, Gilles & Eve Sweetser (eds.). 1996. *Spaces, worlds, and grammar*. Chicago, IL: University of Chicago Press.

Fukada, Chie. 2008. Embodiment and objectification in Japanese mimetics. In Kazuhiro Kodama & Tetsuharu Koyama (eds.), *Linguistic and cognitive mechanisms: Festschrift for Professor Masa-aki Yamanashi on the occasion of his sixtieth birthday*, 229–245. Tokyo: Hitsuji Shobo.

Fukada, Chie. 2011. Ehon ni kakusareta shiza to shisen, shintaiteki keiken: *Shiroi Usagi to Kuroi Usagi* no imisekai [Viewpoint, gaze, and bodily experience in picture books: The world of *Shiroi Usagi to Kuroi Usagi*]. *Sapientia* [The St. Thomas University Review] 45. 157–174.

Golden, Joanne M. & Annyce Gerber. 1990. A semiotic perspective of text: The picture story book event. *Journal of Reading Behavior* 22(3). 203–219.

Johnston, Rosemary Ross. 2012. Graphic trinities: Languages, literature, and words-in-pictures in Shaun Tan's *The Arrival*. *Visual Communication* 11(4). 421–441.

Kasanuki, Yoko. 2010. Ehon ni okeru 'kurikaeshi' to suki-ima ['Repetition' and Schema in Picture Books]. In Hiroshi Yoshiba, Kazuo Nakazawa, Shin'ichi Takeuchi, Shigeo Tonoike, Tomohiro Kawabata, Tadao Nomura & Shihoko Yamamoto (eds.), *Current studies for the next generation of English linguistics and philology: A Festschrift for Minoji Akimoto on the occasion of his retirement from Aoyama Gakuin University*, 157–169. Tokyo: Hitsuji Shobo.

Kita, Sotaro. 1997. Two-dimensional semantic analysis of Japanese mimetics. *Linguistics* 35. 379–415.

Kojima, Takatsugu, Chie Fukada, Teppei Tanaka & Masashi Sugimoto. 2013. Ehon dokusha no shiza/shisen ni honbun ga oyobosu eikyo: Ehon *Shiroi Usagi to Kuroi Usagi* o mochiita gankyu-undo sokutei ni yoru kento [The effect of text on the viewpoint and gaze of a picturebook reader: From the measurement of eye movement of the readers of *Shiroi Usagi to Kuroi Usagi*]. *Proceedings of the Japanese Society for Cognitive Psychology: The 11th Conference of the Japanese Society for Cognitive Psychology* 64.

Kress, Gunther & Theo van Leeuwen. 2006. *Reading images: The grammar of visual design*. London: Routledge.

Matsuoka, Kyoko. 1965. *Shiroi Usagi to Kuroi Usagi* [The white rabbit and the black rabbit]. Tokyo: Fukuinkan Shoten.

Matsuoka, Kyoko. 1987. *Ehon no sekai, kodomo no sekai* [The world of picture books, the world of children]. Tokyo: Japan Editors School Press.

Nakamura, Toshie. 1995. Ehon no yomikikase ni kansuru shinrigakuteki kenkyu (III): Yoji no monogatari rikai ni oyobosu wadaijoho no eikyo [Psychological studies on reading picture books to young children (III): Effects of topic information on young children's story comprehension]. *The Science of Reading* 39(1). 16–23.

Nikolajeva, Maria & Carole Scott. 2001. *How picturebooks work*. New York: Routledge.

Oka, Natsuki, Xia Wu, Chie Fukada & Motoyuki Ozeki. 2013. Concurrent acquisition of the meaning of sentence-final particles and nouns through human-robot interaction. In Minho Lee, Akira Hirose, Zeng-Guang Hou & Rhee Man Kil (eds.), *Neural information processing: 20th International Conference, ICONIP 2013, Daegu, Korea, November 3–7, 2013, Proceedings, Part I (Lecture Notes in Computer Science)*, 387–394. Heidelberg, Germany: Springer.

Rubba, Jo. 1996. Alternate grounds in the interpretation of deictic expressions. In Gilles Fauconnier & Eve Sweetser (eds.), *Spaces, worlds, and grammar*, 227–261. Chicago, IL: University of Chicago Press.

Sanders, José & Gisela Redeker. 1996. Perspective and the representation of speech and thought in narrative discourse. In Gilles Fauconnier & Eve Sweetser (eds.), *Spaces, worlds, and grammar*, 290–317. Chicago, IL: University of Chicago Press.

Snowden, Robert, Peter Thompson & Tom Troscianko. 2012. *Basic vision: An introduction to visual perception*. Oxford: Oxford University Press.

Tamori, Ikuhiro & Lawrence Schourup. 1999. *Onomatope: Keitai to imi* [Onomatopoeia: Form and meaning]. Tokyo: Kuroshio Shuppan.

Vandelanotte, Lieven. 2009. *Speech and thought representation in English: A cognitive-functional approach*. Berlin: Mouton de Gruyter.

Williams, Garth. 1958. *The Rabbits' Wedding*. New York: HarperCollins Publishers.

Yamaguchi, Haruhiko. 2009. *Meisekina inyo, shinayakana inyo: Waho no nichi-ei taisho kenkyu* [Quotational clarity and flexibility: A contrastive study of speech and thought representation in English and Japanese]. Tokyo: Kuroshio Shuppan.

Eve Sweetser and Kashmiri Stec

Maintaining multiple viewpoints with gaze

Abstract: Co-speech bodily gesture has remarkable flexibility in displaying or enacting viewpoint, since – unlike speech but like signed languages – it deploys multiple relatively orthogonal articulators, including head and gaze, two arms and hands, and torso posture. Combined with the viewpoints expressed in the linguistic track, this allows oral narrators to embody viewpoints of two characters at once, or to embody both narratorial viewpoint and an embedded character viewpoint simultaneously. This paper examines video data of semi-spontaneous personal narratives told by speakers of American English. We observe some of the ways in which gaze specifically is used to mark and maintain either the narrator's or some character's viewpoint (including the narrator's Past Self as a story character) even while other articulators may be marking a different viewpoint. These include discourse uses of gaze marking memory access, or "checking" for approval from an interlocutor, as well as content uses such as alternation between enacted characters' gazes. It is always the storyteller's own eyes and face doing the gaze-enaction, but the understood meaning attributes a particular gaze to one of a complex of narrative viewpoints. This is transparent to listeners/viewers because they have access to the complex set of mental spaces evoked, not just to the physical space.

1 Introduction

Unlike the linear sound sequence of spoken language, co-speech gesture and signed languages involve the simultaneous visible use of relatively independent articulators. Two hands, torso posture and orientation, head orientation, facial expression, and gaze are among the articulators which are regularly relevant in linguistic communication – especially for indicating viewpoint shift (see Parrill 2012 and Stec 2012 for reviews, and McClave 2000 for an indication of the multifunctionality of head movements in discourse). Although manual gesture is the most studied of these, and indeed gesture is often used specifically to mean manual gesture, we will be using a more inclusive definition of 'gesture' which includes all multimodal articulators. These multimodal articulators are both externally observable and centrally involved in everyday action and attention in the world, not just in communication. Looking at someone's bodily action and motion tells you what they are doing and attending to. And gaze, the topic of this paper, plays a unique role in discerning communicative action, attention and intention (e.g. Rossano 2012, Sidnell 2006, Schegloff 1998).

Consider the case of a person working at her computer, who turns her head and gaze leftwards to address a colleague entering her office – but keeps her body facing the computer, with her hands held above the keyboard, as she speaks with the visitor. She is providing clear evidence to the visitor both that she is attending to him, and that she is embedding this temporary attention in a longer stretch of ongoing work which will be resumed. The effect would be extremely different if she instead also turned her whole body and gaze towards the visitor as she addressed him, removing her hands from the desk. And it would be different yet again if, for example, she kept her head, gaze and body turned towards a skype session on the computer, but perhaps silently stretched out a hand towards the (peripherally visible) visitor – to hand him a document she knows he wants, or instead greeted him with a palm held up to request that he wait. Perhaps most interestingly, even if she turned her body and face and arms towards the visitor, if her gaze repeatedly strayed towards the computer screen (or towards her watch), a sighted visitor would still quite strongly feel the effect of divided attention. This has been called *body partitioning* (Dudis 2004) or *body torque* (Schegloff 1998), and it shows not only what activities a person is currently engaged in (or currently engaged in representing, cf. the dual viewpoint gestures discussed by Parrill 2009), but also how ongoing discourse is re-structured as a result of such partitioning.

Of course, in a speaker/gesturer, the speech track is the dominant informational channel – which is why, unlike a signed language, co-speech gesture is not generally interpretable on its own. But in oral narrative, gesture provides very complex support for the viewpoint structure of the spoken content, in particular where a narrator is voicing and embodying multiple characters, while also maintaining interaction with her real-world interlocutor. This work is an initial attempt to pin down the role of gaze in this very multi-track multimodal set of affordances for an oral narrator. Our guiding questions are: How does gaze contribute to meaning differently from hands, body posture, position, and head movement? And what can this tell us about viewpoint in oral narrative?

We might think of narrative embedding – the embedded expression of a character's utterances and thoughts in a narrator's expression – as being a kind of combining and embedding of activities, somewhat like that of the person being interrupted by the visitor to her office. But the activities involved in narrative include representation of multiple – embedded, or contrasting – viewpoints. Instead of attention-sharing between the interactions with the computer and with the visitor, the writer of a narrative is dividing linguistic resources between author-reader interaction, narrator-reader interaction, and of course the content of the story space, including different characters' viewpoints embedded in the narrator's viewpoint. It is fairly well understood by narratologists that combining linguistic forms appropriate to the narrator (e.g. 3rd person and past tense, since the narrator is recounting past events about other people) with forms appropriate to a character's point of view (descriptions such as *that rat* or *Daddy*; deictic forms like *now* and *here*) will result in a tight embedded viewpoint which is sometimes called Free Indirect Style or Free Indirect Speech and Thought (Genette 1980); other combinations of forms produce different narrative effects (Vandelanotte 2009, 2012; Dancygier 2012).

The oral narrator, however, is dividing not just her linguistic resources, but also her gesture space, her movements and actions, and her attention resources, between representing the content of the Story Space, including particular character viewpoints, and the real world interaction with her interlocutor. One way of talking about this is to talk about representation of different mental spaces, using the framework introduced by Gilles Fauconnier (Fauconnier 1994[1995]; Fauconnier and Turner 2002). Following other work in this framework on both gesture and signed language (e.g. Liddell 2003; Dudis 2004), we will refer to the shared physical space of the actual Speaker and Hearer as the Real Space. Gesture space is one aspect of Real Space.

Parrill and Sweetser (2004) noted that in gesture, as well as in signed languages (Liddell 2003; Dudis 2004) it is normal for sub-areas of physical gesture space to be devoted to different topics or characters. And Guntner et al. (2015) have used experimental paradigms with EEG to demonstrate that interlocutors not only recognise these distinct uses of gesture space, but expect them to be there after only minimal prompting. Sweetser and Sizemore (2008) and Stec and Sweetser (2013) have noted the functional division of gesture space, with the Speaker-Hearer line as the locus of Real Space interactional gestures, while a space to one side of that line would normally be allocated to the narrative.

Sweetser (2013) and Stec and Sweetser (2013) have argued that viewpoint-alternation and viewpoint-embedding can be achieved in extremely complex ways, since part of the narrator's body may be engaged in the part of the gesture space devoted to the narrative, while other simultaneous aspects of gesture may take place along the Speaker-Hearer line and engage in interaction in the Real Space.

Looking at gaze, Thompson and Suzuki (2014) have used the relationship between original and reenacted events to argue that gaze is an important means by which speakers jointly create reenactments with their listeners and differentiate events which took place in the here-and-now (or Base Space, to use our terminology) vs. in the reenactment (or Story Space), specifically to manage transitions between narrative proper and reenactment. Like Sidnell (2006), they found that gaze is moved away from interlocutors during reenacted sequences, and returned to interlocutors at the end of such sequences. Moreover, they found that the direction of the averted gaze depends on the kind of reenactment, with gaze resting in central, neutral spaces during phone call or text reenactments, or more peripherally for face-to-face reenactments. At the same time, however, Holler et al. (2014) used an experimental task to demonstrate that listeners are sensitive to the direction of speaker-gaze: Listeners who were gazed at process speech better than listeners who are not gazed at. This suggests that there are comprehension costs inherent to speaker shifts in gaze. Nonetheless, as Thompson and Suzuki (2014), Sidnell (2006), and Park (2009) suggest – and as we show below – speakers do systematically avert and return gaze in ways which are related to the partitioning of Real Space, and to managing ongoing discourse.

Anchoring the body in one Real Space allows for easier transitions to other Real Spaces and therefore mental space. As we will show, gaze is one of the means by which this is accomplished. Of course, there are others. Sweetser (2014) argues that the orthogonality of gestural articulations allows the simultaneous physical maintenance of elements from different mental spaces, thus physically representing space embedding structures. As mentioned above, narratologists have long noted that the effect of combining linguistic markers appropriate to a higher space and an embedded space can give particular narrative effects (Genette 1980; Banfield 1982; Fleischman 1990; Sanders and Redeker 1996; Dancygier 2012; Vandelanotte 2009, 2012; Nikiforidou 2010, 2012). More specifically, Free Indirect Speech and Thought is conventionally represented by past tense and third-person reference to story characters, combined with character-based deictic forms (*here*, *now*) and character-based descriptions. Thus, a sentence like *She knew that by now he would be telling Daddy all about it* shows the Narrator's past tense and the Narrator's *she* to refer to the viewpoint character; but *Daddy* and *now* refer to the viewpoint character's father and temporal present, not the Narrator's. The result is an experience of active viewpoint embedding: the narrator's viewpoint is not abandoned, but rather maintained as constant background to the foregrounded viewpoint-character's space. Sweetser noted cases where a gesturer simultaneously maintains gestural depiction of a story character's body, and interacts (often with face/gaze as well as voice) with the real-world interlocutor, somewhat like the way Thompson and Suzuki (2014) and Park (2009) note that speakers can treat their interlocutors as Story Space characters for the purposes of reenactment. Both narratorial body and character body are enacted simultaneously, and the result is a vivid embedding of one embodied viewpoint within another.

Now that we have given an overview of the different issues involved in multimodal viewpoint embeddings, we will give an overview of the rest of this paper.

In Section 2, we briefly describe our data and the narratives used in our analysis. Following that, in Section 3, we discuss how gesture space is partitioned in our narratives. And then we discuss particular uses of speaker gaze to manage viewpoint embeddings within ongoing discourse: Character enaction (Section 4), Narratorial gaze (Section 5), Visual "checking" (Section 6), and to access memory (Section 7). Throughout, we will consider how gaze works to manage discourse functions whether in coordination with or separately from other multimodal articulators, and how it contributes to understanding oral narratives more broadly.

2 Data for the present study

Our data come from a video corpus of semi-spontaneous speech which was collected by the second author on the West Coast of the US in January 2012. All participants were native speakers of American English who brought a friend to the recording location, where they told and requested personal narratives in a relatively naturalistic way. Stec et al. (submitted) describes our recording procedure. Our corpus is comprised of 26 speakers (17F, 9M) and a total usable corpus length of approximately five hours. There are 85 narratives in the entire corpus – we only discuss three here, but the behaviours we note are present throughout the corpus.

In Stec and Sweetser (2012), we offered a quantitative analysis of the spatial distributions of gestures in these narratives, and correlations between different aspects of gesture, gesture space and mental spaces. In this paper, we will be focusing instead on qualitative analysis of a few complex clips, all of which involve the simultaneous representation of more than one viewpoint. We will be deepening the tentative analysis offered in Sweetser (2014) of partitioned gestural viewpoint as a representation of narrative embedding, but we will focus specifically on the role of gaze in such partitioned structures.

For this analysis, we will focus on three narratives from the corpus (about which more below): License, Snow, and Cats. For each narrative, we will identify participants by the colour of the shirt they wear. A representative screenshot from each narrative, with speakers circled, is provided in Figure 1. For relevant examples, we will provide a transcript and a figure composed of stills from the video-recording.

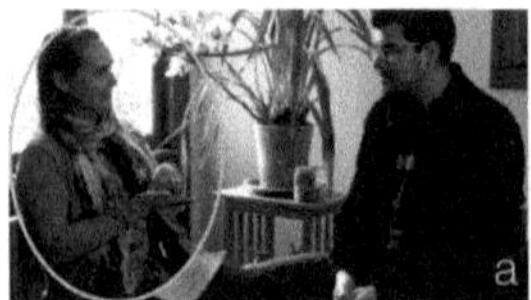

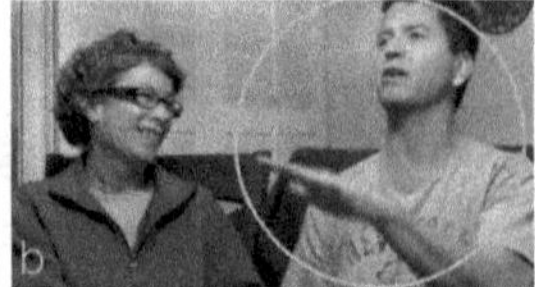

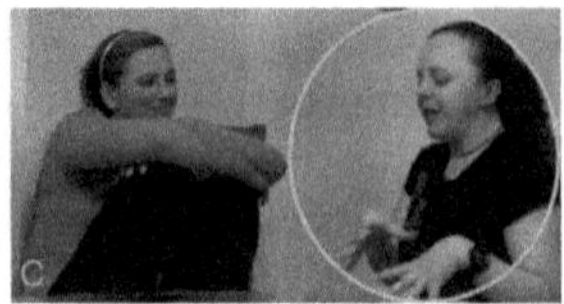

Figure 1: A representative still from each narrative, with primary narrators circled. License is shown in panel a, with Green identified on the left of the frame. Snow in panel b, with Grey identified on the right of the frame. And Cats in panel c, with Black identified on the right of the frame.

But first, a brief summary of the three narratives: In License, the narrator, Green, located on the left of the frame, tells the story of going to a town hall of a small town with another woman and requesting a marriage license from an official there. As she tells the story, she enacts her own Past Self and the Official, sometimes simultaneously – and she also interacts directly with her Real Space interlocutor. In Snow, Red on the left and Grey on the right are a married couple, and Grey is recounting the story of a long-past difficult drive through a blizzard which they made together, in more or less the same relative spatial configuration of the original event (since Red is seated to Grey's right in Real Space, and Grey was the driver in the Story Space). Grey is simultaneously reenacting both of their past selves, and also sharing enjoyment of this favourite story in the present with Red. In Cats, the narrator Black, located on the right of the frame, describes how her boyfriend likes to put a laundry basket over her cat to see what will happen. She enacts her Past Self, the Boyfriend, and even the Cat in this narrative, while also intermittently sharing appreciation of these events with her real interlocutor Pink.

As we shall see, in all narratives gaze plays a crucial role in allowing the narrator to simultaneously engage in more than one level of meaning building. License involves lengthy manual gesture holds and the use of gaze to facilitate transitions between the Story Space and Real Space. The rich co-narration involved in Snow, as the couple re-live their past experience, offers a great deal of gaze use as a way to maintain that shared experience in the present, even while one of them narrates the past.[1] Cats involves two very interactive friends, and offers special evidence of other ways in which meta-interaction takes place alongside narrative content. They also offer unusually vivid character-viewpoint depictions, with both positional alterations and partitioning of the body to depict multiple characters.

1 For more information about the co-construction of gestural space in narratives, see Stec and Huiskes (2014).

3 Partitioning of the gestural body, and of gestural space

In one sense, gesture is simple: a human body moves in Real Space. But why does it move the way it does, and how does anyone interpret co-speech bodily activity as contributing to communicative meaning? The answer is both simple and complicated. First, much of gesture is interpreted as building content relative to mental spaces other than the current Base Space, the Speaker and Hearer's overall real world of which the Real Space is a part. The interpretive trick, then, is to figure out to which space a gesture is contributing meaning. This is, of course, in a way no different than the problem of interpreting language; someone listening to a story in the past tense has a good clue from the tense that the events described are not about the here-and-now Base Space, but about a Story Space whose content is past relative to the Base Space. In the case of gesture, things are a bit more complicated. Someone telling a past-tense narrative could gesture about running, as she described past running events; she could also put up a hand to stop interruption from the Real Space interlocutor, without any linguistic markers of doing so from the Story Space.

However, spatial partitioning gives crucial and complex clues. As is normal in co-speech gesture, our narrators regularly used the Real Space area directly between the Speaker and Hearer (the Speaker-Hearer line) as the locus for real-world interaction between them. They normally picked an area in physical space to one side of that line as the one used to represent the mental space of the narrative content (the Story Space). This partitioning of space is illustrated in Figure 2, where each dyad's use of gestural space in these three narratives is depicted.

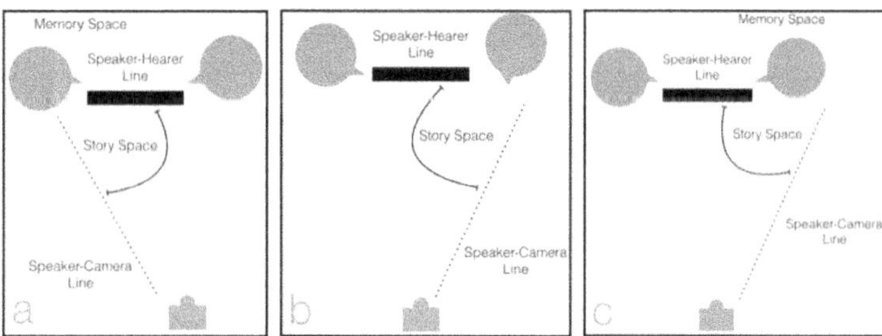

Figure 2: The partitioning of gestural space used by each dyad in the three narratives considered here. License appears in panel a, Snow in panel b and Cats in panel c. In each case, both interlocutors and the camera are identified, as well as the Speaker-Hearer line and the location of the narrator's story space. In addition, the Memory Spaces used by Green (panel a) and Black (panel c) are identified.

Gestures depicting events in the past tense Story Space occur in the physical part of the gesture space allotted to the story, while gestures towards the real-world interlocutor occur instead along the Real Space Speaker-Hearer line. Very often, given the physical setup, speakers chose to place the Story Space on the camera side of the Speaker-Hearer line, though not directly facing the camera. This had the practical advantage of not letting gestures be obstructed by the physical surroundings of the recording locations – as well as of treating the filming observer as a third participant. That is, if there had been a third person actively taking part in the conversation (as in, e.g., Özyürek 2002), the narrator would certainly not have chosen to locate the Story Space either right on that Speaker-Hearer line, or completely outside the shared three-way interactional zone, but rather in some neutral and accessible space in between. Because of this, the Speaker-Camera line was avoided as a primary Story Space locale. Özyürek (2002) has shown that narrators prefer to avoid the Speaker-Hearer line in miming at least some kinds of story event content. Özyürek asked participants to watch Looney Tunes cartoons and re-tell them to two naïve listeners. Placing her participants in a triangular array with the two listeners, she found that some subjects enacted event descriptions like *She threw the cat out the window* with a backwards over-the-shoulder throwing motion. This was a poor representation of the content being expressed, since in the video being re-narrated, the character threw the cat forwards out the window. However, the backwards-gesturing speaker thus avoided *throwing the cat* into the personal gesture spaces of her hearers or onto the shared Speaker-Hearer communicative line. Perhaps our storytellers, therefore, were avoiding both the communicative line between themselves and the filmed auditor, and also the "communicative line" between themselves and the camera.

Because gesture uses so many more independent articulators than speech, it is also less sequential: different gestural articulators of a narrator can simultaneously enact different parts of a scene, or different characters in the scene. The terms Character Viewpoint and Observer Viewpoint have been used to characterise the contrast between iconic gestures that represent the actions of a character's body with actions of the gesturer's body (e.g., using gesturing hands to mime grasping a steering wheel or climbing up a drainpipe), and those which use the gesturing body rather to represent objects or aspects of the overall viewed scene (e.g. two hands with facing palms to represent two participants in the story) (Parrill 2009; Liddell 2003; McNeill 1992). It is now also well recognized by both signed language and gesture analysts that body partitioning (Dudis 2004a, b) is an ordinary feature of communicative bodily action. For example, as we will discuss below, a speaker's gaze, head direction and facial expression may represent those of one narrative character, while that speaker's hands and body represent those of another character. Supposing these enactions to be accompanied by utterances attributed to the two narrative characters, and to be carried out in the physical gesture area of the Story Space, neither the narrator nor the listener will have any trouble in appropriately interpreting them as representing the emotions and actions of the story character, rather than the emotions and actions of the speaker herself.

4 Character enaction

A narrator's gaze can readily represent the gaze of a character rather than that of the actual speaker, when it is in the Story Space rather than directed at the Real Space listener. This is equally true in ASL, as Liddell (1998) showed in his analysis of a signed recounting of a Garfield cartoon, where the signer's gaze alternately enacts the cat's upwards gaze towards the owner, and the hapless cat owner's downwards gaze at the cat. This phenomenon in co-speech gesture is well exemplified by the sequence in License where Green describes a past interaction with a town-hall bureaucrat. This is shown in Transcript 1 and Figure 3. In the story, she tells us that her birth certificate erroneously says "male" with a stapled-on correction saying "female" – this of course confuses the Official. The narrator's gaze alternately represents the Official's sceptical gaze (going back and forth between an imagined birth certificate, and the narrator's Past Self as they discuss it), and Green's Past Self's gaze (directed towards the official) and facial expression. Throughout the sequence, the narrator's hands represent the Official's hands, holding the document – even when her face and gaze are representing her Past Self, who is clearly not holding the document. In these cases, we have two distinct Character viewpoints, simultaneously represented by the narrator's partitioned body.

As can be seen in the stills in Figure 3, Green is using the space in front of her and to her right to enact the story; her Real Space interlocutor is to her left, away from the camera, and she turns head and gaze towards him for Real-Space interaction. Within the Story space in front of her, she alternately enacts the two story characters (Past Self and the Official).

```
Transcript 1: License, excerpt 1
1  Green:   and finally someone turned over the stapled part of my
            birth certificate
2           and saw that it said female
3           and they were like nope that's why you can't
```

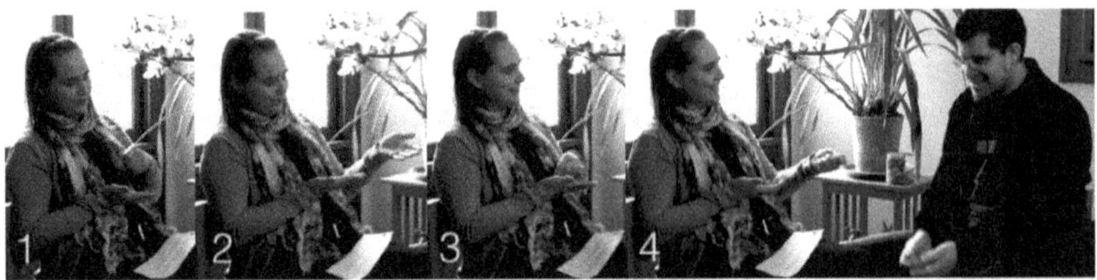

Figure 3: Stills from License. Images 1–2 correspond to line 1 of the transcript (Green enacts the Official manipulating her birth certificate). In image 2, Green underlines the part of the transcript that says "female" and in image 3, she shows the triumphant Official returning the birth certificate to her Past Self. Apart from looking at the document in images 1–2, Green looks at her interlocutor, Black, throughout this sequence.

Green's interlocutor, Black, clearly has no trouble understanding Green's partitioned representation as showing the two characters, and viewers to whom we have shown this material have also effortlessly reached the same interpretation. This interpretation depends first of all on the pre-constructed relationship between physical space and mental spaces; without the pre-establishment of a physical gestural subspace (to the right of the Speaker-Hearer line) devoted to the Story Space, these gazes would be not only meaningless but socially problematic as they might indicate that the speaker was not fully attending to the current speech interaction. After all, none of them are directed towards the real-world interlocutor, Black. And of course without the quoted speech sequence of the two characters within the Story Space, the actual physical gazes would mean nothing, since they are hard to interpret as the speaker's current gaze.

Fascinatingly, note that once a narrator is "inside" the Story Space and enacting interaction between characters, a new Speaker-Hearer line develops inside the Story Space. That is, the Past Self and the Official, both enacted in turn by the narrator of License, are imagined to be at opposite ends of this communicative axis, and we mentally rotate/displace Green's representations, blending them alternately with the Official's end of the axis and the Past Self's end. This looks very much like the kind of 180-degree virtual "rotation" between interlocutor-viewpoints described by Janzen (2013) in ASL storytelling.

Another example of this comes from Cats, and is shown in Transcript 2 and Figure 4. Here, the narrator Black, on the right of the frame, alternately enacts her past self and her boyfriend's past self in narrated speech exchanges. Her head and gaze go upwards and to her right as she enacts her shorter self talking to the taller boyfriend, and downwards and leftwards as she enacts the boyfriend. Similarly, her gaze is downwards as she enacts both Past Self and Past Boyfriend looking downwards at the cat. This is shown in Figure 4.

```
Transcript 2: Cats, excerpt 1
1  Black:   but she's not
2           sssssh
3           ok but she's not
4           sssssh (0.5)
5           ok but she's not doing anything
6           not (0.5) yet
```

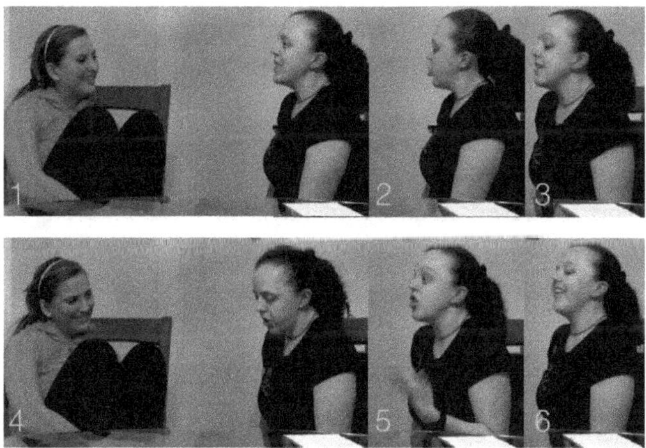

Figure 4: Stills from Cats. Image 1 corresponds with line 1 in the transcript, image 2 with line 2, and so on. Throughout the series, Black is oriented towards her Story Space and makes a left/right and up/down distinction with her head movements and gaze to differentiate quotes made by her Past Self and her boyfriend in the story.

Again we must alternately blend the narrator's bodily behaviours as well as her speech track with the two interlocutors, who are of course not construed as being in the same location – despite the fact that the speaker does not shift her overall seated location. This looks very much like the most-described kind of signed-language role shift (e.g. Quinto-Pozos 2007), which involves actual partial body rotation (not imagined 180-degree rotation) when enacting a quoted character, and partial rotation in the opposite direction to enact that character's interlocutor, as well as character-viewpointed signing and averted gaze.

And, as we've noted, more than one character can be represented simultaneously by the same body – in License, Green keeps her hands in a document-holding position representing the Official holding the Document, even as she switches her gaze from representing that of the Official to that of Past Self, and even (as we shall see below) when her head and gaze revert momentarily to her present self in real-world interaction. (This is also true in signed language; cf.

Dudis 2004a,b and Dudis 2007.) In Cats, the Boyfriend's physical features, such as his height and position relative to Black's Past Self, are retained during enactment of Past Self's utterance and gaze, as well as during Black's performance of her Boyfriend's utterances and gaze.

We note that facial expression and gaze tend to go together here. License regularly involves representing character facial expression together with gaze – the Official examining the document with a dubious expression, the Past Self looking at and responding to the Official with a cheery, hopeful expression even while the speaker's hands remain those of the Official holding the Document. Similarly, in Cats, the alternation between representations of the two characters' speech coincides with alternations between enacting their gazes and their facial expressions simultaneously. This is something to examine closely in future work. Although gaze and facial expression are certainly separable in principle, in practice they seem tied – perhaps more strongly than gaze is tied to head direction, even. Or, as one reviewer put it: Body partitioning is fine – and even common (see, e.g., Schegloff 1998, Dudis 2004, or Parrill 2009) – but face partitioning is not.

5 Narratorial gaze as itself

Of course, the Real Space of actual interaction is always present in oral narration. This is why listeners don't feel offended by divided attention when the narrator's body and gaze vividly represent characters – they know that all of this is in the service of a meta level of attention to the narrative, which constitutes the current phase of the narrator's Real Space interaction with the listener. As evidence of this, Sidnell (2006) and Thompson and Suzuki (2014) document the extent to which reenactments (by which is generally meant, quotative utterances) are preceded and followed by gazes directed to interlocutors, but the reenactments themselves are produced with averted gaze. This behaviour is so entrenched that, as Thompson and Suzuki show, speakers purposefully seek their interlocutors' gaze to make sure proper attention is paid to the reenacted sequences. Normally, shared gaze is used to indicated shared attention (cf. the joint gaze discussion in Tomasello 2000) – so it is in some sense bizarre that joint gaze is sought specifically to enable averted gaze. The fact that it happens during these reenacted sequences with quoted utterances (and therefore, explicit conceptual viewpoint shifts, cf. Parrill 2012) makes some sense insofar as the pattern bears resemblance to standard role shift sequences in sign (e.g. Quinto-Pozos 2007) and enables the iconic representation of another viewpointed body (Sweetser 2012). But what about elsewhere?

The narrator's gaze can of course always remain (or revert to being) just the actual speaker's gaze within the current interaction – even while other parts of the speaker's body are not representing her real-world self. Often, but not always, this use of gaze is packaged with head movement, while the hands and body are the ongoing placeholder (or buoy, in the terminology of Liddell 2003) maintaining the embedded space, including embedded characters. This is how we would characterise the sequence in License in Transcript 1 and Figure 3, above. There, the narrator's hands continue to represent the Official's document-holding activity in the Story Space area, even when the narrator's face and gaze are turned away from the Story Space towards the Real Space interlocutor to answer an interpolated question. Just like the person at the desk whose body and hands remain directed towards her computer while she turns her head to respond to a visitor in her office, this narrator is showing clearly that she is still telling her story and will return to it after the meta-interaction is over.

```
Transcript 3: License, excerpt 2
Green:   and so she scoots her chair back from her desk
         like really abruptly
         and just sits there for a second
         like wondering what she's going to say
```

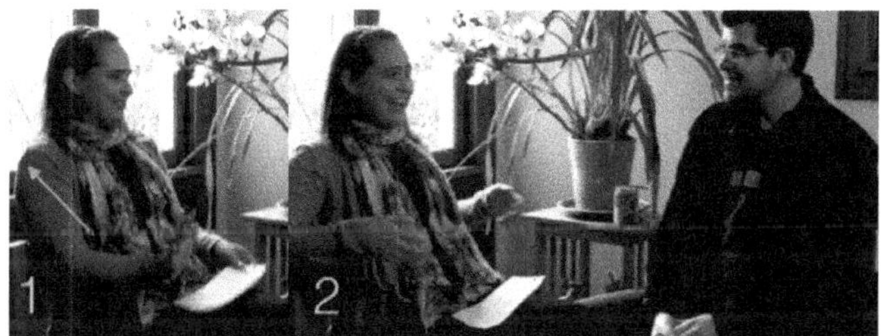

Figure 5: Stills from License. Green shows how the Official scooted their chair back (lines 2–3 in the transcript) and then sat there, wondering what to say (lines 3–4). Green gazes at her interlocutor throughout this sequence.

License is another good example – Green is enacting the described official's pushing back of her chair, while her gaze and head direction maintain direct connection between herself as speaker and the real-world addressee. This is shown in Transcript 3 and Figure 5. Similarly, later in the narrative, her hand is enacting the described character's telephoning a colleague, while gaze and head direction are Base Space interaction. This is shown in Transcript 4 and Figure 6. And in Cats, Black's hands hover in the Story Space area, prepared for narrative content expression, while gaze and head direction are already directed towards the Story Space. This is shown in Transcript 5 and Figure 7. On line 2/image 2, Black's head moves towards Pink along the Real Space Speaker-Hearer interaction line, as the two actual interactants joke before the story starts – but her gaze and face maintain orientation towards her Story Space. This is shown in Figure 7. At the end of such a "meta" stretch, a narrator returning to narrative content often also linguistically marks the return with a linguistic resumptive marker (*anyway, OK, so*) as gaze and head direction return to the narrative space.

```
Transcript 4: License, excerpt 3
Green:   so we went over there and in the meantime
         she had phoned over to the
         I think it was to the magistrate of the court
```

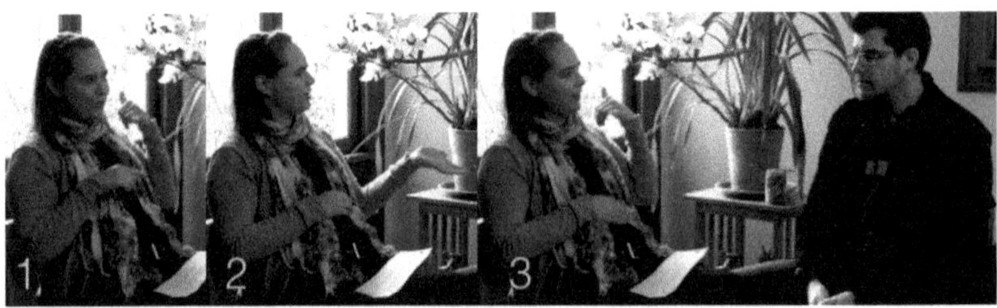

Figure 6: Stills from License. Green's head and gaze are oriented to her interlocutor while her hands produce character-viewpoint gestures which elaborate the Story Space.

```
Transcript 5: Cats, excerpt 2
Black:   go to bed
         eat your tea
Pink: eat your tea
Black:   so (0.5)
         so my sweetie and I
```

A point to note here is that we have observed an extremely tight link between gaze and facial expression; we haven't seen examples where a narrator's gaze represents one viewpointed entity, while her facial expression represents another character or entity. Gaze can be detached from direction of head/face, but not from facial emotion expression – as in License, where Green's gaze and facial expression shift together between representing the Official, the Past Self, and the present narrator, even while her hands and body direction are partitioned and may be representing another character or space. As we saw earlier: a body can be partitioned in multiple ways, but not a face.

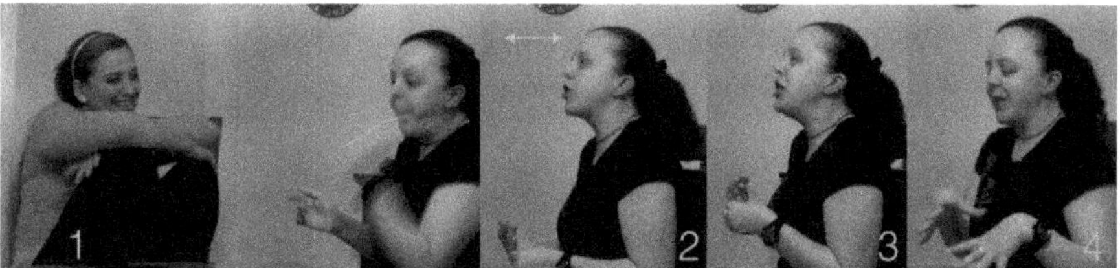

Figure 7: Stills from Cats. Pink and Black joke before Black starts her narrative (line 1–3 in the transcript, images 1–2 in the figure). When Black says line 2, her head and gaze are already oriented towards the Story Space, and hands are already raised (image 3 in the figure). Black reclaims the floor in line 4, and in line 5 (image 4) manages to start her narrative. During the entire exchange, her gaze is oriented away from Pink and towards her Story Space.

And, as we said above, a vivid form of viewpoint embedding is achieved by this combination of bodily enactment of Character with Real-Space narratorial gaze and speech. It would be hard to argue that this is less complex than, say, Free Indirect Speech and Thought representation in language – it is certainly very rich, and we cannot even claim to have isolated all of the relevant parameters involved. It is certainly like Free Indirect Speech and Thought in that it is easy to process these multiple viewpoints simultaneously – interlocutors are not confused by the complexity. And gaze is a crucial component.

6 Visual "checking"

We mentioned above that at any point a narrator can choose to go "meta" and return from the narrative performance in the Story Space to the Real Space interaction. If she needs to address the listener in the midst of the narrative, she will almost certainly turn her head and gaze towards the listener during that time, even while perhaps maintaining hands and trunk in the physical area allotted to the Story Space. This does at least somewhat break the embedded storyline. However, we also observed instances of very brief gaze/head re-direction towards the addressee, while the verbal content and the rest of the gestural body remained related to the embedded Story Space. This was used as an interactional device of "checking" with the listener without interrupting the embedded verbal flow of narrative. Since no real interruption is involved, no linguistic resumptive devices such as *anyway* are needed either.

As we mentioned earlier, in Snow we see Grey telling the story of a past drive which he and Red, the current Real Space interlocutor, took together years before.

As Grey enacts both sides of a past conversation during the drive, he very briefly turns his head and meets Red's eyes, both right before and right after quoting her past utterance (lines 2 and 4 in the transcript). This is shown in Figure 8, images 2 and 4. At the second head-turn, he actually "checks" linguistically as well (line 4), but the first one has no linguistic concomitant.[2]

```
Transcript 7: Snow, excerpt 1
1  Grey: oh let's turn around
2           and [Red]'s going
3           no no no just go just go
4           remember
```

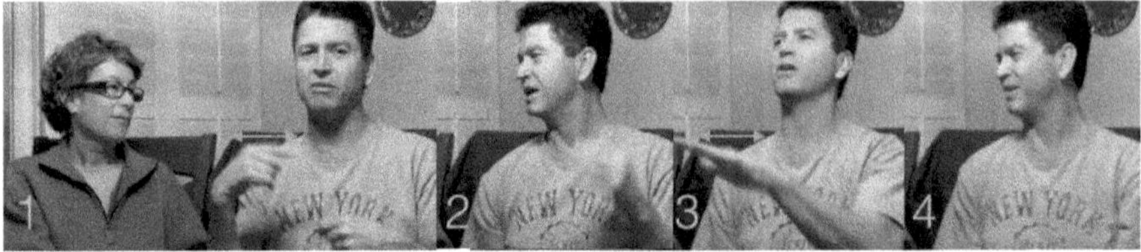

Figure 8: Stills from Snow. Grey turns his head and meets Red's gaze both right before (image 2) and right after (image 4) quoting her.

The closest parallel we can think of to this is back-channeling (or Japanese *aizuchi*), where small utterances (*yeah, OK, right, no way, wow*) or gestures (e.g., nods and headshakes) help to manage the listener's side of the interaction and maintain interparticipant connection, while not claiming the floor or interrupting the speaker. For example, during the narrative about their drive through the blizzard, Grey very briefly turns his head and meets Red's eyes, not claiming the floor or interrupting her interjection. In a similar way, one might say that this visual "checking" avoids self-interruption by avoiding actively returning the communicative floor to the Real Space interaction. And it allows both the overall linguistic track and the overall gestural track (with this momentary divergence) to stay in the narrative space, while still maintaining Real Space Speaker-Hearer connection.

2 Park (2009) discusses quoting a co-present character, such as Red, in naturalistic Korean discourse. There, he notes that the co-present character withdraws their gaze from the speaker during the quoted utterance. We don't see that kind of behaviour with our English speakers.

7 Memory spaces

Averted gaze can often represent access to a Memory Space. McCarthy et al. (2008) demonstrated that the direction varies cross-culturally, with Canadian speakers preferring to look upwards in communicative contexts and downwards otherwise while Japanese speakers generally prefer to look downwards. And Glenberg et al. (1998) demonstrated that averted gaze improves cognitive processing in non-communicative situations, such as problem-solving. But as these and Holler et al. (2014)'s finding suggest, gaze is tricky – and not least of all for the huge individual variation in gaze patterns and use. For example, unlike McCarthy et al.'s Canadian speakers who varied gaze aversion patterns depending on context, the American speakers in our corpus – all of whom were in communicative contexts – averted gaze by looking either upwards *or* downwards. More important than the choice of direction was the fact of the action itself, which demonstrates "thinking" to the addressee and thus also holds the floor for the speaker. At the same time, it partitions gesture space – "thinking" doesn't happen on the Speaker-Hearer line or in the Story Space, but elsewhere.

For example, in Cats, Black glances up as she is remembering, before telling the story. This is shown in Transcript 6 and Figure 9. Often access to the Memory Space involves little head or no movement – it is specifically the eyes which move.

```
Transcript 6: Cats, excerpt 3
1  Pink: can I hear the cat and the laundry basket story
2  Black:   yes yes you can
```

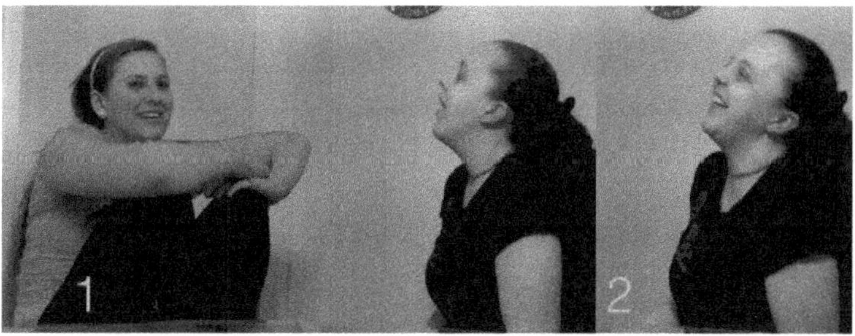

Figure 9: Stills from Cats. Black, the narrator, looks towards Pink as she requests the story in image 1 and then looks up as she prepares to tell the story in image 2.

These memory gazes bring to the fore an issue which pervades gesture studies overall: how intentional and how conscious is meaningful gestural behaviour? Although all of the behaviours we've been talking about are potentially observable, it's not clear exactly how conscious speakers or listeners are about them. It's true that a listener might subsequently say, if questioned, that the narrator was being vivid, or "acting out" past characters and scenes. But would they be able to bring to consciousness facts like the allotment of physical gesture space to different functions (narrative content, meta-interaction)? In the case of the upwards gaze for gathering memories together, however, we seem to be seeing a communicative discourse signal to the listener that the speaker is "searching" or "consulting" her memories, rather than (for example) just being silent. This is interestingly parallel to hesitation markers (see James 1973, Clark 1996 ch. 9) – while *um* or *uh* seem to simply indicate floor-holding during linguistic formulation, *oh* (as in, *There were, oh, about thirty people at the party*) specifically seems to mark memory searching – and hence to mark evidentially the fact that the speaker has personal memories to search.

8 Conclusions

We hope to have laid out in this paper at least some of the ways in which gaze contributes to the maintenance of multiple viewpoints in the gestural structure of our English oral narratives. Gaze in narrative would be uninterpretable without mental space mappings: *whose* gaze is understood as being involved or represented? An essential component in such interpretation is the partitioning of the gesture space: if the gaze is directed into the Story Space, we know it is not the Real Space narrator's gaze that is meant (since the Story Space sector of Real Space does not have real addressees in it). And the partitioning of the body itself is equally crucial: is the gaze to be interpreted as belonging to the *same* viewpointed person as other gestural components?

Like anything about gesture, gaze is meaningful primarily because of how the mental spaces are constructed relative to the Real Space. Some of this is really general – for example, the Speaker-Hearer line of the Real Space or of an embedded discourse space, or the "up-there-ness" of memory. And some of it is very locally built – we always need to know where the speaker "put" the Story Space (in all our examples), and may need to know things like the relative heights of characters (e.g. the upwards and downwards head turns in Cats), as well as what they are saying/doing within the narrative, etc.

As we suggested in Stec and Sweetser (2013), particular aspects of gesture are not all equally orthogonal to each other. Hands and body positioning often go together. And as we have noticed in this paper, gaze and facial expression seem particularly tightly tied to each other. This is clearly just a beginning, since the richness of viewpoint structures in even these narratives has not been fully analysed – but we hope it is a helpful beginning as we start to look at the role of gaze in multimodal narrative viewpoint.

Acknowledgments

We thank members of the Gesture and Multi-Modality Group at UC Berkeley and participants at ISGS 2012, ICLC 2013 and ISGS 2014 for helpful comments made on earlier stages of this work. Kashmiri Stec's contribution was funded by grant number 276.70.019, which was awarded to Dr. Esther Pascual by the Netherlands Organization for Scientific Research (NWO).

References

Banfield, Ann. 1982. *Unspeakable Sentences: Narration and representation in the language of fiction*. Boston: Routledge and Kegan Paul.

Clark, Herbert. 1996. *Using language*. Cambridge: Cambridge University Press.

Dancygier, Barbara. 2012. *The language of stories: A cognitive approach*. Cambridge University Press.

Dudis, Paul. 2004a. *Depiction of events in ASL: Conceptual integration of temporal components*. University of California, Berkeley dissertation.

Dudis, Paul. 2004b. Body partitioning and real-space blends. *Cognitive Linguistics* 15(2), 223.

Dudis, Paul. 2007. Types of depiction in ASL.Ms., Gallaudet University.

Fauconnier, Gilles. 1994[1985]. *Mental Spaces*. Cambridge: Cambridge University Press.

Fauconnier, Gilles & Mark Turner. 2002. *The way we think: Conceptual blending and the mind's hidden complexities*. New York: Basic Books.

Fleischman, Suzanne. 1990. *Tense and narrativity: From medieval performance to modern fiction*. Austin: University of Texas Press.

Genette, Jean. 1980. *Narrative discourse: An essay in method*. Ithaca: Cornell University Press.

Glenberg, Arthur, M., Schroeder, Jonathan. L., & David A. Robertson. 1998. Averting the gaze disengages the environment and facilitates remembering. *Memory & Cognition* 26. 651–658.

Gunter, Thomas C., J. E. Douglas Weinbrenner & Henning Holle. 2015. Inconsistent use of gesture space during abstract pointing impairs language comprehension. *Frontiers in Psychology* 6(80). doi: 10.3389/fpsyg.2015.00080

James, Deborah. 1973. Another look at, say, some grammatical constraints on, oh, interjections and hesitations. Papers from the Ninth Regional Meeting of the Chicago Linguistic Society. 242–251. Chicago Linguistic Society.

Holler, Judith, Louise Schubotz, Spencer Kelly, Peter Hagoort, Manuela Schuetze, & Asli Özyürek. 2014. Social eye gaze modulates processing of speech and co-speech gesture. *Cognition* 133(3). 692–697.

Janzen, Terry. 2012. Two ways of conceptualizing space: Motivating the use of static and rotated Vantage point space in ASL. In Barbara Dancygier & Eve Sweetser (eds.), *Viewpoint in language: A multimodal perspective*, 156–176. Cambridge: Cambridge University Press.

Liddell, Scott. 1998. Grounded blends, gestures and conceptual shifts. *Cognitive Linguistics* 9(3), 283.

Liddell, Scott. 2003. *Grammar, gesture and meaning in American Sign Language*. Cambridge University Press.

McCarthy, Anjanie, Lee, Kang, Itakura, Shoji& Darwin W. Muir. 2008. Gaze Display When Thinking Depends on Culture and Context. *Journal of Cross-Cultural Psychology*39(6). 716–729.

McClave, Evelyn Z. 2000. Linguistic functions of head movements in the context of speech. *Journal of Pragmatics* 32(7). 855–878.

Nikiforidou, Kiki. 2010. Viewpoint and construction grammar: the case of past + now. *Language and Literature* 19(3).265–284.

Nikiforidou, Kiki. 2012. The constructional underpinnings of viewpoint blends: The Past + now in language and literature. In Barbara Dancygier & Eve Sweetser (eds.), *Viewpoint in language: A multimodal perspective*, 177–197. Cambridge: Cambridge University Press.

Özyürek, Asli. 2002. Do speakers design their cospeech gestures for their addressees? The effects of addressee location on representational gestures. *Journal of Memory and Language* 46(4). 688–704.

Parrill, Fey. 2009. Dual viewpoint gestures. *Gesture* 9(3). 271–289.

Parrill, Fey. 2010. Viewpoint in speech-gesture integration: Linguistics structure, discourse structure, and event structure. *Language and Cognitive Processes* 25(5). 650–668.

Parrill, Fey. 2012. Interactions between discourse status and viewpoint in co-speech gesture. In Barbara Dancygier & Eve Sweetser (eds.), *Viewpoint in language: A multimodal perspective*. 97–112. Cambridge: Cambridge University Press.

Parrill, Fey & Eve Sweetser. 2004. What we mean by meaning: conceptual integration in gesture analysis and transcription. *Gesture* 4(1). 197–219.

Park, Yujong. 2009. Interaction between grammar and multimodal resources: quoting different characters in Korean multiparty conversation. *Discourse Studies* 11(1). 79–104.

Quinto-Pozos, David. 2007. Can constructed action be considered obligatory? *Lingua* 117(7). 1285–1314.

Rossano, Federico. 2012. Gaze in social interaction. In Jack Sidnell & Tanya Stivers (eds.) *Handbook of Conversation Analysis*. 308–329. Malden, MA: Wiley-Blackwell.

Sanders, Jose and Gisela Redeker. 1996. Perspective and representation in speech and thought in narrative discourse. In Gilles Fauconnier & Eve Sweetser (eds.), *Spaces, worlds and grammar*. 290–317. Chicago: University of Chicago Press.

Schegloff, E. A. 1998. Body Torque. *Social Research*, 65(3). 535–596.

Sidnell, Jack. 2006. Coordinating gesture, gaze and talk in reenactments. *Research on Language and Social Interaction* 39(4). 377–409.

Stec, Kashmiri. 2012. Meaningful shifts: A review of viewpoint markers in gesture and sign language. *Gesture* 12(3). 327–360.

Stec, Kashmiri & Mike Huiskes. 2014. Co-constructing referential space in multimodal narratives. *Cognitive Semiotics* 7(1).

Stec, Kashmiri, Mike Huiskes, Alan Cienki & Gisela Redeker. Submitted. Annotating bodily indicators of perspective shifts in conversational narratives.

Stec, Kashmiri & Eve Sweetser. 2012. Significant breaks: Space and viewpoint transitions in gesture. Paper presented at the 2012 International Gesture Studies Conference, in Lund, Sweden.

Stec, Kashmiri & Eve Sweetser. 2013. Managing multiple viewpoints: Coordinating embedded perspective in multimodal narrative. Paper presented at the 12th International Cognitive Linguistics Conference, in Edmonton, Alberta.

Sweetser, Eve. 2012. Introduction: Viewpoint and perspective in language and gesture, from the Ground down. In Barbara Dancygier & Eve Sweetser (eds.), *Viewpoint in language: A multimodal perspective*, 1–2. Cambridge: Cambridge University Press.

Sweetser, Eve. 2014. Creativity across modalities in viewpoint construction. In Mike Borkent, Barbara Dancygier & Jennifer Hinnell (eds.), *Language and the creative mind*, 239–254. Stanford CA: CSLI Publications.

Sweetser, Eve and Marisa Sizemore. 2008. Personal and interpersonal gesture space: functional contrasts in language and gesture. In Andrea Tyler, Yiyoung Kim & Mari Takada (eds.). *Language in the Context of Use: Cognitive and Discourse Approaches to Language and Language Learning*. 25–51. Berlin: Mouton de Gruyter.

Thompson, Sandra A. & Ryoko Suzuki. 2014. Reenactments in conversation: Gaze and recipiency. *Discourse Studies* 16(6). 816–846.

Vandelanotte, Lieven. 2009. *Speech and thought representation in English*. Berlin/New York: Mouton de Gruyter.

Vandelanotte, Lieven. 2012. 'Wait till you got started': How to submerge another's discourse in your own. In Barbara Dancygier & Eve Sweetser (eds.). *Viewpoint in language: A multimodal perspective*. 198–218. Cambridge: Cambridge University Press.

Verhagen, Arie. 2005. *Constructions of intersubjectivity: Discourse, syntax and cognition*. Oxford: Oxford University Press.

Maria Josep Jarque and Esther Pascual

Mixed viewpoints in factual and fictive discourse in Catalan Sign Language narratives

Abstract: This chapter is based on in-depth qualitative analysis of original elicited and naturalistic narratives from 20 native signers of Catalan Sign Language. Signed languages are especially interesting for the study of mixed viewpoints, since their grammar is characterized by viewpoint shift (Herrmann and Steinback 2012). They also lend themselves particularly well for the study of conversational constructions, such as direct discourse, as they are typically used in situated intersubjective interaction.

We focus on the use of role shift to set up non-genuine quotes in Catalan Sign Language narratives. In particular, we examine multifunctional or polysemic direct discourse, which per definition involves (mixed) viewpoints. In signed languages direct discourse may serve to represent a referent's utterances, actions, thoughts, emotions, attitudes and source of information. We show that despite its complexity, "constructed action", which involves multiple perspectives, is a central component of Catalan Sign Language narratives. In fact, although alternative descriptive constructions do exist, native signers consider constructed action as the most unmarked (cf. Quinto-Pozos 2007). We further propose that the structure of mixed viewpoints in narratives – and in grammar – mimics the mode in which language is mostly used, namely intersubjective conversation, characterized by constant perspective shifting.

1 Introduction

This chapter stems from the assumption that thought, grammar and discourse are not only embodied, as generally assumed in cognitive linguistics (Wilcox and Xavier 2013, inter alia), but also inherently intersubjective (Voloshinov [1929] 1986; Vygotsky [1934] 1962; Verhagen 2005; Zlatev et al. 2008), and hence *viewpointed* in nature (Dancygier and Sweetser 2012). More specifically, the assumption is that the structure of narratives as well as language's pragmatic functions and grammatical meaning are intimately related to and partly modelled by face-to-face interaction (Voloshinov 1929; Verhagen 2005; Zlatev et al. 2008; Pascual 2006, 2014; Pascual and Sandler forthcoming). The central question addressed is: how is the basic interactional pattern of turn-taking reflected in grammatical structure? And, since turn-taking involves the alternation of viewpoints, how is viewpoint shift and the resulting mixing of viewpoints reflected in grammatical and discursive structures used in narratives?

The focus is on the form and function of conversational structures such as the use of direct discourse, which involves viewpoint shift and thus a mixture of viewpoints. Consider for instance this extract from a 1997 interview in Dutch with the then crown prince of the Netherlands. There, the future king illustrates his empathic capacities with a story on his visit to the victims of a crashed building:[1]

(1) *Met name na het bezoeken aan, aan het flat zelf, het samenkomen in de sporthal, waar de meest vre-se-lijke ellende door je heen gaan. Maar gewoon, het kunnen geven van een* **gevoel** *van er wordt aan* **ons** *gedacht, Nederland leeft met* **ons** *mee.*
'Especially after visiting the- the apartment building itself, getting together in the sports hall, where the most ter-ri-ble things go through your$_i$ head. But just being able to give this **feeling** of ***we***$_j$*'re being thought of, The Netherlands is with* ***us***$_j$.'

In (1), the narrator characterizes the kind of feeling he gave the victims he visited through an embedded enunciation ascribed to the experiencer of such a feeling. This involves the presentation of two mixed viewpoints in one and the same grammatical phrase. The embedded utterance "***we****'re being thought of, the Netherlands is with* ***us***" is produced from the victim's perspective and thus the first person plural refers to them rather than to the utterer in the here-and-now. At the same time, this characterizing 'utterance' is produced from the narrator's perspective, as this is his interpretation and presentation of an emotional state of his interlocutors. Note, too, that the string in italics is not a genuine utterance factually uttered by the victims in unison, but rather an enactment or non-genuine 'demonstration' (Clark and Gerrig 1990). It is not only an instance of constructed choral speech (Tannen 1986), but also of *fictive interaction* (Pascual 2006, 2014). Its ontological state is between reality and fiction and it characterizes a non-conversational referent in conversational terms, as a kind of verbal exchange between the agents involved.

We suggest that all instances of direct discourse involve the fusion of different viewpoints, regardless of whether they present factual or fictive speech or writing. Such intersubjective structures occur in a great number of unrelated lan-

1 Link at: http://nos.nl/koningshuis/video/189536-prins-willemalexander-over-de-troonswisseling-1997.html (min. 4:22, 4:37–4:57). All italics, bold and underlinings in the examples are ours.

guages (Pascual 2006, 2014; Pascual and Sandler forthcoming). In fact, a vast cross-linguistic study of direct speech for non-quotations across a large number of spoken languages from different families found no single language without this construction (Pascual 2014: ch. 4). There are, however, important differences in their degree of grammaticalization. Non-quotational direct speech constructions, which more often than not involve mixed viewpoints, all seem to be the more engrained in the grammar of a language, the more their speakers rely exclusively or mostly on oral communication among them. In fact, the only languages lacking an indirect speech construction tend to be languages without or with a limited writing system (Pascual 2014: ch. 4). When a language has both direct and indirect speech, direct speech is also used more frequently in spontaneous situated interaction as opposed to monologic writing (Tannen 1982, 1986, inter alia). The role of speech, voice and turn-taking naturally becomes less prominent in a written society, and consequently the role of conversation also becomes less exclusive as a locus of language change (see Pascual 2014: ch. 4 for references).

Mixed viewpoints in non-quotational direct speech appear fully grammaticalized in many unrelated spoken languages of the world with no or a poorly used writing system. These may serve to express: mental states (thoughts or the result of thoughts), emotions, desires, intentions, attempts, states of affairs, causation, reason, purpose and even future tense (Pascual 2014: ch. 4; ; Spronck forthcoming; van der Voort forthcoming).

The present chapter builds up on these studies to examine non-quotational direct discourse in signed languages. Languages in the visual-gestural modality are particularly interesting for our purposes since they have viewpoint or role shift as a critical feature of their grammar and discourse structure. To quote Herrmann and Steinback (2012: 222): "Only in sign languages has role shift become a genuine part of the grammatical system, because the visual-manual modality, unlike the oral-auditory modality, offers the unique property of grammaticalizing manual and non-manual gestures". Sign languages are further interesting to our goal because they show the characteristics of oral and written languages. They are used (mainly) in face-to-face interaction by (mainly) literate individuals.

Our hypothesis is that the in-between position of signed languages on the orality continuum also places them in an in-between position in the grammaticalization of interactional structures continuum. In other words, we believe that signed languages will show a use of non-quotational direct discourse that is more grammaticalized than their counterpart constructions in spoken languages with established writing, but less grammaticalized than those in spoken languages with limited or no writing.

The non-quotational use of construed action or dialogue in signed languages is further particularly interesting for the study of mixed viewpoints, since, according to some authors, it is characterized by a combination of direct and indirect speech features (Herrmann and Steinback 2007; Quer 2011, among others).[2] As Herrman and Pfau (2012: 213) state, "role shift seems to be part of a continuum between indirect and direct speech, most probably closer to direct speech". Thus, in signed languages the construction under discussion per definition involves mixed viewpoints of the individual 'reporting' or being 'reported' and the 'reported' issuer.

2 Direct discourse in signed languages: Constructed action

In the sign language literature the visual-gestural direct discourse construction used to (re)present mixed viewpoints has been identified as *role shift*, *reference shift* or *role switching* (Lillo-Martin 2012). From a cognitive/functional perspective, the term *constructed action* is preferred, since it involves an enactment or *demonstration* (Clark and Gerrig 1990) that does not have to equate what actually happened, as described for spoken languages by Tannen (1986) and others.

Constructed action has been defined as "the reporting (usually via a demonstration) of another's actions" (Quinto-Pozos 2007: 1288). Constructed action is a grammatical and discourse strategy used widely in signed languages, in which the signer uses his/her face, head, body, hands and/or other non-manual cues to represent a referent's actions, utterances, thoughts, feelings and/or attitudes (Metzger 1995; Liddell and Metzger 1998; Wilcox and Xavier 2013 for ASL; McClearly and Viotti 2010 for Brazilian Sign Language – LIBRAS; Ferrara and Johnston 2014 for Australian Sign Language – AUSLAN; Cormier et al. 2013 and Smith and Cormier 2014 for British Sign Language – BSL).

Metzger (1995) distinguishes between *constructed action* (a signer's representation of a referent's actual or perceived actions) and *constructed dialogue* in the sense of Tannen (1986), that is, a language user's (re)presentation of a referent's discourse. We will regard *constructed action* as the overarching phenomenon and *constructed discourse* as a subtype or a specific function of it. As will become apparent in the next pages, in LSC narratives constructed action involving mixed viewpoints is used to present: referent events (4.1) and discourse (4.2) as well as

2 Such constructions with characteristics of both direct and indirect speech are also found in languages with a written code used in a predominantly oral community, such as ancient Greek and some African languages (see Pascual 2014 for references).

cognitive states, such as mental (5.1), emotional and attitudinal states (5.2), and source of information (5.3).

3 Methodology

This chapter is based on a qualitative analysis of our own corpus of narratives in Catalan Sign Language (*llengua de signes catalana*, henceforth LSC). A poorly studied language, LSC is used by the signing deaf and deaf-blind community of Catalonia, in North-East Spain.

The data for this chapter were collected from 10 deaf adult signers in Barcelona. All are Catalan-born, between 40 and 68 years of age, and with LSC as their most frequently used language. They are all native or early signers, that is, they either come from a family in which LSC has been the native language for two to three generations, or they come from a hearing family, but acquired LSC before their sixth birthday. Almost all informants are trained as LSC instructors and most of them actually work as LSC instructors. All of them are in regular contact with written language (in Catalan or mostly in Spanish). Their written and especially reading competence is rather high.

Our Catalan Sign Language corpus includes narrative texts and narrative fragments from expository and argumentative texts. The data combine naturalistic discourse and elicited data. The naturalistic data come from personal video blogs, conversations between friends, and specially a LSC news website, including short news, documentaries and tales. The elicited data are narratives using different kinds of elicitation stimuli: (i) Mayer's (1968) *The Frog Story*; (ii) on one occasion: the short wordless movie *The Pear Story* (Chafe 1980), which is another story successfully used in a variety of studies; and (iii) five so-called made-up narratives of personal experience, considered the optimal technique to elicit the archetypical narrative (Labov 1984).

4 Direct discourse in Catalan Sign Language

4.1 Constructed action for reporting events in LSC

In Catalan Sign Language the expression of constructed action occurs through manual and non-manual markers (i.e. the upper part of the body, the head and the face). Signed constructed action may refer to the different characters in a narrative, thus showing simultaneous mixed viewpoints. Note for instance example (2). This corresponds to the episode of *The Frog Story* narrative when the narrator describes how the boy character reacts when realizing that what he thought was a tree is actually a deer, now running and approaching the cliff (Jarque 2011: 88).

(2) *The Frog Story: The running deer*[3]
< $_{\text{CA: boy}}$ DC:“the boy is on the deer while tree branches passing through” > TILL DC:“plain landscape” DC:“there is a cliff” < $_{\text{CA: boy}}$ DC:“the boy is scared since the deer's body is approaching to the cliff” DC:“the boy calms down when the deer's body stops just before the cliff >

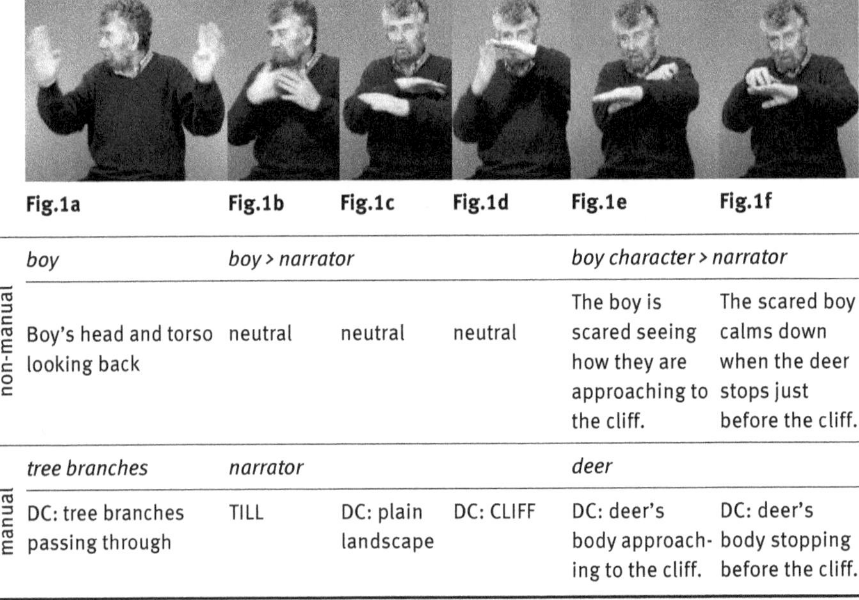

	Fig.1a	Fig.1b	Fig.1c	Fig.1d	Fig.1e	Fig.1f
	boy	*boy > narrator*			*boy character > narrator*	
non-manual	Boy's head and torso looking back	neutral	neutral	neutral	The boy is scared seeing how they are approaching to the cliff.	The scared boy calms down when the deer stops just before the cliff.
	tree branches	*narrator*			*deer*	
manual	DC: tree branches passing through	TILL	DC: plain landscape	DC: CLIFF	DC: deer's body approach-ing to the cliff.	DC: deer's body stopping before the cliff.

3 The glosses appear in two different rows in order to show the simultaneous or consecutive combination of mixed viewpoints. We first specify the narrator or character(s) perspective, followed by the action demonstrated. In all LSC examples, lexical and grammatical signs are glossed in upper case. Numbers attached to verbs with hyphens indicate points in the signing space that correspond to the grammatical person. The signs “< >” mark the scope of the report or demonstration. “CA:xx” stands for *constructed action* where *xx* identifies the agent. “DC” stands for depicting construction in the sense of Liddell (2003) or *polycomponential verb* (Slobin et al. 2003), or just classifier, and it refers to the spatial verb type in other typologies. The meaning of the DC is described between inverted commas. Gestures and the meaning of DC are described in lower case. Hyphens separate morphemes within a sign. “ASP” stands for aspect, “PLU” for plural, and “^” indicates that the sign is a compound.

Lit.: 'The boy was on the deer, looked back with his head and torso, as they were moving (seeing tree branches passed through) and became scared when he saw they were approaching the cliff.'

'The boy was sitting on the deer, looked back while the deer was running forward and became scared when seeing they were approaching the cliff.'

In Fig. (1a) the narrator first assumes the boy's viewpoint, acting as a so-called 'surrogate' of the boy's (Liddell 2003) by turning his torso, head and face, as the boy does in the story. At the same time, his hands produce a depicting construction with a spatial verb representing the static branches of the trees around, which seem to move when the boy on the deer moves forward. One of the main mechanisms signers use to relay information about referents in narratives is verbal morphology.[4] LSC verbs include: (i) simple, (ii) deictic, and (iii) spatial verbs (Morales-López et al. 2005). Whereas all types of verbs may include morphemes expressing aspect[5] and adverbial information regarding the different states of things, the three types differ in the perspective that may be adopted, as well as in the morphological expression of semantic notions such as agent, patient, theme, instrument, locative, etc. Simple verbs basically convey lexical information, whereas deictic verbs further include agent and/or patient/goal information, activating – through a change in the handshape orientation and/or movement direction – indexing meaning (always personal deixis, but in some contexts also social and spatial deixis) (Morales-López et al. 2005). When using constructed action with a deictic verb, the signer will adopt the *protagonist's perspective* (Slobin et al. 2003), also called *character perspective* (Özyürek and Perniss 2011), and the verbal predicates will show first person morphology (as agent or patient), resulting in a demonstration or enactment, and not third person morphology, as expected in a descriptive discourse.

Finally, in Morales-López et al. (2005) spatial verbs correspond to *policomponential verbs* (Slobin et al. 2003) or *depicting predicates* (Liddell 2003). Using this type of verbs, signers may select either the narrator's or the *protagonist perspective* (Slobin et al. 2003), also called *character perspective* (Özyürek and Perniss 2011), according to the type of depicting construction: entity (as in Figure 1a) or handling construction (as the manual predicate in Figure 1e or 1f). In (2), the

4 Contrary to common practice in the signed language literature, we will not speak of verbal inflection, since, from a typological perspective, it does not follow the established criteria (see Bybee 1985; Bybee, Perkings and Pagliuca, 1987, among others). The arguments are: (i) these agent and patient morphemes are not present across all verbs in LSC; (ii) different types of morphemes occur according to the type of verbs, and (iii) the morphemes do not seem to be obligatory.

5 See Jarque (forthcoming) for references on aspect and its expression in LSC.

signer produces a depicting construction adopting a *character scale*, that is, the signer uses the space surrounding him as if he was acting or interacting with people or objects in a real-world scale (see Aarons and Morgan 2003 for South African Sign Language; Özyürek and Perniss 2011 for German Sign Language and Turkish Sign Language; and Smith and Cormier 2014 for British Sign Language; also see Swetser and Stec, this volume).

Subsequently, the signer makes eye contact with the addressee, as he produces the lexical sign 'STILL', as shown in Figures (1b) to (1d), indicating that he is taking the narrator's viewpoint. This is followed by an entity construction, as he represents the landscape (i.e. the cliff). In (1e) there is a break of eye gaze, which shows that the narrator enacts the referent once more. The signer again uses his own facial expression to represent the referent's face (in this case, the boy), who is scared because of the cliff's proximity. The signer's head and torso represent the boy's head and torso movements, as well as his posture. At the same time, as shown in (1e), his hands produce a depicting construction: the right hand adopts an entity handshape that corresponds to a four-leg animal (i.e. the deer), whereas the left hand represents a plain entity (i.e. the ground). The signer simultaneously conveys two spatial scales and thus two mixed viewpoints: (i) the deer's running action (with manual articulators) from a *narrator's perspective* and (ii) the boy (with face, head and torso) from a *protagonist's perspective*. Whereas both hands produce a given type of linguistic material, the non-manual articulators are responsible for the gestural part, representing the constructing action as such, thereby creating a composite utterance (Enfield 2009; Ferrara and Johnson 2014).

4.2 Constructed discourse in LSC

As is true for other signed languages (Lillo-Martin 2012; Herrman and Steinback 2012), the formal marking of constructed discourse in LSC may include a constellation of non-manual markers co-articulated with the (re)presented utterance (cf. Quer 2011):

i. Eye gaze change towards the locus of the addressee of the quoted utterance, and thus temporal interruption of eye contact with the actual interlocutor.
ii. Body leaning over, including a sideward movement of the upper part of the body towards the locus of the quoted signer and a midsagittal body shift towards the locus of the addressee of the reported utterance.
iii. Change of head position towards the locus of the addressee of the reported utterance.
iv. Facial and bodily expression associated with the quoted issuer conveying affective and attitudinal components.

These non-manual markers are produced more prominently by non-native signers (see Costello et al. 2008 for Spanish Sign Language). Moreover, together with prosodic pauses, they constitute the unmarked devices for introducing embedded constructed reports in LSC, rather than subjunctions or a marker as BE+LIKE, as described for American Sign Language (Ferrara and Bell 1995). It should be noted, however, that not all these markers are mandatory. Eye gaze change and temporal interruption of eye contact with the actual interlocutor constitute the most frequent kinds of marking. Consider example (3). This piece of dialogue describes an anecdote in which a man goes to visit a friend in a working-class neighbourhood, notorious for its many robberies. The signer narrates how the visitor's motorcycle is stolen in front of his friend's apartment.

(3) *The stolen motorcycle story*

a. [DEAF [OF LIVE INDEX:$_{\text{neighbourhood}}$]$_{\text{-relative}}$]$_{\text{-topic}}$ KNOW-ASP.PERF SEE-ASP.HAB INDEX:$_{\text{neighbourhood}}$

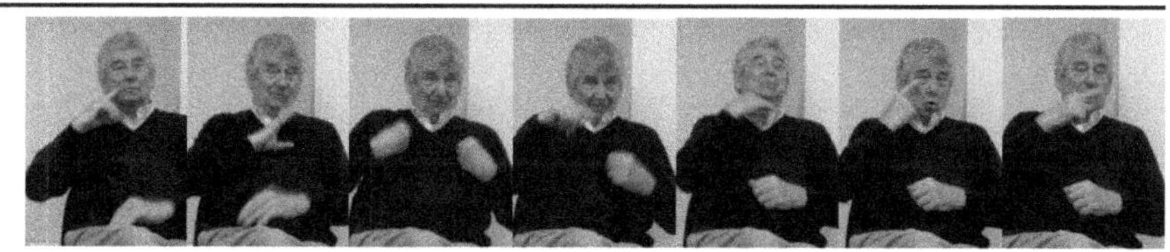

non-manual	narrator				narrator		
	[			]-topic			
		[		]-rel			
manual	narrator				Narrator		
	DEAF	OF	LIVE	INDEX-there	KNOW-ASP. PERFECTIVE	SEE-ASP. HABITUAL	INDEX-there

Lit.: 'The deaf man (that) lives there (in that neighbourhood) knew (that the motorbike could get stolen), since he had often seen (that happen) there (in that neighbourhood)

'The deaf man living there (in that neighbourhood) was aware of it (the risk that the motorbike get stolen) (since) he knew about (the neighbourhood's bad reputation).'

b. <$_{\text{CA: deaf host}}$ PITY 2-TELL-1, MOTORBIKE SAVE WELL >

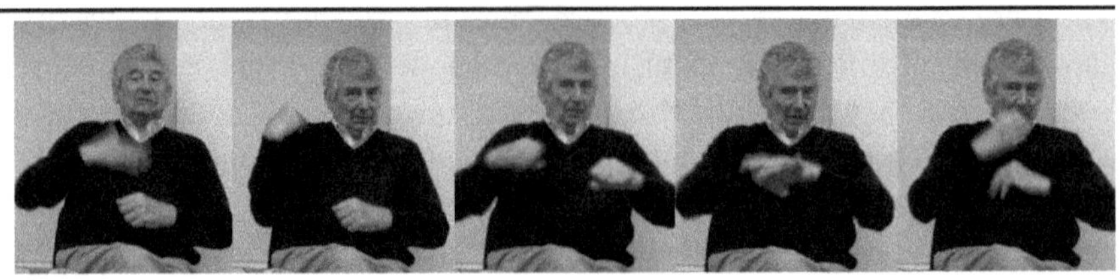

non-manual	character: deaf host				
	facial expression of "pity"	facial expression of "obligation"	[facial expression of "counterfactual"		]-topic
manual	character: deaf host				
	< PITY	2-TELL-1	MOTORBIKE	SAVE	WELL >

Lit.: '...he [the deaf host] said: *"Pity. You (should) have told me and (I would have) kept the motorbike in a safe place".*'

'...he [the deaf host] said it was a pity and told (the other man) that he should have told him (about the motorbike) and he would have taken it somewhere safe.'

c. [DEAF]$_{\text{-topic}}$ <$_{\text{CA:guest deaf}}$ INNOCENT >$_{\text{pause}}$ DEAF [OF LIVE INDEX-there]$_{\text{-relative-topic}}$ <$_{\text{CA:hosting deaf}}$ WAIT >

Lit.: 'The (other) deaf (man) answered: *"I didn't know that!"*. (Then) the deaf who was living there said: *"Wait"*...

'The other deaf man answered that he didn't know that. Then the deaf living there said: *"Wait"*...'

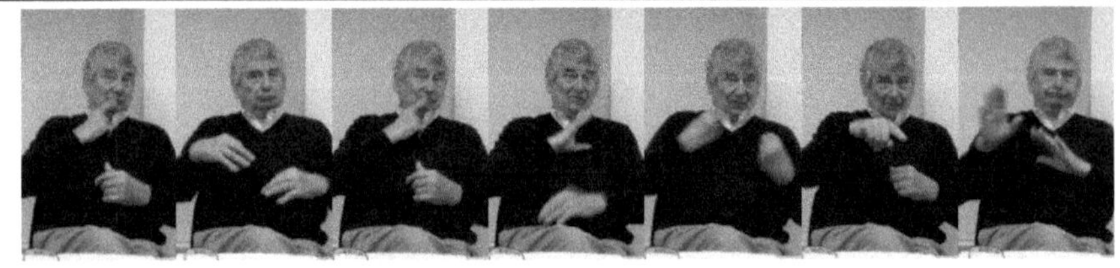

non-manual	narrator	Deaf guest	narrator				Deaf host
	[ ]-topic		[			]-topic	
				[		]-relative	
manual	narrator	Deaf guest	narrator				Deaf host
	DEAF	INNOCENT	DEAF	OF	LIVE	INDEX-there	<WAIT>

Lit.: 'The (other) deaf (man) answered: *"I didn't know that!"*. (Then) the deaf who was living there said: *"Wait"*...

'The other deaf man answered that he didn't know that. Then the deaf living there said: *"Wait"*...'

The markers of viewpoint shift in (3) are not very prominent. Moreover, several mechanisms frame the constructed action, marking its beginning and end (see Cornier et al. 2013 for British Sign Language). Along the narratives, we observe different framing strategies: contiguous reference, non-contiguous reference and subject omission. Contiguous reference (a noun phrase referring to the character portrayed by the constructed action followed by that constructed action) was preferred with an introductory function, but also for reintroduction (switch reference). Note examples (3a) and (3c), where an NP is followed by a relative clause for viewpoint switch. In a switch reference context, a pattern of overt subject expression is generally preferred in LSC, with body leaning over, change of head position/orientation, and/or other non-manual markers, as well as break of eye gaze, especially when there is only a break of eye gaze. Moreover, subject omission was favoured when the subject was co-referential with the subject of the preceding clause, or in a shift reference context with body leaning over, change of head position/orientation, and/or other non-manual markers, as well as break of eye gaze.

Apart from serving to set up reports of actions and utterances, constructed action may also be used in LSC narratives as an unmarked means of presenting fictive discourse ascribed to character(s).

5 Fictive discourse in LSC

In Catalan Sign Language, a non-genuine action or fictive discourse constitutes an unmarked linguistic construction with discourse and grammatical functions, such as the expression of thoughts and intentions (5.1.), emotional states and attitudes (5.2.), and source of information (5.3.).

5.1 Fictive discourse for mental states

Just as is the case for the pragmatics of a large number of spoken languages with established writing (so-called 'chirographic languages'), and the grammar of various spoken languages with no or restricted writing (so-called 'oral languages'), direct discourse in LSC may also serve to present thoughts and intentions. Consider example (4) from a tale about an old lady having troubles with a fly:

(4) *The spider tale*[6]
[OLD PERSON FEMALE$_{i}$]$_{\text{-topic}}$ <$_{\text{CA:old woman}}$ LOOK.FOR.A.SOLUTION-DURATIVE.ASPECT gesture: "she thinks for a while" [THINK]$_{\text{facial.expression.of.'aha!'.moment}}$ [INDEX:$_{\text{spider}}$ SPIDER]$_{\text{-topic}}$ SPIDER-GO EAT(fly)...>

Lit.: 'The old woman goes: *"What can I do?"* (She goes like) thinking for a while (and then says): *"I got it. If the spider eats (the fly then)..."*'.

'The old lady wondered what to do. She thought for a while and then got an idea: If the spider ate the fly then...'.

In (4), the signer first establishes the referent with a topicalized nominal phrase, and then produces the constructed action that includes both thought representation (i.e. enacting the sign cluster 'LOOK.FOR.A.SOLUTION') and gestural enactment (the external attitude that accompanies the thinking process). This is followed by a cognitive predicate functioning as a framing device (i.e. the enacted 'THINK') introducing the reported thought (lit. '*I got it. If the spider ate (the fly then)...*').

Other cognitive predicates that frame constructed action for thoughts and intentions are THINK, BELIEVE, WORRY, etc. This is also the case of zero manual marking, as in (5) below. This piece of LSC direct discourse, from the beginning of the deer episode of *The Frog Story*, illustrates the expression of intentions.

(5) *The frog story: The huge rock*
ROCK DC: "There was a huge rock" DC: "There were branches all around the rock" [SEE INDEX-there THERE.BE FROG]$_{\text{raised.eyebrows}}$

6 For reasons of anonymity, we did not include the pictures in this example.

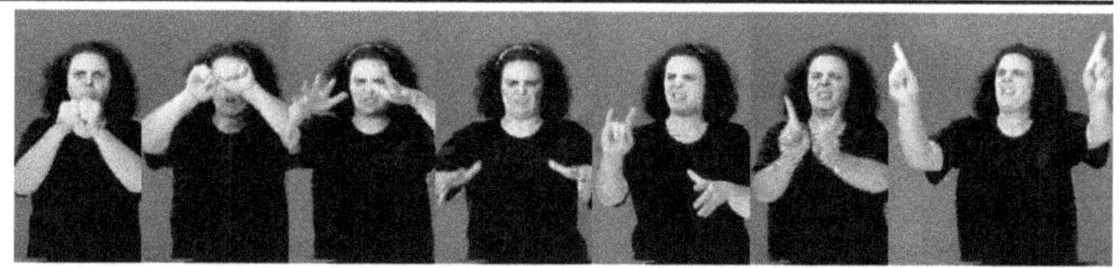

non-manual	narrator		
	neutral	facial expression of massive quantity	facial expression of massive quantity
manual	narrator	narrator	narrator
	ROCK	DC: huge rock	DC: branches all around the rock

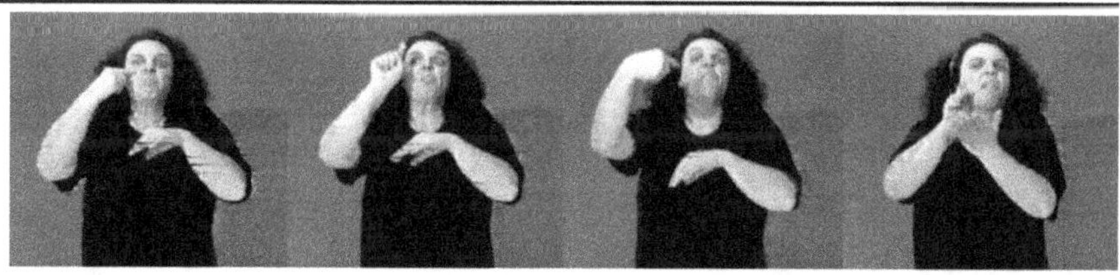

non-manual	boy character			
	facial expression of intention		facial expression of possibility	
manual	boy character			
	SEE	INDEX-there	THERE.BE	FROG

Lit.: 'There was a huge rock, taller than the boy, surrounded by branches. The boy said to himself: *"Let's see if the frog is there"*.'

'There was a huge rock, taller than the boy, surrounded by branches. The boy decided to go see if the frog was there.'

After the token of the manual depicting construction describing the branches and the rocks, the string in direct discourse (i.e. "<SEE INDEX-there THERE.BE FROG>") represents neither reported action or dialogue nor actual dialogue. Instead, it presents the thoughts of the boy in the story, as constructed by the signer. The boy is not really talking to himself. Rather, the signer expresses the boy's intention out loud for the sake of the signer's interlocutor, temporarily turned in effect into the fictive bystander of the boy's fictive enunciation. The interplay of mixed viewpoints hence includes both the character (the boy) and the narrator (the female signer).

5.2 Fictive discourse for emotional and attitudinal states

The use of a non-genuine piece of discourse for presenting emotions and attitudes is very common in a wide range of spoken as well as signed languages (Pascual 2014: ch. 4). Consider the LSC example in (6).

(6) *The Frog Story: The frog family*
< $_{\text{CA:boy}}$ DC: "the boy and the dog are looking at the frog family"> FEEL.EMOTION < $_{\text{CA:boy}}$ FEEL.EMOTION DC: "the boy and the dog are looking at the dog family" > [DOG]$_{\text{raised.eyebrows}}$ < $_{\text{CA:frog}}$ (frog's parents)-LOOK.AT-(boy.and.frog)>

	Fig. 7a.	Fig. 7b	Fig. 7c	Fig. 7d	Fig. 7e	Fig. 7f
	boy	narrator	narrator>boy	boy	narrator	frog
non-manual	The boy and the dog are looking at the frog family with a happy expression.	facial expression of happiness	facial expression of happiness	The boy and the dog are looking at the frog family.	[ ] topic	facial expression of intentions
	boy and dog	narrator	narrator	boy and dog	boy	
manual	DC: two entities with eyes (the boy and the dog) are looking at the frog family	FEEL.EMOTION	FEEL.EMOTION	DC: the boy and the dog are looking at the frog family	DC: FROG	(frog's parents)-LOOK.AT-(boy.and.dog)

Lit.: 'The boy and the dog were looking [at the frog family]. "*Exciting, happiness!*", the boy thought.

'The boy, looking at the frog family, got really excited and happy.'

In (6) the signer narrates how the boy and the dog in *The Frog Story* find the family of the lost frog. She does so by a demonstration. In this fragment she uses all of the non-manual markers available in LSC, mentioned in 4.1 and 4.2, for coding the mixed viewpoints of both herself as narrator and the boy as discourse character.

5.3 Fictive discourse for source of information

The last function of constructed action we will address involves the use of direct discourse from different viewpoints as a discourse strategy to present information from different sources (see Shaffer 2012 for a similar use in American Sign Language).

The semantic domain regarding the coding of source of information is referred to as *evidentiality*. It may be fully grammaticalized as an inflectional category in some spoken languages (Aikhenvald 2004), or be less grammaticalized and adopt a lexical, periphrastic and syntactic expression in other languages (Bermúdez 2005). The evidential function is relevant in narratives since it constitutes a deictic phenomenon of non-discrete nature. It expresses the speaker's point of view and is based on both the context of utterance and the speaker's relationship with the interlocutor and the conceptualized scene (Bermúdez 2005), including the participants and/or the characters in the narrative. Evidentiality is particularly relevant for the characterization of mixed viewpoints, since it allows the utterer to guide the interlocutor to the pragmatic interpretation of the state of affairs presented, based on the qualification of its source.

Consider example (7), from a news webpage addressed to the Catalan signing community, on a demonstration against social exclusion of the deaf. The narrator presents the contradictory report on the number of attendees given by the organizers and the police through a fictive dialogue between the two groups, a mixed viewpoint discourse structure, each speaking in unison.

(7) *The success of unity*[7]

a. [ORGANIZATION OF DEAF.FEDERATION ENTITY]$_{\text{i·topic}}$ <$_{\text{CA: Deaf Federation}}$ 1$_{\text{contralateral}}$-LOOK-INDEX$_{\text{:demonstration}}$ SAY$_{\text{i}}$ COUNT SAY$_{\text{i}}$ ROUGHLY 2-THOUSAND PERSON-PLU PARTICIPATE-AT.1 DEMONSTRATION INDEX>

Lit.: 'The Catalan Federation for the Deaf looked at the demonstration and said: *"We count (and) two thousand people participated at our demonstration".*'

b. [BUT]$_{\text{advers.}}$ [OF POLICE^TRAFFIC INDEX$_{\text{:demonstration_z}}$ POLICE INDEX$_{\text{j}}$]$_{\text{-topic}}$ 1$_{\text{ipsil}}$-LOOK-INDEX$_{\text{:demonstration}}$ SAY$_{\text{j}}$<CA: $_{\text{POLICE}}$ [NO]$_{\text{neg}}$ ROUGHLY THOUSAND 5-HUNDRED A.LITLE MORE ROUGHLY>

Lit.: 'But, the traffic police looked at it and said: *"Not really, roughly one thousand five hundred, (or maybe) a little bit more approximately".*'

'The Catalan Federation for the Deaf estimated that two thousand people participated in the demonstration. However, the traffic police claimed one thousand five hundred, or a little bit more, approximately.'

This piece of news is construed as a narrative in which the perspective of the narrator and the two quoted characters are thoroughly interwoven. After establishing the agent entity, the signer adopts the perspective of the Federation for the Deaf, by shifting his body slightly and producing the verb 'SEE' from a contralateral side. The sign begins from the signer's body and ends at the point in space that corresponds to the deaf demonstration. The body orientation shift thus encodes both subject and object (Morales et al. 2005). This spatial orientation of the verb provides information about the signer taking one of the character's voices. In indirect discourse, the verb would have to include an intermediate locus to mark the third person reference (i.e. the Federation for the Deaf).

This example illustrates possible variations in the use of the non-manual markers in LSC in order to encode role shift via constructed action. The signer changes his position and bodyshift into the perspective of the two 'reported' entities (i.e. the Deaf Federation and the traffic police), by adjusting his body and head position as well as his eye gaze and facial expression. His eye gaze changes towards the locus of the demonstration rather than towards the locus of the addressee of the quoted utterance, as one may expect. After assuming the perspective of the Deaf Federation (7a), the signer assumes the perspective of the

7 For anonymity reasons, we did not include the pictures in this example.

traffic police (7b). He does so not only by giving them 'voice', but also by presenting them as directly confronting the Deaf Federation in a discussion that never took place. In (7), an approximate number of attendees is presented through a fictive argument between two groups, each giving their estimation 'as one voice' that contradicts the other. By doing so, the signer manages to present both a piece of information and the source where this information comes from. The fictive dialogue set up thus serves an evidential function.

Critically, this is not a rhetorical device, like the presentation of a contemporary philosopher as debating with the long-deceased Kant in order to teach philosophy students (Fauconnier and Turner 2002). Quite differently, in LSC this is an entirely unmarked means of presenting information. The narrator indicates the source of information upon which his statement is based (see also Chafe and Nichols 1986; Aikhenvald 2004). By doing so, through conversational implicature, the news reader manages to present the degree of commitment in the information reported to the interlocutor (i.e. the viewer of the news), thereby giving it epistemic value.

6 Discussion and conclusions

In this chapter we showed that Catalan Sign Language signers use a schematic linguistic unit called *constructed action* (sometimes in combination with other linguistic devices, such as depicting constructions or framing cognitive predicates), by setting up multiple perspectives within a narrative. Signers enact a character's actions and discourse – both a factual previous one and an entirely created one – by using non-manual articulators as well as body shifts in space, indicating viewpoint shift.

Instances of constructed action in LSC are *composite utterances* (Enfield 2009), combining different manual and non-manual components (linguistic and gestural ones). Although conventionalized and entrenched to a degree, some elements of their form and meaning are dependent on specific instances of use, as observed by Ferrara and Johnson (2014) for Australian Sign Language. They seem to be in-between purely pragmatic and obligatory grammatical structures. Since many constructions in Catalan Sign Language – and in signed languages in general, for that matter – are still in a conventionalization and entrenchment process, most signed language users being non-native signers, and since the transmission process is horizontal and discontinuous, we consider it more accurate to speak of unmarked rather than a (totally) grammaticalized viewpoint shift.

Despite its complexity, constructed action is a central component of LSC narratives and grammatical structure. Its effective use requires a mastery of non-manual facial features, verb morphology, pronoun reference, use of space, as well as the understanding that these mixed viewpoints can serve to express a wide range of meanings or functions (characters' events, discourse reports, expression of emotional and attitude states, as well as thoughts and intentions, and evidentiality). Signers are able to simultaneously express multiple physical and conceptual viewpoints in unique ways, since human bodies have relatively independent articulators, and signers may use space in complex ways (Janzen 2012).

Although alternative descriptive constructions for these same functions do exist and are used, LSC native and early signers consider those involving constructed action as more unmarked, necessary and genuine ones, in line with what is reported by Quinto-Pozos (2007) for American Sign Language. Based on the first author's notes from participant observation in the Catalan Deaf community for over twenty years, as well as our informants' explanations on the structure and discourse of LSC, we suggest that signing deaf people in Catalonia show a clear preference for demonstration or enactment, rather than description in narratives when referring to characters events and discourse. This has been an important issue in discussions on LSC interpreters training programs and LSC courses as L2 for the hearing at university level as well as in college programs.

We further propose that the structure of mixed viewpoints in narrative (as well as in a language's grammar) mimics the mode in which language is mostly used, namely intersubjective conversation, characterized by constant perspective shifting. This seems to confirm our hypothesis that relates the use and grammaticalization of conversational structures, such as direct discourse, to orality. The fact that languages without or with limited use of writing share a massive use of *unmarked* interactional structures, which are also vastly – if maybe less so – present in signed languages, further raises issues on grammaticalization.

It should further be noted that this preference for enactment or demonstration presents a challenge for cognitive theories of language representation, not only for amodal theories defending a propositional nature of mental representations, but also for grounded or embodiment theories. The embodiment approach to cognition suggests that the meaning of linguistic entities (words and constructions) are tied to perceptual experience, rather than derived from relationships between abstract, amodal symbols (Barsalou 1999). We argue that this perceptual experience is grounded in intersubjective action.

Constructed action is a schematic linguistic unit, a grammatical and discourse construction that evokes sensorimotor affordances of the entity referred to. Affordances of such entities are set up for ease of identification of (sometimes) simultaneity and multiplicity of mixed viewpoints expressed in narrative. This increases efficiency in communication, not only regarding viewpoint identification but also informativity (Özyürek and Perniss 2011), and especially concerning the emotional content required for a better comprehension.

The data discussed in this chapter show that the several specific constructions – not only character events or direct discourse, but also for the expression of mental states and evidential meaning – activate perceptual and motor information in the form of mental imagery. Direct action and discourse in LSC involves mental images, which rely on simulations of perception and action, simulation of the interaction – on occasions focusing on smaller pieces simultaneously, as in *The Frog Story*. The signer produces a text analogue to visual perception, shaped by action, both in genuine uses (reporting events and discourse) and in fictive ones (the expression of thoughts and intentions, as well as emotional states and attitudes, and source of information), giving support to grounded theories of cognition.

Grounded theories of language comprehension and production suggest that our environment, physical experiences, situated action, the body, social interaction, and simulations in the brain's modality specific systems (perception, action and introspection) interact and ground cognitive representations (Barsalou 2008; Horchak et al. 2014). Future lines of research may consider data from signed languages in order to test the role of sensorimotor experience in language production and comprehension, since in the signed modality the symbolic and embodied representation converge in the same linguistic elements. Critically, in signed languages both symbolic and embodied representation are often presented simultaneously, usually standing for different viewpoints.

Acknowledgments

This study was supported by a Vidi grant by the Netherlands Organization for Scientific Research (NWO), awarded to Esther Pascual (276.70.019), who was also supported by the 'Hundred Talents Program' of Zhejiang University, China. The work in this chapter is further embedded in the research group *Grammar and diachrony* (AGAUR 2014 SGR 994) and the research project FFI201 3092-P (Spanish Ministry of Economy and Competitiveness). Informed consent was received from the two signers from whom images are reproduced.

References

Aarons, Debra & Ruth Zilla Morgan. 2003. Classifier predicates and the creation of multiple perspectives in South African Sign Language. *Sign Language Studies* 3(2). 125–156.

Aikhenvald, Alexandra. 2004. *Evidentiality*. Oxford/New York: Oxford University Press.

Barsalou, Lawrence W. 1999. Perceptual symbol systems. *Behavioral and Brain Sciences* 22. 577–609.

Barsalou, Lawrence W. 2008. Grounded cognition. *Annual Review of Psychology* 59. 617–645.

Bermúdez, Fernando. 2005. *Evidencialidad. La Codificación Lingüística del Punto de Vista.* Stockholm: Stockholm University.

Chafe, Wallace (ed.). 1980. *The pear stories: Cognitive, cultural, and linguistic aspects of narrative production*. Norwood: Ablex Publishing Corporation.

Chafe, Wallace & Johanna Nichols (eds.). 1986. *Evidentiality: The linguistic coding of epistemology*. Norwood, NJ: Ablex.

Clark, Herbert H. & Richard J. Gerrig. 1990. Quotation as demonstration. *Language* 66(4). 784–805.

Cormier, Kearsy, Sandra Smith & Martine Zwets. 2013. Framing constructed action in British Sign Language narratives. *Journal of Pragmatics* 55. 119–139.

Costello, Brendan, Javier Fernández & Alazne Landa. 2008. The non- (existent) native signer: Sign language research in a small deaf population. In Ronice M. de Quadros (ed.), *Sign languages: Spinning and unraveling the past, present and future*. Petrópolis, RJ, Brazil: Editora Arara Azul.

Dancygier, Barbara & Lieven Vandelanotte. 2009. Judging distances: Mental spaces, distance, and viewpoint in literary discourse. In Geert Brône & Jeroen Vandaele (eds.), *Cognitive poetics: Goals, gains and gaps*, 379–382. Berlin: Mouton de Gruyter.

Dancygier, Barbara & Eve Sweetser (eds.). 2012. *Viewpoint in language: A multimodal perspective*. Cambridge: Cambridge University Press.

Dudis, Paul G. 2004. Body partitioning and real-space blends. *Cognitive Linguistics* 15(2). 223–238.

Engberg-Pedersen, Elisabeth. 1995. Point of view expressed through shifters. In Karen Emmorey & Judy S. Reilly (eds.), *Language, gesture, and space*, 133–154. Hillsdalle, NJ: Lawrence Erlbaum.

Enfield, Nick J. 2009. *The anatomy of meaning: Speech, gesture, and composite utterances*. Cambridge: Cambridge University Press.

Fauconnier, Gilles & Mark Turner. 2002. *The way we think: Conceptual blending and the mind's hidden complexities*. New York: Basic Books.

Ferrara, Kathleen & Barbara Bell. 1995. Sociolinguistic variation and discourse function of constructed dialogue introducers: The case of BE+LIKE. *American Speech* 70(3). 265–290.

Ferrara, Lindsay & Trevor Johnston. 2014. Elaborating who's what: A study of constructed action and clause structure in Auslan (Australian Sign Language). *Australian Journal of Linguistics* 34(2). 193–215.

Herrmann, Annika & Markus Steinbach. 2012. Quotation in sign languages: A visible context shift. In Isabelle van Alphen & Ingrid Buchstaller (eds.), *Quotatives: Cross-linguistic and cross-disciplinary perspectives*, 203–228. Amsterdam/Philadelphia: John Benjamins.

Horchak, Oleksandr V., Jean-Christopher Giger, Maria Cabral & Grzegor Pochwatko. 2014. From demonstration to theory in embodied language comprehension: A review. *Cognitive Systems Research* 29–30. 66–85.

Janzen, Terry. 2012. Two ways of conceptualizing space: Motivating the use of static and rotating vantage point space in ASL discourse. In Barbara Dancygier & Eve Sweetser (eds.), *Viewpoint in language: A multimodal perspective*, 156–175. Cambridge: Cambridge University Press.

Jarque, Maria Josep. 2011. Lengua y gesto en la modalidad lingüística signada [Language and gesture in the signed linguistic modality]. *Anuari de Filologia. Estudis de Lingüística* 2. 71–99.

Jarque, Maria Josep. [Forthcoming]. The coding of aspectual values in periphrastic constructions in signed languages. In Mar Garachana, Sandra Montserrat & Claus D. Pusch (eds.), *From composite predicates to verbal periphrases in Romance languages*. Amsterdam/ Philadelphia: John Benjamins.

Labov, William. 1984 . Research methods of the project on linguistic change and variation. In John Baugh & Joel Sherzer (eds.), *Language in use: Readings in sociolinguistics*, 28–53. Englewood Cliffs, NJ: Prentice Hall.

Liddell, Scott K. 2003. *Grammar, gesture, and meaning in American Sign Language*. Cambridge: Cambridge University Press.

Liddell, Scott K. & Melanie Metzger. 1998. Gesture in sign language discourse. *Journal of Pragmatics* 30: 657–697.

Lillo-Martin, Diane. 2012. Utterance reports and constructed action in sign and spoken languages. In Roland Pfau, Markus Steinbach & Bencie Woll (eds.), *Sign language – an international handbook*, 365–387. Berlin: Walter De Gruyter.

Mayer, Mercer. 1969. *Frog, where are you?* New York: Dial book for Young Readers.

McClearly, Leland & Evani Viotti. 2010. Sign-gesture symbiosis in Brazilian Sign Language narrative. In Fey Parrill, Vera Tobin & Mark Turner (eds.), *Meaning, form, and body*, 181–201. Stanford: Center for the Study of Language and Information.

Metzger, Melanie. 1995. Constructed dialogue and constructed action in American Sign Language. In Ceil Lucas (ed.), *Sociolinguistics in deaf communities*, 255–271. Washington: Gallaudet University Press.

Morales-López, Esperanza, Rosa Boldú-Menasanch, Jesús A. Alonso-Rodríguez, Victoria Gras-Ferrer & M. Ángeles Rodríguez-González. 2005. The verbal system of Catalan Sign Language (LSC). *Sign Language Studies* 5(4). 529–532.

Özyürek, Aslı & Pamela Perniss. 2011. Event representation in sign language: A crosslinguistic perspective. In Jürgen Bohnemeyer & E Pederson (eds.), *Event representation in language: Encoding events at the language-cognition interface*, 84–107. Cambridge: Cambridge University Press.

Padden, Carol. 1986. Verbs and role-shifting in American Sign Language. In Carol Padden (ed.), *Proceedings of the Fourth National Symposium on sign language research and teaching*, 44–57. Silver Spring, MD: National Association of the Deaf.

Pascual, Esther. 2006. Fictive interaction within the sentence: A communicative type of fictivity in grammar. *Cognitive Linguistics* 17(2). 245–267.

Pascual, Esther. 2014. *Fictive interaction: The conversation frame in thought, language, and discourse*. Amsterdam/Philadelphia: John Benjamins.

Quer, Josep. 2011. Reporting and quoting in signed discourse. In Elke Brendel, Jörg Meibauer & Markus Steinbach (eds.), *Understanding quotation*, 277–302. Berlin: Mouton de Gruyter.

Quinto-Pozos, David & Sarika Mehta. 2010. Register variation in mimetic gestural complements to signed language? *Journal of Pragmatics* 42. 557–584.
Quinto-Pozos, David. 2007. Can constructed action be considered obligatory? *Lingua* 117 (7). 1285–1314.
Shaffer, Barbara. 2012. Reported speech as an evidentiality strategy in American Sign Language. In Barbara Dancygier & Eve Sweetser (eds.), *Viewpoint in language: A multimodal perspective*, 139–155. Cambridge, MA: Cambridge University Press.
Slobin, Dan I., Nini Hoiting, Marlon Kuntze, Reyna Lindert, Amy Weinberg, Jennie Pyers, Michelle Anthony, Yael Biederman & Helen Thumann. 2003. A cognitive/functional perspective on the acquisition of 'Classifiers'. In Karen Emmorey (ed.), *Perspectives on classifier constructions in Sign Languages*, 271–296. Mahwah, NJ: Erlbaum.
Spronck, Stef. Forthcoming. Evidential fictive interaction in Ungarinyin and Russian. In: Esther Pascual & Sergeiy Sandler (eds.). *The conversation frame: Forms and functions of fictive interaction*. Amsterdam/Philadelphia: John Benjamins.
Smith, Sandra & Kearsy Cormier. 2014. In or out?: Spatial scale and enactment in narratives of native and nonnative signing deaf children acquiring British Sign Language. *Sign Language Studies* 14(3). 275–301.
Tannen, Deborah. 1982. Oral and literate strategies in spoken and written language. *Language* 58(1). 1–21.
Tannen, Deborah. 1986. Introducing constructed dialogue in Greek and American conversational and literary narratives. In Florian Coulmas (ed.), *Direct and indirect speech*, 311–322. Berlin: Mouton de Gruyter.
Vandelanotte, Lieven. 2009. *Speech and thought representation in English: A cognitive-functional approach*. Berlin/New York: Mouton de Gruyter.
van der Voort, Hein. Forthcoming. Recursive inflection and grammaticalized fictive interaction in the southwestern Amazon. In: Esther Pascual & Sergeiy Sandler (eds.), *The conversation frame: Forms and functions of fictive interaction*. Amsterdam/Philadelphia: John Benjamins.
Verhagen, Arie. 2005. *Constructions of intersubjectivity: Discourse, syntax, and cognition*. Oxford: Oxford University Press.
Voloshinov, Valentin N. 1986 [1929]. *Marxism and the philosophy of language* (trans. L. Matejka and I.R. Titunik). Cambridge, MA: Harvard University Press.
Vygotsky, Lev S. 1962 [1934]. *Thought and language*. Cambridge, MA: MIT Press.
Wilcox, Sherman & André Nogueira Xavier. 2013. A framework for unifying spoken language, signed language, and gesture. *Revista Todas as Letras* 11. 88–110.
Zlatev, Jordan, Timothy P. Racine, Chris Sinha & Esa Itkonen (eds.). 2008. *The shared mind: Perspectives on intersubjectivity*. Amsterdam/Philadelphia: John Benjamins.

Barbara Dancygier

Concluding remarks: Why viewpoint matters

The research presented in this volume allows a number of generalizations, regarding the range of mixed viewpoint phenomena, the most effective approaches, and the role of viewpoint in cognitive linguistics work. Whatever the limitations of this sample, it offers sufficient grounds for suggesting research directions and highlighting some issues.

Viewpoint is clearly a conceptual phenomenon, and we can only study its manifestations, which imposes some limitations on what can be worked on. However, even within this volume, one can see how widespread viewpoint phenomena are and how unlikely it is that linguistic investigation will identify what would be some cross-linguistically common level of viewpoint expression. In the studies featured here, viewpoint is represented by a wide range of forms: particles and other function words, lexical items such as verbs and adverbs, constructions and longer stretches of discourse, multimodal artefacts and, last but not least, embodied aspects of communication such as sign, gesture or gaze. The breadth of viewpoint types and the variety of forms they take suggest the importance of viewpoint studies, but also the need for work at and across all levels of linguistic structure, and much cross-pollination between studies of various forms.

The variety of forms of viewpoint expression also suggests that there may soon be a need for two research streams to develop. On the one hand, we might study more specific types of viewpoint, and on the other we should start looking for more generalizations. Some viewpoint phenomena are well covered already – to mention only deixis, modals, evidentials, epistemic stance, or various constructions of represented speech and thought. But much of the existing work is primarily concerned with subcategories – it is enough to think about classifications of modals or massive work on reported speech, focused to a large degree on identification of types and subtypes. While this work definitely helps us see the complexity and variety within areas of expressions of viewpoint, it does not directly address the question of the nature of viewpoint as a general conceptual and linguistic category that may be present in many more phenomena than the 'usual suspects' – a question that is certainly equally important.

Narratives are still commonly considered the most fertile ground for viewpoint studies. They are expected to represent a somewhat narrower range of viewpoints, as they are typically described with respect to sentential level constructions containing markers of temporal viewpoint, epistemic stance of the reporting participant, and the degree to which the viewpoint represented is that of just one participant (let's say, narrator's viewpoint) or more participants (combining signals of the narrator's and character's perspective in a construction, as in Free Indirect Discourse). However, even in this relatively well-described area, an extended view seems to be required. Vanderbiesen, for example, puts the issue in a broader context of quotatives and reportives in general and talks about a cline of forms (rather than specific categories); Izutsu and Izutsu show complex cases of oral narratives edited as texts for publication, where multiple viewpoints are represented through conflations of typically less complex concepts of addressee/ audience vs. narrator/teller. They make it clear that in narratives which inherit features of orality in spite of being accessible as textual printed stories, viewpoints rely on various kinds of grammaticalized blends, built out of written and spoken features of narratives. Also, van Krieken et al. show viewpoint representations in less constructionally salient instances, through implicit means. Finally, Dancygier and Vandelanotte discuss recent (mostly internet-based) forms of reporting, which present new challenges to the interpretation of reporting forms and their meanings, as they inherit only some of the standard reporting features and use them in new ways.

What the variety seems to be indicating is that looking at viewpoint in narratives through the lens of speech and thought representation constructions may not be the most effective approach. Much of what counts as constructionally salient signals of viewpoint is possibly best described in terms of individual forms and (potentially) relevant clusters of forms, but the expectations brought about by the term 'construction' seem to be too stringent. What appears to be more important in all these cases is the discourse type and its requirements, while specific grammatical viewpoint markers (tense, pronouns, or deictics in general) may appear in different clusters in different genres. To continue working on reporting forms, a fruitful direction might be working towards a structured list of common reporting means, which one can match expressions against to determine language-specific strategies or discourse options. Understanding viewpoint cross-linguistically could benefit from such an effort.

We are also becoming much more aware of the complexities of viewpoint in cross-linguistic and cross-modal analyses. As Lu and Verhagen suggest, there may be language-specific viewpoint phenomena that emerge in translation and point clearly to the fact that viewpoint expressions may not only be language-specific, but they are deeply immersed in the entirety of the language system, especially since there may be expressions dedicated to a type of viewpoint strategy in one of the languages involved – the specific case they discuss is viewpoint shift from narrator to character. Foolen and Yamaguchi further suggest that cross-linguistic comparison of the expressions of what they refer to as 'enactive viewpoint' will also contribute to a better understanding of the knowledge required in the context of translation. A rich cross-linguistic approach to viewpoint is a must.

Theoretical approaches represented in the volume are clearly connected to the type of form discussed. At one end of the spectrum, there are grammaticalized forms of complex viewpoint expression, and they occupy an important role in any kind of discourse – 'construed action' in sign language story-telling (Jarque and Pascual), oral stories (Izutsu and Izutsu), and basic colloquial discourse (Engberg-Pedersen and Boeg Thomsen). But grammaticalization is not the only path to expression of multiple viewpoints. As Dancygier and Vandelanotte point out, viewpoint marking is not restricted to dedicated particles or classifiers. In English, they claim, grammatical expressions such as articles, possessives, and demonstratives, typically not considered viewpoint expressions first and foremost, may also develop viewpoint functions in appropriate discourse contexts – and it is hard to claim that this is a result of grammaticalization; rather, these instances are possibly best treated in terms of polysemy triggered by features of discourse. Generally, then, we can see viewpoint marking in dedicated grammaticalized forms, but also in discourse-specific uses of other grammatical expressions. We do not mean to argue that these cases are essentially different – rather, they may exemplify various degrees of salience and discourse-reliance. Naturally, deictic expressions such as demonstratives (which are semantically complex in any language) are better suited to marking discourse phenomena, and a similar case can be made for English articles. This seems to confirm the earlier suggestion that in spite of the existence of dedicated systematic viewpoint markers, discourse phenomena play an important role.

The other approach represented in the volume is that of mental spaces and blending, which turns out to be useful in representing viewpoint in complex narrative configurations, and whose applications go beyond typical examples of represented speech and thought. In fact, the approach seems to go beyond basic representation of discourse configurations signalled through sentential means and syntactic embedding, works well for general pragmatic phenomena such as irony, and is particularly useful in multimodal contexts (body/text, text/image, etc.).

Not surprisingly, viewpoint phenomena cannot be divorced from issues of embodiment. Dedicated embodied aspects of oral story-telling, such as co-speech gesture, linguistic sign, gaze, and body posture, use various ways of body-partitioning and space distribution to allocate different viewpoints to different aspects of embodied behaviour and different parts of the communicative space. However, as Sweetser and Stec point out, it would be an overstatement to assign particular viewpoint categories to just one type of embodied expression, as there are some systematic correlations as well (for example, using hands often correlates with body-positioning). But also in image representations, as in the picture book discussed by Fukada, depicted body posture and facial expression of animal characters follow expected forms of embodiment.

Another aspect of embodiment is the representation of a person's experience (rather than their discourse). Foolen and Yamaguchi introduce the concept of 'enactive' viewpoint, where the issue is a representation of experiential viewpoint, rather than of any propositionally salient content. The category is important, not only with respect to the translation data that Foolen and Yamaguchi discuss. In a recent discussion of experiments by Brunyé et al. (2009), which tested the influence of personal pronouns on the conceptualization of situations, the issue of experiential viewpoint became fundamental. Among other results, Brunyé et al. have shown that subjects aligned themselves more closely with experience of events when these events were described from the first person perspective, but only when the events were simple, and represented by one sentence, such as *I am slicing a tomato*. When more details were added to the discourse (the speaker's age, occupation, etc.) the alignment effect disappeared. There may be various speculations as to why that happens, but possibly the most illuminating comments were offered by Sanford and Emmott (2013). They suggested that looking at pronouns and discourse length was not sufficient, since the experiential ('internal') perspective is more reliably triggered by verbs of perception and depiction of embodied experience. The discussion will most certainly continue, but it seems crucial that discussions of viewpoint include the experiential and enactive perspectives, not always realized grammatically or constructionally.

Given that different communicative modalities can be co-opted into representing different aspects of viewpoint, it is important to think about the very choice of the term 'mixed' viewpoint versus 'multiple' viewpoints. Neither choice seems to unambiguously clarify the nature of the phenomenon. 'Mixing' suggests that there are situations where several viewpoints are merged into one, while 'multiplicity' may evoke the understanding that the viewpoints remain independent and do not cohere in a communicatively salient way. Whichever term gets used in further research, it should be used with certain assumptions clearly spelled out. For example, 'mixing' assumes that there is more than one viewpoint expressed by a form of expression under consideration – be it a particle or a construction of reported speech. In the case of a particle, 'mixing' would mean that the one form discussed represents a certain specific viewpoint configuration, involving more than one perspective. In the case of a construction, such as Free Indirect Discourse, this would refer to the overt expression of more than one viewpoint category within a sentence. For example, a sentence such as *Tomorrow was the day of the wedding*, where the represented speaker's view of the future is profiled by the word *tomorrow*, while the past tense is aligned with the current speaker's perspective, the viewpoints may be seen as 'mixed' on the sentence level. As is generally agreed upon, the narrative does not really prompt a conflation of the represented speaker and the current speaker/narrator, so talking about 'mixed' viewpoint may be misleading until it is clarified that the 'mixing' is true of the grammatical choices at the constructional level.

Choosing 'multiple' rather than 'mixed' acknowledges the complex viewpoint configurations that underlie all kinds of grammar choices (particle, tense, pronoun, etc.), but is also better suited to properly representing cross-modal viewpoint configurations, where the constructional level is less salient. For example, marking different viewpoints in speech and in gesture is truly 'multimodal' and it would not be accurate to talk about mixing in such cases. Still, in these instances, it needs to be made clear how a coherent understanding is arrived at, in spite of multiplicity. There are some suggestions in the volume, especially in Dancygier and Vandelanotte, where an additional level of processing is postulated so that the viewpoints can be reconciled. Inclusion of such a level is also needed to clarify ambiguities in the use of specific forms (for example, different narrative referents of deictic pronouns), which cannot be easily addressed with the 'mixing' concept.

We also need to note that viewpoint research addresses a steadily growing range of phenomena, especially in the language of the internet and creative contexts. In these examples, the analyst cannot be restricted to a well-defined linguistic form. For example, Dancygier and Vandelanotte discuss examples from film, TV shows, and video art which are not naturally identifiable as constructions – especially in cases resembling irony. These are interpreted in the context in which they appear, but are not well aligned with more standard forms of linguistic expression. Again, discourse seems to clarify the nature and configuration of viewpoints expressed.

This brings us to the issue of evidence of viewpoint. In the case of clear grammatical distinctions – such as the distinction between proximal and distal or present and past – the analyst has reliable tools. But, as Engberg-Pedersen and Boeg Thomsen point out, in the case of complex meanings grammaticalized into simple expressions, like particles, one needs to be ingenious. They seek additional evidence from comparisons between standard colloquial discourse of young language users and discourse of autistic children, whose conceptualization of viewpoint may be impaired because of weakened social cognition skills. In the context of the concept of viewpoint, a saliently cognitive concept, such correlations are particularly telling.

Another interesting source of evidence of viewpoint is to compare modalities – which is possibly why studies of gesture and sign language have been particularly strongly engaged with viewpoint analysis. Still, there are some complex configurations to be sorted out. For example, when McNeill and then Parrill (2012) describe viewpointed gesture in narratives in terms of three categories (narrator's viewpoint, observer viewpoint, and character viewpoint), they make these distinctions against the background of the gesturing speakers consistently relying on tense (the usual past or conversational narrative present) as the standard form of story-telling. In other words, different viewpoint choices in gesture are still accompanied by one standard choice in language. Examples like these suggest that cross-modal observations can not only tell us more about viewpoint types, but also show (at least in English) how discourse and grammar choices may not be well suited to representing the same variety. Overall, looking at narratives suggests that the use of past tense, at least in English, is a choice so predictable as to be hardly informative any more – but that does not mean that there is no hidden viewpoint iceberg underneath that tip.

Finally, evidence may come from looking at a single phenomenon, not necessarily a saliently viewpointed one, in a range of pragmatically interesting or creative contexts. One such example is direct discourse. Various examples in the volume show how this basic communicative form (it is only a construction in the context of reported speech) can take on different meanings when the words remain the same, but the viewpoint changes (for examples, see Jarque and Pascual). It should, under normal circumstances, simply represent the speaker's authentic words and thoughts, but in fact it often does not – in fictive interaction, in what has been described as demonstration, or in irony. Finally, Dancygier and Vandelanotte describe a video art piece portraying a speaker engaged in direct discourse, but obviously using another speaker's words verbatim, without any signal of reporting or intersubjective construal. All these examples pose interesting questions about the assumed viewpoint of the typical alignment between the speaker's body and her words, and make it clear how much is in fact assumed about what constitutes typical viewpoint. Looking at the contexts where the pattern is tweaked uncovers important underlying assumptions. But also, relying on cases of various combinations of modalities (gesture, text, embodiment) seems to provide good evidence of viewpoint categories which otherwise remain elusive.

The choices mentioned above are generally representative of multiple viewpoints in the sense of simultaneous representation of the same content from different perspectives. But viewpoint generally applies to a speaker aligning herself with various salient aspects of a situation – time, proximity or distance, and first-hand experience versus reported experience. The speaker (or signer) may also use her body to express further aspects or dimensions of alignment. But another crucial aspect of viewpoint expression is the way in which the speaker orients herself with respect to other participants. In reported speech, it is typically the case that the speaker/narrator represents the discourse of another participant, who may not be present. Intersubjectivity thus seems to be another important aspect of viewpoint, where the speaker either relies on discourse of others or presents events in a certain way for the benefit of others and taking their (stated or unstated) viewpoint into account.

There is a whole range of phenomena related to this, some of which have been mentioned throughout the volume. The primary underlying one is of course deixis, as the interacting participants' basic alignment with time and location of an event (current or reported, proximal or distal). Other phenomena include epistemic and emotional viewpoint, intersubjective coordination, fictivity, using discourse as demonstration, the various alignments within a viewpoint network, etc.[1] What this suggests is that the term 'viewpoint' can refer to very different linguistic phenomena, which include (but are not limited to) lexis, grammar, and specific constructions. This might raise the question whether the concept of viewpoint is too broad to be useful at all. Our answer is that it is useful, precisely because it allows us, as analysts, to capture complex linguistic choices. If viewpoint were to be dismissed as too general a concept, we would have some difficulty describing the coherence across various co-aligned choices. For example, when using an epistemic verb such as *think* as a viewpoint choice, the speaker is not committing herself to knowing the facts. But in a negated construction or discourse marker such as *I don't think so* a number of viewpoint dimensions need to be taken into account together. It is intersubjectively salient, as it refers to an opinion voiced by another participant, it aligns the speaker with less than positive epistemic stance, and it uses negation to reject the proposed claim (though with less-than-complete conviction). There are constructional, lexical, grammatical and discourse-related components here, which together place the speaker in a complex network of viewpoints – the level of certainty, acceptance/rejection, intersubjective negotiation, etc. It is useful to be able to discuss such constructions as complex viewpoint configurations, since it is then possible to extend the analysis to other phenomena. As a result, viewpoint becomes a concept as indispensable as the cognitive linguistic reliance on the body – we may talk about 'the body' in its entirety, but we also distinguish the roles of vision, touch, responses to temperature, spatial dimensions, gaze, gesture, etc. Viewpoint is becoming a concept which is used in similar ways – to capture a range of distinct, but related phenomena.

Viewpoint thus seems to be an important concept, coordinating a number of linguistic facts and offering coherent explanations of interrelated (though otherwise independent) types of usage. More research is (obviously) needed, to

1 See Fillmore (1990), Dancygier and Sweetser (2005), Verhagen (2005), Pascual (2006, 2014), Clark and Gerrig (1990).

uncover language specific choices, connections to grammar, implications for discourse, and the nature of multimodality. The range of issues is extremely broad, but we need to work on a manageable methodology to include the relevant data. The work is exciting and productive – as, we hope, this volume shows clearly.

References

Brunyé, Tad T., Tali Ditman, Caroline R. Mahoney, Jason S. Augustyn and Holly A. Taylor. 2009. When you and I share perspectives: Pronouns modulate perspective taking during narrative comprehension. *Psychological Science* 20 (1). 27–32.

Clark, Herbert H., & Gerrig, Richard. J. 1990. Quotations as demonstrations. *Language* 66 (4). 764–805.

Fillmore, Charles. 1990. Epistemic stance and grammatical form in English conditional sentences. *CLS* 26. 137–162.

Parrill, Fey. 2012. Interactions between discourse status and viewpoint in co-speech gesture. In Barbara Dancygier and Eve Sweetser (Eds.), *Viewpoint in language: A multimodal perspective*, 97–112. Cambridge: Cambridge University Press.

Pascual, Esther. 2006. Fictive interaction within the sentence: A communicative type of fictivity in grammar. *Cognitive Linguistics* 17(2). 245–267.

Pascual, Esther. 2014. *Fictive interaction: The conversation frame in thought, language, and discourse.* Amsterdam/Philadelphia: John Benjamins.

Sanford, Anthony J. and Catherine Emmott. 2013. *Mind, brain and narrative*. Cambridge: Cambridge University Press.

Verhagen, Arie. 2005. *Constructions of intersubjectivity: discourse, syntax, and cognition.* Oxford, UK: Oxford University Press.

Index

Authors and artists discussed

www.ingramcontent.com/pod-product-compliance
Lightning Source LLC
LaVergne TN
LVHW010854110826
845149LV00005B/1403